Germany Divided

An Atlantic Monthly Press Book

Germany Divided

THE LEGACY OF

THE NAZI ERA

by

Terence Prittie

With a Foreword by

Sir Ivone Kirkpatrick

G. C. B., G. C. M. G.

WITH ILLUSTRATIONS

LITTLE, BROWN AND COMPANY · BOSTON · TORONTO

LIBRARY OF CONGRESS CATALOG CARD NO. 60-11642

FIRST EDITION

The author wishes to thank the following:
For permission to quote passages: The Editor, *Sunday Express,* London,
for quotation from A. J. P. Taylor; Professor H. J. Iwand, Bonn University; Professor L. B. Namier, Oxford University.

For permission to use newspaper cartoons: Michael Cummings, Osbert
Lancaster, *Daily Express,* London; "Vicky" (Victor Weiss), *Evening
Standard,* London; "Herblock" (Herbert L. Block), *The Washington Post,*
Washington; *Die Welt,* of Hamburg, Berlin and Essen, for cartoons by
Szewczuk and Hicks; Köhler, *Frankfürter Allgemeine,* of Frankfort; Soro,
Le Rire, Paris.

ATLANTIC–LITTLE, BROWN BOOKS
ARE PUBLISHED BY
LITTLE, BROWN AND COMPANY
IN ASSOCIATION WITH
THE ATLANTIC MONTHLY PRESS

*Published simultaneously in Canada
by Little, Brown & Company (Canada) Limited*

PRINTED IN THE UNITED STATES OF AMERICA

To
THE YOUTH OF GERMANY

*The future of their country is their trust, and their
responsibility. A clear knowledge of the German
past will enable them to discharge their task.*

On April 26, 1960, the East German Ministry of Cultural Affairs issued an order signed by an obscure Undersecretary with the name of Tiedt. He was so obscure that no one in West Germany had heard of him before, or even knew his Christian name. The order was simple and straightforward — the word "Germany" would not henceforward be used in East German atlases, or on maps published in East German books, newspapers and periodicals. The two German States would be marked as the "German Democratic Republic" and "West Germany."

Herr Tiedt added a footnote. The frontier running through the heart of Germany should be marked in exactly the same way as the other frontiers which separate one state from another. For this interzonal, all-German frontier is no longer "provisional." It is the most lasting legacy of the Nazi era and of Hitler's war. It is not the symbol but the hard fact of Germany's division. And that division will be Europe's, and possibly the world's, most dangerous and delicate problem in the years ahead.

Foreword

Anglo-German relations have understandably generated a great deal of emotion on both sides of the Channel. But in the present state of the world, indulgence in prejudice and emotion is a luxury we cannot afford; and if we have any regard for our safety, we shall be well advised to base our policy on rational thinking. Generals are often accused of wishing to fight the last war and we should be making the same mistake if, rooted in the past, we failed to perceive what changes time has wrought in the international scene. There are, in particular, four considerations to which I should like to draw attention.

In the first place, it is undeniable that recent technical progress has made it impossible for a nation of sixty millions, however highly developed its industry, to pursue an independent foreign and military policy. We can apprehend from our own experience how impossible it is for Germany to create her own nuclear armory, rocketry, armored divisions, navies and all the other equipment which a modern belligerent requires. With every year the task becomes more massive, and it may soon strain the resources of America with all her Nato allies.

The conclusion to be reached is that Germany singlehanded does not present the same danger as she did in 1939. On the other hand, Germany represents an important accession of strength to the Western Alliance; and conversely, the position of Russia would be enormously reinforced if Germany could be attracted into the Soviet orbit. In these circumstances it would be madness so to conduct our affairs as to drive Germany away from the West and into the arms of Russia.

Secondly, although we may have an instinctive dislike of German rearmament, we must face the alternatives. We could decide — and this would suit German opinion very well — that Germany should be defended solely by Anglo-American forces. This would impose an intolerable burden, particularly on Britain, whilst Germany, dispensed from military obligations and placed by an act of our own volition in a favored economic position, would be free to capture our overseas markets. We are apt to resent Germany's present wealth, but we should remember that it is largely due to the circumstance that for nearly a generation she has, at our behest, not been burdened by an army, a navy and an air force.

Or we could decide that West Germany should not be defended at all. In that event, we should not have long to wait before seeing the whole of Germany disappear behind the Iron Curtain. If, however, Germany is to contribute to her own defense, we must recognize that German troops must have access to the same weapons and equipment as their allies. No troops in the world will fight if they are deliberately placed in line with weapons inferior to those of their opponents and of their allies on either flank.

Thirdly, honor and self-interest demand that we should continue to press for German unity. Unless we wish to repudiate our treaty obligations, no other course is open to us; and the considerations of self-interest are cogently stated in this book.

Lastly, we are often told that Germany has not changed. Whatever one may think about the Germans, this is demonstrably untrue. For example, the attitude of the people towards rearmament has undergone a fundamental alteration. Whereas in 1919 all Germans, including the Socialists, were conspiring to rearm, today the youth, the women, the trade-unions, the Evangelical Church and the industrialists have all combined to delay rearmament. Under the Bonn and Paris agreements Germany undertook to provide twelve divisions, a relatively small force. Over eight years have elapsed since these treaties were signed and the twelve divisions have not yet appeared. Nevertheless I was warned by emotion-mongers at the time that if Germany were once allowed to create twelve divisions, it would not be long before, by one expedient or another, she created thirty-six.

Of course the transition to a democratic regime in Germany has not been without its problems and difficulties. But there are today a very large number of men and women who are sincerely attached to democratic ideals. What they require from us is sympathy and support, particularly when opponents of democracy raise their heads. The ex-Nazis and the Communists are doing all they can to break existing ties with the West; we should be doing their work if we indulged in indiscriminate condemnation of all Germans and thus led the masses to believe that there was no future in a Western association. There is an International of ex-Nazis which gives moral and, if required, financial support to the small remnant of the Nazi Party in Germany. Democrats should surely be as active in sustaining the much larger and more important German democratic forces.

There is much in Terence Prittie's book with which I do not agree. Or perhaps it would be more accurate to say that I should have presented facts and reflections in a different way. I should, for example, have preferred a stronger appeal to reason. Yet I think that, in the main, his conclusions tally with mine; and they will possibly have greater force, since they obviously come from a man who cannot throw emotion overboard. I should be happy if readers would carry away his last sentences:

"The Germans lack no human quality, no capability needed to weld them into a community which can make a huge contribution to the free world. They are being given the chance to discover their own soul, not self-consciously, nor in any spirit of arrogance or abasement. But they face strains and stresses in the years ahead which will test them sternly. It should be the duty and the privilege of the other free nations to help them along their road."

IVONE KIRKPATRICK

June 1960

Contents

Contents

Germany Divided

FÜHRER BEFIEHL!

HICKS, *Die Welt*

1945
["Führer's Orders!"]

-1-

The New Germany

> In the German soul, in the art, philosophy and literature of her people, there is a lack of understanding of what life really is, of what constitutes its charm and greatness; and there is a sort of morbid and Satanic attraction for death.
> — GEORGES CLEMENCEAU, Prime Minister of France,
> 1917-1920

> The Germans . . . a vast population of brave, competent and cruel people.
> — ALFRED DUFF-COOPER, later Lord Norwich

> My crime is that I had faith in Germany.
> — ALFRED DELP, a member of the Roman Catholic
> Resistance to Hitler

I T is a common German habit to use an English word to describe a thought, a detail, a habit of mind, or an intricacy of some game or sport. The Germans use those English words because they are descriptive, and short. The English-speaking peoples do not consciously use German words so often. But today they use one very often — the *Wunderkinder,* in reference to those members of the post-1945 generation of young German industrialists who have helped to create the "German Economic Miracle." That "miracle" has blinded a great many people to the fact that it has done no more than provide a material basis for the life of a people which has, for at least sixty years, suffered the afflictions which spring from pride and uncertainty of mind, power, and a total lack of sense of fulfillment.

The *Wunderkinder* — it sounds like a phrase from a fairy tale. In practice, it means such mundane heroes as Max Grundig, who

3

has built up a radio set, television and typewriter empire on an indigestible diet of sausage and sauerkraut; Josef Neckermann, who cannot escape from the countinghouses of his mammoth mail-order business; Berthold Beitz, who sells Krupp products in underdeveloped countries and canvasses American good will per Boeing; Hans Thierfelder, who has devised the slinkiest advertisements for sheer nylon stockings and who lives on the end of a telephone line.

Too many books have been written about "The Germany of Today" which have really been about the *Wunderkinder* and their works. This is, indeed, reducing a terribly difficult problem to a mere table of statistics. The operative facts of the "German Economic Miracle" can be dealt with in a very few sentences. In 1945 Germany was destitute. By 1960 a West German population, whose intense, unresting energies had been diverted into a single field, was producing, in terms of sheer worth, two and a half times as much as twenty-five years earlier. Eastern Germany was producing about one and a half times as much. And the West German economy was setting the pace — only just in time — for a community of European nations which has only now begun to understand that the very survival of Europe depends on the high development of industrial techniques and on acceptance of a code of usefulness dedicated to the world as a whole.

The German *Wunderkinder* and the "German Economic Miracle" have their place in European history — an important place. But their place in strictly German history is incidental. For the "German problem" is a human problem, and I shall try to write about it in human terms. People matter. The German people matters. The German problem is a very serious problem, and has not begun to be solved. Briefly, it is the problem of an immensely industrious, restless and competent people, which has had the geographical misfortune to find itself in the very middle of Europe, and the political ineptitude to infuriate Europeans of every political color and every state of social development — and thus to be left divided between two world blocks after Europe's worst war since 1648.

Why should the German problem be so complex? Leaving

4

geography and — as far as possible — history, too, aside, here are a few human reasons.

During the last fifty troubled years, Germany has failed to develop a settled, properly fused society. German society is in theory classless — and in fact the most class-conscious in Europe. The German aristocrat who has not suffered from the war is buried in his estate, or immersed in the affairs of his cosmopolitan cousins-by-marriage; if he has lost his estates, he is buried in a job or a garret. The German industrialist is generally divorced from all the rest of the human race — a sort of twentieth-century Neanderthal Man. The German middle class is acutely conscious of its waning strength and prestige.

The German civil servant has remained a model of efficiency and an emblem of honest service. But his social status has suffered bitterly from the introduction of a new scale of values, based on sheer earning power. The civil servant is sadly underpaid; in a starkly materialistic society that is, in itself, a slur. There is not one of "the professions" which has not been adversely affected by the Nazi era. Lawyers and teachers were all too often swept up in the far-flung net of the Nazi Party. Men of exceptional intellect compromised with the Nazi regime, and with their own consciences; it is hardly surprising that German humanists, historians, philosophers are today still mentally, morally adrift. The medical profession strove, indeed, to keep itself free of the Nazi taint; one result is that that great body of German-Jewish doctors has vanished, while anti-Nazi "Aryan" doctors were put, like Uriah the Hittite, in the forefront of the battle. German medicine has suffered a setback from which it will take fifty years to recover.

To complete the picture of an un-co-ordinated society, the German worker remains too undemanding, too much aware of his "place" in the social scheme of things. Democracy, indeed, has come to Germany — in the shape of a code of behavior. But democracy as a living spirit of endeavor, responsibility and self-respect is only just beginning to root itself.

Democracy should begin at the bottom. But the "little" Ger-

5

man's picture of himself, as someone who is not remotely responsible for what goes on around him, still persists. Politics, so many "little" Germans still believe, are something for politicians. A superior being still orders his immediate inferior around. (Once upon a time, it was generally believed that every German kicked the German directly "below" him; now he merely reminds him where he belongs.) The usual picture of the social order in the mind of the average German is a stereotype: he is aware most of his "position" in it and of the *Obrigkeiten,* the powers-that-be.

These powers-that-be are still very much alive to their own authority. Here, for instance, is the story of the German citizen who was called a "grinding idiot" by the Lord Mayor of his village. He sued the Lord Mayor for slander, and lost the case.

His legal counsel made a final appeal to the judge.

"Your Honor," he said, "would you not consider it an insult if I were to call you a grinding idiot?"

The judge did; and the lawyer was sued for contempt of court and sent to jail for a month, with the option of a fine. Naturally, it was a straightforward matter — in the new, democratic Germany — for a judge to sue a mere citizen lawyer. Whereas the original plaintiff had tried to sue a Lord Mayor, who was an *Obrigkeit,* one of the powers-that-be.

The *Obrigkeiten* have, in Germany, their own rules of behavior. Here are three appropriately absurd examples.

The Federal Minister of the Interior from 1949 to 1953 was Dr. Robert Lehr. He built himself a new house in Düsseldorf, and chose to place it on a piece of ground with only a single road and a sloping meadow between it and the Rhine. Unfortunately, a side road turned off at a right angle to the Rhine, just past his front door. It branched just beyond it, and one fork described another right angle thirty yards on. Children played along these lanes, and motor cars had to sound their horns continually. Dr. Lehr suggested to the police that they should post up notices forbidding tooting outside his Ministerial home (putting it in the same category as a hospital). With sound democratic prescience, the police refused.

The Federal Minister of Finance from 1949 to 1957 (he then became Minister of Justice) was Dr. Fritz Schaeffer. He considered that it was unnecessary for his chauffeur to observe the fifty-mile-an-hour speed limit which the American military authorities imposed on the Frankfurt-Heidelberg stretch of *Autobahn* (since the speed limit has been lifted, it has become known as "Death Alley"). One day an American military police patrol car overtook the Minister who had been going at around seventy-five miles an hour, shepherded his car into the side, warned his dutiful chauffeur not to do it again.

Chattering, no doubt, with rage, Dr. Schaeffer waited until the Americans had departed in the opposite direction. Then he told his chauffeur to put his foot well down and make up for lost time. But, farther down the road, the American police car had turned again and was very quickly on his trail. This time the speed cops took him to an American command post for questioning. They were genuinely concerned to learn that he really was a Minister of State; for they could not believe that a Minister of State would so blithely break the law.

The Federal Minister of Defense after 1955 was Herr Franz-Josef Strauss. One day he was paying a call on the Federal Chancellor, in the latter's official offices in the Palais Schaumburg. The policeman on duty outside the Palais Schaumburg held up the Ministerial car, which had to cross the main artery of the Coblenzer Strasse. This outraged the Minister, who told his chauffeur to drive on. By great good fortune he just failed to collide with a tram. Franz-Josef Strauss had to appear in court, with an unconvincing alibi.

This sort of example is not calculated to make the "little" German regard himself as a very responsible person. Lack of responsibility may, in turn, have encouraged his already ingrained

7

tendency to forget the past — if it happens to be embarrassing or irksome. But, then, the "little" German is not alone in this respect; forgetting the past is a German occupational disease.

Early in 1959 a letter appeared in the Free Democratic weekly *Fortschritt* attacking a columnist of the British daily newspaper the *Daily Mirror*, William Connor. Mr. Connor, who writes under the pseudonym of CASSANDRA, has never tried to tell his readers anything of the slightest interest about the Germans. He has employed his own, ultrasimple technique — to revolt and enrage readers with distorted, nightmarish pictures of "the German." CASSANDRA has never considered that the average German is, today, the recognized ally of the West, who is trying to get on with the job of being a junior, often embarrassed partner in the Atlantic Alliance, and who is at last aware of his need for firm friends among the Western democracies.

Intelligent Germans could have produced crippling criticisms of CASSANDRA, who writes for a leftish-Labor newspaper but who is the epitome of myopic, hidebound British insularity. But the correspondent to *Fortschritt* based his case against CASSANDRA on one argument only — that Britain had engineered two world wars in order to smash a Germany which was poised and groomed to lead Europe. The letter was signed WOLBER.A.D. LEVERKUSEN. This was revealing. The letters a.d. stand for *ausser-Dienst*. The writer was a retired officer, and felt bound to remind readers of the fact. He was unable to visualize himself as a normal citizen.

Equally revealing was a recent interpretation of the 1938 Munich Agreement by the weekly paper *Heimkehrer*, which circulates among former prisoners of war and has close connections with the German Red Cross. The *Heimkehrer* explained that the Munich Agreement was equitable, that it "did not create a wrong" but "offered compensation for a wrong which had already been committed." Well, the Munich Agreement led directly to the ruthless dismemberment of Czechoslovakia; in the long term, it encouraged Hitler to attack Poland and made the Second World

War inevitable. Twenty years later, the *Heimkehrer* could see only one aspect of Munich — it removed a German-speaking community from Czech control and placed it under Hitler's. It was, the *Heimkehrer* argued, the inalienable right of every German-speaking person to belong to Germany. The enforcement of such a "right" would have given Germany the whole of Austria, four fifths of Alsace, two thirds of Switzerland, four towns in Belgium, and enclaves all over Central Europe.

Munich, the *Heimkehrer* argued, "righted the wrong of Versailles." For Versailles "gave Hitler the chance to pose as the champion of justice." Given that chance, of course, Hitler then was able to fool the German people too.

German readiness to forget the past inspired one masterpiece of illogic from the pen of Paul Sethe, still in 1960 the historian of the editorial department of *Die Welt* — the most-read serious daily paper in West Germany. After years of mature reflection, Sethe was able to write about the contradictions of the 1922 Treaty of Rapallo between Weimar Germany and Bolshevik Russia, evaluate its mistakes, and yet conclude in contemporary terms: "For the sake of keeping the peace, a free Germany should play an important mediatory role between the remainder of the West and Russia."

An "important mediatory role"? One is left gasping. The Germany of Dr. Adenauer signed on unreservedly with the West, has even been an impediment in the negotiations of that "remainder of the West" with the Soviet Union. The Germany of Dr. Adenauer has utterly, if inevitably, failed to establish worthwhile relations with the Soviet Union, and has been scrupulously ignored by it on the international diplomatic level. More important, the Germany of Dr. Adenauer is only progressing now, after more than ten years, towards self-aware, self-reliant statehood.

The primary duty, even of a reunified Germany, would be to live unobtrusively on good terms with all of its neighbors, indefinitely, in order to allow memories of Hitler's atrocities to wither with the sheer passing of time. If ever a myth needed destroying, it is that of a Germany which is a ready-made "bridge between East and West." Such a Germany has not existed since the breakup of the Holy Roman Empire.

Plenty of Germans are still subject to schizophrenia. Forgetting the past is only one of the characteristics of the schizoid. I have heard the same reasonably well-informed and averagely intelligent German commend the Western Powers for their understanding of German interests, and then, almost in the same breath, castigate the West for "exploiting" its half of Germany. An excellent example of the less harmful type of German schizophrenia was supplied in 1952, when something like a national campaign was worked up against the use of a sandbank off the North German coast, the *Grosse Knechtsand*, as a bombing-practice target for NATO planes. German parliamentarians, who were all for NATO, denounced the bombing (mainly with dummy missiles) as "an affront to Western civilization" and "a deathblow to the European idea." Yet these people knew that American and British planes were using more than forty similar targets off the coast of Britain, and that this single uninhabited sandbank was the equivalent German contribution towards keeping the air forces of the West in a state of preparedness.

Seven years later there was a ludicrous sequel to the *Knechtsand* story. Germans living near the *Knechtsand* "observed" twenty-three "attacks from the air" which allegedly took place on a single day. At once every German newspaper and political party jumped to the conclusion that the British were carrying out bombing practice again. "Is this the way for an ally and partner to behave?" one newspaper asked; others castigated the Federal Minister of Defense, Herr Strauss, either for giving the British permission to bomb, or for not preventing them from doing so. The Defense Minister carried out a hasty, anxious inquiry. All that he learned was that not one German had seen or heard a single plane when the mysterious "attacks" took place. The story was a hoax; yet the whole German press believed it.

German schizophrenia is partially based on the haunting belief that there are conspiracies against Germany without end and beyond computation. This belief blossoms with tropical violence at moments of stress. Sir Ivone Kirkpatrick, a Briton with great experience in Germany, remarked that: "A man from Mars reading a German newspaper would get the impression that the German people wanted to pick a bone on every issue with both Russia and the Western Powers and that there was no desire to establish particularly friendly relations with anyone." Four years after Kirkpatrick made this statement, a leading, middle-of-the-road West German newspaper, the *Frankfurter Allgemeine,* wrote that the Allied bombing of Dresden — it was the tenth anniversary of the event — was just as discreditable to the West as to the Russians. The paper suggested that 200,000 people were killed during the bombing (the highest informed estimate was 30,000). Other newspapers wrote that the Americans and British bombed Dresden in order to murder defenseless women and children, and so break the morale of the unbeaten German Army. East German Communist propaganda on the subject of Dresden has taken precisely the same line.

An equally unhappy German characteristic, which may only disappear after decades of democratic self-government, is that of blaming others for their own failures, and refusing responsibility for their own governments. The outbreak of the First World War was "Austria's fault"; the losing of it was the work of the Kaiser and the mutinying Kiel sailors, who "stabbed Germany in the back." Hitler came to power because the Western Powers "did not stop him" (Dr. Adenauer, among others, holds this view); the Second World War, in turn, was lost because of Hitler's lunacy (*Wahnsinn*) in fighting on two fronts. And the division of Germany was the fault of the Western Allies, who allowed themselves to be "duped by Stalin."

The Western Powers were to blame, so the German legend runs, for the failure of the German Resistance to Hitler. They "did not give the word" to the resisters to act. They failed to weaken Hitler's position by not offering stiffer diplomatic resistance to him. They undermined the Resistance by insisting on "unconditional surrender" at Casablanca. To make confusion more complete, a leading member of the Resistance, Ulrich von

Hassell, wrote in his diary in 1939: "I told Henderson [British Ambassador in Berlin] that one of the most dangerous notions circulating here in Germany was that England would no longer deal with Hitler at all. If this thought took root, it might result in the lining-up of the whole of Germany behind Hitler." Quite right! This would, indeed, have been no more than the normal reaction of a proud and powerful nation — whatever the *arrières pensées* of Dr. Adenauer twenty years later. As for "unconditional surrender," no German pauses to consider that failure to insist on it could have entailed leaving Nazis at the helm, to negotiate peace and re-entrench themselves afterwards.

The tendency to blame others has persisted since the war — over the German problem as a whole, over Berlin, over the alleged failures of the West to come to satisfactory terms with the Russians in 1952 and again in 1955.

When the radical right-wing Socialist Reichs Party won a notable success in the 1951 Lower Saxony *Land* (state) election, a usually sensible German politician told me that this was "the fault of the Western press."

Astonished, I asked him why.

"Because the Western newspapers built up the S.R.P. leaders, made them appear important in the eyes of the electorate. That was what got them so many votes." The same man had told me that *The Times* of London had made a criminal mistake in "not warning the world about Hitler"!

The tendency to blame others, moreover, has certainly helped to induce a nationwide lack of sense of responsibility, that lack of *Zivil-Courage* which Germans themselves note and deplore. This may, in turn, have encouraged an unpredictability which afflicts even the cleverest Germans. They are liable suddenly to say something so ill-conceived, muddleheaded and tactless that one cannot believe one's ears. Thus Professor Walter Hallstein, Chairman of the European Economic Community since 1958, once told an American audience that the German aim was "to unify Europe up to the Urals." A French paper promptly nicknamed the unwarlike professor the "Ural Expansionist"; the effect of his statement on Russian opinion can be imagined. Dr.

Hermann Schaefer (a Cabinet Minister without portfolio) once accused Denmark of financing a fifth column inside German borders, in order to secure the annexation of North Schleswig — at a time when Western Germany and Denmark were on the best of terms. Even Dr. Adenauer produced the amazing remark that "the worst Nazis of the lot were the Austrians," when the two governments were negotiating an agreement on property claims of Austrian and German citizens arising out of the war.

And the kindly, correct Federal President of the time, Professor Theodor Heuss, sent a telegram of congratulations to Konstantin von Neurath, the former Nazi "Protector" of Bohemia-Moravia, when he was released from an Allied jail for war criminals. In his monumentally tactless message, Heuss expressed his sympathy for von Neurath's "martyrdom."

It may seem carping to begin a book on Germany by listing the human failings of the Germans — or some of them. Yet it is convention to look at the bad side of a problem first. There have always been happy and hopeful features of German life — even in the darkest days of the Nazi era — but it has been Germany's misfortune that so many of its best citizens have been un-co-ordinated individuals swimming bravely but hopelessly against the tide of German history, epic in their way, but usually regarded as *Aussenseiter* — outsiders.

There were the men and women of the Resistance to Hitler, like those infinitely gallant young Munich students, Hans and Sophie Scholl, who believed that it was their duty to protest — although they knew what their fate afterwards would be. There was Count Ulrich von Schwanenfeld, who left instructions in his will that a cross should be erected over the mass grave of people murdered on his Sartowitz estate, with the words on it: HERE LIE 1400 TO 1500 CHRISTIANS AND JEWS. MAY GOD HAVE MERCY ON THEIR SOULS, AND ON THEIR MURDERERS.

The epic German may be less spectacular, more casual than such dedicated people. He may be an awkward individualist, like Ernst Rowohlt, the head of the Hamburg publishing house.

1 3

Rowohlt disliked the Nazis and emigrated at his leisure — he was neither a Jew nor an active politician — to South America. There he built up a new business, and lived in extreme comfort, introducing Hemingway and Faulkner to a Latin-American public. He needed only to sit tight. But when the war was at its height and his city of Hamburg a shambles of smoldering ruins, Rowohlt "ran the blockade" in the reverse direction, back into a Germany which was in its death throes and where he was a "wanted" man.

Why did he do it? I asked him. He shrugged his huge shoulders. He had to "be in at the death." If his country were going down in red ruin — well, he ought to be there. There might have been something that he could do, to help. . . .

Equally individualistic was Pastor Martin Niemöller, the submarine commander who turned pacifist, opposed Hitler, and was sent to a concentration camp. His record is an essay in miniature in the contradictions of the German character. In 1919 he refused to accompany the German High Seas Fleet on its voyage of surrender and scuttling in the British naval base of Scapa Flow. This ruthlessly efficient submarine officer became a devout churchman. He opposed the Nazis with immense courage, yet wrote from a concentration camp to Grand-Admiral Raeder offering his services to the submarine navy in Hitler's war. On release he became a complete pacifist, deciding that he could not reconcile the taking-up of arms with the Sermon on the Mount (which had been a part of his regular reading for thirty years). In May 1959 he said that it was better for the peoples of the free world to be ruled by Communism than to fight a nuclear war. But he admitted that he himself would "sooner be dead than red."

Kurt Schumacher, the first postwar leader of the West German Social Democratic Party, was another individualistic German. No man suffered more outrageous buffetings of fate, nor bore them so uncomplainingly. He had lost an arm in the First World War. The Nazis imprisoned him in concentration camps, and wrecked his already uncertain health. Two years before his death, in 1952, he had to have a leg amputated. He died in harness, commanding his party from his sickbed — courageous, resolute, even heroic.

This innately shy, humorous and friendly man is too often remembered as the waspish and frustrated opponent of collaboration with the Western "occupation," of European integration and of Western Germany's logical, gradual emancipation as a sovereign state. Schumacher would have asked for too much, too soon. He could not see why German Social Democrats, who had never capitulated to Hitler, should not at once be treated as friends and equals by the Western Powers. He could not understand that the hatred and bitterness aroused by the Nazis was bound to remain focused on the whole German people, at least for some time to come. Yet Schumacher's services to German democracy were immense — he kept the Social Democrats independent of the Communist-controlled "Popular Front" (the Socialist Unity Party, or S.E.D.) in Eastern Germany, and he brought back life and purpose to the only German party with a solid and continuous democratic tradition.

It is a sad circumstance that Germans of stature and character fail so often to fulfill themselves, that their great qualities are dissipated in the frustration of opposition and the sourness of defeat. Success — possibly especially in present-day Germany — tends to be a fattening, soul-destroying business, making for flabbiness. The surviving heroes of the Resistance to Hitler still bear an aura of glamour; the *Aussenseiter* still wins an often unwilling admiration; but the successful German — who used to become pompous and proud — tends today to be busy, and a bore.

Yet there have been signs of grace at all levels of German life since 1945. Dr. Konrad Adenauer, Chancellor of the Federal Republic of West Germany since 1949, has cultivated the friendship of the Western nations with immense initial patience. His ministers have generally given him the sort of team support which Hitler never enjoyed and never much encouraged. A civil service, a police force, an army have been built up anew on democratic principles and the rule of law. A great mass of simple

Germans have made at least one binding vow which should hold good in the future — *Nie wieder Krieg*, "no more wars."

There have been special signs of grace at unexpected moments in post-1945 German history. Here are some examples.

In September 1953 Dr. Adenauer — on the bad advice of two of his closest confidants — decided to create a Ministry of Information which would have borne a frightening resemblance to the Nazi Propaganda Ministry of Dr. Josef Goebbels. The new Ministry was to co-ordinate and control all organs of information. It was to control all broadcasts to foreign countries and to organize a "Government Press Summary," which was to be quoted, without comment, by German newspapers and radio networks. It was to sponsor press and radio laws, whose disturbing drafts already reposed in the desk of the Federal Minister of the Interior. It was to monopolize Government public relations, censor films, deal with all "publicity" connected with the new German armed forces, eventually control television. In advance of its official birth, it was already being given the title of the *Überministerium* — the "Ministry above all other Ministries," which could in time become the "Ministry to end all Ministries."

The reaction of the West German press and radio (it was still too early to talk about "German public opinion") was remarkably prompt and robust. Sitting in his holiday hotel in the Black Forest, Dr. Adenauer received the blueprint of the *Überministerium* on September 24. By the evening of the next day he was aware of the hubbub which the plan was causing. That night he sent the draft back to Bonn and issued a hasty statement that he had "never been in favor of a Ministry of Information." A dangerous experiment died stillborn, denounced by every responsible West German newspaper in ringing tones and with much common sense.

Another sign of grace: In May 1955 the *Land* Prime Minister of Lower Saxony appointed, as Minister of Education, a certain Franz Schlueter, one of those curious Germans who first interested himself in Nazi ideas after the war had been lost, the Nazi Party dissolved and Hitler's ashes shoveled away into an unnamed resting place. Schlueter had formed connections with the radical right-wing political parties which sprouted and withered away like so many sickly toadstools in the early postwar years; officially he belonged to the Free Democratic Party. He had become a successful publisher, and his firm, the Göttingen Verlagsanstalt, specialized in the memoirs and apologia of former Nazis and their widows.

On the news of Schlueter's Education appointment, 3000 out of the 4800 students of Göttingen University — many of them familiar with the stench of Schlueter's literary pigsty — took part in a silent torchlight procession through the streets of the town. They followed this up with a students' strike; and, as a gesture of solidarity, the rector of the university, Dr. Woermann, and eighteen of the professors resigned their posts. Herr Schlueter held office for just one week. The *Land* Minister then sent him tactfully "on holiday." Later, under pressure, he resigned. Thus, by a spontaneous demonstration of their beliefs, students and professors prevented the appearance in political life of an intensely ambitious, potentially dangerous man who could have exercised a shocking influence on the teaching of the young.

In October 1958 the Federal President, Theodor Heuss, paid his first state visit to London. He guessed beforehand that it might not go as smoothly as, for instance, visits to America and Italy where he had been assured of a friendly welcome by a large section of the population. The British are notoriously slow to forget, and the length of their memories can have an embarrassing as well as a salutary effect. Heuss was treated with scrupulous but somewhat distant courtesy in London; there was never any question of an enthusiastic reception. West Germans took umbrage; they wrote angry letters to the papers and to British newspapermen in Germany. They considered that their country had been slighted.

All this did not for a moment diminish or dilute the solid good sense of Theodor Heuss. In London he displayed a charming blend of tact and humor. Driving through its streets, he did not take off his hat to the phlegmatic crowds, but to the young Queen, whose carriage he shared. When a German Embassy official nervously remarked that there had been "a lot of cheering," Heuss replied: "Come, now! Nearly all of them were cheering their Queen. Most of the others were cheering the fine horses which pulled our carriage. Of course, there were the members of the German colony in London." He was not in the slightest degree worried or offended, and later remarked: "What did anyone expect? The English did not run after me, and I did not run after them." He could not have said anything more likely to commend him to people who, as they saw it, had treated him with only an understandable reserve.

In November 1958 Mr. Khrushchev launched his threat to Berlin. The Red Army, he declared, would withdraw its garrison from East Berlin and would hand over control of West Berlin's communications with the Federal Republic to the "sovereign" East Germans. Khrushchev asked that West Berlin should become a "free city," deprived of Allied garrisons and economically dependent on its East German hinterland. He set a six-month time limit, expiring on May 27, 1959, for the beginning of "constructive" negotiations among the Great Powers on the Berlin problem.

The people of Berlin could well have been seriously alarmed by this brutal threat. I was in Berlin only a day or two after Khrushchev delivered it. There was not the faintest sign of concern on the broad, whimsical faces of the Berliners. "We have to stick it out here, anyway," was the stock answer to any questioner. "And we shall do so. We've had one Russian occupation and one Russian blockade. We know when we're up against it. We shall see it through." "Business as usual" — as in the London Blitz of 1940 — was the Berliners' motto in 1959. Yet even if there were no bombs falling, they faced a more subtle menace — the slow sapping of hope by the passage of time and ceaseless Communist pressure on and along the city boundaries.

The fortitude and sturdy independence of the Berliners are certainly not the least among the signs of grace which I have listed. Fortitude is badly needed in West Germany, and for a long time to come. While an Ulbricht regime sits in East Berlin — and the Russians can always find a personal successor to Walter Ulbricht — the West German community will suffer the worst of all strains, the frustration springing from the division of Germany. And this is only one strain among many others — the difficulty of coming to terms with the past, the lack of social coordination, the pressure of material needs and a materialistic ethic, the slow digesting of eleven million refugees, the hesitation of the outside world to treat Federal Germany as an entirely trustworthy friend and ally. In the circumstances it will be an added strain that the West will continue to expect Federal Germany to "work her passage" and contribute to the Western world.

Here are some of the forms that such a contribution may take:

West Germany can go on proving herself a loyal and resolute partner in the Western Alliance. She has already done so during the first eleven years of the "Adenauer era"; the Chancellor's greatest achievement has been to give West German policies clarity, conviction and continuity. West Germany, again, can set an example of firm and intelligent administration for her neighbors of the East. This will do more to win the Cold War than a dozen Western notes to Moscow or a dozen halfhearted attempts to find a solution to the German problem. West Germany can go on integrating a refugee population which deserves sympathy and admiration for its thrift, hardihood and undimmed energies, but which should not be encouraged to expect Western backing for a new German colonization of the lost eastern provinces.

West Germany can continue to act as pacemaker for the rest of Europe in a continuing era of economic progress. For in doing so she can contribute to Europe's very survival. Failing greater technical progress and the more rational use of her resources, Europe cannot maintain her position of social and economic leadership in the Old World. West Germany can act as a trade broker between the Western world and the underdeveloped countries — shorn of the stigma of "colonialism" by the loss of her colonies in 1919. In areas on the fringes of the Cold War, German economic genius and drive can do a tremendous amount to compete with applied Soviet economic penetration.

West Germany can and should continue to propagate the cause of peace. For it is in her interest to do so; her people, her cities and her very soil have no chance of surviving a third world war waged with nuclear weapons.

It may be that the division of Germany will continue to dominate all other issues in Central Europe for a lifetime to come. Is it, perhaps, presumptuous for a mere foreigner to counsel Germans to practice patience and loyalty to the West? It might be more appropriate to quote the words of warning of a German — the Bonn University theologian, Professor H. J. Iwand — written in 1959 just after refugee organizations had staged a "Homeland Day" in Bremen and had listened to fierce words from the Federal Minister for Refugees, Professor Theodor Oberländer. Professor Iwand wrote:

> I read the reports about Homeland Day with horror and indignation. It seemed to me that the speeches came from the repertory of that period of misguided nationalism which has cost us German soil and German honor. . . . Where is the right to a homeland, when we expelled our Jewish fellow citizens who had been living in Germany for centuries? Did the Federal Minister who used such strong language at Bremen do or say the least thing when it was a matter of preventing that expulsion?
> Where is the right to a homeland when many Polish noblemen and other landowners were liquidated in order to make room for Germans of the same class? Those who trampled on other peoples' right to a homeland should at least be silent today. . . . God cannot be ridiculed. Man reaps what he sows. When I pointed this out . . . I myself was deprived of my right to a homeland. I shall not join in now, when the murderers assemble at the graves of the murdered. For not others, but we ourselves — our German thinking and German ideology — have forfeited the inheritance of our fathers.

This is sober if bitter truth. It may be that the Germans have as great a duty to recognize the facts of history as the Western Powers have to strive unceasingly to enable a new Germany to fulfill itself in peace and honor. This book will endeavor to set out some of the problems which confront Germany, and some at least of the most operative facts which form the background to these problems. This book will aim to explain the German problem for the mutual benefit of Germany and the outside world. For the two must belong together; the alternative is unthinkable.

- 2 -

The Poultice of Allied Occupation

The task of engendering in Germany a new spirit of self-government and a new social order — whether by example or decree or a combination of both — was clearly the most arduous and exacting that had faced the Grand Alliance since before the dark days of El Alamein and Stalingrad.
— BASIL DAVIDSON, in *Germany, What Now?*

The Germans of this generation labor under a burden of ill fate; proclaiming that they were the bringers of salvation, they have actually brought a curse upon the world.
— PROFESSOR THEODOR HEUSS, speaking on
"The German Character"

We were much freer in 1945 than in 1918 to begin a new life, but we were much weaker too. Man is usually strong enough to admit to occasional mistakes, but not to a whole lifetime of error.
— COUNT KURT BLÜCHER, in *Know Your Germans*

It is a very difficult thing to administer a foreign country. It is bad enough trying to administer one's own.
— ERNEST BEVIN, British Foreign Secretary, in the
House of Commons, September 1948

ON May Day 1933 I was lucky enough to attend the first May Day celebrations under Nazi rule in the placid southern German town of Freiburg, as the guest (paying) of a stout and friendly ex-Colonel who had fought under General von Lettow-Vorbeck in German East Africa fifteen years earlier. At least those celebrations fixed the mood of a people in my mind. My host sent me to the parade with his son and his daughter — one a lumpish member of the *Jung-Stahlhelm,* which was in process of

Soro, *Le Rire*

"Plus Ça Change . . ."

being incorporated into the *Hitler Jugend,* the other an over-serious and devoutly Nazi seventeen-year-old who regarded her blue-and-white *Hitler Mädel* uniform as the most important part of her sacred vocation to serve the Fatherland.

I cannot remember exactly what I had expected to see (I had only arrived in Freiburg three days before), but it was certainly not half of the town's 80,000 inhabitants lining the Kaiser Josef Strasse. Nor had I visualized the build-up of emotional excitement which greeted the marching columns of Brownshirts as they swung into view, nor the great roar of acclamation which swept along with them like a tidal wave. The boy with me shouted himself hoarse (though he came of a solid Army family which affected to look down on the Nazis as parvenus); his sister was very soon blubbering with joyful emotion.

All through that march — punctuated with the lilting "Horst Wessel Song" and the more dignified strains of *"Deutschland Über Alles"* — women cried openly, unashamedly and copiously. My escorts explained to me, afterwards, that they had cried because they were happy; and they were happy because troubled times were over and Germany would again be great. For Germany had found a Leader who would act.

In a way they were right. On the next day, Hitler dissolved the trade-unions and a week later he stole the funds of the Social Democratic Party. Next he reabsorbed the Saar. Five years later he had attacked and overrun two neighboring countries and was preparing to butcher a third, Poland. And always the sun shone, as it had on that first May Day. "Hitler weather" — until Stalingrad — was the inevitable accompaniment of every one of the Nazis' key moves, major occasions and successes.

Twenty-five years later I watched the traditional May Day celebrations in Düsseldorf. Hundreds of people straggled into the Hofgarten in order to listen under the lime trees to the old slogans of the labor movement: "We must have a fair return, comrades, for our labor . . . the product of that labor must not be converted into instruments of destruction . . . social justice means the forty-hour week and wage rates adjusted to keep pace with the rising cost of living. . . ."

Long before the guest speaker had finished, the crowd was flaking away towards the Rhine and the shopping streets, on the lookout for coffee and Coca-Cola stands and paddle boats, and with a comfortable jingle of spendable money in their pockets. May Day was merely an outing for them, and they brought their children to the rally. There was as little evidence of an embattled working class as there was of revolutionary fervor. One big fellow, humping a trombone off on his own when he had got tired of his role in the Metalworkers' Union brass band, summed it up with, "As good a way as I know of working up a thirst."

The German people was quite ready to discard its false gods, muddled ideals, and children's party-cracker mottoes in 1945. It was not ready to put anything in their place, apart from the understandable desires for material prosperity and political security. For Germans in 1945 the most lively memories were of inflation, unemployment, a limited dose of dictatorship and the worst war for three hundred years. Their need for peace and plenty was understandable; so was their political apathy.

Of all the Allied statesmen who had to deal with the Germans after 1945 none understood them better than the British High Commissioner from 1950 to 1954, Sir Ivone Kirkpatrick. He had served in the British secret service against Germany during the First World War, had two tours of duty in Germany in the period between the wars, when he built up a wide but precise knowledge of the Nazi leaders, and headed the German section of the Foreign Office after 1945. It is Kirkpatrick's unhesitating view that the course of affairs in Germany ran much more smoothly after 1945 than after 1919. Why? In his own words — "The principal factor was the decision to occupy Germany and assume government of the country. . . . In 1945 the whole country was occupied, public order was assured, and stable political and economic conditions were gradually created in which a government had a reasonable chance of survival. Many Germans have told me that we were wise to have handed over responsibility by stages."

In 1919 only the Rhineland was occupied. An inexperienced

German Government was left — again in Kirkpatrick's words — "to sink or swim in the tumultuous seas of postwar disorder. It eventually sank." After the First World War no German Government was able to compete with the organized lawlessness of the Free Corps and the Black *Reichswehr,* with the mailed power of General von Seeckt and the General Staff, with the unrepentance of Prussian landowning Junkers and the sheer ruthlessness of the Ruhr industrialists. After the Second World War the victor nations did not repeat their earlier mistake of allowing free play to the unregenerate passions which swept away the democracy of the Weimar Republic.

Kirkpatrick's view was confirmed by what I regard as one of the most informed opinions that one could find in postwar Germany. In the town of Siegburg-Mühldorf there lived a former Sergeant of the British regiment of the Coldstream Guards (by rights, the oldest regiment in the British Army, for it was formed by the Parliamentarian General Monk before the restoration of Charles II in 1660). Joseph Gardiner was born in Brighton in 1888. He served through the First World War and came out to Germany with the British Army of Occupation. In 1923 he was demobilized, and settled with his German wife in the Rhineland. He clung to his British passport, continued to regard himself inwardly as British, but was given German nationality papers a year or two before the Second World War. Still, the people of Siegburg-Mühldorf continued to call him *der Engländer,* a tribute to his sturdy independence of character and tenacious Brighton-Cockney accent.

Sergeant Joseph Gardiner became Herr Josef Gärtner in the course of time, but that did not change his character. He came through the Second World War unscathed — by a miracle, for he continued to say what he thought about the Nazis and refused to serve as an air raid warden. The American military authorities were first on the postwar scene in this part of the Rhineland. They made him Lord Mayor of his town, although they found his Brighton accent hard to understand. Thanks to his impartiality and honesty, he was re-elected by the people of Siegburg-Mühldorf a year later.

Josef Gärtner had little doubt, years after the end of the war, as to what was the worst mistake committed by the Western Allies in their treatment of a defeated Germany. He enumerated some of the obvious but minor mistakes of the "Occupation" (and what occupation of a foreign country can be anything but a failure?); but his principal contention was that it was wrong to hand back too quickly too many powers to the Germans. He believed that, after the shocks of the Nazi era and the lost war, a period of political convalescence was vitally needed for the German people. There was no implied condemnation of their powers of recuperation or personal efficiency in this summing-up; there was no suggestion of lack of patriotism for the country to which he had joined himself. It was his considered, constructive opinion — and he had lived just half of his life in England and half in Germany. His view was a balanced one.

It may have been significant that it coincided with that of the cleverest member of any Allied Occupation administration in Germany whom I ever met. In the early years after the war the head of the French military government's cultural affairs department was a woman. She told me that the Western Powers continually forgot one factor in their appraisal of the necessary "re-orientation" of the German people. They remembered the need for advice, for material assistance, even for human sympathy; but they always forgot the more obvious factor — time. In her view, an Allied Occupation with constructive ideas ought to project them for twenty years. This would ensure that new generations of Germans would grow up in a democratic state, with Parliamentary representation, but — far more important — in a state in which they would be encouraged to think for themselves. One particular German tradition had to be destroyed. This was that if you were not, specifically, a politician, you were *unpolitisch;* and if you were *unpolitisch* you ceased to bear any responsibility for what happened in your country. Twenty years of absolute Allied administration in Germany, this Frenchwoman believed, would be best of all; but twelve years might well prove to be sufficient. And if Allied influence remained considerable, Allied executive control might not be needed.

It is a truism that when somebody suffers from a deadly disease he is the worst possible judge of his own symptoms and of the gravity of his case. This was so with the Germans after 1945. German society had not simply suffered from the effects of the war; it had degenerated into a human jungle. This was not because of the occupiers of Germany — at least of West Germany. Although it would be hard to find a German fifteen years after the end of the war who would admit the fact, he and his fellows were treated as potential members of a civilized Western community from very early days. On May 8, 1945, Field Marshal Montgomery, commanding all British troops in Germany, promulgated an order which read: "I have ordered that the armed forces are not to purchase or requisition any foodstuffs from the civil population. The latter will need these for themselves." In July, Montgomery told his troops: "We ourselves are well off in Germany; we must not flaunt our well-being in the sight of the impoverished and hungry inhabitants." Yet only a few months later responsible Germans were saying that British Army officers' messes had refused to have lace curtains hung in the windows of their dining rooms, "so that we should look in and see what they are eating and drinking, and suffer."

A salutary little account has been given by a member of the British Control Commission, Mr. J. A. Cole, in his book *My Host Michel*. He was determined to "get to know" Germans better, and, in spite of the difficulties in early days over "fraternization," asked some in for a drink. This was his obviously honest story of what happened (for his book was essentially friendly to the Germans, and appreciative of them).

> Visits to my flat dispelled illusions and created a certain disappointment, summed up by a German lawyer who, after surveying my quarters and eating a rationed meal, referred to his staff service in Brussels and said, "We knew how to occupy." It would be pleasant to record that Germans were impressed by my modest circumstances, but I

27

do not think many were. They looked at my uncarpeted floors with evident distaste. . . . Eventually they came to the conclusion that I could not be the important person they had supposed me to be.

A German side of the story has been given by Richard Tuengel, in the weekly *Die Zeit*, eight years after the end of the war. This in brief is his version:

There were many Germans who had never served the Nazi Party and who were only too ready to come forward to play their part in the reconstruction of their country. The Allies refused to give them a chance to help. Instead, the Western Powers forced their own forms of thought and action on every section of German society, beginning at the bottom with the smallest municipalities and villages. The Allies then carried out a "de-Nazification program" which was a mockery. People who had simply been Nazis, but who had not committed any crime, were punished for their "formal" political affiliations. The Allies, according to Tuengel, encouraged the creation of an elite composed mainly of Communists and fellow travelers and of the *Konjunkturritter* — those who grew fat out of the post-1949 industrial revival.

From this elite grew the West German political parties. The political parties treated each other as deadly enemies, as each of them regarded itself as the heir of Allied illusions. German laws and observances of long standing were disregarded, and a chaotic form of society was the result. In such a society it was impossible for a genuine form of public opinion to assert itself. German society was gelded by the Western Powers before it was ever given the chance of evolutionary functioning.

The above Tuengel interpretation of the first postwar era should be put in its true perspective. In 1945, Germany was defeated and devastated. Its towns were heaps of rubble. Its people were physically shrunken and mentally demoralized. One American journalist called postwar Germany "a country where the men had lost all honor, and the women all shame." Germans denounced each other to their conquerors. They lost all sense even of human solidarity. Farmers sat down to luncheons of roast duck and apple pie, while refugees living in one room in their farm-houses managed on a handful of ungarnished potatoes. One German politician told me how his own chauffeur was systematically and secretly pilfering part of the sandwich lunch which he took with him on visits to Ruhr factories. Germans never failed to have *eine kleine Bitte* — a little request — to put to the occupiers of their country. It ranged from food and cigarettes to a new flat, a car, a job or the tactful expunging of a political past.

No one should be too quick to blame them. They had lost three million killed in the war and another seven million prisoners of war or missing. They had lost over three million homes, which had housed nine million people. There were over one million war cripples. Millions of East Germans were pouring in from territories occupied by the Poles, the Czechs or the Russians. A detailed account of the miseries of the Germans is unnecessary; it has been given very often before now. But misery is not best exemplified by a gloomy record of statistics. Let one story illustrate the degradation of the postwar in Germany.

Two years after the end of the war, the people of the towns of West Germany were still half-starved (the Western Powers imported foodstuffs within their limited capacity; but the villains of the story were the German farmers, who did not deliver reasonable quotas of farm produce but traded all that they could in the black market). In one Ruhr town a suspicion arose that people were literally vanishing, and could not be traced by the police. Invariably these were young refugees, usually girls, who found temporary refuge in the religious and other charitable missions of the main railway station. They were "in transit" and were not registered by the police; therefore their very disappearance was a matter of some uncertainty. They could have simply moved on, unexpectedly.

The story unfolded itself as follows. An old man, wearing blue-lensed glasses and carrying the conventional heavy stick of the blind man, frequented the main railway station of this town. He used to hang about in the subway, below the platforms. He always accosted young German refugees, male or female but generally the latter, and he did so in the most harmless possible way:

he was catching a train in twenty minutes' time and had left his ticket where he had lodged, only four minutes' walk from the station entrance. That was, at least, his story.

Could the young lady fetch his ticket for him? She could. And she went to an address from which she never reappeared — until one day the police, suspecting nothing worse than white slavery, followed a refugee girl to the address to which all of her kind were sent. They broke in after she had been several minutes inside. And they found a butchers' shop in the basement, well stocked with joints of human flesh.

The purpose of this vignette is not to suggest that such cannibalism was widespread throughout postwar Germany. This incident was so unique that it was possible to hush it up. But it shows how desperate the situation often was in the early postwar years, before the reform of the currency in 1948 and the first results of the Marshall Plan.

After the First World War, Douglas Reed was able to write truthfully in *Insanity Fair:*

> I looked for the crushed and starving and desperate and bled-white Germany. I never found it. I found a country that had never known war on its own land . . . that had called the war off when the inevitable defeat impended . . . that by this apparent surrender had warded off decisive military defeat . . . a country that was beginning to hope that it had outwitted its foes.

After the Second World War Germany was never like that.

Another vignette, too, may be illustrative. Five years after the end of the Second World War I paid an extended visit to the Cologne Carnival. I wanted to write something about this ebullient and not altogether attractive example of an organized German *joie de vivre.* I attended various staged functions. They proved nothing more than the fact that Germans are able to be happy, when they are determined and directed to be. But one night I walked down a Cologne side street with no other purpose than to buy a drink at the end of the road.

It was still early in the evening, but the moon was already dominating the still night sky of a frostbitten March. Just off the main thoroughfares was an unbroken silence. Side streets were still nothing more than meandering paths, through and over mounds of rubble; some of them were mildly precipitous.

Along one of these rambling tracks I watched a strange procession make its way to the gay, garish, alcoholically befogged Excelsior Hotel. It was led by a figure with the head and long flapping ears of a donkey. There were crimson bows on his (its) ears. Behind came a woman in heliotrope tights — she was too old for them, or they were too young for her — and she was leading a mean little figure who had, most inappropriately, dressed himself as Mephistopheles. Behind, again, were Harlequins and Columbines, and clowns with immensely long noses, brightly colored but beaming out no more than a pale saffron glow in the light of the pallid moon. All these creatures walked in silence — on enjoyment bent, but temporarily restrained by their surroundings. They hurried down the final slope, into a friendly bar serving schnapps, beer and Coca-Cola.

When one is hungry one will eat. . . . When one wants to enjoy life one will trail one's way through ruins of the past. . . . These vignettes prove nothing, are intended to prove nothing. They are set five years apart, and five years later again, in 1955, I would suggest a very different picture as being typical of the contemporary German scene. Between 1950 and 1955 West Germany made mainly steady, but often spectacular economic progress. The national income rose by an average of 12 per cent a year; exports moved ahead even faster; new homes began to be built at a rate of half a million a year, or 50 per cent more than in Britain and three times the rate in France; in five years unemployment dropped from two and a half million to nine hundred thousand. As Federal Minister of Economics, Professor Ludwig Erhard instituted one of the most sensible of systems; his "Free Market Economy" was designed to let Germans work off an immense surplus of energy in order to buy the immense backlog of consumer goods which they so badly wanted, after six prewar years of Nazi austerity, six years of war and four years of postwar want. The "Free Market Economy" — based on cheap imports, boosting exports, tariff reductions and the liberalization of trade, with steadfast avoidance of labor disputes — paid handsome dividends. By 1955 West Germany was the most prosperous country in western Europe.

Rich countries have to be able to afford rich citizens. Already in 1952 the Social Democratic Party began complaining about West Germany's "105 postwar millionaires" (there were many more by 1960). The party's complaints were founded on a misconception. The occupying powers had taken steps to limit the financial power of Germany's prewar millionaires — because these people had been enabled to take a hold on the economic body of the German State as resolute and unshakable as that of a cancer in the body of a human being. The analogy is not complete: a cancer is an unthinking organism, which has not sought to give itself a premium on everlasting life; the prewar German millionaires intended to live off the German body politic in perpetuity.

But the postwar German millionaires were — initially — men who reaped the rewards of their own industry and prescience. It was foolish to chatter about their very existence, and in doing this the Social Democrats showed that lack of discrimination which has helped to condemn them to the political outer wilderness of opposition for the first post-1949 decade. It would have been wiser to select later genuine examples of unfettered antisocial capitalism, which are certain to be forthcoming in any age of dynamic economic expansion. Such examples were already available then. The most obvious was that of Hermann Krages, the son of an obscure Bremen timber merchant, who decided that he would acquire industrial power by sheer speculation and work himself into the "dynastic" aristocracy of German industry.

Hermann Krages was born in 1909. His father's firm owned a timber business in Bremen and had branches in Lübeck and the Rhineland (Siegen). In 1948 Hermann Krages was only a junior partner in the family firm. But he had ideas of his own, the most important of them being that he ought to be able to secure fat pickings by buying shares of big German steel, chemical and engineering firms which had suffered from restrictive Allied legis-lation. As Krages saw it, the prices of shares of these firms were unnaturally depreciated; allowance was being made for a further period of restrictive Allied control, as well as for the normal haz-ards of any major enterprise which has to get on its feet again after a lost war. Krages decided that the Western Powers would relax their already casual hold on German industry, would en-courage its growth as part of the Western effort to contain Com-munism in Europe, and would eventually seek to boost its further expansion by every means within their power. In 1948 he was taking what seemed to be a very big risk; but it worked out right.

Krages began by buying thirteen million shares in the steel combine of the Vereinigte Stahlwerke, which under the Nazis controlled roughly half of German steel and coal production. The Vereinigte Stahlwerke was in process of being split up by the Western Powers into nearly twenty "successor companies." Many of its plants had been dismantled and sold as reparations. Her-mann Krages was not deterred; he knew that its surviving plant and, more important, its good will, was worth a lot of money. It is believed that he sold a part of his shareholding in 1950 for forty-two million marks (ten million dollars) and that he sold other but smaller blocks of shares in later years even more ad-vantageously.

Hermann Krages made his next killing by buying and selling shares of the Rheinische Stahlwerke. This firm had major hold-ings in other Ruhr coal and steel plants, and it was in these that Herr Krages was primarily interested. He hoped that, by buying Rheinische Stahlwerke shares, he would eventually be able to ac-quire a controlling share in the Erin Coal-mining Company and the Bochumer Verein Steel Company. He failed in both objec-tives, but in the meantime he made at least a 300 per cent profit on his shares. He reinvested in the Gelsenkirchner Coal-mining Company, which had holdings in steel plants, shipyards, trading companies and chemical works, in addition to its four major coal mines. Krages wanted to gain control of the Gelsenkirchner Com-pany.

Deviously he collected shares worth roughly one hundred and fifty million marks (thirty-seven million dollars) in this company, amounting to a 25 per cent interest in it. It is fairly sure that at that date (1955) Krages owned other shares worth another one hundred and forty million marks (thirty-five million dollars). But the steel men of the Ruhr were horrified at this invasion by an "outsider"; they closed their doors against him. The Gelsenkirchner Company increased its capital, sharply. It prevailed on the Thyssen steel firm to sell its eighty-seven-million-mark holding privately, so as to keep these shares out of Krages's hands. By promising a further capital increase, the company froze Krages out. But it had been a near thing, and Krages, undiscouraged, made further efforts to gain control of both the Conti Gas and the Rheinrohr Steel firms of Düsseldorf. He failed each time; but he remained a multi-millionaire. He is the perfect example of the asocial capitalist, whose purely selfish determination to get rich has nothing to do with the lifework of industrial pioneers and managers, has nothing to do with the contribution of industry to the life of a nation. One West German paper, *Die Zeit*, referred to Herr Krages as the "woodworm." The name is not unfairly chosen.

Krages was symptomatic of an age of plenty secured in a great hurry. Yet his brilliant speculations tell only one side of the story of that comfortable poultice of Allied occupation, under which Germany was encouraged to work, earn, produce, recover a radiant economic health. Equally typical is the story of the little Rhineland town of Jülich. I first saw it in the desolate winter of 1946-1947. Two years earlier the river Roer, on which Jülich sits, had for long months been the front line between the American Army and the German. The Americans had occupied the old castle on the western bank of the river till German guns pounded it into ruin. American shells had reduced the main part of the town to rubble; out of its 4732 houses, 4644 were more than 65 per cent destroyed. On December 1, 1944, the population of this previously thriving town of 12,000 inhabitants was officially listed as — zero.

In the winter of 1946-1947 Jülich was known to the thousands of American and British troops who traveled the Brussels-Cologne road on convoy duty as the "town of three houses." No troops could be quartered in it, and its only link with the Allied Occupation was a solitary British official who lived in an intact house reached through streets of ruins — utterly solitary. Fourteen shells had penetrated even this roof, but most of them had failed to explode. One million dollars had to be spent to clear away the rubble, dredge the canals, repair the sewers and patch the roads through the town. Then, amid the ruins, little two- and three-room houses sprang up, built from the scattered bricks which had belonged to three- and four-story predecessors. Shops, banks, churches, hospitals and a town hall followed in due course. To-day, in 1960, Jülich is rather bigger and more prosperous than before the war, with a population of 14,000, two sugar-beet factories, and an active trade in the agricultural produce of its rich hinterland. A minor miracle has been performed.

Miracles should arrest the attention of their beholders, encouraging them to analyze what has happened and to illustrate, in the written and spoken word, their understanding of the hard and hopeful lessons of their history. This has not happened in Germany to any appreciable, reasonable extent. For one thing, events moved too fast. The black days of 1945-1947 were followed by only a short period of burgeoning hope, in which there could have been profitable reflection over the mistakes of the past. By 1950 West Germany was — thanks to Marshall Aid, the scaling-down of Allied reparations claims, and the single-minded concentration of its government on material reconstruction — progressing so fast that it was the envy of European countries who had fought for the Allied cause, had defended their freedom and independence, and had suffered quite as much as Germany in the process.

The tempo of German reconstruction defeated one of the primary purposes of the Allied Occupation, which was to bring home to Germans that only by careful and unbiased study of their own past could they ever hope to secure a peaceful, prosperous and genuinely happy future — for only by study of their past could Germans realize what monstrous crimes they had perpetrated against their European neighbors; only by fair and unbiased analysis of those crimes could they learn how to live with these neighbors.

What effort at analysis has there been? The Oxford historian, Sir Lewis Namier, wrote in 1952: "The first things that will reach the wider [German] public will be one-volume memoirs and romanticized biographies. These the Germans are producing by the dozen; some write them to furbish up tarnished reputations; others to make money; and all alike to make out a case for the German nation." Sir Lewis is a Jew and might be held to be biased against the Germans; but he is also a scrupulous historian, who knows that the twisting of truth is like a botched dental operation. It may seem to work at the time, but it leaves behind fragments of bone, abscesses and decay.

Sir Lewis maintained that "the first Germans to publish their memoirs are men who served Hitler but who now try to prove that in reality they opposed or even sabotaged him." The list which he offered is a striking one — General Franz Halder, Hitler's Chief of Staff; Herbert von Dirksen, former ambassador to Tokyo, Moscow, London; Ernst von Weizsaecker, State Secretary to the German Foreign Office from 1938 to 1943; Erich Kordt, Ribbentrop's secretary; Otto Meissner, who managed — with more than usual bureacratic prescience — to be chef-de-cabinet to Presidents Ebert (Social Democrat), Hindenburg (Nationalist) and Hitler (Nazi).

Halder complained querulously of Hitler's interference with the strategic planning of the German General Staff. This is about the only valid point which he made in his lamentable memoirs. His case was that Hitler robbed the generals of any possibility of "honorable action" once the Russian campaign began. But the generals were utterly obsessed with fighting battles; Hitler, to them, was merely an irritating and too often "inspired" Commander in Chief. He was not Lucifer; he merely prevented them from winning their war.

Von Dirksen was an apostle of Russo-German alliance, which could bring such immense benefits to two power-hungry nations and could solidify that great European "Land-mass" stretching from the Rhine to Vladivostok. Von Dirksen joined the Nazi Party, "as I did not wish to evade declaring my allegiance to the regime which I served." He was a violent nationalist, an anti-Semite, and a mildly hysterical man who gave much thought to the "humiliations" of the Treaty of Versailles and the reasons why a "proud and passionate German patriot" should strive to "obliterate" that treaty (which his own government had signed).

Von Weizsaecker's interpretation of European history is summed up in the words: "We Germans were not destined patiently to build our house, bit by bit, and then enjoy in peace the fruit of our labors. Again and again, other Powers have attempted to rearrange Europe by creating a political vacuum in Germany." Well! Could it have been knowledge of a hostile wish to create a "German vacuum" which led Count von Schlieffen to propagate his famous plan for invading neutral Belgium in 1914? Or a similiar unkind hostility towards Germany which led Hitler to attack, in turn, neutral Czechoslovakia, Poland, Denmark, Norway, Belgium, Luxembourg, Holland, Yugoslavia? So far from wanting a political vacuum in Germany, other European powers are terrified of it; because they know that Germans, rich in courage, craftiness and destructive imagination, would pack a vacuum full of political dynamite. But Weizsaecker was full of Germany's "legitimate" demands; he was in favor of a "chemical process of disruption of the Czechoslovak political structure"; he called the Munich Agreement "the last happy day of my life"; and in 1941 he wrote to Ribbentrop: "If every Russian city reduced to ashes were as valuable as a sunken British warship, I should advocate the German-Russian war for this summer. But . . . the sole decisive factor is whether this project will hasten the fall of England . . . England is close to collapse."

Halder, Dirksen, Weizsaecker — they, and others like them, are regarded in Germany as fair, genuine and honorable witnesses to what happened in their generation. So are von Papen, Schacht (Hitler's banker), Dietrich (Hitler's press chief), Hanfstaengel (Hitler's liaison officer with the foreign press), Schellenberg (Hitler's secret service chief). The written word has a more than ordinary fascination for Germans, who are apt to evolve their own history by the most unorthodox means. Sir Lewis Namier has described how Erich Kordt used long passages of Hansard, the official British Parliamentary Report, as his own "thoughts" in his reports to the German Foreign Office. In one place in his most untrustworthy "memoirs" Kordt printed the text of an imaginary letter from Mussolini to Hitler, allegedly sent on August 25, 1939. He left this letter out of the second edition of his book, presumably because he himself knew that it had never been written and had found that other people were aware of this too. But Paul Schmidt, Hitler's interpreter, had meanwhile borrowed the letter from the first edition of Kordt's memoirs, and had used it in his own book! Other German "historians" did the same. "In short," Sir Lewis was able to write, "it has become a fixture in German historical literature."

The memoirs of Field Marshal Erich von Manstein — sometimes considered to have been Germany's great military strategist during the Second World War — were a best-seller in Germany after von Manstein came out of a war criminals' prison in 1955. They are revealing. I met von Manstein when he was still a prisoner in the British-administered war criminals' jail of Werl. I was not impressed by his sort of sly, amoral approach to every problem which was mentioned to him. He claimed that he had fought "strictly as a soldier" in the Russian campaigns, and that the massacres of Jews, gypsies and Red Commissars which took place in his area of command had "nothing to do" with him. He claimed that he had been unjustly imprisoned and that the Allies' overdeveloped sense of justice would rebound on their own heads when they had to raise a German Army again. I believe that he had spent most of his time in prison thinking out justifications for everything that he had ever done, and excuses for much of what Hitler had perpetrated. The fruits of his long hours of thought and the committing of it to paper were harvested in his memoirs, *Lost Victories*.

In this book he excused himself and his fellow generals for going to war with the greatest enthusiasm in 1939 with the thought that Hitler had achieved one objective after another without the slightest difficulty — "look at Czechoslovakia!" The Poles should have given way, instead of fighting. For the British guarantee of Poland was "inoperative," and this made the Polish position "hopeless." But the Poles really brought their defeat on themselves — "No one in Poland ever quite realized in what a dangerous situation the country had landed itself by enforcing its unjustified territorial demands on the neighboring states of Russia and Germany."

What territorial demands had Poland "enforced"? Heaven knows! Poland was, indeed, awarded certain frontiers by the Treaty of Versailles — a very different matter. But Manstein could not leave Poland alone, for his real object was to show that Hitler was justified in attacking, overrunning, splitting up and brutally maltreating that country. Another passage in his book reads, "People in Poland had undoubtedly spent far too long in the years of Germany's military weakness dreaming of a chance for aggression against the Reich." In Manstein's view, "the Poles should have come to terms on the Danzig and Corridor questions." In fact, Hitler was right to attack the Poles, who were guilty of "dreaming" and had failed to hand over to Germany Danzig (which was, in any case, under League of Nations control) and the Corridor (which was Poland's only outlet to the sea and was mainly inhabited by Poles).

Like so many Germans, von Manstein evidently regarded Poles as some form of *Untermenschen*, subhumans who deserved very much less consideration than "superior" Aryans of Germanic stock. But this was not the full extent of his lunacy. He writes repeatedly of his "plan" for waiting until the Western Powers violated Belgian and Luxembourg neutrality, so that Germany could then "fight an offensive on the rebound." It does not seem to have occurred to this man, with his brilliant, logical, military brain, that the Western Powers could never have brought themselves to attack small, friendly neighbors in Europe. What was in the German mind must necessarily be in the mind of the enemy too — so he reasoned.

Manstein repeats General von Rundstedt's puerile myth that Hitler "let the British Army escape" at Dunkirk. He repeats Hitler's propaganda fantasy: that he wanted a "decent" peace with Britain, and as a result never evolved a war plan designed to beat Britain. He explains the attack on the Soviet Union as a "preventive war" — when Stalin was in his Seventh Heaven of certainty of German friendship, refusing to listen to any warning that Germany might betray him.

The sort of rubbish that Manstein has written is believed by a great many Germans. One of them explained why to me. "After all," he said, "it's all very well to attack the Marshal, but he was the outstanding military brain of his time. It was he who worked out the plan for the break-through on the Meuse, and the defeat of France!" (As if Manstein's mastery of the *Kriegspiel* could justify his blatant ignorance of political facts and political morals!)

All too many Germans have written in quite as criminally foolish a way. The Refugee Press Service has explained that the brutal partitions of Poland in the eighteenth century occurred only because Russia was rapacious, and Prussia and Austria took only their "fair share" of Polish territory, in order to safeguard their own frontiers. Poland, moreover, had "shown herself incapable of resisting Russian interference." In 1922 General von Seeckt, the creator of the post-1919 German Army, wrote: "Poland's existence is intolerable, and incompatible with the needs of Germany. She must disappear." Von Seeckt would hardly have held different views had he lived in 1772, at the time of the first partition of Poland.

The editor — Erich Dombrowski — of the *Frankfurter Allgemeine,* one of the most reputable daily papers in West Germany today, wrote, long after the war, *It Was Not as Bad as All That.* He sought to show that France had caused the war of 1870 and was primarily responsible for the war of 1914; that it was a mistake to delve too much into the past, and that each country was bound to be prejudiced about its own history. "For what is history," the editor wrote rhetorically, "save a sequence of stories, a ripple on the tides of eternity?" This would not be an unfair description of the approach of the Germans to the history of their own country.

The "historian" of the *Deutsche Zukunft* — the leading weekly of the officially respectable Free Democratic Party — Egmont Roth, called on the Western Powers to "keep on Prussia's side." He maintained that Britain had fought far more wars of aggression in Europe than Prussia, and that the British policy of a balance of power in Europe was a dangerous lie. Its purpose was to slap down any European nation which was taking its rightful place in the political firmament. Did not Britain attack the *Gesundende Deutschland*, the Germany "on the road to health," in 1939?

It is not necessary to labor the point that history is persistently and perniciously rewritten and miswritten in Germany, even today. One should not grudge von Manstein his ultimate hour of triumph, when he can explain how he would have won the war but for Hitler's antics, or Egmont Roth his belief that there would have been everlasting peace if only the Allies had allowed Hitler to go on taking what he wanted. What is more important than the ramblings of these, and of a host of other authors of "popular" memoirs, is the effect of such badly written or unwritten history on young Germans, who are growing up genuinely anxious to know what happened, what "went wrong," and to draw their own conclusions.

These young Germans are still told that Germany was bled white by the victor nations after the First World War. (In reality, Germany eventually paid a net payment of 3100 million marks in reparations; 33,000 million marks had been borrowed abroad.) Young Germans are still told that those same victor nations who poured capital into Germany imposed a "hunger blockade" on their country in 1919.

There were roughly twelve million German school children under the age of sixteen in 1959. The picture offered to them of the immediate past of their own country was fragmentary and, possibly, deliberately distorted in some of its details. It is perfectly true that German school children are worked very hard, are probably overworked judging by the standards prevailing in, say, American and British schools. German children must, at seventeen, take twelve subjects for their *Abitur,* or school-leaving certificate of proficiency. History is an optional subject in some of the West German *Länder* (states); in others it is skimped. Young Germans whom I know have admitted, rather sadly, that they never "quite get to the end of their history book." This means, generally, that they get to around 1910 or, maybe, to 1925 — with a badly cockeyed version of what the First World War and the Treaty of Versailles were about. In May 1959 the *Welt am Sonntag* published the results of an inquiry among school children of school-leaving age as to what they knew about Hitler. The most frequent answers were: the man who built the Autobahns, the ruler who eliminated unemployment, the builder of millions of new homes, the man who ended juvenile delinquency and made people realize that crime doesn't pay.

A different inquiry showed that most young Germans are not encouraged to know what the Nazis did to the Jews. In the *Land* of Baden-Württemberg a textbook in use in 1959 was *Geschichte der Neuesten Zeit,* by Ernst Klett. It purports to "cover" history up to 1955, and it devotes five sentences in all to the Jewish problem in Germany. These read:

> In November 1938 there occurred an especially shameful event. An emigrated Jew shot a German diplomat in Paris, who had been anything but an enemy of the Jews. This deed was excessively exaggerated by the Nazis and used as an excuse for a vigorous persecution of the Jews. By order of Goebbels the dependents of different organizations of the party burned the synagogues. They also mistreated many Jews and damaged the Jewish stores and apartments more or less severely.

Nothing was said of the pre-1938 Nazi persecutions of the Jews, or of the Nuremberg Laws which deprived Jews of citizenship, or of the concentration camps.

A history book used until 1956 in Bavarian schools described the persecution of the Jews by the Nazis in these words: "It is impossible to ascertain the exact number of people who lost their lives during the Jews' uprising in Warsaw and in the gas chambers of the concentration camps, but they were probably very many." The author of the book intended, originally, to suggest that "several million" Jews lost their lives, but the Bavarian Ministry of Education had the passage expurgated.

In the secondary schools (up to seventeen years) of North Rhine Westphalia, in 1959, children were once again being taught the fable of "hostile powers" organizing the "encirclement" of a peaceful Germany. They were being taught that Germany's violation of Belgian neutrality in 1914 had already been explained by the German Chancellor of that time — it was the result of "emergency needs." They were being taught that Alsace-Lorraine was "rightfully German."

The standard history book for the seventeen-year-olds, *Erbe des Abendlandes*, devotes thirteen lines to the persecution and annihilation of European Jewry. No figures at all are given. (One German schoolmaster told me, in all good faith, that this was "because the figures were so horrific that nobody would ever believe them — not even children"!) *Erbe des Abendlandes* skips away from the Jewish problem in order to examine the causes of the Second World War. "All Germans rejoiced," it believes, when Hitler reoccupied the Rhineland. (It is an interesting reflection that Dr. Adenauer told me personally that all "good" Germans would have backed Allied intervention, "in order to stop Hitler.") Only "German areas" were annexed after the rape of Poland in 1939 — an obvious and childish untruth. Hitler's attacks on Denmark and Norway are justified on the grounds that they were "to secure air and naval bases and make a blockade of Germany more difficult." *Erbe des Abendlandes* makes no mention of the fact that Denmark and Norway were neutral and friendly neighbors of Nazi Germany — as were Holland, Belgium and Luxembourg.

This is how young Germans were, in 1959, being taught about their country's past. This is why, in May 1959, a spokesman of the Evangelical Church Council described the failure to teach young Germans the truth about Hitler as "an almost incredible breakdown" of the educational system. History, he suggested, was "being allowed to stop at Bismarck." The only word which must be challenged in that sentence is "allowed." History was and is being halted at Bismarck. The same generation of dead-headed Ger-

43

man schoolmasters, which declaims against the corrupting power of cheesecake, does not want young Germans to know what happened to their country, or why.

This is an undeserved affront to German youth. Undeserved, in particular, because a new generation of Germans is growing up who are open-minded, alert, and intent on getting to know the outside world and divorcing themselves from the stale atmosphere of mock-heroics, party-cracker slogans and false gods. The natural curiosity of young Germans cannot be set at rest by a deliberate or spontaneous failure to teach them about what happened. For they know full well that something went seriously wrong, and they are suspicious of elders who drifted on the deadly tide of Nazi daring and destruction.

And under what disadvantages German youth has had to face the future! Nearly one and a half million young people lost their fathers in the war; ten years after the war, another 200,000 were living with one parent as a result of a divorce; 200,000 more were in hutted camps; 40 per cent of all youths who were medically examined were found to be suffering from some form of neurosis; the proportion of young people convicted of sex crimes had multiplied four times since prewar; prostitution of girls under fourteen had multiplied ten times; overall youth-criminality was 10.4 per thousand, against 4.2 per thousand twenty years earlier; and countless young Germans were living with a mother and an "uncle" who did not marry her because both of them worked and could each, singly, claim maximum taxation relief.

Fifteen years after the war, I made the following notes about the terms of existence of the 120,000 young Germans at universities and technical colleges. Over 15,000 of them came from the lost territories east of the Oder-Neisse line, and another 15,000 from families who had fled from the East German Republic; 20,-000 were fatherless; only one student in seven received more than 150 marks a month ($36) in state grants and direct financial help from his family — one student in five had less than 50 marks a month ($12); 60,000 students worked through the four months' summer vacation, and 40,000 of them took odd jobs or even regular work during term-time. Every second student suffered from some kind of nervous disability; one in three needed regular medical treatment; and one in five was classified as needing sanatorium treatment (he did not always get it).

The average university student, I found, did not take part in any organized form of sport, was lonely and isolated, obsessed with getting a degree and then a job, was badly dressed and mildly undernourished. Most students to whom I have talked admitted that they generally eat only a ten-cent plate of vegetable soup in the middle of the day, that they drink no alcohol and can seldom afford tea or coffee. They have a tendency to wear their fathers' converted army uniforms and Afrika Korps forage-caps, and they are sometimes so ill-dressed that they are mistaken for tramps when they try to thumb lifts on the Autobahns. On the other hand, young Germans were open-minded and receptive, keen to travel (37 out of every 100 were going abroad at least once a year), interested in Europe (it was German students who first demonstrated near Strasbourg against the carrying of passports). They were not at all anti-Semitic — since the war, students have always taken the lead in openly showing disapproval of ex-Nazis and their works and sayings. They did so once again after the desecration of the Cologne synagogue at Christmas, 1959.

One Frankfurt student told me that nearly every member of his law class of thirty-eight spent at least two months a year out of Germany — setting out with a few marks in their pockets, begging lifts, doing odd jobs in order to earn enough for their next meal, but seeing the world and coming into close contact with the people of other countries. "We want Europe," one member of an Evangelical Youth Group told me. "What we can at once do in order to help unite Europe is to learn about it. Almost all of us over the age of eighteen have crossed at least one frontier. Just not to have been at least once to England is becoming positively unfashionable." One German professor, Dr. Horst Adamietz of Arnsberg, began collecting the names of young people who wanted to correspond with contemporaries in other European countries. After a few months he had collected 30,000 names and

45

was forwarding forty to fifty letters a day abroad. The desire of young Germans to learn has resulted in almost every youth hostel's having to organize its own library for "overnight" readers.

It would be wrong to paint an idyllic picture of West German youth, which is mildly cynical, immensely inquisitive, yet politically uninformed, stereotyped, and a little uncertain of itself after the stresses of the postwar period and continuingly tough terms of existence. There have been outbreaks of teen-age violence, which reached a peak in an epidemic of riots at the end of 1956 in Cologne, Hamburg, Brunswick, Osnabrück, Duisburg and other towns. Increased incidence of youth-criminality — although primarily the result of young people "growing up quicker" — continues to cause concern. Cynicism was aptly illustrated by one public-opinion inquiry. It produced remarks like these: "The Fatherland is no longer an intelligible concept for me" . . . "How can I pledge my life to my people and my country, when so many have been so senselessly sacrificed in the past?" . . . "The ideas of freedom and patriotism can only make one laugh when there are so many war graves, so many war cripples." Young people have too little time to inform themselves about politics, and political disinterest is often very evident on the surface. What was Hitler's mistake? — To lose the war. What are the benefits of democracy? We are living quite well, so it must be all right. How important is reunification? Oh! Important all right; but I cannot remember any Germany save a divided one.

Yet most young Germans with whom I have talked have struck me as sensible and matter-of-fact, with a healthy urge towards independence and self-reliance. They work hard but enjoy their leisure. Many of them have carried out their one year's service in the *Bundeswehr* uncomplainingly and in the belief that a citizen should be prepared to defend his country. (Some even complain that the discipline is too lax!) Their ready spirit of inquiry is in marked contrast to the attitude of mind of regimented East German youth, best illustrated by a member of the Communist "Free German Youth" who answered a question about the dictates of his own conscience by producing a booklet and saying, "Answer is on page 18, at the top."

Young West Germans may seem a little colorless, a little lacking in individual ideas, or in physical sparkle. They may suffer from worry complexes, extreme preoccupation in their future careers, from a lack of time to think. But they are growing up among the good citizens of Europe, and may develop into the best. Here, again, the poultice of the Allied Occupation has helped to some extent. Old-fashioned German parental tyranny is a thing of the past; for the elder generation of Germans failed conspicuously to support and strengthen good government, to oppose dictatorship with real moral courage, to make and value real friends in other nations. Young Germans recognize this, and the Allied Occupation may have helped them to grow up with ideas of their own.

The Allied Occupation, indeed, did the Germans very little harm, save to leave them with no recognizable ideal beyond a general desire to "belong to the West." The Allied Occupation neither helped nor discouraged the development of the new deadness of intellect and concentration on material self-interest. These were the products of the division and political impotence of Germany; and these, in turn, were the products of Hitler's war. Bonn, the West German Federal Republic's capital, is the emblem of this latter-day Germany, with its endless round of dreary cocktail parties, its ministerial rabbit warrens, its bureaucracy, provincialism, banality. Only the occasional thoughtful utterances of Theodor Heuss, the Federal President from 1949 to 1959, have broken its steady, soulless rhythm of technocratic existence.

The correspondent of *Die Welt*, Peter Grubbe — who spent nearly ten years in London up to 1958 — has described feelingly his impressions on his eventual return to his own country. He found that people were obsessed with a lack of time. Everyone was in a hurry, and nobody seemed to listen any more to what his fellow had to say. Businessmen and civil servants demonstrated an almost demented pride in the fact that their engagement books were so well filled-up for so long ahead, showing that they were using every minute of the day. The urge to be prosperous was producing all sorts of side effects — the workingman looked like a well-to-do member of the middle class and left a tip for the waiter; the coal miner put on clean clothes in an excellent changing-room and never showed a grimy face on the street; the diner-out drank wine with less appreciation but at three times his previous speed; any self-respecting citizen expected to take his holiday abroad. In 1954 Düsseldorf had five travel bureaus; in 1959 it had twenty-three.

When a community has crumbled into chaos like that of Germany at the war's end, there is no ready answer to the question as to how and in what form it can be re-established. The Allies (apart from the Russians) did not come to Germany of their own free will, but because a madman had threatened European civilization with annihilation. The mistakes which the Allies made in Germany were the sort which could be expected. No German has ever explained to me how things could really have been better organized — he has only outlined, in detail, his personal complaints about occupation.

No harm is done by admitting that the Allies made mistakes; it should render the Germans more aware of their own. It is equally obvious that the Allies did not come to Germany in a co-operative frame of mind. The French were stirred by memories of past sufferings, and by the periodic pulse of an inferiority complex. The British felt a cold distaste and the unspoken resentment caused by losing the status of a Great Power. The Americans were animated by a sharp irritation at having once again been forced into an unwanted, unnecessary, catastrophic war. Self-examination can be salutary if it helps towards solving "the German Problem." And there, at least, the Western Powers and the fifty-two million West Germans are united by the pursuit of a common objective — the emergence of a viable, peaceful, civilized German community, with a tremendous role to play in Europe and the Western world.

Day of Judgment

The strong men, the masters . . . regain the pure conscience of a beast of prey; monsters filled with joy, they
can return from a fearful succession of murder, arson, rape
and torture with the same contentment in their souls as if
they had indulged in some student-rag. . . . How can one
fail to perceive, deep down in all noble races, rapacity; the
splendid blond beast that stalks its prey and prowls in
search of victory?
— FRIEDRICH NIETZSCHE

In the camps for Russian prisoners they have begun to
eat each other. This year alone between twenty and thirty
million people will die of starvation in Russia. Perhaps this
is as well, for certain nations must be decimated.
— AIR-MARSHAL HERMANN GÖRING, to Count Ciano,
1943

IN the winter of 1942, many hundreds of British officers who
were prisoners of war witnessed one of the most pitiful proces-
sions imaginable. A column of around two hundred Russian prisoners was marched past the British compound at Warburg camp
into a separate wired-off enclosure. Reeling with physical exhaustion and hunger, some of them wounded, unshaven and
filthy, they were penned into an open space surrounded by
ten-foot-high wire which was picketed by raised sentry-boxes
manned with machine-gun crews. There the Russians settled
down to death by slow starvation.

Their German captors had not yet decided what was going to
be done with them. So many hundreds of thousands of Russian
prisoners had been captured that it was not possible to put them
to work at once. And in the meantime it was hardly worth feed-

SZEWCZUK, *Die [...]*

Their Free and Secret Choice — without
Permission of the East German Regime

ing them. Big zinc urns filled with watery soup and a few shreds of potato peel and turnip were wheeled into the Russian compound and the prisoners were left to feed themselves as best they might. German guards laughed merrily as starving men fought like animals over the miserably inadequate food. Usually one or more urns would be upset during the frantic struggle.

The British officers did what they could. Their senior officer complained to the German Commandant that Russians were literally starving to death in plain view of their British allies. The answer was a shrug. Could the British, the Commandant was asked, be allowed to contribute some of their own food to the Russians? The answer was, "No. If you did that it would mean that we were overfeeding you. And we would cut your rations accordingly." At one point the Russian and British compounds were separated only by two double rows of wire and a ten-yard-wide corridor in between. British officers began throwing food over the wire, only desisting when German sentries opened up with machine-gun fire over their heads.

The Commandant issued an order that sentries would in future fire to kill, both on the British who threw the food and the Russians who snatched it up. British lives were protected, in some degree, by the Geneva Convention; Russian lives, on the other hand, were as good as worthless. But the Commandant relented so far as to agree that the tubs of swill which left the British camp would be diverted from Westphalian hogs to the Russians. Individually and in groups British officers worked out a new plan: they put whole potatoes, half-loaves of bread, already-opened cans of meat into the swill. The German riposte was to insert rusty razor blades into the good food and watch the Russian prisoners cut their mouths and tongues to bits.

I watched this happen. I was as much amazed as horrified. I need not have been. For the Germans carried their innate gifts for bestial and sadistic cruelty to a high pitch during the years of the Nazi era. Their conquerors were horrified to find, in almost every Gestapo headquarters from Norway to the Spanish frontier and from the Channel coast to the steppes of the Ukraine, diabolical instruments of torture which would have shamed the Spanish

Inquisition in their infinite variety. They found clamps for crushing testicles, thumbscrews and drills, specially constructed pads for electrocuting penis, anus or testicles. They found the written records of their use — for Germans have an incurable habit of committing everything to paper and refusing to destroy records. More than one criminal has been caught because of this.

Wing Commander Yeo-Thomas, the "White Rabbit" of the British Air Force, had his testicles systematically crushed and was repeatedly "drowned" and revived after being held down in baths of ice-cold water until his lungs began to fill. German girl secretaries of the Gestapo looked on and howled with laughter. The French Resistance heroine "Odette" had her toenails pulled out one by one. A friend of mine, a Channel Islander, was beaten up morning and evening in a Frankfurt jail. His teeth were smashed and his hair torn out in handfuls. After each beating he was placed in a steel cage, which was hoisted ten to twelve feet up from the ground. He contracted diphtheria and went blind. By some fluke he did not die; by another he was released. He was seventeen at the time, and he had refused to "confess." This was quite simply because he knew nothing.

German cruelty was matched by German efficiency in hunting down their often totally harmless victims. In White Russia and the Ukraine S.S. troops or the ordinary soldiers who did the job for them were given instructions like these:

"Even if there is no cellar in a house, a large number of people may be found in the little space between the floor and the ground. In such places it is advisable to lift the flooring and send in police dogs." (S.S. Report, Pinsk, 1942.)

As a prisoner of war I remember a German guard showing me pictures in an illustrated paper of an S.S. roundup in the Lublin area of Poland. One S.S. unit, so the story ran, had on a number of occasions been unable to track down people whom they saw moving about in the night and who were challenged, shot at, but got away. The S.S. unit sent out patrols with dogs. Quite by chance they stumbled on the hideout of a score of Jews. A shaft had been dug fifteen feet down into the ground, and a chamber excavated at the bottom of it. A trap door, with grass sods packed on top of it, opened onto the side of a manure heap. The Jews laid in a stock of potatoes, and only came up at nighttime to find water.

The illustrated paper which published the story complimented the S.S. men on their courage and cunning. It showed the group of shivering, terrified Jews in pictures which carried captions like, *"Rats dug out of their stinking hole! You can smell a Jew even when he's under a manure heap!"*

Those Jews were doubtless among the six million whom the Germans murdered during the Nazi era. Nine Germans out of ten would probably still deny today that anything like that number of Jews died, just as they claim that they had never heard of the concentration camps. (Dachau was one of the first such camps, and even before the war nine out of ten citizens of Munich — population 800,000 — knew of Dachau's existence.) A decade after the war the story of the concentration camps was still popularly regarded as a "fable" invented by the victor nations. (A weekly paper claimed that the first gas chamber which ever came to Germany was a mobile unit brought to Dachau by the United States Army in order to pin guilt on innocent Bavarians!) By inference, if no crimes had been committed there could be no properly convicted war criminals. From 1951 onwards a violent campaign for their release was whipped up by Germans who ought to have known better.

In January of 1951 a delegation from the Bundestag called on the United States High Commissioner, Mr. John McCloy, and asked that an act of amnesty be passed for the 1100 war criminals still held in Allied jails in Germany and in Western countries. The Federal Minister of Justice, Dr. Thomas Dehler, made an impassioned plea for mass release. The death sentence, he pointed out, had been abolished in the West German Federal Republic. Too long an interval had elapsed between the sentencing to death of a small minority of the war criminals and implementation of the sentences. Many sentences, both to death and to imprisonment, were, in Dr. Dehler's view, unjust. Finally, he questioned the legality of the Allied courts which had tried Germans.

In Landsberg, where the American-administered jail held twenty-eight Germans who had been sentenced to death, the Lord Mayor told demonstrators: "The time for silence is past; now we must act. We must tell the Jews to go back where they came from." A small delegation of Jews attending the demonstration and trying to make their voices heard were howled down with, "*Juden Raus!*" ("Jews, get out!") On January 31 the American authorities commuted 21 out of 28 death-sentences to imprisonment, but still no one was satisfied. Agitation for the commuting of the remaining seven death sentences went on. The seven included men like Otto Ohlendorf, who freely admitted that he had authorized the murder of over 90,000 people, mostly Jews and gypsies and including many children; Paul Bloebel, who naïvely suggested that he had organized the killing of "only" 30,-000 and not 60,000 Jews in the two-day massacres at Kiev; and Oswald Pohl, who ravaged the Jewish ghetto in Warsaw, killed or deported 56,000 people, and personally selected dozens of them for hideous medical experiments.

On June 7 a right-wing member of the Bundestag, Franz Richter, interrupted a debate in order to announce that the seven men had been executed and that any further cooperation with the United States should be impossible. One paper, the Düsseldorf *Mittag*, wrote that the Western Powers had "allowed these men to suffer unspeakable tortures which had been almost indefinitely prolonged," and that the story of Landsberg was "a deadly sin against all principles of humanity." In reality, defense counsels had held up their appeals — and there were a number of them — until the last possible moment. In this way they hoped to string out the time spent in jail by their condemned clients to the maximum. For they knew that they were guilty, but hoped that the time factor — failing all else — might save them.

National hysteria over war crimes produced some curious incidents. On October 24, 1951, a Cologne court acquitted an S.S. doctor who had helped to put to death more than eighty insane children at Sachsenburg Hospital between 1941 and 1944. The doctor maintained that he had killed only incurable idiots and so was able to save the lives of less afflicted infants. This was a ludicrous argument; in practice, he began with the maddest because they were the most trouble to look after. In any event, he was implementing the official Nazi policy of "getting rid of the useless mouths." But the court found him not guilty, even of manslaughter. This might still be excused on the grounds that he undoubtedly had acted under orders and had killed the children as painlessly as possible. But the court went even further; it added a rider, expressing its sympathy with an unhappy man, who had only done his duty!

Early in 1952 a former official of the German Foreign Ministry, Franz Rademacher, appeared before the Nuremberg criminal court charged with having helped in the deportation during the war of 80,000 Jews from Rumania and another 108,000 from France. Nearly all of them were sent to the Ausschwitz concentration camp, and four out of every five were gassed or disappeared. Rademacher's defense rested mainly on his assertion that he had really wanted the Jews sent to Madagascar (he could offer no explanation as to how or why the French authorities in a purely French colony would be prepared to receive them). While still on bail Rademacher was smuggled out of Germany by his friends in the S.S. and reached Cairo. This was the first notable success of the S.S. "escape route" to the Middle East, which five years later was functioning perfectly.

In October 1952 a stranger and more significant drama took place. At the end of August 1952 two war criminals, Hans Kuhn and Wilhelm Kappe, escaped from the British-administered jail of Werl. These were two of the men for whom West German parliamentarians, churchmen and newspaper editors raised anguished voices. Kuhn was serving a twenty-year sentence for murdering three captured Allied airmen. The three were members of a party consisting of one British Royal Air Force officer and three crewmen of a Canadian Air Force bomber shot down near Solingen on November 5, 1944. A German Luftwaffe guard was escorting the men to jail when its way was blocked by a crowd of civilians and S.A. storm troopers (Brownshirts). Kuhn, who was on leave from the Russian front, pushed two Luftwaffe guards aside and opened fire on the party of prisoners, killing three of them. Kappe had been sentenced to twenty-one years' imprisonment for killing a Russian prisoner of war in cold blood at Wilhelmshaven in 1941.

The two men slipped away from a Werl working party sent out to collect firewood. Kuhn gave his story to a German illustrated paper in Hamburg, *Der Stern*. He claimed that he received no legal aid at his trial (this was demonstrably untrue), had been half-starved (the rations at Werl amounted to twenty-five hundred calories a day and the prisoners did only a little light work), and had had several teeth knocked out by "the brutal Sergeant Brunner of the Essex Regiment." Kappe was more discreet. He vanished, and the British authorities vainly pasted up notices all over Western Germany bearing a picture and description of him.

On September 29 Wilhelm Heidepeter, a fishmonger in the little Friesland town of Aurich, was buttonholed in the street by a man called Ballin, a mere acquaintance, who had evidently been drinking. Heidepeter, a quiet, friendly man, was a person of some importance in Aurich. He was a town councilor and a prominent member of the local branch of the Social Democratic Party. He owned a smart little shop and a thriving business, and in the town square he was well known and well liked, with his long white apron, his ready smile and his range of freshly caught North Sea fish to sell.

Ballin told him that he had been drinking with an escaped criminal. From this tipsy clodhopper Heidepeter gathered that the man had freely admitted that he had been convicted of murder. As it happened, there were two murderers (other than Kappe) at large in Friesland, and police notices had been put up on the walls of the town-hall. Heidepeter instantly informed the police of what Ballin had told him. Patrols were sent out, and stopped and questioned anyone on the roads who did not belong to the neighborhood. Kappe was arrested at the village of Nadoerst, a few miles north of Aurich. He was brought back to the police station, questioned and identified. The British authorities at Werl were informed.

The police admitted that they were "terribly embarrassed"

when they found that they had captured a man who had murdered "only" a Russian prisoner of war. They gave him cigarettes and apples, while the British escort from Werl was driving the one hundred miles to Aurich. Later the Aurich police chief was to be sued by an ultra-patriotic Dortmund chemist for "crimes against humanity," and was to remark ruefully, "We are just not taught to distinguish between criminals and war criminals — we merely have to rope in wanted men." But the police saved their honor as good Germans when the British escort arrived. They moved Kappe into a room with an unbarred, open window and left him there, while they offered the British coffee. Kappe, rather naturally, escaped.

On the next morning a threatening crowd gathered outside Wilhelm Heidepeter's house. They propped a notice board against it which bore the words "Here lives Heidepeter, a Traitor." They spat in the face of his assistant, Emil Zagowski, when he tried to set up the fish stall in its usual place in front of the shop. When Heidepeter himself appeared, "Friesian fists were raised, and Friesian voices shouted, Down with him and his fish stall!" — as a local paper put it. One newspaper called him "the Judas of Aurich"; another launched a fund for Kappe and his wife, although Kappe's sole connection with the place was one visit to the police station and another to a beer hall. Heidepeter's life was threatened. He and his family left house, home town and the fish shop, and moved over one hundred miles away to a place whose name could not be disclosed for years.

The Heidepeter story proved that Germans were just not prepared to believe that their own people had committed hideous crimes in the past, and were even less disposed to find out about them. A nationwide campaign to "set the prisoners free" was instituted. Its moving spirit was the deputy chairman of the Free Democratic Party, Dr. Erich Mende, who had held colonel's rank at the end of the war and had been decorated with Hitler's "Knights' Cross." Mende said that his purpose was to "reaffirm the honor of the German soldier." He stated explicitly that only 12 out of 105 war criminals still in Werl in January 1953 were genuinely guilty of a criminal act. One of the elder statesmen of his party, Dr. Ernst Achenbach, went further; in his view there was not one single convicted German war-criminal who would be regarded as a criminal in the eyes of the law.

The truth was that, out of the 105, 64 were men who had served on the staffs of concentration camps, where murder — ordered or individually inspired — was a daily event; another 39 had been convicted of individually undertaken murders of Allied nationals, outside the concentration camps. The remaining two men were General "Panzer" Meyer and General Falkenhorst, who had countenanced atrocities in their areas of command.

Mende's campaign was less than honest. He encouraged a mass of other accusations against the Western Powers who continued — against their understandable inclination to be rid of an awkward problem — to hold German war criminals. He accused the British, for instance, of holding men who were chronically ill. The answer, in 1953, was that one man was a worrying medical case. Ex-Marshal von Manstein was released on bail in August, 1952, and sent to a Kiel clinic for treatment for cataract in one eye. Only one war criminal in Germany died in 1952, and only one of those in British hands was over sixty-five — although the "Set the prisoners free!" campaigners maintained that people were being held until they were at death's door.

In May 1953 von Manstein's conditional release was made final. He was restored to his home and his family and, it must be admitted, behaved with a fair degree of discretion. At the elaborate celebration organized in his honor at his home village of Allmendingen, in Württemberg, he consented to listen only to an address of welcome by the Lord Mayor and to the singing of the German National Anthem. The Prussian virtues are liable to assert themselves at unexpected moments. But von Manstein's premature release should never obscure the justice of his original conviction. In the Crimea Manstein had told his troops: "A large part of the population will have to starve. None of the goods that the Fatherland gives us, at the cost of privations, may out of a sense of mistaken humaneness be distributed to prisoners and to the population." To eradicate a sense of pity from the minds of a whole army of soldiers is a cruel thing. And while Manstein did alter some parts of the infamous High Command Order to the German Sixth Army in Russia in October 1941, he did not touch the following passage: "The soldier in the eastern territories is not merely a fighter according to the rules of war, but also the bearer of a ruthless national ideology . . . therefore, the soldier must have an understanding of the necessity of a severe but just revenge on subhuman Jewry."

Eighteen years later a German, who was asked by a friend of mine why he had returned so late from a Soviet prison camp, explained that he had been in the Waffen S.S. But he had a consolation. "You see," he said, "I was privileged to watch the executions of Jews and partisans in Sinferopol by Marshal von Manstein's troops." Privileged!

The Mende campaign reached its climax at the time of the 1953 Federal elections. This, indeed, was exactly as intended. American officialdom dissolved — as sometimes happens — into a state of acute embarrassment over policies which no longer seemed to dovetail with political expediency. The British were quicker to answer the German accusation that innocent soldiers, who had "only done their duty," were being treated as scapegoats for a lost war. Out of nearly 100 war criminals left in British hands, just 8 had served in the German Army and another four in the armed Waffen S.S. A full list of answers was given to German complaints that the Werl inmates were not being generously treated. It was shown that their conditions of existence were at least 50 per cent better than those of convicted Displaced Persons, who occupied the section of the prison which was under German management. But those Displaced Persons had, at the very worst, robbed a German bank or hit a policeman who tried to carry out an arrest by the usual German frontal tactics. They were not murderers.

The Tank Corps ex-general, Heinz Guderian, asserted: "It was not the honor of the German prisoners that was ever in question, but that of their Allied jailers." Well, the consciences of the Allied jailers rest easy, for all that.

It is a misfortune for all Germans that their leaders — when

59

leadership is vitally needed — are apt to fail them, and fail them badly. In the summer of 1953 the Federal Chancellor, Konrad Adenauer — bowing to the storm blown up by his Free Democratic Party allies in the Government and Parliament — told the Bundestag that every possible effort would be made to secure the release of all war criminals. There is no exact parallel to such a statement. The nearest possible one would be if the Mayor of New York should tell his electors that he would contrive to empty the city jails. Almost on appointment, the Federal Minister for Foreign Affairs, Heinrich von Brentano, asked the Western Powers in the fall of 1955 to free the war criminals. The doyen of the Roman Catholic hierarchy, Cardinal Frings of Cologne, sent a similar request to Queen Elizabeth. And as we have seen, the Federal President, Professor Theodor Heuss, sent a message of heartfelt congratulation to Baron von Neurath when the latter was released from the "major" war criminals' jail of Spandau in 1955.

War crimes should not be looked on solely as affairs of individual brutishness. Big German industries employed slave labor, with an untroubled conscience and with a heartfelt relief at the thought of how little it would cost them. The armaments and steel firm of Friedrich Krupp employed slave labor on a large scale — knowing that used-up foreign workers would be moved on to concentration camps and extinction, in the gas chambers or otherwise. So did Heinkel, Demag, AEG. Also I. G. Farben, Europe's biggest chemical combine, was a bad offender. It actually built a big plant — the Monowitz Buna works, next door to the Ausschwitz concentration camp — in order to benefit from an inexhaustible supply of cheap and expendable labor. The basis for the deal between I. G. Farben and the Nazi Government was a very simple one — I. G. Farben technical know-how was to dovetail with the Nazi "extermination through work" program, by which Jews and others were simply transferred to the gas chambers when their performance fell below the level set by their employers. It was nonsensical for I. G. Farben executives to deny that they knew anything of what was planned — every detail of the deal had to be thrashed out beforehand.

Yet in February 1955 directors of I. G. Farben called on me in order to protest their innocence (their animating reason was not simply self-justification, but the worry caused by claims for compensation brought against them by former slave employees who had miraculously survived). It was revealing to listen to what these ordinary, businesslike, self-satisfied gentlemen had to say.

I. G. Farben, they told me, had been "instructed" to establish its Buna plant at Ausschwitz-Monowitz. It was part of the Nazi plan to "bring industry" to the dreary plains of Poland, and Ausschwitz was out of range of Allied bombers. I. G. Farben was "forced" to take slave laborers from Hitler's biggest concentration camp. Its directors, in fact, had to take orders from local S.S. commanders.

The plant was set up in a "veritable desert." It was tough work. Why, "even the German employees" had to sleep in their cars or in tents to begin with! Of course, to give slave workers a "proper" supply of food in this remote, evil spot was impossible. Ration scales, for that matter, were laid down by the Ausschwitz camp command. And the method of using these slave laborers was — well — "unfortunate." They were worked at high pressure until they were too weak to carry on. When they were lined up for selection for the gas chambers, it was little use for them to stick out their chests and pretend to be physically fit. The S.S. guards walked round behind, and their buttocks, their pitifully wasted buttocks, always gave them away.

"Frankly it was a nasty business," one I. G. Farben director told me, "it was simply not nice at all" — a magnificent understatement if intended to describe so horrible an episode. But — "We Germans were torn in two. Things were done which we didn't necessarily approve of. But Germany, after all, had to win the war." No, it would have been no use at all protesting, I was told. "Why, they might have put people like us in the gas chambers, too! After all, the whole of Germany had in a sense become one big concentration camp by then. And we were to all intents and purposes prisoners too."

Anyway, a director summed up, their firm was ready to offer a lump sum in compensation to those who survived their "employment" by the biggest and ostensibly most reputable chemical combine in Europe (to do I. G. Farben justice, it did produce a sum of around 35 million marks at a later date, but this was partly because individual claimants for huge damages had begun to assert their rights in the German law courts). Finally, I was told, the Federal Government had signed a reparations agreement with Israel, and didn't this constitute the end of the whole affair? Like many other Germans (the editor of the Düsseldorf *Mittag* wrote the same thing as late as March 1959) the I. G. Farben directors believed that the German payment to Israel wiped out individual claims for loss of limbs and livelihood, the murder of all members of a family, incredible cruelty and prolonged suffering. The German-Israeli agreement did nothing of the kind; it provided funds for the resettlement in Israel of European Jews who had been uprooted from their homes by Hitler.

I met the directors of I. G. Farben in 1955. Their attitude towards all that had happened was fairly typical of the German community as a whole. Concentration camps were just not a subject which was discussed in polite society. A German friend explained why to me. The Germans, in their turn, had suffered bitterly at the hands of Russians, Poles and Czechs, and millions had been driven from their homes. One evil "canceled out" another, and comparison of the wrongs done by the Germans or their enemies was purposeless. The Germans had already suffered too much emotionally — had they not survived two lost world wars, two inflations and the Allied Occupation? It was not "fair" to burden them with a permanent load of guilt; their "nerves" wouldn't stand it.

In October 1955 a Professor Karl Clauberg returned from a prisoner of war camp in Russia, as a result of the agreement reached a month earlier when the Federal Chancellor, Konrad Adenauer, visited Moscow. He was greeted by former members of the S.S., regaled with food and drink, allowed to broadcast from the prisoners' transit camp at Friedland, and even appeared on television. He was promised a payment of six thousand marks (fifteen hundred dollars) as compensation for long detention as a prisoner.

Clauberg had served as a doctor at Ausschwitz. But what a doctor! To what purpose did he swear his Hippocratic oath to heal? Clauberg occupied himself at Ausschwitz devising and putting into practice new methods of mass sterilization. Before applying them, he carried on a lively correspondence with Heinrich Himmler, Reichsfuehrer of the S.S., on their efficacy. He claimed that a twelve-man unit would be able to sterilize several thousand people a day "comparatively painlessly." In reality Clauberg's methods were primitive and indescribably cruel. All of his victims suffered hideously from internal burns, and scores died in agony from them.

Clauberg's arrival in West Germany and his story aroused scarcely a ripple of interest, but meanwhile developments were taking place which hastened the day of judgment for the blood-guilty of Hitler's Reich. The Western Powers handed over their war crimes files to the German authorities. British Intelligence officers, quite by chance, unearthed a mass of material on the concentration camps — especially Sachsenhausen — in the villa of an S.S. officer at Aachen. The old German weakness for clinging on to records had asserted itself once again. German law courts — spurred in many cases by Ministers of Justice of various *Länder*, who had themselves suffered under the Nazis — were beginning to take action against unpunished war criminals. The former deputy commandant of Dachau, Zill, was sentenced to life imprisonment. So was Kramer, the former commandant of a Jewish forced-labor camp in Poland.

The German conscience was beginning to stir. For the grisly sufferings of the concentration camps were coming alive again — in print. Germans learned of the prewar camps — in Friesland, where a sullen, soulless population had found no difficulty in shutting its ears to their sounds of horror; or at Buchenwald, where in 1938 the camp loud-speakers announced: "Any Jew who wants to hang himself must put a piece of paper with his number in his mouth, so that we may know who he is." Germans learned of the recreational activities of the S.S. in Poland, how they used to break into Jewish homes, force all occupants to strip naked and dance with each other, then make them wash their jack boots and drink the filthy water.

Germans began to learn of some of the medical experiments practiced on harmless, helpless victims; how the cultured, charming Dr. Sigmund Rascher of Dachau used to put prisoners in a sealed van, extract the air progressively and watch them die of hemorrhages of lungs or brain through an observation window. They began to learn how other prisoners were put into ice-cold baths, how blood was extracted from their necks and tested as their temperatures sank to freezing-point, and how they were "brought alive" by being taken out of the bath and "sandwiched" between two (non-German, of course) prostitutes. They began to learn of the true horror of the gas chambers, when poison gases were not applied in sufficient strength and massed crowds of prisoners took one hour, two hours to die, spattered by their own and their neighbors' urine and excrement, blue, naked and reduced by this obscure cruelty to the last stages of bestial degradation.

Yet the German conscience is famously resilient, and it was not until 1958 that a series of trials shook it finally into life. In August ten former officials of the S.S. and Gestapo were sentenced to terms of imprisonment ranging from three to fifteen years at Ulm. They had assisted in literally thousands of murders of Lithuanian Jews, when serving with the *Einsatzgruppen*, the special service squads of the S.S. The sentences imposed were by no means severe, and the case attracted less attention than might have been expected. Often the Ulm courtroom was less than half full. But another trial, which ran concurrently in Bayreuth, excited far more interest. This was of Martin Sommer, known as "The Hangman of Buchenwald," and up to that moment the most atrocious war criminal who had been brought before a German court.

Sommer was the son of a well-to-do butcher, who used the profits of his business in order to buy land and stock it with pigs and cattle. Martin Sommer joined the Nazi S.A. in 1931 and three years later volunteered for an S.S. instruction course at the "Blackshirts College" in Dresden. After a year's training he was sent to the Sachsenburg concentration camp and stayed there until it was shut down in 1937. The Sachsenburg inmates mostly went to Buchenwald, and Sommer went with them.

At Buchenwald Sommer was given a free hand with his countless victims. He devised a special "whipping machine" on which prisoners were strapped naked and beaten, often to death. As a sadist of the most terrible kind, Sommer took a keen personal interest in the weapons which he used on these occasions — finely wrought steel rods; sticks trimmed from the hardest hazelwood; a rhinocerous-hide whip; a broad, pliant strip of gristle cut from beneath a bull's spine. He enjoyed his task so much that he was known to have beaten fifty prisoners in succession. Those at the end of the queue came off more lightly — and Sommer told the Bayreuth court how he sometimes suffered himself from "thoroughly unpleasant blisters of the hands."

Sommer denied that he "beat to kill"; if his victims died later it was simply because they were in poor physical shape anyway. He denied, indignantly, that when he grew tired he used to strike deliberately at spine and kidneys, furious that he could no longer lacerate flesh to his taste. But when asked if he whipped women as hard as men, Sommer answered, "Of course." He agreed placidly that he used to make his victims count out the strokes aloud, until they were screaming unintelligibly. Then he often made them start again, from "one." And in jail he spent much of his time modeling a miniature version of his Buchenwald whipping block.

Sommer used, too, to hang people from the branches of trees or from stout poles, with their hands tied behind their backs and their bound wrists taking the full weight of their bodies. "In theory," he told the court, "their toes were meant to touch the ground. But generally they were not tall enough." Sommer tortured the hanging men and women by burning them with cigarette butts, ripping their ears and noses with his signet ring, beating them in their vitals with an iron bar. But not really hard, he insisted, for he could recall only one man suffering a slightly torn ligament. Sommer himself named this place of execution "the Singing Wood."

Sommer, finally, was accused of killing twenty-one people individually by giving them injections. He injected intravenously with kerosene and gasoline, even with air. This was "in the interests of science" and he watched the death agonies with an avid interest shared by the camp's chief doctor, Hans Eisele, who managed to flee to Egypt in July 1958, with the Bavarian police too slow on his trail. Eisele and Sommer between them poisoned several people, who went blind and were "put down," like a dog with rabies, by shooting. By a curious perversion, Sommer used to keep corpses under his bed — for "physiological observation," as he explained to the court.

German nerves were still lacerated by the revelations of the Sommer trial when two yet more frightful sadists came before a German court. "Iron" Gustav Sorge and "Pistol" Wilhelm Schubert were brought before the *Land* Court in the Federal Capital of Bonn, where the highest in the land could take an interest in the case, if they so wished (in practice, virtually none of them went near the courthouse during the four months that the trial ran). Sorge and Schubert were *Blockfuehrers* in Sachsenhausen concentration camp during the war. They were accused of 102 and 67 individual murders respectively, between 1938 and 1943. They were found guilty of 67 and 46 murders, and of having participated in thousands of others. They were sentenced to imprisonment for life on February 6, 1959.

It was an unforgettable experience to listen to the two men giving evidence, who must have been among the most brutal and persistent murderers of the Nazi era. Sorge was a mere five feet four inches tall, a lightweight of around one hundred and thirty pounds. With his high cheekbones, ugly gash of a mouth, receding forehead and cold, predatory eyes, he had a close physical resemblance to Dr. Josef Goebbels, that prototype of the undersized bully. He gave his evidence in a soft, level tone, answering questions with academic exactitude. There was a nightmarish quality about the dispassionate way in which he sometimes corrected the court — no, he had not beaten three men to death that day, but only two — or, identified the photograph of a murdered man, remarking on the fact that he died on his very first day at Sachsenhausen.

Schubert was a far more typical specimen of a Nazi storm trooper squad, with his straight back, broad shoulders and forceful chin, and with the contempt with which he flung back his head and stared his judges down when he did not intend to answer one of their questions. Stocky but upstanding, Schubert wore a neatly folded handkerchief in his breast-pocket, brushed his hair well back sleekly and smartly, answered questions in clipped monosyllables until the trial was far advanced and the appalling weight of his guilt began to become apparent to him. Until then he radiated unregeneracy, glowered at his questioners, shrugged his shoulders in silence or answered back harshly and with unconcealed impatience. Where Sorge sought anonymity, Schubert was full of aggressive spirit. Each man took what he believed was the most favorable line of behavior for the conduct of his defense.

Both men came of very ordinary, worker families. Both men joined the Nazi Party in their teens, Sorge in 1931 and Schubert in 1933. Both found their way into the S.S., in each case two years after becoming Party members. Both men volunteered to work in the concentration camps. Here resemblance ended, save in the scale of their brutalities. Sorge was a fanatical Nazi, who regarded brutality as a means of striking terror into the hearts of his country's enemies, who tortured publicly for that reason, and who was granted some dim perception of his bestial guilt when his country went down in defeat. Schubert murdered at the orders of his superiors and then, feeling a sense of power, murdered on his own account. Sorge, the more rational of the two, decided to make a clean breast of his crimes; he was continually prompting, helping the court. Schubert maintained for as long as he could the fiction that he was still bound by his oath of loyalty to the Nazi Reich, and that he would give no evidence which cast any discredit on the Nazi regime. If he had killed, it was because he carried out orders, and rightly, to "execute" prisoners.

The story of their brutalities has to be told, for one simple reason — the German people has to be reminded of these things, over and over again, if they are not again to be driven by racial lunacy and ingrained arrogance over the abyss which separates civilization from barbarism. The story should be terrible enough to stick in the German mind.

The two men helped to destroy 10,800 Russian prisoners of war in 1942, but this was the least horrific of their crimes. For the extermination of the Russians was carefully, coldly ordered, and it was carried out as a military operation. The men were shot in the back of the neck; the bodies were carted away. It was a straightforward S.S. version of a slaughterhouse — except the carcasses were human. Sorge and Schubert were tried by a Soviet military tribunal after the war and shipped off to Siberia to work in the salt and coal mines of Vorkuta as convicts. They were returned from there as "non-amnestied" war criminals, in 1956.

At Sachsenhausen the two men had unlimited opportunity to display their brutality. These were some of the ways in which they murdered:

The whipping block. A "normal" punishment was twenty-five strokes administered with an oxhide whip. Prisoners were usually unconscious long before the whipping was completed. Often they received up to sixty strokes. Then they died.

The "frozen death." In winter both the accused used to chain prisoners to posts and at intervals pour icy water over them. The winters of 1941-1942 and 1942-1943 were terribly cold. Prisoners were sometimes frozen into solid blocks of ice. Needless to say, they died.

"Recreational exercise." Sorge and Schubert liked to use prisoners to "test" a new type of boot or shoe. They made them run up to twenty-five miles in them. Other prisoners were made to "frog-hop" round the camp with sacks of cement on their backs. They had to assume any ludicrous position ordered by their guards, do knee-bends and press-ups until they collapsed. "Some of the prisoners," Sorge said, "went *kaput* sooner than others. Very few lasted three days. They all went *kaput* in the end."

Boiling alive. This was a variant of the "frozen death," and prisoners were hosed with scalding water until skin and flesh flaked away and their bones were uncovered. So that they should not collapse too quickly, they received periodic jets of ice-cold water which revived them. Sometimes they took an hour or more to die.

Bursting open. The prisoner was chained and had his hands bound. Then the nozzle of a hose was forced down his throat, and the water turned on full, either hot or cold. The prisoner's stomach was ripped out, but he might not die until some time later.

Both men also trampled prisoners to death, kicking then literally to pieces with their heavy jack boots. They supervised the giving of intravenous injections of gasoline and air. They flung prisoners into open cesspits and watched them suffocating in liquid manure. They set one old man's beard alight and prevented him from beating out the flames. Sorge made prisoners take maggots from their festering wounds and feed the guard company's goldfish with them. Schubert turned the radio full on so that prisoners could be beaten up to the strains of gypsy music. His comrades encouraged him to give his ghoulish humor free rein. On one occasion a batch of new prisoners found banners over the camp gate with the words, "Welcome to Sachsenhausen! And a Happy Easter!" Unsuspectingly the new arrivals walked through the gate. Just inside they were set on by a horde of jack-booted S.S. men, beaten, kicked and stoned. One of them died the same day.

Startling confirmation for the theory that a suprising number of Germans are schizoid was forthcoming when the court heard evidence of the characters of Sorge and Schubert. The former's wife — although admitting that she wanted to divorce him after hearing what he had done — described him as a kind, loving and faithful husband, and father of a family (so was Himmler, and Hitler was notoriously fond of children and animals). Frau Sorge could only recall one occasion on which her husband had chastised one of his own children — "And then he, and not the child, cried." In the prisoner of war camp in Siberia, one fellow prisoner declared Sorge had been a loyal and popular comrade. Another said, "He was altogether a decent, honest chap. A war criminal, you say?" He shrugged his shoulders. "Quite possibly." Gustav Sorge was not the only schizophrenic in court that day.

Schubert's family always thought him "quite ordinary." He was looked on in the S.S. as something of a buffoon, perhaps a little bit weak in the head but fond of a good joke, of a drink, of a girl. Girls, in fact, were very much an interest of his, and he took great pride in showing off photographs of his latest "pick-up." "He hadn't really had time to grow up," one acquaintance remarked.

The mammoth Sorge-Schubert trial — it lasted four months, and four hundred witnesses were called — had all sorts of salutary results. It cast an interesting light on the ability of some Germans to shelter behind a cloak of respectability. One witness was a Dr. Gustav Ortmann, once an S.S. doctor at Sachsenhausen and at the time of the trial a highly-paid practitioner in the town of Kippenheim in Baden. Dr. Ortmann, oozing self-esteem and bourgeois respectability, was asked about medical facilities at Sachsenhausen. He described them as "entirely adequate." What of the food given to prisoners? It was good. "Better, in fact, than many people outside the camp had." And the treatment of the prisoners? A shrug, a polite smile — "Perfectly correct."

Why was it then, the public prosecutor asked, that so many prisoners died? Dr. Ortmann was quite prepared to answer — "Many of them were injured when out on working parties." But was it true, or not, that prisoners were manhandled? Dr. Ortmann decided to compromise — "Occasionally." And had he ever treated a prisoner after a whipping? A long pause, and a barely audible "Yes." What sort of state would a prisoner be in then?

Dr. Ortmann, who found the treatment of prisoners "entirely correct," paused for a long time before answering. Then he said, "Usually his whole backside was cut into ribbons."

The public prosecutor and the judges (at the time of the trial three out of four judges in Western Germany had been trained or served under the Nazis) were in for an unpleasant shock too. One of the witnesses was the seventy-five-year-old Karl Vollmershaus, from Coblenz. He concluded his evidence by saying, "I have given evidence in no spirit of revenge or hate. But the spiritual mentors of Sorge and Schubert should be prosecuted too. Sorge and Schubert were only their tools."

"And where would you look for them?" the public prosecutor asked.

"Among you gentlemen, too," Vollmershaus answered.

The President of the Court expressed his scandalized amazement, but the witness was only pointing an obvious moral. Sorge and Schubert did not represent the S.S. only, but the German community as a whole. Excrescences are not separate from the bodies that grow them. One of the most apt commentaries on the German community was provided by ex-Admiral Karl Doenitz, who remarked petulantly that it was a disgrace that he had not been informed about the concentration camps. Equally revealing was Frau Sorge's admission that she had lived a few hundred yards from the gate of the Sachsenhausen camp and had never once asked what went on inside.

The Sorge-Schubert trial — along with those of the Ulm murderers and Martin Sommer — produced a flurry of activity among hitherto untried war criminals and hitherto uninterested law courts. The police inspector, Artur Genath, took poison in his cell at Ulm and died. The town clerk of Gelsenkirchen, Paul Gerber, hanged himself in order to avoid arrest and trial. Another police inspector, Hans Artschwager of Fallingbostel, attempted suicide, botched it. Two former S.S. men shot themselves. In Nuremberg, proceedings were opened against August Kolb, a Sachsenhausen guard who had thrown an eighteen-year-old Polish girl to Alsatian dogs which tore her to pieces. In Munich, S.S. friends warned Dr. Hans Eisele to flee from his Pasing home and flourishing panel practice. His wife subsequently sold the house for eighty-five thousand marks (twenty-one thousand dollars) and has doubtless transferred the money to her husband's swelling bank-account in the United Arab Republic, best of all convalescent homes for Nazi criminals.

The Sommer and Sorge-Schubert trials were responsible for Dr. Gorgas's being refused permission to practice in Frankfurt by the *Land* government of Hesse, and for the inquiry into the case of

Dr. Herta Oberhaueser. During the war she took part in medical experiments in the women's concentration camp of Ravensbrück. She was sentenced to twenty years' imprisonment, but released after five years in 1952. She then set up successfully as a doctor in the town of Stocksee, in Schleswig-Holstein. Protests by the British Medical Association helped to get her license withdrawn by the *Land* government in August, 1958. Thanks to the activity of the association of former inmates of Sachsenhausen camp, information was lodged with the German courts about a dozen untried criminals who had committed atrocities almost as bad as those of Sorge and Schubert. Finally, Ministers of Justice of the *Länder* decided, in October 1958, to set up a central office at Ludwigsburg to collate information about Nazi criminals who were still at large. According to one German authority, there were at least one hundred and fifty dangerous Nazi criminals in West Germany who had never been tried.

Those who wanted to do so now began to reflect on one cardinal problem. Why should Germany — with so many fine traditions and so many honest, kindly inhabitants — produce the most atrocious sadists and the most dreadful acts of cruelty in modern European history? For the cruelty which is practiced in Iron Curtain countries differs from Nazi cruelty in one vital respect — it has been applied for a special purpose, not for its own sake.

Germans have well-developed powers of scientific deduction. If they care to apply these powers to this particular problem, they will certainly be able to find the answer. But they have shirked doing so. I can suggest only these inconclusive thoughts.

Young Germans are not natural sadists; they are not brought up to be. But like small animals, they will pick on the "weakest of the flock," the runt of the family, the creature least able physically to defend itself. The coefficient of worship of strength is despising helplessness. The Nazis canalized this instinct. For the basis of their entire philosophy was belief in the Germanic *Herrenmensch* — the superior being who was destined to rule Europe and direct the future of the world. Young Germans, according to Nazi philosophy, had to be brought up as *Herrenmenschen* from the cradle. In the meantime, Germans of every age should be mobilized to do their duty — however daunting or even horrific.

Service as concentration camp guards was only one duty which Germans might be called upon to carry out. Possibly it was the most despicable imaginable. (Himmler commented on this in sentimental terms!) Yet the Nazis knew that they would find ready volunteers. No secret here. The Germans have an almost unbelievable capacity for service — if they decide that they are serving the State. This capacity was forged in the Bismarckian era, and on the indescribably gory battlefields of the First World War. Hitler canalized this capacity too, as well as the rankest of human emotions: he encouraged Germans to be bullies. He succeeded; he succeeded so well that it may take several generations to breed this instinct for brutality out of the German community.

The most salutary effect of the war crimes trials was on the ordinary German public. The Bonn Court was bombarded with letters after the Sorge-Schubert trial ended. Only one of them came from a racial crank who asked why any Jews had been allowed to survive. Others expressed shame, sorrow and an honest desire to make amends — if only by learning the lessons of the past and by teaching the present generation of young Germans about the sins of omission and commission of their elders. One German friend who had told me how well Russian prisoners of war had been treated on the farms was thunderstruck. Another almost wept as he told me how appalled he was by the cruelties committed in the name of the German people. He added with unconscious irony, "I wouldn't have joined the Nazi Party if I had known what they were doing." It was the first time he had admitted to me that he had been a Party member. Every seat available to the public was filled at the Bonn trial and the West German press certainly gave it a fair amount of play.

And yet, and yet . . . there were some false notes which jarred the harmony of this paean of overdue repentance. Governments of some *Länder* continued to refuse to hand over to the others their documents relating to war criminals. (Schleswig-Holstein was a bad offender in this respect.) The cry was heard that, "It was the fault of the Western Powers — they should have dealt with all the criminals long ago." One writer to the daily paper, *Die Welt*, took an opposite view. Why, he asked, was "harmless" Rudolf Hess still being held in prison under Four-Power control in Berlin when all he had done was to fly to Britain in the war and try to fix up a peace treaty? Dr. Karl Weinrebe of Hamburg might have asked himself what part Hess played in the murders of the "Roehm Blood Bath" of 1934, the beatings-up of thousands of Jews on the *Kristall-Nacht* of 1938, the planning of World War II. He might have recollected that Hess flew to Britain because he wanted his Germany to be free to attack the Soviet Union without having to fight a war on two fronts.

A Rhineland student wrote in the same paper that the German people had already suffered enough as a result of the war — a war which had been "brought about by groups in which we mostly had no real part." By what right, he went on, did the British go on talking about German war crimes? It was a pity that the war criminals of other nations escaped scot-free. This was "a part of the creed of the victors." And a Munich bishop, Dr. Johannes Neuhauesler, said, "The German people knew nothing about the concentration camps." It would have been better if this good and sincere man had told them instead to find out.

Just how many Germans refused, even fifteen years after the war, to believe that such a thing as a German war criminal ever existed? The Germans — as the Federal President from 1949 to 1959, Professor Theodor Heuss, warned — are apt to develop a "cult of forgetfulness." Psychologically, this is not hard to explain. Their reactions to the blood-bespattered pages of their own country's past history are much the same as that of a hedgehog who sticks his nose out to look at the world and finds that it is not good to look upon. The German nose is buried in the present. "Even the Anglo-Saxons talk about burying the past," one editor once said to me. "So why should we Germans not do so?"

A more appropriate reflection for the German people was suggested by the story of the party of Polish children who arrived at Sachsenhausen in 1943. Several were kicked and beaten to death on arrival. A prisoner who was bolder than most (he was a Russian from Leningrad) asked one of the guards, "Which is the true Germany? This (pointing to the corpses), or that?" "That" was the camp loud-speaker out of which was coming the glory of Beethoven's Ninth Symphony.

More than ten years after the war I went back to Dachau — once again as a mere casual visitor. A bitter, black frost gripped the dreary plain of the *Dachauer Moos* which stretches up to the gates of the former concentration camp. I walked through into the garden which surrounds the crematoria. Nothing had changed. There, still marked with its convenient cross, was the "Gallows Tree," from which prisoners were suspended, garroted, slowly strangling to death. There, still, was the "Blood Ditch," scooped out behind the "Execution Range" in order to drain off the blood of thousands of martyrs, typical of the schizoid German instinct for marrying the tidy with the ghoulish.

There, still, was the "Mass Grave of Thousands," a nondescript, grass-covered mound. There were the "old" and the "new" crematoria, which were run up by slave laborers who, no doubt, were later shoveled out as ashes from their red brick, suburban walls. And there, inside, were the infinitely pathetic inscriptions and messages — *Les Soissonais à leurs Martyrs, Stanley Joachimiak was once here*, a cross, a pierced heart, a Star of David. And there was silence in that man-made desert, save for the echoed laughter of children who played outside its walls innocent of all knowledge of all that had ever happened there.

When I went away from Dachau that evening there was a blood-red sun sinking beyond the black, empty plain. And behind me the tall chimneys of the crematoria loured into a sky which was the color of ashes. The earth lay mute in the frost's embrace, as unyielding as the hearts of those who had murdered with such cold, crazy science in this dismal place. And it seemed to me that to forgive but never to forget was the smallest tribute that one can pay to the memories of the mountains of the dead. For time is no finite thing; and their cries of pain and terror should haunt this corner of Germany until the world's end.

VICKY, *Daily Exp*

"Ach, Painting Swastikas AND Getting Caught —
What Would the Führer Have Said . . . ?"

Lost Homes

Thanks to the existence of the East German Republic,
we shall never see Dr. Adenauer on our frontier, unless he
should exchange the Crusader cloak which he symbolically
wears for the mantle of repentance, in order to come and
beg our forgiveness for all we have suffered from German
militarists and war-criminals.
— PRESIDENT CYRANKIEWITZ, of Poland, in Warsaw,
March 1959

Let us strike the Poles until they lose the courage to live.
— BISMARCK

The Western statesmen who allowed the Slav Governments to expel fourteen million people must be held responsible for the deeds of the Russians. Most Germans are
intelligent enough to lay the blame for the expulsion from
Eastern Germany, the death of four million on the trek
to the West, the destruction of Dresden, and many other
atrocities, at the door of those who were their spiritual authors. They regard the Eastern Powers as the tools, but
the Western Powers as the instigators.
— WILHELM, BARON VON RHEINBADEN, in the
Frankfurter Rundschau, April 1952

FOURTEEN years after the war Germany was full of marvels of physical reconstruction, of self-made millionaires, of "economic miracles." Tucked away in an obscure corner of Bavaria is
one of the more outstanding of them, the town of Neu-Gablonz.

Four hundred years ago the Bohemian glass industry had been
founded in the town of Gablonz, nestling in the friendly foothills
of the Erzgebirge, in what is today the northeastern corner of

Czechoslovakia. Out of this glass industry — an aristocrat among handicrafts — grew the manufacture and trade in artificial jewelry. Gablonz delivered to the outside world superb "crusted," cut and colored wineglasses, decanters, bowls, along with jewelry which included first-class workmanship and trash with an undeniable charm and elegance. In the first quarter of this century trade expanded very quickly. Gablonz was a thriving town of over 35,000 inhabitants when Hitler annexed the Sudetenland in 1938.

A few years later it was little more than an empty shell. The Czechs expelled the bulk of the purely German population of Gablonz and, with a fine disregard for economics, put most of the survivors to work in the neighboring salt mines. Gablonz, for that matter, ceased to exist; it became, in good Czech, "Jablonec," once and for all time. Czech settlers arrived in a trickle and were unable to maintain the glass industry. By the middle of 1946, all but five thousand of the German Gablonzers had left their homes and had been dispersed into every corner of western Germany. Nearly all of those who remained were old people. One little scene in the huge tragedy of the depopulation of the "German East" had been enacted.

German clannishness, which is at least as potent as German patriotism, reasserted itself. Early in 1946, a small group of Gablonz Germans was given makeshift quarters a mile and a half outside the Bavarian town of Kaufbeuren. These refugees were housed in adjoining parts of the old halls and hangars where Hitler's "secret weapon," the V-1, had been built. Most of them had no work. A few found temporary employment with the farmers of this poor and sandy part of Bavaria. The sole factors in the lives of the remainder were the miserably inadequate rations (about thirteen hundred calories a day) and the equally wretched Poor Relief (about fifteen dollars a month in depreciated Reichsmarks).

With astonishing pertinacity, the Gablonz Germans set out to refound their old industry. They wrote letters to friends and relatives in other parts of Germany. Hitchhiking, traveling "black" on freight-trains, the first of the Gablonz craftsmen began to arrive. They raised small sums of money from the banks in order to buy the tools of their trade. They attracted the interest and sympathy of the virtually bankrupt Bavarian *Land* government.

In November, 1946, Neu-Gablonz housed four family firms, with a total employ of twenty-two people. Two years later there were 156 handicraft firms, employing 1500 people. Many of them were "cottage craftsmen," working in their own makeshift homes. By 1959, the population of Neu-Gablonz had swelled to over 10,000 of whom 95 per cent were former inhabitants of the old Gablonz, or their offspring. Another 3000 ex-Gablonzers were living and working in neighboring Kaufbeuren, and several hundred more in Markt Oberdorf, five miles farther south.

"We began," the owner of one of the biggest firms in the town told me, "with next to nothing. Most of our tools were homemade. We lived and slept eight or ten to a room, and although we were making glass we had none to spare for our own windows. Every pfennig we earned was plowed back into our traditionally small, compact firms of skilled craftsmen. We were lucky to have American troops in this area. They bought our stuff, for they had the cash and, if we were very lucky, they sometimes gave us coffee and cigarettes instead."

The new Gablonzers concentrated at first on artificial jewelry, for they could make this with the cheapest glass and other materials; it appealed, too, to members of the Allied Occupation forces, and quick sales were a necessity. Within a few years their goods were being exported to the Congo and the Mato Grosso, Brazil, as well as to every country of western Europe. Within a few years they were again making the same delicate cut glass, colored by the same processes that their forefathers had used — "smoked" rose, translucent blue, pale amber. By 1954 their trade had a turnover of more than ten million, and by 1959 of between thirty and forty million dollars a year. By then they had built three churches, cinemas, shopping districts and two thousand model homes. And the most remarkable thing of all about their achievement was that they had ceased to regard it as a miracle at all.

It would be next to impossible not to admire these sturdy, rather shy, unassertive Sudetenlanders. Their performance is epic. They have reassembled families and a whole community, with the minimum of fuss and with positive advantage to their Bavarian hosts. It is not hard to sympathize with them too. For most of them know that there is only the most slender chance that they will see their old homes again. Their children are growing up with no clear memory of those old Sudetenland homes, and are intermarrying with the intensely locally patriotic Bavarians. A heritage has been lost, the Sudetenland as home is being forgotten; the older members of the community are beginning to admit as much.

It is the stark fear that this is happening which has prompted the desperate efforts of a minority of the nine million East German refugees in the Federal Republic to keep alive memories of the "Homeland" and hopes of a return there. Their efforts are untiring, and are backed by every sort of argument. Often enough they sound convincing. Thus a compelling argument was advanced by Dr. Hermann Rauschning, himself a native of East German Danzig, when lecturing at a university in America, his adoptive home. This is how it went.

Germans, Rauschning explained, had good reasons for being unable to accept the Oder-Neisse line frontier as final. This was not simply because, without her eastern provinces, Germany was reduced to a "torso," an unfinished structure. It was not simply because Germany, and Europe, had lost a valuable buffer against the East, or even because the march of history and of Western civilization — as typified by the Teutonic Knights and their fortresses, by the rapacious Frederick the Great and his Prussian colonists — had been reversed. For, said Rauschning, the current theory that Germans entered these provinces as conquerors was a "foreign fairy tale." They were the exponents of a "cultured expansion" eastwards, which he compared with the movement in the opposite direction of the American pioneers during the nineteenth century. Rauschning maintained that the loss of the eastern provinces "upset the balance of Europe." The fall of Prussia was comparable with the dissolution of the Hapsburg Dual Monarchy. "Politically," he declared, "Germany and eastern Central

Europe is the core of a middle zone between East and West." His conclusion was that a strong, vital, evolutionary Europe could best be served by the creation of a strong, whole Germany — the potential link and "mediator" between East and West.

Rauschning's basic argument was echoed by the vocal representatives of the nine million East German refugees or "expellees" (who are distinct from the three million who fled between 1945 and 1960 from the Soviet Zone to the west); and support for the revision of the Oder-Neisse line frontier does not necessarily mean having once lived east of it. A Sudeten German cannot visualize ever returning home if the Oder-Neisse line has not previously been adjusted; but many a Saxon or Brandenburger cannot visualize any "final" eastern frontier within fifty miles of Dresden and Berlin. This has made it easier to organize refugees into their provincial *Landmannschaften* organizations, which have fostered local traditions, literature, habits of speech and love of the "Homeland." It has made it easier to build up an immense, intense "refugee literature," whose primary aim is to preach "the Return" and to keep revisionist aims alive.

Twelve years after the war there were nearly 250 "refugee" newspapers and periodicals in West Germany with a circulation (in 1959) of 1.6 million. The *Landmannschaften* contributed to 170 of these; there were over 50 for the Sudetenland alone; and over 40 for Silesia. Fourteen refugee papers were published abroad. Their task, wrote a Dr. Durth in the Refugee Press Service, was clear. Many refugees were becoming "spiritually integrated" in West German life. Each one of these represented "a loss to us by assimilation." Dr. Durth went on: "We must win two new kinsmen for every one we lose. We must recruit for *Ostdeutschtum* — East-Germanism. We must tell the world what eastern Germany means to its own country and to Europe as a whole."

How should this be done? One method is by extolling the very real beauties of the "German East," the blue horizons of the rolling Riesengebirge, the rich pastures and the Renaissance and baroque jewels of Silesia, the dales and valleys of the Sudetenland, the lakes and forests of Pomerania and Prussia. This was the land of the *Trakehnen* horses, of the dappled black-and-white cattle, of the long dunes of the "amber coast" of the Samland Peninsula and the Kurisches Haff. This was the land, not only of warriors, landlords and slaves, but of thinkers like Herder and Kant, Copernicus and Kleist, of painters like Adolf Menzel and social reformers like Gustav Freytag. Silesia was the richest province of Germany, and if Napoleon called Prussia "a land of six months' winter and six months without summer," the Prussians still loved it. Germans can wax lyrical over even the dreary flats of Posen and the Warthe, and these too have one advantage — space. It is lack of space which has made it so hard for many of the East Germans to settle down in suburban West Germany: they complain that they cannot breathe there.

Another method of propagandizing the Return is by arguing the impossibility of Poland's ever effectively colonizing the German East. Where once nine million thrifty Germans lived and worked, there were in 1959 no more than four and a half million Poles. ALDERS AND BRIARS COVER OUR POMERANIAN CORNLANDS is a typical headline in the Refugee Press Service, and 40,000 ACRES IN THE LEBA VALLEY RELAPSE TO DESERT. In the once flourishing little Baltic seaport of Heydekrug, we are told, it was impossible in 1959 to buy a rusty nail. The meadows of the *Warthegau* (Hitler's name for a mainly Polish area) were a mass of thistles and weeds four feet high, and the tidy villages of East Prussia had been turned into pigsties, with slops, rubbish and manure littering the main street and pavements disintegrating into ruts and holes in the muddy ground.

Here are headlines carried by a single issue of the Refugee Press Service: HUGE LOSSES OF STATE SALES ORGANIZATIONS IN THE ODER-NEISSE TERRITORIES . . . SUPPLY FAILURES IN THE BALTIC SEASIDE RESORTS . . . ONLY SEVENTEEN NEW COMBINE-HARVESTERS IN THE WHOLE OF EAST PRUSSIA . . . STETTIN AND BRESLAU TODAY — NEW RECORDS IN FILTH. Ten years after the war, according to one refugee paper, there was only one school for every 1147 inhabitants, against one for 715 before the war. The school population in the Oder-Neisse territories under Polish occupation was down from 1.6 million to 560,000. Once there was a theater or cinema for every 130 people, but under Polish occupation one for every 1050. Hospital accommodations dropped by 40 per cent after 1945. These stories — apart from often enough being true — serve the object of awakening the German instinct for progress and orderliness, and of strengthening the refugee's desire to return to his old home and throw out the evil forces of nature as well as the "Eastern barbarians." This is the way in which the idea of a new Teutonic Crusade could be born.

The German aptitude for rewriting history with little regard for historical fact has inevitably played a big part in the German demand for the restoration of its eastern territories. An article written for the Refugee Press Service by a Professor Laubert in 1953 was typical. He saw no reason why the future Germany should be restricted to its 1937 frontiers. He therefore analyzed the three partitions of Poland, at the end of the eighteenth century, in terms of Teutonic logic.

By joining in the first partition of Poland (along with Russia and Austria), wrote Professor Laubert, Frederick the Great earned the gratitude of all Europeans by restricting Russia's gains. In any case, by seizing part of Poland, Prussia only righted the wrong done to her at the Treaty of Thorn, three hundred and six years earlier.

The second partition of Poland, in 1792, Professor Laubert considered, was "entirely the fault of the Poles themselves." They had allowed their pro-German reform party to be defeated by the pro-Russian landowners.

The third partition was "merely the result of the Polish uprising of the year before." Prussia, according to the professor, was "forced" to compensate herself for Russian and Austrian gains and "even" contented herself with less than they did — a mere 2,635,000 inhabitants. And at the 1815 Congress of Vienna Prussia was "compelled" to hold on to her gains by England's Castlereagh and France's Talleyrand.

A newssheet circulated privately, but subsidized by the B.H.E.[1]

[1] *Bund der Heimatvertriebenen und Entrechteten* ("League of the expelled from their homes and deprived of their rights").

Refugee Party in West Germany, made the following claims in 1957:

> The Germans lived in harmony with the Slavs all these hundreds of years (since A.D. 921) until they were expelled in 1945.

> The forefathers of those who were expelled then were in their ancestral homes in eastern Germany before the Anglo-Saxon forefathers of the English people were in the British Isles.

> Bohemia and Moravia have been the homes of German settlers for more than 1300 years. The German Samo liberated the Slavs living there and was raised by them to the kingship in A.D. 623.

> Pomerania was a thoroughly German land for thousands of years until Russians and Poles drove out 98 per cent of the native Germans from their homes. The Western Allies agreed to this out of their blind hatred of Germany at that time.

The "historical" argument has been advanced by the leaders of the B.H.E. Refugee Party: that both the British and French Governments recognized Hitler's annexation of the Sudetenland in 1938 and offered no objection to the annexation of Memel one year later. The corollary, by German reasoning, is obvious: German's territorial claims must include both these areas, and Austria. A B.H.E. spokesman said in 1958 that any renunciation of these maximum claims should be treated as high treason.

The "historical" argument is the basis of action for the Schwerte Press Service, which circulates in both America and Britain. Its March 1955 issue contained these gems of reasoning, within a few lines of one another:

> The new railways and roads built by the Germans, after the founding of the Second Reich through the genius of Bismarck, made East Prussia one of the most important transit lands for commerce between East and West. . . . By facilitating international business between East and West, it could become a factor for world peace.

> The wild hatred of the mere name of Prussian, instigated by ultra-chauvinistic propaganda, has kept people in

the dark about what Prussia has always been — a barrier against barbarous invaders, such as Tartars, from the East.

Trade channel or barrier — which was East Prussia? It could scarcely be both. In 1959, the same press service was still churning out the same nonsense, blaming the results of Hitler's war on the Western Allies, threatening attempts to revise the Oder-Neisse line by force or by negotiation with the Soviet Union, declaiming against the Polish and Czech states and pouring out "facts" and figures about the expulsion of Germans from their homelands.

It is easy enough to paint a black picture of the endless, extravagant refugee propaganda. It is often forgotten that a love of one's own home is an honest, intelligible emotion. Two German refugees with whom I have talked have expressed this love in very different terms. One of them was born in Danzig and became a Düsseldorf businessman. "There are too many professional refugees," he told me. "They are people who will not accept the facts of history. Their numbers are going down every month, every day, as members of the German community filter west to rejoin the remainder of their families. A claim to a mass return to Prussia, Silesia and the rest makes no sense. Most of us do not want to go back anyway, but a desire to see one's old home is a different matter. That may never be lost."

An exactly contrary opinion was that of a former Silesian landowner who today likewise lives in the Rhineland, after a period of exile in England. In a letter to *The Times* of London this man, Baron von Richthofen, claimed that it was illusory to think that the East Germans would ever settle down, for good, in the "soft" German West. The only ones who were really satisfied were "opportunists" who were lining their pockets. For the rest, "A strange light comes into their eyes as soon as they can speak with others from their own homeland, as here they never feel at home, never feel satisfied." Privately, he told me that the Poles and Czechs really wanted the Germans back, for they could not deal with their unwanted heritage and were obsessed by the feelings of *Vorläufigkeit*, of the provisional position they enjoyed. In his view, the Return was inevitable, and would lead to Germans and

Poles living in friendship together in a more peaceful, happier Europe.

This man's arguments were not intentionally "irredentist" or "expansionist." He was genuinely unaware of the legacy of hatred for all things German which Hitler's armies and S.S. men left behind them throughout the whole of eastern Europe, and he did not realize how many Poles loathe Germans even more than Russians — because they had expected so much more of them. He was typical of the class of German who misunderstands history and misapplies its lessons, but with complete well-meaning.

Less typical is the sort of local association of East Germans which was still maintaining itself intact in 1959 and which will probably last as long as the lives of its present founder members. Such a one is the association of former inhabitants of the two West Prussian communities of Schlochau and Flatow, which sat almost on the German-Polish frontier of 1918-1939. Like other associations, it has a virtue which has nothing to do with morality: it is a part of German history.

Schlochau and Flatow are just north of the railway junction of Schneidemühl, in typical West Prussian countryside where moor and forest mingle with pasture and arable land, whose farmers used to be justly proud of their livestock and sugar beet crops. Up to the eighteenth century this was an unpromising land of sandy plain and trackless marsh which Brenckenhoff drained and Frederick the Great recolonized. It was German *Grenzland*, frontier country, which Teutons, Wends, Slavs and Baltic Barons had striven for centuries to master. In the third century before Christ the Teutons were dominant; in the third century of the Christian era the more Slavonic "Prusiai"; in the ninth century the Wends, and in the thirteenth the German Counts of Pomerania. Ever and again the surge of Polish invaders and colonizers swept over these flat lands, only to recede as a fresh counter-thrust came from the West.

Prussia captured the area in 1772 — finally, it seemed, but in fact only in order to usher in a new era of struggle. The Treaty of Versailles left it to Germany, with a small Polish minority but a pronounced German character. The Potsdam Agreement handed it over to Polish safekeeping which was supposed to be provisional but seems to be becoming permanent. There is scarcely a German left in the area today, and the citizens of Schlochau and Flatow are grouped in little colonies all over western Germany. At festive seasons and especially at Whitsuntide they gather together, exchange news, carouse and go their different ways again. They are mostly imbued with intense local loyalty, and pretty well all who were born before 1925 have a distinct preference for mixing with their "own kind." They harbor little resentment over the great trek westward, the years spent in hutted camps and converted air-raid shelters (in 1951 nearly two million refugees were in makeshift quarters in Western Germany; in 1959 still 300,000), the postwar lack of food, jobs and other essentials to life. But they still remember their old homes with a deep longing.

They have their own monthly paper, the *Schlochauer und Flatower Kreisblatt,* which circulates to several thousand readers. It is a modest affair, averaging ten small pages and printed in the Holstein town of Heide. The annual subscription is DM 6.60, or around $1.50. Its main circulation is in Gifhorn and Northeim, the two West German towns which "adopted" Schlochau and Flatow for a period of exile with no foreseeable end, and which give them a warm welcome for their annual reunions.

This little paper illustrates in cameo the feelings, frustrations and hopes of each and every "expellee" — no East German likes to regard himself as a mere "refugee," for only force could have made him leave his old home — and all of the expellee communities now in West Germany. Its salient feature is love of the old "homeland," endemic in every part of the paper. There are Joachim von Muenchnow's editorials, preaching the inviolability of the expellee's claim to the home, soil or corner of the street which once belonged to his family. There are the photographs of the "family parties" of the 1890's and 1900's, with the men in Edwardian boaters and bow ties, the women with jutting jaws in black dresses and button boots, the children out in front in their sailor suits. There are the advertisements for books like *The Teutonic Knights and Their Castles,* and the pictures of villages and churches, farms and forests, of the high school at Hammerstein, where Napoleon fought one of his bloodiest battles, of the Garzer Lake at Peterswalde (Petřvald now), of the statue of the stag in the town hall square at Flatow.

Each month there are five solid pages of "local" news of the widely scattered families, of births and deaths, jubilees and funerals. There are plenty of hints of the horrors of war, and the sadness of severance from home. There are entries like "Who was a soldier serving with my son, Günther Hass of Pollnitz, last heard of in Breslau in 1945?" or "I am looking for my two sons, Hans and Horst Semrau, of Hammerstein." To the bare announcement of a death is often added: ". . . who died so far from home." There are tragic references to the dead of the war — "Bertha Janke, beaten to death by Poles in Flatow prison camp, 1945," or "Melita Thiede, of Stegers, shot by the Russians 1945, aged fourteen." There are grim serials of the Russian invasion: "The Red Assault on our Brandenburg . . ."

The *Kreisblatt* is a record of rugged endurance. West Prussians revere *Ausdauer* — that power and instinct for survival with fortitude, so needed during centuries of struggle. Prussia was a tough country. Frederick the Great was imprisoned by his own father for indiscipline at Kuestrin, twenty-five miles east of Flatow, when his less fortunate boon companion, Lieutenant von Katte, was beheaded. Many of the Prussians who arrived in the West German Federal Republic were penniless: today they are mostly well-dressed, physically fit and decently prosperous. One told me, in 1946: "We can make do with a handful of potatoes. In time we shall run West Germany." Many of them helped to found some of the 3250 "expellee firms" in West Germany, which employed over a quarter of a million people in 1960.

West Prussians believe they are more God-fearing, hard-working, and mentally more stable than the Germans of the Rhine and Bavaria. Their *Ausdauer* is expressed in physical terms today by longevity and — even in exile — by big families, as well as by a tradition of sporting activity which makes them the truest contemporary disciples of that rugged gymnast, "Turnvater" Jahn, who played so big a part in propagating the ideal of German unity in the nineteenth century. It is expressed by readiness to travel the length of the West German Federal Republic in order to meet an old friend, and halfway across Central Europe to catch a glimpse of their old homes. The spiritual aspect of this *Ausdauer* was latent in a letter written to the *Kreisblatt* by a Flatower: "My good friends: I have built a new home in the West, but I do not believe that any coals, any fire can burn so fiercely as my love for my old home in the East." It was latent in one of von Muenchnow's editorials: "There are two conditions for a return to the old *Heimat*. It can be done if we do not give up hope, and this hope must be kept alive by the sheer determination of old and young alike to go back, with God's help."

The West Prussians have always been a practical people, and one of their oldest sayings is: "If you drop your broom in the morning, no good will come on that day." There was a laudable common sense in that 1945 train-convoy of Flatowers on their way to the West German Federal Republic, when they were confronted by an East German notice board reading: "In the West there is only hunger and want. Stay with us here!" The Flatowers laughed loudly and continued their journey. West Prussian sober reasoning shows itself in a 1958 issue of the *Kreisblatt*:

> We have been twelve years parted from our homes. Our children no longer regard themselves as Pomeranians or Silesians, East Prussians or Schneidemühlers. They belong to their second homeland, and they identify themselves with the places in which they live today. But these young people must carry our banners when we veterans are gone. They must never let the demand for the German East lapse.

It would be less than human to give up hope. These Prussians are still not resigned. They know that they will not return home tomorrow, or the next week. They take no comfort from the tales of the decay of agriculture in their old homelands, or from the election of a German girl — Barbara Krol — as beauty queen of renamed Wroclaw (Breslau). It is precisely the Prussian virtues — determination, loyalty, courage and an abiding love of their own homes — which make it impossible for them not to hope for the Return, for which they are prepared to wait a long time. And it is equally impossible not to feel admiration and sincere sympathy for people who have such a pertinacious faith.

The West German Federal Government has been put in an awkward position by the claims of the refugees and by the political failure of the B.H.E. party. When the party was founded in 1950, it looked as if it would lap up the whole refugee vote. The B.H.E. made immediate headway in Schleswig-Holstein and Lower Saxony, two out of the three "refugee-ridden" *Länder* (the third was Bavaria, but there a majority of refugees had quickly come to regard their new *Land* as a second home, *Zweiter Heimat*). In 1950 the B.H.E. captured 23 per cent of the votes in the Schleswig-Holstein *Land* election, in 1951 17 per cent of the votes in Lower Saxony. At the 1953 Federal election the B.H.E. leaders were still talking in terms of securing over three million votes and around 12 per cent of the poll. In the event, their vote was 1.6 million, or 5.9 per cent of the poll. Their hopes of holding the political balance between the two big parties, the Christian Democrats and Social Democrats, faded. The B.H.E. has lost votes at every subsequent federal or state election.

The failure of the B.H.E. was of itself a healthy sign, for it was primarily a pressure group which sought to attract the "have-not" vote (the "E" stands for *Entrechteten,* or "Unprivileged," and the B.H.E. added the word only in order to secure support from ex-Nazis). The emergence of a strong B.H.E. would have been somewhat analogous to the position of Parnell's Irish Party in the British Parliament towards the end of the last century. If ever in a position to hold the political balance, a strong B.H.E. would have been able to exact terms which would have had nothing to do with the ordinary processes of government. It could, for instance, have made its support conditional on a future government undertaking of an active diplomatic campaign for the recovery of the lost provinces. It could have bargained for increased financial aid for its own adherents.

Yet the failure of the B.H.E. has forced every other political party to bid for the refugee or "expellee" vote. Few responsible politicians have done this blatantly. The Federal Minister of Transport, Hans Christoph Seebohm, is an exception and his wildly inflammatory speeches are partly due to his having been a joint chairman of the German Party, which has its main strength in Lower Saxony, and partly to his personal connections with the Sudetenland. (He was born near Eger and worked as a mining engineer in Bohemia.) But the refugee vote could win or lose an election for either the C.D.U. or S.P.D. The revision of the Oder-Neisse line has, as a result, become an article of political faith, a dogma. It does not matter how obviously unattainable it may be, or may become. Up to 1960, it was truthful to say that a West German politician's career would be ended if he once made it clear that he believed the Oder-Neisse line had come to stay.

Early in 1956 the Federal Foreign Minister, Heinrich von Brentano, said in London that the German people might someday have to decide whether they should renounce their claims to the lost eastern territories — in order to set the seventeen million Germans of the D.D.R.[2] free. Within a few days Professor Carlo Schmid, the chief foreign affairs expert of the S.P.D.,[3] said much the same thing. Brentano was forced to eat his words, which were henceforward conveniently and more succulently described as "a slip of the tongue," and in May 1956 he sent a heart-warming message to the Sudeten Germans — "The right of every man to his own home must be the basis of a solution of the German refugee problems." Carlo Schmid was more dignified; he simply failed to mention the Oder-Neisse line again for a long, long time.

The Brentano *gaffe* had its sequel. The Federal Foreign Office decided to clarify its own views. It told inquisitive newspapermen that Brentano's London statement (although still officially a "slip of the tongue") had been designed to set British fears at

[2] *Deutsche Demokratische Republik* (German Democratic Republic).

[3] *Sozialdemokratische Partei Deutschlands* (Social Democratic Party).

rest. The British, it supposed, were afraid that NATO might be used by the Germans for their own territorial ends; the British had been asking for "new ideas" from the Germans; the British were interested in a détente in Europe and had ceased to give real support to plans for the reunification of the Federal Republic and the D.D.R. The Federal Foreign Office produced a simple formula for Government policy on the Oder-Neisse question. The right of every German to his old home was inalienable and no government could abrogate it by any declaration. The question of the Oder-Neisse line as an actual frontier, on the other hand, would be regulated only by a future German Peace Treaty. This had been agreed by the Allied leaders at the Potsdam conference in 1945. In any event, there could be no question of any revision of frontiers being carried out by force.

It seems surprising to find the official Foreign Office spokesman advancing precisely the same arguments as the refugee associations — although not quite so surprising, perhaps, when it is remembered that he was a Silesian and had a large map of his home town of Breslau hanging up in his office. Many of these arguments were sound, others were based on that "lunatic logic" which makes so many Germans proof against all applied reason. For instance: "The Poles did not regard 700 years of German occupation of these provinces as irrevocable. Why, then, should we Germans regard a dozen years of Polish occupation as irrevocable?" Useless to point out that Polish occupation was fragmentary, feudal, and not, as today, backed by the strongest state power in the world. Useless to point out that Poland has today copied the technique of mass deportation of populations introduced into its own country by Hitler, or that the Soviet Union regards the Oder-Neisse line as of the utmost strategic importance in warding off possible attack from the West.

Equally misleading was the Federal Foreign Office's argument that, since only global reasons could induce the Soviet Union to allow reunification of the Federal Republic and the D.D.R., then global reasons might induce it to readjust Germany's eastern frontier. Reunification may, some day, be the price which the Soviet Union is prepared to pay for German friendship. But this would be at the direct expense of nobody else. Readjustment of the eastern frontier would make a lasting enemy out of Poland, would gravely alarm Czechoslovakia, and would lead to the disintegration of the satellite bloc.

Even more unreal was this German's suggestion that Poland could be offered "compensation" for a withdrawal from at least a part of the old German eastern provinces by giving her back a part of the territorially larger area surrendered to Russia in 1945. What the Western statesmen were unable to retain for Poland in 1945 they will certainly be unable to regain for her at any future date. And this Foreign Office spokesman's final contention was that the Western Powers had a "moral responsibility" not to recognize Russian or Polish annexations. If they did not honor this responsibility, Germany might have to "turn East" in order to secure a fair solution of her frontier problem. This is a bad, dangerous argument; it could have many purposes but only one result — lasting Western distrust of Germany.

As Germans saw it, the need for a "firm" policy on the subject of the Oder-Neisse line was underlined by the publication, at this time, of Miss Elizabeth Wiskemann's book *Germany's Eastern Neighbors*. Scholarly and convincing, it aroused a storm of protest in Germany. For the lesson which the book taught was clear enough: a mass movement of population had occurred which could not foreseeably be reversed, and the Oder-Neisse line was bound to become Germany's final eastern frontier.

A howl of rage went up from the refugee associations and many other Germans beside. The author quickly became known as "the Wiskemann," a genteel jeer which marks modified German contempt. Some newspapers suggested that she had been bribed to write her book, others that she was animated by an intense hatred of Germany in which unspecified personal reasons played a big part. Even so moderate and middle-of-the-road a newspaper as the Hamburg *Die Zeit* (August 1956) roundly condemned the book, but for reasons which may seem incredible to the normal reader. Miss Wiskemann's book did not represent a serious contribution to history, because it was based on "references to old, yellowed documents." (How else does a real historian work?) And *Die Zeit* condemned the book because it "lacked passion and penetration" and had "sprung from the British tendency to recognize a reality as a reality." (What better basis for research?) Finally, Miss Wiskemann identified herself with National-Socialist ethics by wanting a "final" frontier drawn with "brutal simplicity." This was precisely what Hitler never did: every frontier which he "arranged" was intended to be revised to Germany's advantage at a favorable moment in the future.

Miss Wiskemann's reasons for regarding the Oder-Neisse line as final were simple enough. She argued that Germany, even in the days of the Weimar Republic, never ceased to play with ideas for another partition of Poland. The allegedly democratic Stresemann considered doing exactly what Hitler did, but without war. His aim was a "compression" of Poland rather than its virtual destruction by stages. When Hitler applied deportation, deprivation, sterilization, enslavement and mass murder to Poland he sowed the seeds for future vengeance. (A single quotation suffices to pass down a picture of the German Occupation to posterity. Governor Hans Frank said, "If I had to hang up posters about every seven Poles we shot, there would not be enough forests in the whole of Poland to make the necessary paper.")

Miss Wiskemann decided that the Poles had demanded only what was logical in the Oder-Neisse line, since it was the Nazis who had explained that there was no natural frontier between the Oder and the Vistula (of course, this was to prove the justice of their annexations in Poland in 1939-1940). She decided that the East German Government had been equally logical in recognizing the Oder-Neisse line under the Goerlitz Agreement of July 1950. And she summed up in one devastating sentence: "Since, however, the West German population is predominantly old, top-heavy and tending to decline, while its prosperity tends to increase, it is difficult to feel that there is a very strong case for any further interference with the incidence of population." On the whole, this summing-up is too coldly logical to be swallowed without bitterness. Her case could have been stated with more tact and human feeling, and it could have been more lastingly true. The resources of Germanic vitality are tremendous.

Her book will still do good in the long run. It will help towards correcting that appalling German habit of miswriting their own history by basing their studies on — as *Die Zeit* would have it — "passion and penetration." It will rub home the lesson that a monstrous retaliation sprang from a yet more monstrous episode of German aggression and brutality. It will undo some of the harm done by Germany's well-wishers. Two cases deserve mention.

In 1954 the Göttingen Refugee Research Committee published a small book, *Documents of Humanity*, which gave a picture of the kindly acts done by non-Germans to Germans at the end of the war. Many of the stories are moving, some only banal. But the abiding impression given is that of a vast, nightmarish and utterly unjustified expulsion of a harmless German civilian population. In his foreword Dr. Albert Schweitzer does no one — including the Germans — any good, by giving no explanation in order to put the situation into perspective.

Dr. Schweitzer's foreword includes the sentence, "Incitement to hatred had erupted in these countries of Eastern and Southeastern Europe, where hostility had deeper historic roots and where lack of education had rendered the inhabitants less resistant to violence than in other areas." This is not just unfortunate: it is dreadful! For it panders to that age-old Germanic concept of a *Herrenvolk* which is superior to its "barbaric" neighbors to the east. The expulsion of the East Germans, with its details of pillage, rape and death, makes terrible reading. But it does not compare with the story of what the Germans did in Poland — in which six million noncombatants were tortured and murdered; in which a minor, generally forgotten detail is the death-by-starvation chamber at Ausschwitz concentration camp, where prisoners were incarcerated and feasted on each others' corpses under the eyes of their German guards.

Equally ill-advised was the Whitsuntide message to the Sudetenlanders in 1956 from Cardinal Spellman, in which he wrote: "I believe that all those who have been forced to leave their homeland, or who have been expelled because of their faith, should join you in your efforts to reach your goal." The postwar "goal" of the Sudetenlanders has become the return of their homelands to Germany, and the recognition of Hitler's 1938 annexation. Could it be that Cardinal Spellman really believed that Sudetenlanders were expelled in 1945 because of their "faith"? Here is the burgeoning of a new myth, which should call forth the shades of Hitler and Henlein, who plotted the rape and destruction of Czechoslovakia, and of "Protector" Heydrich, who slaughtered the men, women and children of Lidice.

One of the most infuriating aspects of their woes, for the refugees, is the apathy of the average West German. When the weekly paper, *Der Spiegel,* asked two thousand West Germans where the Oder-Neisse line was and what territories it divided, only 22 per cent answered even approximately correctly. The West Germans' apathy — the product of extreme preoccupation with their own affairs — is often charged with resentment. More than once I have visited farmers' houses, where a dozen refugees have been crammed into two rooms and the farmer's family of five has had ten rooms for its own use, or where the refugees have had to use the pump in the yard for all washing purposes.

A Munich newspaper editor, on one occasion, began to recount to me the horrors of having "Prussians" billeted on Bavaria. I suggested that he was demonstrating a localized aspect of German race consciousness.

"Nonsense," he replied. "Your Londoners regard people from Lancashire as strange, and any Southerner in America thinks the same of Yankees."

"But we all like each other well enough," I answered.

"Ah," he said, looking very serious. "I think you're forgetting one thing. Prussians — are — all — swine."

Two other stories may illustrate how refugees from the German East are often regarded in West Germany.

An old refugee woman arrived early one morning at Düsseldorf railway station. She went into the railway restaurant to rest for a while. As with so many of her kind, her luggage consisted of half-a-dozen assorted papier-mâché "suitcases," brown-paper parcels and rolls of blanket.

The waiter approached her suspiciously. "If you want to sit here," he said, "you must order something. Otherwise you must get out!"

The old woman studied the bill-of-fare, chose the cheapest item on it, a cup of "mixed" coffee, mainly *ersatz* but with a blend of a little "real" coffee. She drank it as slowly as possible, then began to doze.

The waiter came over to her table, rapped it sharply, "You can eat, drink and smoke here," he said, "but not sleep!"

He went off, and after a time she looked round nervously, then settled down to doze again. The waiter was waiting his chance. This time he tipped her chair violently into the table. He then ordered her out of the restaurant. Meekly she went, gathering her many bundles. German character cannot be expected to change very quickly.

The second incident concerned the lease of a hunting lodge in the Eifel Hills, which was taken each year by the officers of a British regiment. They paid nothing, but undertook to keep the building in first-class order. In 1955 it seemed high time to them that they should pay some rent. They asked the owner — a rich German lady who lived in Cologne — to lunch, then broached the subject tactfully.

She flatly refused to take any rent, but wanted the British officers to keep the lodge on the old conditions. She had only one reason: "If you did not take it, the housing authorities would put refugees in, and they would very likely be Communists; in any case they would be bound to be Prussians."

Of course, there are other Germans who have done a great deal for their less fortunate fellow countrymen. A classic instance is that of the Bismarck family. After the Second World War, the grandson of the Iron Chancellor decided to turn over a large part of his 20,000-acre estate at Friedrichsrüh, outside Hamburg, to East German refugees. His own mansion had been destroyed by Allied bombs, and he and his family moved to a smaller house in the grounds. Farms, outhouses and barns were converted for the use of the refugees. I saw three comfortable if unconventional little homes which had been created out of a single barn; cottages which had once been cattle stalls; prefabricated wooden houses, each with its own garden.

The Bismarcks built their own sawmill and a small distillery. They started carpet-weaving and other cottage industries with looms and other equipment sent from Swedish well-wishers. A staff of twelve sorted and distributed gifts which came from a dozen other nations. Two thousand refugees were housed and found work on the estate by 1952, and the Bismarck Project adopted two of the poorest and most refugee-ridden villages in the whole of Germany, Klempau and Schwartzenbek. Help as practical and unstinted as this will never be forgotten.

The Bismarcks, and other well-doers, have naturally only touched on the fringes of the problem of integrating the East German refugees in the West German community. Nor can any summary of facts and figures show how far integration has been successful. For this is a spiritual as well as a material matter. The following considerations are at least relevant.

Only one out of four East German refugees who were once independent farmers today farm their own land (99,000 out of 400,000). One in seven, again, is employed on the land. These approximate figures are not as distressing as they may sound. For a great many East Germans who once owned their own farms have died since the war, and a great many more will die during the next decade. This is not meant to sound heartless; no one deserves more sympathy than the man who has lost the very land to which he dedicated his life's work.

One out of every two East Germans who were "white-collar" workers in their old homes has found the same employment in Western Germany; so has one out of every three East Germans who used to be civil servants. In 1956 the Federal Minister for Refugees, Professor Oberländer, estimated that 50 per cent out of nine million expellees had been "fully integrated" and that 40 per cent were in process of being integrated. The final 10 per cent would never be. In 1959 three out of every four refugees had been integrated, in the material sense, in the West German community. But 330,000 were still living in camps, which cannot all be closed down before 1963.

That is not a discouraging picture; by all rights, it should be an outstandingly optimistic one. No other European country but Germany would have been capable of absorbing an extra 30 per cent of population, putting it to work, welding a bigger, more efficient community with its help. This German performance would appear to be conclusive. Yet such is not the case.

For a solution of the expellee or refugee problem depends, ultimately, on the desire of the whole German community to see it solved. What solution does the bulk of the German community consider reasonable? These are some of the opinions I have read or heard:

A Hamburg businessman: "It is untrue that an overwhelming majority of the expellees are prepared to give up their claims to return to their old homes. It is not even true that they would do this, if the Soviet Union allowed the reunification of the two German states in freedom. However much we want reunification, the renunciation of our right to return to our old homes would be too high a price to pay."

Hermann Ehren (a refugee from Silesia), writing in the *Frankfurter Allgemeine Zeitung:* "I am speaking in the names of twelve million expellees when I say that our Federal Government's duty is to reject every suggestion that the Oder-Neisse line should be recognized as a final frontier. This view cannot be regarded as illusory. For us Germans, Breslau is, as long as there is no peace treaty, a German town."

Baron von Richthofen: "It is not true that, as we older East Germans die out, love of our homelands will die out too. We have been at pains to ensure that this should not happen, and that our children should have the same love of the homes which they may, indeed, hardly remember today. And we have been successful! Today the young people are taking the biggest part in the work of the *Landmannschaften;* they are keenest of all for the return."

The Schwerte newsletter: "Failure to solve the expellee problem might bring a third world war. Ignoring this question does not help to pacify Europe or ensure world peace. If the natural and inherited longing for home is not finally appeased, there will be an unceasing inner restlessness. One day a future generation, which has not experienced the horrors of war, may attempt to win back its ancestral homes by force."

Wenzel Jaksch, S.P.D. member of the Bundestag (writing in *Die Welt*): "The formal renunciation of the right to their homelands of the Sudeten and Eastern Germans would merely strengthen the Communist regimes in Prague and Warsaw. Based on this strengthened position, the Eastern bloc could apply its full forces in negotiations on the German problem."

Statement of the Federal Ministry for Refugees: "The expellees have been assisted, but all assistance must be regarded as provisional as long as the basic cause of their need has not been solved and they and their children have not been enabled to return to their old homes. This remains the unalterable objective for all German effort."

Federal Chancellor Dr. Adenauer in a personal message to the Breslauers: "I hope that you will soon be able to resume your historic task."

Some voices, admittedly, have been raised in favor of recognition of the *fait accompli* of German expulsion from the old eastern provinces and the Sudetenland. The evangelical pastor, Martin Niemöller, said in the spring of 1957 that the territories east of the Oder-Neisse were being systematically and industriously settled by the Poles and that no other frontier could conceivably be agreed on at a peace conference. At about the same time the Lord Mayor of Hamburg, Dr. Karl Sieveking, told a somewhat startled audience at a press conference that the Oder-Neisse line had come to stay and that the movement of populations which had taken place could not possibly be reversed. In an article in the *Frankfurter Allgemeine Zeitung* in January, 1959, Nikolas Benckiser suggested that recognition of the Oder-Neisse line could be made a powerful bargaining counter at a peace conference, and that the great majority of the West German population would accept it as the price for reunification. This was an explicit restatement of the thought in Heinrich von Brentano's mind three years before.

These voices are few and far between. For although the older refugees are dying out, the weight of propaganda for "the Return" inevitably has a snowballing effect. Week after week the Göttingen researchers pour out facts and figures to show that it must take place sooner or later. In April 1959 they published the "Refugees' Bible," a mighty, one-thousand-page tome entitled *Das Oestliche Deutschland* (*Eastern Germany*). Here were all the classic arguments against acceptance of the existing eastern frontiers — they were not based on treaty, they were contrary to the Atlantic Charter and to international law, they were founded on conquest, confiscation and brute force. All too often the Göttingen group produces propaganda of the most blatant kind. Some trenchant examples were given by the Stuttgart paper *Arbeiterpolitik* in February 1959. They showed that some West Germans have still not forgotten how to apply the Goebbels technique of the "big lie." Yet the work of the Göttingen group is supported by the Federal Foreign Office, the Federal Ministry for Refugees, the Federal Ministry for All-German Affairs. The same Ministries provide money for the *Landmannschaften* and for the *Bund der Vertriebenen*, which, with 2.5 million members, had by 1959 become the next largest organization in Germany to the United Trade-unions.

Maps of the lost territories still hang in the offices of half-a-dozen Federal Ministries. The official Government Bulletin still issues instructions that maps of Central Europe should not suggest that present frontiers are permanent, but should mark the Oder-Neisse territories as "under Polish administration" and northern East Prussia "under Soviet administration." A schoolmaster was able to return an expensive atlas (costing thirty-two dollars), on which he had paid only a first installment, because these areas were "wrongly marked." Ever and again the Ministry for All-German Affairs issues reminders that the D.D.R. is not "eastern" but "middle" Germany (*Mitteldeutschland*). The Bulletin urged the marking on all maps of the old German place names, "and only those new names should be added (in brackets) which were artificially created for postal purposes by the present administrative powers."

There are also many other organizations to help the Federal Government and the Göttingen group — the Norddeutsche Akademie in Lüneburg, the Herder Institute at Marburg, the East German institutes at Stuttgart, Munich, Freiburg. Their work has borne fruit in the Gallup polls which have been held on the problem of the eastern frontiers. In 1953, 66 per cent of those asked believed that the lost provinces would one day be German again. In 1955, 69 per cent of those asked said that they would not accept reunification in return for renunciation of the German East. In 1956, 57 per cent of the refugees asked said that they would be prepared to return to their old homes, and only 22 per cent said that they definitely would not. The organizers of these Gallup polls never asked anybody how the Return could ever be made remotely possible.

The lesson of President Eisenhower's visit to Bonn in August 1959 should be recalled. With the connivance of the town authorities, the refugee associations hung huge banners over the road down which he drove after arrival. It is doubtful whether the President ever noticed them, but their purpose was clear — to gain unlimited American support for their claims to the old homelands.

Is there any solution of the question of the eastern frontiers other than acceptance of them as they stand? For a time, the Federal Foreign Office played with the idea of a Polish-German "condominium" in the lost provinces. (Such an arrangement has never worked anywhere in Europe — although it has been put to the test again in Cyprus.) The leader of the Sudeten refugees, Dr. Lodgman von Auen, produced a "plan" which foresaw the creation of a Central European "Federation" after the German refugees had been allowed to return to their old homes. Early in 1959, spokesmen of the *Bund der Vertriebenen* proposed that the refugees should return home, if they wanted to; that the "debatable" territories should be put under United Nations trusteeship for ten years; and that their future should be settled by a referendum.

All such plans are more or less chimerical. Historical facts can be brutally final. The operative facts are that Nazi Germany murdered around ten million East Europeans and deported fourteen million more for slave labor; that Hitler carried out a monstrous, cruel and arbitrary rearrangement of the map of Central Europe; that the Slav world took a bitter revenge in 1945; and that the Soviet Union will never tolerate an eastern frontier for a united Germany beyond the Oder and Neisse, or south of the Erzgebirge. The operative facts are that probably only half a million people with any claim whatever to German nationality remain in the "German East" in 1960; that 104,000 left in 1957, and 119,000 in 1958; and that Poland is colonizing its new western provinces with nationalist fervor and with the backing of a rising birthrate. To the Western Powers, therefore, German plans for the Return have all the qualities of a dream. On March 25, 1959, General de Gaulle — in other respects the staunchest ally of the West German Government — said: "The reunification of the two parts into a single Germany seems to us the normal destiny of the German people, provided that the Germans do not reopen the question of their present frontiers to the west, the east, the north and the south." There are no Western statesmen who would not, in their hearts, endorse this statement.

Prussia has gone — the Prussia which Theodor Häcker called "that gluttonous colony, which devoured us and gnawed the marrow from our bones." The concept of a Prussia that stood guard on Europe's eastern fringe "in shining armor" is relegated to its proper realm of cheap mythology. Prussia can never be re-created out of the rump of Brandenburg and western Pomerania. Prussia's doom was not written by the Allied statesmen at Yalta or Potsdam, but by Hitler himself when he signed his robber's pact with Stalin in 1939. For Hitler invited Russia into Europe, and handed away eastern Poland. The simple Russian reflex has been to push Poland farther west. No one, even if cleverer than Churchill or Roosevelt, could have prevented this. Hitler, for that matter, only carried on a fifty-year-old German tradition of *Drang nach Osten*, expansion to the east. This expansion was always intended to be built on force: "It is necessary that our civilization should build its temples on mountains of corpses, on an ocean of tears, and on the death-cries of men without number," wrote General Count von Haeseler in 1893. The code of brute force has rebounded on the heads of the Prussians who preached it so blithely.

Four final thoughts on the question of the German expellees may be relevant. The first is that the old German desire for space to live (*Lebensraum*) may — although dormant today — revive in days to come. That urge for *Lebensraum* was never a population problem; it was the product of a German desire for conquest, a German ability to give that desire active expression, and a typically German disgust over the failure of East Europeans to develop their own territorial resources. But today — as opposed to Hitler's era — West Germany really is becoming thickly populated, and yet all Germany may well remain divided for half a century to come. The old, bad German arguments which sought to justify stealing land from other nations could therefore be invoked once again.

The second thought is connected with the East-West struggle. Thanks to intense propaganda, a renunciation of the lost eastern provinces by a German Government will represent a real sacrifice on the part of the German people. The West has the right to ask the Soviet Union for major concessions in return for such a renunciation. For the West will have to bear the brunt of German anger if and when such a renunciation has to be made. Any West German Government is, for its part, justified in reserving the question of the eastern frontiers for a peace conference, and in maintaining a discreet silence in the meantime. Nor should it be forgotten that the German loss of the German East forced the Western Powers to assist in the re-creation of a highly industrialized West German state, in double-quick time. Rump Germany could not feed itself, it had to earn in order to buy its food. This fact — which was due to the Soviet "push to the west" — should never be forgotten when nailing the Russian lie that the West re-organized Federal Germany for its own ends.

The third thought is that a settlement of Germany's eastern frontiers must, when it comes, be explicitly final. There are still all too many unteachable Germans — who still think only of the wrongs done to them and never of the wrongs they inflicted on others — who will say, with a certain complacency, that Hitler's war was fought to save Europe from the "barbarians" of the East and that the Waffen S.S. was the first "European Army," united by comradeship, blood and a high ideal. The days for romantic jargon are past; when a fair price has been exacted for renunciation of the German East, the German claim to it must be dropped forever. When the Germans are asked to recognize this, there may be a crisis in German-Western relations. But that crisis must be faced when it comes.

The last thought of all is that there are many refugees who have no direct responsibility for the loss of their own homes. The refugee mother who never touched politics, the refugee child who was too young to do so, the refugee Christian or Social Democrat who never pandered to Hitler and his works — these people deserve only sympathy and understanding. Germans are not as ungrateful as their critics would have us believe. West German newspapers printed glowing accounts, in September 1959, of the one hundred and forty-six million marks' worth of private parcels received from abroad by Germans in the postwar years. Private parcels do not solve political problems. Nor does mere sympathy; but it can, with time, help to heal the real grief of the German refugees.

WEST GERMANY

EAST GERMANY

HERBLOCK in *The Washington*

"Why Don't You Move Out And Stop Torturing
This Poor Guy?"

5

The Power of Fear

The specters which the Nazis invoked will haunt Germany, and all of us, forever. Luther unintentionally rent Germany into a northern and southern half; Hitler rent it into a western and eastern half. The Germans have nailed themselves to this cross.

— AN EMIGRATED GERMAN-JEW in a letter to the Refugee Press Service

The people over there [in East Germany] are Germans just as we are, and are as much a positive part of Germany's intellectual, political and economic history. But they are locked up in a prison of atrophy. We know, and they know too, that we alone cannot liberate them. It is the most appalling heritage of Hitler's policies that between the Fulda of Boniface and the Wartburg of Luther — two places geographically so close to one another — there is a demarcation line of barbed wire and ideology which is entirely alien to all Germans.

— PRESIDENT THEODOR HEUSS in a farewell speech to the German people, 12 September, 1959

For all of us European states there is only one important problem — not to be swallowed up by Communism.

— PIETRO QUARONI, Italian Ambassador in Bonn, 1959

THE Iron Curtain between the free and the Communist-dominated worlds is not just a metaphor of speech or a political concept. It is as real as any other fact in Central Europe. It does not merely cut through the grazing or grain fields belonging to a particular peasant, leaving old neighbors separated by twelve-foot-high barbed wire which forces them to make a two-hundred-mile trip in order to meet; nor does it merely cut through human friendships and economic facts. It is the boundary between two different worlds, even where it divides one country like Germany in half.

A faintly ludicrous example of how East Germany is becoming Eastern in thinking as well as Eastern in political orientation was provided by a visit which I paid to Leipzig four years after the end of the war. East Germany was barred to foreign journalists except during two weeks of the year. Then it was possible to visit the spring and autumn trade fairs in Leipzig, and to capture — if not any sort of working knowledge of what went on throughout East Germany — at least a little of the atmosphere of reservation, suspicion and fear which has come there to stay.

Hotel rooms were difficult to find in bleak, bombed Leipzig. I had to share one with another British journalist. In the middle of our first night, the door of our bedroom opened stealthily, and a candle, held in a shaking hand, wavered in the doorway. We both woke up at that moment, both shouted "Get out!" and both went to sleep again without saying anything to one another at the time.

In the morning my companion asked me if I remembered what had happened during the night. I did. Had I noticed whose face was behind the guttering candle? We agreed on the face, and decided to ask its owner what the big idea was.

We found the proprietress of the hotel in the dining room, where she was supervising the serving of a breakfast of black bread, acorn coffee and inferior liver sausage. I asked her why she had forced an entrance into our room in the very middle of the night. She was first indignant, then apologetic — it was the first time she had done this, and she had not gone into any other room.

"But just why did you do it?" I persisted.

"Well, I was ordered to by the Russians." (There were Russian officers and soldiers stationed in each hotel at that time.)

"In that case why did you, or they, pick on our room?"

She was quite sure of her ground there. "Oh, that is easily explained. You were the only people who did not lock your door.

The Russians thought that very suspicious indeed. They guessed that you were foreign agents."

This sort of experience is all very well if you carry an American or British passport. It would have been very frightening for the East Germans themselves, then or later. For they knew that the rule of fear introduced when the Red Army arrived in eastern Germany was destined to last as long as Communist domination. Typical of this rule of fear was the little known story of the Liberal students of Leipzig University, whose struggle to maintain freedom was broken in November 1948.

In 1947 the student councils elections at Leipzig University went, from the point of view of the Russian military administration and the Communist-sponsored Socialist Unity Party (S.E.D.), sadly wrong. The S.E.D. had over 1100 members among the students but polled only 600 votes at the elections. The Liberals (L.D.P.) had just over 300 members, yet polled 570 votes. The Christian Democrats (C.D.U.) had 320 members and polled 670 votes.

The Soviet authorities were scandalized. They had known that the universities of eastern Germany constituted one of that region's chief obstacles to Bolshevization. (Around 60 per cent of the students, for one thing, had served during the war, and a great many of them had fallen into Russian hands. This did not make them easy subjects for Soviet propaganda.) The German universities have a strong liberal tradition, and it was not possible at once to replace teachers when all that was available was a sprinkling of Communist intellectuals and a heterogenous mass of old-guard Communist Party hacks. The students' clubs, councils and debating societies remained a resisting, moderating political force.

The Communist attack against Leipzig University opened as soon as the 1947 student council elections were over. It began at the top. A new rector, Professor Friedrich, was installed by the *Land* Saxony Minister of Education, Herr Holtzhauer. At the installation Holtzhauer said, "Yesterday we had the chance of deciding for or against war criminals and Nazis. Today the choice is one for or against war — tomorrow it will be for or against the Soviet Union." The pro-rector, Grimmer, was eased out of his administrative posts. He was forced to resign when he opposed the *Land* Government's scheme for making admission to the university dependent on the approval of a "packed" student committee of eleven members, nine of them from the S.E.D.

Next on the list for "liquidation" was the bursar, Dr. Tritzschler. He was forced to resign, and an S.E.D. nominee was put in his place. His two administrative assistants, Herr and Frau Lippert, were accused of fraud and fled to Western Germany. The President of the University, Dr. Wandel, was induced to accept a new entrance scheme, under which "the sons of workers and farmers" were given special allowances — based on possession of a Party membership card and not on their means — and a 60 per cent guaranteed proportion of all vacancies. But he insisted on introducing an amendment under which candidates would be subjected to a normal, competitive examination as well. The S.E.D. students thereupon appealed to the *Land* Ministry of Education, on the grounds that the amendment was "an affront to our democratic government and to the Soviet Occupying Power."

The *Land* Government ordered the rejection of the amendment and the holding of fresh elections to the student councils. Voting slips were to be "scrutinized" in order to avoid "forgeries." The Liberals and Christian Democrats tore up their voting slips and an S.E.D. council was returned. Its first action was to approve the appointment of a new official, a curator, who was to act as liaison between the students and the *Land* Government. He was an old-guard Communist, Herr Eichler. In the course of a few weeks, "reactionary" professors were bitterly attacked by this man, and were continuously interrupted during their own lectures by S.E.D. students who told them, "Now, Herr Professor, what you say isn't right at all. Marx and Lenin say . . ."

The Communist *Land* Government had appointed a docile rector and pro-rector; it had packed the student council; it had control of finances and examinations; and in October 1948, 85 per cent of the university entrants at Leipzig were "sons of workers and farmers" whose candidatures were approved by the S.E.D.

authorities. Yet still it was not content. The Liberal students, in particular, remained a rallying-point of all those who sought to keep education free from Communist infiltration and ideology. In November the S.E.D. struck at this last, infinitely gallant remnant.

On November eleventh, 1948, the leader of the Liberal students, Wolfgang Natonek, was arrested. Natonek's family had a fine record of resistance to the Nazis, and his father had managed to escape from Germany during the Nazi era and migrate to America. He was still living there when his son was sentenced by a Soviet Military Tribunal to twenty-five years' imprisonment for "sabotage" and "conspiracy." Seven other leading Liberal students were arrested and imprisoned. Similar arrests of Liberal students took place on November 12 at the Universities of Dresden, Halle, Rostock and East Berlin. At Leipzig the Liberal students' committee was dissolved by Russian order, and its student newspaper, *Das Freie Wort*, banned. The Russians secured some measure of co-operation from the Liberal Democratic Party itself. In its executive they found a ready tool in the person of Herr von Stolzenberg, the "Red Baron." On 19 November von Stolzenberg remarked that "We still haven't caught all the people we want."

This was true. Seven of the young Liberals escaped to Berlin, and from there to West Germany. The escape stories of two of them were fascinating.

The first, Heinz Foelsch,[1] was arrested on November 11 at his Leipzig home. A six-cylinder Mercedes drove up to his front door, and at least three men got out. When two of them broke into his bed-sitting room, the resolute, athletic Foelsch picked up a chair and hurled it into their faces. He leaped out of his window into the garden, twisted an ankle, and was caught there.

The Russians who captured him took him to the civil jail, part of which was under Soviet military control. He was left in a cell for three days and nights, then brought before a tribunal of half a dozen Soviet officers for questioning. It soon became clear to

[1] Real name cannot be given.

him that he was not merely being questioned; he was being tried at the same time. The same questions were put over and over again: Why had he been to West Berlin, why had he talked to people there and betrayed important secrets? (He had been to West Berlin, and he had talked to people there. He had betrayed no secrets; he knew none.) Finally, Foelsch was sentenced to twelve years' imprisonment. He was told that he would be taken back to his cell and that he would stay there until fetched. He would spend the twelve years in the Soviet Union.

Foelsch has described to me the utter, weary hopelessness of the next twenty-four hours. All too many German prisoners had vanished into the depths of Siberia and had never reappeared. There would be small chance of escaping on his way East. He would, no doubt, be carefully guarded. He was. An escort of three arrived for him in the middle of the night — a Russian officer, a corporal and a private soldier. They marched him through the gaunt ruins of the town center towards the railway-station.

Halfway there the officer left the rest of the party, after giving a few words of instructions to the corporal. At the next street corner the corporal turned off down a side street. A hundred yards on, the private soldier prodded Foelsch with the muzzle of his rifle, motioned him into another side street. There he gave him a kick behind, and shouted "*Laufen!*" ("Run!"). Foelsch knew that he was going to be shot, "while trying to escape." He set off at a limping canter, never looking back. Behind him the soldier laughed raucously, but he never fired. It was and is still an unexplained incident. But it remained a nightmare to Heinz Foelsch, long after he arrived safely in West Germany.

Foelsch's friend Karl Neumann was a serious, bespectacled, slightly owlish young man who was studying at Leipzig University to become a doctor. One by one his friends among the Liberal students vanished, usually fetched by the crew of the big Mercedes. Less than a week after Natonek's arrest Neumann decided to go to the Liberal Party headquarters, where the party executive and the youth group were holding discussions on social policy. Neumann had an instinctive feeling that something was going to happen that day.

He described to me how inside the party headquarters building he went from one group to another, peering myopically in the belief that he would see someone who had never been there before. He did — a thick-set, flat-faced man wearing a long overcoat with a high fur collar. Desperately, Neumann went up to him, asked him a banal question. The man smiled, shrugged, said nothing. He was a Russian.

Neumann went to the main entrance, looked through. The big Mercedes was waiting outside, with three men inside. He staggered back, past the waiting Russian, was buttonholed by a member of the party executive. "You know, Neumann, you're one of the people who are causing us real trouble! We have got to get along with the Russians from now on. I know you believe in your line, but it's too late for that now. It's probably too late for you, too!"

Neumann had only one idea left; he must make some effort to escape. He had, as it happened, money in his pocket — he had acted according to instinct in leaving not one cent in his room — but he had no plan. He ran down a corridor, rushed into a lavatory, hurled the window open and jumped out. He landed in a cabbage patch; and he told me later how he remained on all fours in it, shivering violently. He was convinced that someone must have been posted at the back of the building to stop so elementary a getaway.

There was no one. He got up, ran through the vegetable garden, climbed a fence out of it and made his way to the railway line. He trudged to the next station, bought a ticket to Chemnitz, climbed into the next train. He did not notice that there were big RESERVED notices on the carriage: it was full of workers who had been deported from their homes and were being taken under guard to the Aue uranium mines. This was the worst part of all of the nightmare. Neumann got out at the next station, bought another ticket, and made his roundabout way to Berlin and safety.

The stories of Foelsch and Neumann are a part of the pattern of oppression and terror which the Russians introduced into eastern Germany as soon as they arrived there. Perhaps the most important part of all was the pressure exerted on youth, for its Bolshevization was to be the essential basis of the existence of the separate East German Republic. Men like Foelsch and Neumann fought for freedom in vain. At Leipzig vital changes were made in the curriculum. In all faculties, lectures on materialist ideology were introduced; examination boards were packed with Communists who asked questions on politics, social science, the teachings of Marx and Lenin. Students were dragooned into joining the S.E.D. study-groups, which were vehicles of blatant Communist propaganda; recruiting for the Communist-sponsored "Free German Youth" (F.D.J.) was pushed ahead; "open" voting was adopted for student elections. Here, as in other universities, such innovations were introduced as radios in the dining and "recreation" rooms, relaying the propaganda programs of Radio Leipzig and the Deutschlandsender in Berlin, and usually played full-blast in order to prevent "seditious" conversation. F.D.J. members were instructed to "report" any talk of this kind. The morale of the young was to be first broken, then standardized and nursed in the Communist tradition.

The regimentation of youth was, of course, only a small part of the Russian-sponsored regime of repression in East Germany. But it was certainly the most significant. On the eve of the Russian Revolution Lenin had written: "Only when we basically transform the organization and education of youth will we evolve a new society which no longer resembles the old." The Soviet plan for East German youth was pressed through with ruthlessness, consistency and with an immensely cunning alternation of force and favor.

Numbers can tell true stories. The F.D.J. was formed in March 1946, and in the course of one year built up to a membership of 400,000. By the end of 1949 this had increased to 923,000, and the F.D.J's junior branch, the "Young Pioneers," had enrolled 800,000 members. By 1952 the two organizations counted 3.3 million members, and the only other youth group in existence

— that of the Evangelical Communities — was in no sense a rival. Membership of the F.D.J. has remained fairly constant ever since.

How did the Russians and the East German Communists build up this monolithic organization? Young East Germans have told me that repression was only one of their weapons. Yet it was a fearsome one. As early as December, 1947, the Evangelical Bishops of East and West Germany sent a letter to the four Allied Military Governors claiming that 2000 young people had been arrested and imprisoned in East Germany during one year. They included 157 under the age of 15 and another 500 under 18. Many of them were sent to the old Nazi concentration camps, Sachsenhausen, Buchenwald, Bautzen, now under Russian management. There were over 15,000 political prisoners in Sachsenhausen in 1949, sleeping on wooden bedsteads without blankets and at first without straw palliasses, living under leaking roofs, washing in ice-cold water even in the depth of winter, half-starved and with no change of clothes. They lived on a diet of black bread, watery soup and a few potatoes. They were kept on parade for five hours at a stretch, and they were kicked and bullied for the least offense (possession of a pencil or paper was one).

In Bautzen around 18,000 people died between 1946 and 1949. Over 7000 lived where there was room for just over 1000. One in five had tuberculosis. Under Hitler's heirs, the East German S.E.D. authorities, prisoners in 1950 for the first time demonstrated and forced the introduction of slightly better living conditions. In 1958 I met a survivor from eight years' imprisonment in Bautzen. He told me of the endless interrogations, often in the middle of the night, the senseless beatings-up of the early days, the everlasting hunger. A year after release this man retained his prison pallor, had a habit of looking over his shoulder, winced when he recalled his worst experiences.

The F.D.J. recruited by offering inducements. F.D.J. membership meant quicker advancement at school and better chances of a good job after leaving school. It was a qualification for entrance to a University or Technical College. It was the sole means of enjoying the best sporting facilities — the F.D.J. controlled the East German Sports Movement, had prior claim on sports-grounds and equipment. Even the East German "Rambling Society" became an F.D.J. monopoly. Life was drab and desolate in East Germany for at least ten years after the war. The F.D.J. offered badges and uniforms (what German can resist either?), march music and military discipline, a sense of comradeship and of solidarity. Along with advantages in learning and recreation, it offered young Germans everything that they most wanted.

The F.D.J. told its members that the future lay with them, that they could repair the faults of their elders who were no longer their betters. It appealed to youth's self-importance and to German youth's intolerance. It offered the chance to lead and to follow. The old weapon of the *Führer-Prinzip* could function in the service of the New Order of a "genuine" Socialist society. And the most appealing part of this New Order was to be the F.D.J.'s blue and gold uniforms, its bronze, silver and gold badges of "Good Knowledge," its display and discipline, and the flight from frustration which it offered.

The F.D.J. is the Communist state in embryo. It has its small secretariat, with a ruling Politburo, its sub-departments which deal with education, sport, labor relations, international affairs, propaganda and "mass agitation." It has its high school, at Bogensee, its district and local schools, its own publishing house, its discussion-group cells, its branches in the factories where F.D.J. members are generally the driving forces of the "Activist" movement, in which F.D.J. training begins with the seven-year-old juniors of the "Young Pioneers" and is intensified from the age of fourteen onwards. Programs of aims are published regularly. In 1950 they were "Unification of Germany and a Just Peace," "Support of the East German Republic" and "Opposition to the Colonial Policies of the West." In 1958 they were "A German Peace Treaty," "Freedom for West Berlin" and "Ban the Atom Bomb." Their programs coincide exactly with the aims of the Soviet Government of the day. With their pre-military and "revolutionary" training, the former members of the F.D.J. dominated the 100,000-strong East German Army and the 75,000-strong People's Police.

A hundred examples could be given of the F.D.J. drive to secure conformity and strangle opposition. As early as 1953 the East German Deputy Prime Minister, Walter Ulbricht, announced that the Christian Churches must declare themselves to be on the side of the Socialist State and against Western imperialists and warmongers. The F.D.J. undertook to "convert" young people to the creed of dialectical materialism. They coined the catchword "God has left the Church and Jesus never belonged to it."

This is how the F.D.J. went about the business of conversion on May 14, 1953, in the town of Ölsnitz, near Plauen. Led by a schoolmaster, Albert Dölling, forty members of the F.D.J. demonstrated outside the St. Jacob's Church. Dölling then led the party inside, where they hurled volleys of bricks at holy pictures and statues, flung everything off the altar, smashed collection boxes and ripped down church notices. The local press complimented them on their "spontaneous demonstration against superstition."

In the same month Pastor Herbert Bohnke of Proschim, near Cottbus, was sentenced to eight years' imprisonment for asking members of his confirmation class not to attend it in F.D.J. uniforms. One of his pupils reported him. A twelve-year-old boy at a Dresden school was reported by his F.D.J. master. He was asked "Do you love your enemies?" "Yes." "And do they include the traitors Eisenhower, Adenauer and General Ridgway?" The boy answered, "Christians should never hate." He was expelled from his school and his parents were threatened with reprisals. Resistance to systematic indoctrination is difficult when it has to begin so early.

This was the sort of story which little seven- to nine-year-old East Germans were reading until 1956:

> Once upon a time in the town of Gori two small boys used to go to school together. The bigger was called Peter and the smaller was Josef. Things went well for Peter —

117

his father was a rich merchant. So he got everything that he wanted. Josef was the son of a poor cobbler. He was only allowed to go to the school at all because he learned his lessons readily and sang sweetly.

Peter was lazy and asked Josef to help him in some elementary cribbing and cheating. Josef refused, for he was honest. Then Josef converted Peter and helped him, not to crib but to learn. And the clever little boy, who always helped others with their lessons, was called Josef Stalin. [None other.]

In 1957 examination questions for East German school children included the following. "Outline the alteration of the soil under the differing impact of socialist and capitalist society, with particular reference to the American prairies and the Soviet steppe and desert."

"In the battle for natural resources give examples of the thieving nature of United States imperialism."

"Which measures of the Western Powers led to the division of Germany?"

"Name the security organ of our Democratic German Republic and prove its democratic character."

Finally: "Give examples of the genial strategy of J. W. Stalin in 1919."

Even problems of algebra and geometry have been given an anti-Western, ideological twist by East German educators. Under the impact of such teaching children become to some extent indoctrinated simply by the constant repetition of the same phrases. A brilliant exception was the examination class of the Kurt Steffel Bauer secondary school at Storkow. On December 27, 1956, sixteen boys and one girl out of a class of twenty fled to West Berlin. Only three girls stayed behind.

These sixteen-year-olds had organized their private protest after the bloody Soviet stamping-down of the Hungarian Revolution. They observed a stony silence and refused to answer questions put by their S.E.D. teacher. The East German Government took this "rebellion" so seriously that it sent down to Storkow — twenty miles east of Berlin — the Minister of Education, Herr

Lange, to lecture the young people on the "true" facts of the Hungarian Revolution. He, too, was received in glum silence. He threatened to debar the children from taking their final examinations. They still remained silent. When the security police arrived on the scene in order to take names and addresses and persecute their parents, the children packed up and left in a body. They finished their studies at the secondary school in Heppenheim, near the West German town of Heidelberg.

The Hungarian Revolution, indeed, brought signs of real resistance among East German youth to the regime's slavish adherence to the Soviet "line." In October 1956 the students of the Humboldt University in East Berlin sent an appeal to their rector, calling on him to carry out a "de-Stalinization" program. They wanted free elections to the student council and the establishment of freedom of speech at students' assemblies. They objected to the amount of Russian language instruction, the Communist social sciences courses, the compulsory attendance at certain lectures, the direction of students to particular universities (German students have traditionally moved from one university to another in order to get the benefit of the particular teaching they desire). Similar objections were voiced at at least four other East German universities. There was particular restiveness in the medical faculties of these universities, and their members asked the most awkward questions at the "Youth Forums" organized by Gerhard Eisler (who fled to the United States from Nazi Germany, and returned to become Minister of Propaganda in Communist East Germany). The Youth Forums were failing in their purpose — which was to have the views of the regime rammed home, without protest or interruption. At Dresden University hundreds of students observed one minute's silence in November 1956, in memory of the dead of the Hungarian Revolution. Twenty of them were expelled, and another twenty from Leipzig University.

On November 29, 1956, an event took place in East Berlin which at the time passed unnoticed in the outside world. One of the established stars of the East German intellectual firmament, Professor Wolfgang Harich, was arrested at the orders of the East German Public Prosecutor. He was accused of "ideological rebellion" — a fatuous phrase, but not necessarily very wide of the mark — and of contact with "Western agents" — which was pure nonsense. The Deputy Public Prosecutor, Bruno Hayd, undertook to prepare the case against Harich and against his three "collaborators" — Bernhard Sternberger, co-publisher with Harich of the monthly *Deutsche Zeitschrift für Philosophie;* Harich's secretary, Irene Giersch; and a young writer, Manfred Hertwig.

Harich was the sort of character who is supremely awkward to handle for the executive officers of an authoritarian regime which happens to be a Communist one. He was a convinced Communist, but felt no special sympathy for the Soviet Union. He loathed the use of brute force and believed that "ideal socialism" must triumph on its own merits. He disliked political oppression, for he believed that "real" Marxism would reject any but intellectual arguments. He was a humanitarian Socialist, who had kept Socialist ideals so resolutely and rigidly a hairsbreadth ahead of his nasal organ that he could not visualize any of the forces which make and break communities and nations. He was probably rather too nice for this world; he was certainly too nice for the ugly little witches' caldron which Walter Ulbricht had made out of East Germany.

Why was the East German regime afraid of this ingenuous (he sent his ideas to the West German Social Democratic Party, not dimly visualizing that this could cost him his neck) and impractical thirty-six-year-old intellectual? One reason, undoubtedly, was that he was a genuine thinker and his ideas could win a host of followers from among people who had never seen or heard him. This, to Communists, is a horrible thing. Intellectuals must be either won over and mobilized, or silenced. Harich had the cocky spirit of the budgerigar. He went on saying what he thought.

Circumstances doomed him. A few weeks before his arrest, an East German weekly paper, *Sonntag,* published a parable which is said to have brought a trace of color to the gray-green complexion of Walter Ulbricht. It ran like this:

Once upon a time, in the village school of Schilda, children were taught that $2 + 2 = 9$. The teaching at the Schilda school was mainly good and the children were keen to learn. But one day the authorities came to the conclusion that the mathematical fallacy involved in this ideologically educative theorem was in danger of becoming a bit obvious. Yet how to correct it? They could not risk too serious a reverse to law and order; at the same time they could not subject young brains to a jarring surprise.

So the schoolteachers of Schilda were told to correct this mathematical fallacy, with tact. They should explain, at first, that $2 + 2 = $ only 8. They could then, in a purely bourgeois manner, reduce this sum to its drearily correct proportions.

The children (and this, after all, was after eleven years of Communist compulsion) failed to react in the right way. When, on the third day, some of them were told to learn that $2 + 2 = 7$, they went into the lavatories and chalked up "$2 + 2 = 4$." It then became shockingly apparent that they had known the right answer all the time.

This parable had immediate repercussions. The editor of *Sonntag*, Gustav Just (he was a friend of Harich's), received a severe reprimand. Just was a present-day disciple of Jean Jacques Rousseau, and his principal complaint against the East German regime was that it did not understand that a human being was part of a natural order, as well as a cog of organized society. So Just had to give his leader writer, Heinz Hoeger, orders to write an article of fierce "self-criticism." The parable, Hoeger had to explain, was the sort of absurdity which originated in countries where the workingman was discredited and reviled, in countries like Hungary where the workingman was exploited in a counterrevolutionary cause. Just backed up the article which he had been forced to inspire. In a public literary "discussion," he explained that it was often not merely inadvisable, but also morally wrong to speak the truth — when the "whole truth" gave the wrong picture.

Harich's influence had spread beyond gay cynics like Just. The people who read his *Deutsche Zeitschrift für Philosophie* were the intellectually most alert in East Germany. The monthly *Auf-*

bau was on Harich's side, and sympathetic articles had been published in *Neue Deutsche Literatur* and the *Wochenpost*, whose editor, Rudolf Wetzel, was another of Harich's personal "circle." Even in the Government and S.E.D.-dominated *Forum*, Gerhard Zwerebz had written, "Who can blame our young people for being embittered and cynical? How many of their basic ideas have had to be shelved in recent years because they were considered to be politically, just politically harmful? Our youth is beginning to realize that truth itself has been slandered."

The Twentieth Congress of the Soviet Communist Party gave the essential impetus to Harich and his friends in East Germany. They assumed that the rejection of the "Stalin Cult" meant the rejection of state interference in the arts and the humanities, and that the Soviet rulers had taken this course because they believed that it was the surest way of guaranteeing the survival and eventual dominance of the Communist system. Thinkers like Anna Seghers, Willi Bredel and Stefan Heym eagerly embraced this opportunity to escape from mulberry-bush-minded Communist ideological thought. The East German Minister for Cultural Affairs, Johannes Becher, was sympathetic. The idol of the Communist artistic world, Bert Brecht, trembled on the brink of a declaration of faith which he never made; instead he died. Even more important, the younger generation at once showed its interest in the broader intellectual horizons of thought which Harich unveiled.

In June 1956 a "Congress of Young Artists" was held in Chemnitz, renamed "Karl-Marx-Stadt." A young writer, Heinz Kahlau, made an impassioned speech on the subject of the "true spirit of realism." Realism, he said, should never be preached and practiced at "the expense of truth." Overemphasis on realism was resulting in "the degeneration of contemporary history into mythology." This mythology "led to the inquisition" (the concentration camps, which were still there, the arrests in the dark hours, the sham confessions and the uncertainty of daily life which accompanied all this). Realism, overdone, brought the "worst" materialism in its train, and the East German regime had begun to base itself on "people who worry about being able to buy a sofa, and officials who live in their official cars." The young poet, Streubel, said that the regime had "inflated all our good ideas. Now peace, freedom, homeland no longer mean a thing. We have shouted ourselves hoarse and deafened everybody to the reality of truth."

Young East Germans, who did not necessarily want to think, had donned jeans and James Dean shirts, had passed through the samba stage and were still dancing the boogie, sometimes read Ernest Hemingway and William Faulkner and interested themselves, in the dabbler's manner, in any sort of Western art which seemed to represent a real protest. They could be found fault with because of their conduct, but not condemned. Young East Germans who were anxious to think waited to hear what was to happen to Wolfgang Harich. They learned that he would be tried on March 7, 1957.

A political trial in East Germany is bound to have the nature of a ludicrous but cruel and terrifying farce. Political trials had, at that stage of history, been brought to a high degree of clockwork efficiency by the Minister of Justice, the vengeful and pitiless Frau "Red Hilde" Benjamin. A woman of masculine power and great courage, Hilde Benjamin became a Communist Party member in the 1920's and was bitterly persecuted by the Nazis, who murdered her husband in Mauthausen concentration camp in 1942. That she survived the war at all was probably due largely to the contemptuous hate which she nursed. In 1949 she became Vice President of the East German High Court, and in her first crop of 67 political cases sentenced 2 people to death, 12 to life imprisonment and the remaining 53 to terms of imprisonment totaling 550 years. Harich stood little chance, with his trial organized by this woman and conducted by Public Prosecutor Ernst Melsheimer (whose wife was nearly raped by the Russians in 1945, and who remarked with unconscious irony, "I could scarcely have blamed them; after all, they are decent Communists.")

Harich's trial in East Berlin lasted two days and a half, and he was sentenced to ten years' imprisonment on March 9, 1957. Bernhard Sternberger went to prison for four, and Manfred Hertwig for two years. They were all found guilty of "conspiring against the State," in front of an audience which was almost entirely comprised of Communist "activists" and which included only a few selected members of the East German Communist Press. All three men had to plead guilty, and their defense was based on the view that they had acted "out of moral weakness and human fallibility." But their real crime was in wanting to think and to express their opinions — however discreetly and diffidently. Intellectual conformity was at least as important to the Ulbricht regime as 100 per cent nationalization of industry or the bypassing of fuel and power bottlenecks in the East German economy.

Where does persecution end? In the Soviet Union it would seem to have been reduced to a matter of periodic purging and disciplining of recalcitrant members of the Communist elite — plus, of course, the regulation of awkward incidents like that of the writer Boris Pasternak. But the Bolshevik Revolution took place twenty-eight years before Bolshevism was applied in East Germany, by carefully calculated degrees, after being exported from the Soviet Union. That was why persecution must needs go on for a great deal longer in East Germany. Conformity is still some way off.

The belief that conformity was especially vital for the youth of East Germany brought the Ulbricht regime into conflict with the Christian Churches. There was, inevitably, friction between the Churches and the civil authorities from 1945 onwards. But there was at first no direct anti-Church campaign, thanks to the firmness and courage of prelates like Dr. Otto Dibelius, Bishop of Berlin and Brandenburg, and Propst Heinrich Grueber, who acted as the special representative of the Evangelical Churches (comprising 75 per cent of the population of East Germany) with the regime. Not until 1953 did the anti-Church campaign begin to take violent forms. In March of that year twenty-three Protestant Sisters of Mercy were arrested in the course of three days and removed from the Paul Gerhard Foundation in Wittenberg. They were accused of having questioned patients while under an anesthetic and of having worked for "Western secret services." In the same month the pastor of the Marienkirche in East Berlin, Reinhold George, was arrested and imprisoned. In Halle a Roman Catholic priest, Father Langer, was sentenced to eight years' imprisonment for showing parishioners copies of West Berlin newspapers. The era of persecution was under way.

To strike at the Christian Churches is comparatively easy; to silence them is not. In April the Ulbricht regime, imbued with its idea of organizing a State Church and stifling all opposition to it, struck repeatedly. A Roman Catholic priest at Velten was sent to prison for five years for "organizing a boycott and misleading the young"; three Protestant pastors were arrested in one week. Throughout the whole Eisleben district the S.E.D. appointed "observers" to attend Good Friday and Easter Sunday services. Their task was to report on the sermons, on instructions to the Christian congregations and on church notices.

At Easter the Church youth groups were forbidden to meet in public or hold religious ceremonies out-of-doors. The thousands of Berliners who habitually crossed the boundaries of Berlin in order to lay wreaths on the graves of their relatives were forbidden access to the cemetery of Stahnsdorf, where 120,000 people were buried. The Communist Free German Youth led the open attacks on the Churches. They "named" priests and pastors for saying that children belonged to God and that atheism was spiritual despair; they reported pastors who, on April 26, read from the pulpit an open letter from the Evangelical Church Council protesting against the "inhuman, inexcusable and unbearable treatment" of the Churches; at Quedlinburg gangs of Communist youths tried to break up two services, struggling with parishioners in the aisle and porch of the church.

On May Day, 1953, the East German Government sent an open letter to all ministers of religion. They were accused of aiding Western "spies," maltreating welfare workers, preventing "freedom to reject religious superstition." In the Marienkirche, his parish church, Dr. Dibelius said that all Christians must unite in preparing for the "terrible times which may lie ahead of us." Propst Grueber had a printed notice fixed to all church doors, warning Christians that worse persecutions than those suffered under the Nazis might lie ahead. On May Day the Marienkirche was closed by the People's Police, and cordoned-off all day. By May Day, 1000 out of 3000 church livings in East Germany were vacant. A cut in government grants had reduced pastors' pay by an average of 45 per cent, to around 220 marks (fifty dollars) a month. Tenants of church lands and houses were being evicted. Travel permits were refused to people who applied to attend Church Assemblies in West Germany.

The regime's plan to create a State Church fizzled out, was picked up again, and then was put on ice for future exploitation. To avoid the impression of undue pressure, the plan had been entrusted to the Prime Minister, Otto Grotewohl, who — unlike Walter Ulbricht — had been baptized and married in church. He believed that he could enlist 3000 out of 7000 ministers of religion throughout East Germany. But only a handful accepted his invitation to discuss the "liquidation of the medieval organization of the Churches." In the summer of 1953, the Soviet High Commissioner, V. S. Semeonov, arrived from Moscow with the "new policy" of killing opposition with kindness and consumer goods. The Churches were to be left in comparative peace for nearly two years.

Total or at least mass conversion to atheism is one of the bases of the East German Government's policy. Its next step was planned in the autumn of 1954, when "Committees for Youth Initiation" were formed all over the country, and all parents were instructed to register children who would be of school-leaving age in the summer of 1955. A Central Committee for Initiation laid down the procedures which would be adopted and the nature of courses of instruction. The courses, and the initiation itself, were to coincide with children's Church confirmation and preparation for it.

Dates for the semipagan ceremonies were announced on January 1, 1955, and full details on January 18, by the secretary-general of the Free German Youth, Werner Lambarz. Courses of instruction were to begin on January 25. They would consist of ten two-hour periods a week of civics, natural history, dialectical materialism and political theory. Instructors were to include S.E.D. activists, "heroes of labor," engineers and F.D.J. officials. The ceremonies would be carried out "in town halls and public buildings with warm sunshine streaming through the windows," inaugurated with "bursts of festive music" and "distribution of colorful bouquets," carried on with "forthright speeches" and concluded with "the march past of the Young Pioneers, singing their stirring melodies."

The Youth Initiation campaign of 1955 was an unqualified failure. Children attended the classes, but their parents kept them away from the ceremonies. Their reason for doing so had less to do with the nature of the classes themselves — which were a mixture of mumbo-jumbo, mild atheism and perfectly normal teaching — than with the fact that Dr. Dibelius issued a pastoral letter proclaiming the campaign to be a deliberate attempt to mobilize youth in opposition to Christian teachings. Dr. Dibelius threatened refusal of church confirmation to all who took part in the ceremonies; the Roman Catholic Church went further, laying down that the sacraments could be denied to parents as well as to children. The ceremonies themselves were farcical. The few children who attended were asked questions over the loud-speaker: "Are you prepared to devote your whole lives to building up the Socialist State?" "Will you do battle for the cause of peace?" Always the children had to answer in chorus, "Yes, we vow to do this." Previously they had been examined in their knowledge of the "atheists' Bible" — the book *Universe, Earth, Mankind,* which was issued in all schools in the fall of 1954. Yet in spite of posters, radio appeals and house-to-house canvassing by the uniformed F.D.J., barely 3 per cent of children of confirmation age attended the Youth Ceremonies of 1955.

The regime would not accept defeat. Pressure was intensified for the 1956 initiation campaign. F.D.J. members were encouraged to indulge openly in blasphemy, in order to damage the Churches by ridicule. Blasphemy reached a peak on February 18, in the town of Brandenburg, when one participant dressed up as Our Lord and put on a tub-thumping act as an evangelist. Another parodied the part of the Capuchin monk in Schiller's play *Wallenstein,* preaching a mock sermon and distributing "blessings." On the next day the local S.E.D. paper, the *Maerkische Volksstimme,* wrote, "The procession yesterday quite rightly included Jesus, who had come down from Heaven to exhort His erring flock, but who found that He had developed a taste for alcohol Himself."

Around 30,000 children were believed to have attended the 1956 youth ceremonies, or about 10 per cent of the children of confirmation age. While they were doing so, Grotewohl was closing down 91 out of 97 church missions at the railway stations, which had done so much to help refugees in transit and the poor people who used their canteens. Half a dozen church weekly papers were banned at the same time and state grants to the Churches cut once more. Typically, this pressure was relaxed later in the year, but intensified as the 1957 Youth Initiation ceremonies drew nearer. According to the Evangelical Churches, whose figures were only approximate, the number of children attending them jumped to 65,000. In 1958 it rose to 90,000, or over 30 per cent of all children of confirmation age. This was largely the result of five months of continuous pressure on the Churches. Religious instruction in the schools was forbidden by the Minister of Education, Herr Lange. A number of pastors were imprisoned (at Christmas 1958 there were at least twenty-five in prison from the Evangelical Churches alone). Bishop Dibelius was forbidden to visit his Brandenburg diocese. The East German Government refused to receive Propst Grueber, who had to resign his post. More church journals were banned, and at Christmas Dr. Adenauer was portrayed kneeling at a manger, with a "newborn babe" in the shape of an atom bomb inside it. The S.E.D. press announced that all children must be told that Father Christmas was supplied with his presents by the State-Socialized industries.

In December 1958 the Evangelical Churches decided to make a strategic withdrawal in their unremitting struggle to maintain the Christian religion. Children taking part in the preparations for youth initiation would no longer be refused religious instruction. But pre-confirmation instruction would end in February and not just before Easter. Instruction would be rounded-off with a religious examination which would not include vows to the Church or admission to communion. Confirmation would be put off until after Easter, and a conflict of loyalties avoided.

In addition, children who continued to attend church after being "youth-initiated" would be able to go to their pastors six months or more afterwards and discuss the possibility of confirmation. If they were considered to have "remained in the Church" in a spiritual sense, pastors would be able to consider confirmation at the following Easter.

Dr. Dibelius and the Evangelical Church Council had good reasons for deciding on this compromise. In one East German town only 3 out of 205 children were confirmed at Easter 1958. Recruiting for the initiation-classes had been stepped up to a new high pitch in December 1958, and about 85 per cent were believed to have agreed to attend courses of instruction. The toughness of East German officials had increased in proportion to their confidence. A West Berlin girl who applied to visit her dying mother in Leipzig was told, "You can wait until she's dead. Time enough to go then." A deaf-mute who lived in West Berlin and wanted to visit his East German parents for the first time in eleven years was told, "Individual cases like yours can only be considered when the Western Powers are ready to negotiate with us as equals." In East Berlin the radio-commentator Karl Eduard von Schnitzler coined the slogans GOD HAS LEFT THE CHURCH and TO PRAY IS NOT AS USEFUL AS TO THINK. In February 1959 the first officially sponsored non-Christian baptismal and burial ceremonies took place.

Pastor Martin Niemöller, the ex-submarine commander of the First World War who subsequently resisted the Nazis, and who turned to "pure" pacifism after the Second World War, believes that the Christian Churches will survive in East Germany. His theory is that the Churches offered open resistance to Communism only because they hoped for an early reunification of Germany. "East Germans lived in a dream," Pastor Niemöller told me in the summer of 1959. "Now they must awaken from it."

Waging a "frontal campaign" against Marxism, backed by the full powers of authoritarian government, was useless. Instead, Christians had to develop self-reliance, depend on Christ and not on His Churches — "It is only in the knowledge and love of Christ that our East German kinsmen can survive as Christians. They will." They may; but the scales are weighted against them.

The Churches are only one part of society which has suffered from Communist persecution. The full story of that persecution is too long to be told in detail here. A few facts give an idea of it.

Every political party has been periodically and systematically purged. In the first three years after the war the East German C.D.U. lost its chairman three times in this way. In January 1953 the C.D.U. Foreign Minister, Georg Dertinger, was sent into long-term imprisonment. Earlier he had told me that his one task was to "preserve what is German." It is questionable whether the best way of doing this was to make his terms with the Devil. The Liberal Democrats were forced to carry out two purges in 1948, another in 1950 and a fourth in 1952. There have even been two major purges in the S.E.D., in 1953 and 1958.

Any semblance of a free election ceased after 1949. The political prisons were never empty, and even in 1959 there were more than 7000 people in them, with 300 or more *Prominente* in Brandenburg prison. With over three million East Germans seeking refuge in West Germany between 1949 and 1959, the Communist regime imposed severe penalties on "flight from the Republic," introduced travel restrictions and cut down contact between East and West. The number of East Germans visiting West Germany dropped from 1.7 million in 1957 to under 600,000 in 1958. All kinds of sufferings arose out of this throttling down of movement. A Thuringian professor, Dr. Flach, who "escaped" to Bonn University in 1958, was sentenced, in his absence, to two years' imprisonment. He committed suicide. A dentist from Uckermende who visited the Ruhr town of Duisburg went on a two-day trip up the river Rhine and sent his relatives picture postcards from various places. His mail was censored and he was sent to prison for three months, on his return to East Germany, for visiting places not specified on his travel permit.

Travel restrictions and a closer watch on the interzonal frontier reduced the number of East German refugees arriving in West Germany from a yearly average of 250,000 to no more than 150,000 in 1959. But the proportion of "intellectuals" leaving for good increased to a remarkable extent. Thus in 1954 only 270 doctors fled west; in 1958, 1242. The corresponding figures for University and Technical College Professors were 28 and 208; for their pupils, 879 and 2522; for engineers 1610 and 2345. The rector of Jena University, Dr. Josef Hämel, fled on the eve of the university's four hundreth anniversary; he said that he was being forced to turn "a great school into the worst kind of Socialistic institution." And all the time contact between East and West Germany was being slowly whittled-down. In 1954, 41 out of every 100 West Germans had friends or relatives on the other side of the Iron Curtain; by 1959 this had dropped to 35. In 1954, 39 out of every 100 West Germans wrote to someone in East Germany occasionally; in 1959 the figure was 33.

What can enable spiritual and intellectual freedom to survive in a state which is being slowly reduced to a conventional Communist pattern? Youth, certainly, has resilience. Young East Germans with whom I have talked have demonstrated a surprising degree of independence of mind. "We don't believe in your sort of capitalism," one boy from Chemnitz told me, "but that does not mean we are satisfied with our East German system. We don't need to believe everything we hear; we don't even need to believe everything we say ourselves." There is a thick vein of cynicism in many young East Germans and at the same time a somewhat masochistic pride in having to be tougher and more enduring than their opposite numbers in the West. Who should blame young people for being cynical, when mild hooliganism may earn a five-year prison sentence, when having a father who is an independent tradesman or farmer may prevent entrance to the university, when failure to conform is a bar to visiting worthwhile holiday resorts, adopting worthwhile professions or even playing football?

Tyranny in East Germany reflects, in cameo, the tyranny which exists in the whole Communist Bloc. That tyranny is based on a Communist hierarchy, which is divorced from all other elements of the community, which is the negation of the Socialist ethic, and which serves Soviet imperialism. Walter Ulbricht has, at least since 1950, been the pinnacle of that hierarchy — just as surely as Khrushchev became the pinnacle in the Kremlin. His record is one of devoted service to Moscow. In the 1930's he even denounced German Communists to the Gestapo, because they pursued a line too independent of the Soviet Union. He — and with him, the East German President, Wilhelm Pieck, and a dozen other key members of the East German hierarchy — has Soviet nationality. As long as Ulbricht remains in power the development of national Communism of the Polish type under Gomulka is unthinkable.

The sense of humor of the simple people may help some freedom of spirit to survive. The East Germans have not forgotten how to laugh. One favorite joke runs: "When Otto Grotewohl fell downstairs one day, his secretary dashed to the telephone and rang up the doctor: 'For Lenin's sake, doctor, come quickly! Grotewohl has busted his backbone!' 'Nonsense,' was the answer, 'he never had one.'"

Or there was the old lady of Leipzig who wrote to Walter Ulbricht to congratulate him on his birthday, adding "I wish you everything that the German people has been wishing you for years." Next day she was arrested for incitement to murder.

There is the story of the beggar and the policeman. The beggar was waiting to see a Communist procession go by when he lost his temper and began to curse the regime and Communism in general. When the policeman came up and proceeded to arrest him, bystanders tried to intervene.

"Don't pay any attention to him," one of them said to the policeman. "Can't you see the man is just plumb crazy?"

"No, I can't," said the policeman. "He's talking much too good sense."

Two unconnected incidents suggest how hard it is to mold the minds of a people traditionally anti-Communist and fixed in its ways. In 1958 I attended morning service in East Berlin's Marienkirche, which acts as substitute for the badly bombed Cathedral. Outside the church, which stands forlornly in waste ground, were exactly five motor cars. But inside was a devout and attentive congregation of around 800. In 1958 the West German nuclear scientist, Professor Werner Heisenberg, visited the East German town of Cottbus to give a lecture. He spoke in the tightly packed Volkssaal, and in the neighboring Klosterkirche an overflow was allowed to listen to a loud-speaker relay. Thousands of applicants for tickets had to be turned away; hundreds more stood in the rain outside.

Communist conformity has been more difficult to achieve than the East German and Soviet leaders may have hoped, or have ever dared to admit. Yet there can be no doubt that the sheer, grinding passage of time must weaken resistance to conformity.

The Soviet Interest

Hitlers come and Hitlers go, but the German people goes on forever.
— JOSEPH STALIN

Whether the Western Powers like it or not, the German Democratic Republic is a fact.
— WALTER ULBRICHT, Deputy Prime Minister of the East German Republic

Today the machines in the factories are still. The shops are shut. The children have a whole-holiday. In the streets workers, men and women, are marching. They carry big placards, on them the words: "All workers are brothers! Work harder, live better!" And they cry out: "We greet the Soviet Union! Long live our President, Wilhelm Pieck!"
— READING LESSON FOR EIGHT-YEAR-OLDS, East German schools 1959

THE division of Germany since the end of the Second World War has been treated by the West German politicians and the West German Press as something unthinkable, unnatural and unheard-of. It is all too easily forgotten that the unity of Germany seemed at least equally unthinkable only a hundred years ago. Even sixty years ago the members of a West German Grand Ducal Court like that of Hesse-Darmstadt used to hold up their hands in horror at the thought of *les Prusses* — those heathenish inhabitants of the marshes and forests of eastern Central Europe, whose military genius had united Germany and whose discipline had imposed a Prussian form of centralism on it.

The cultured, comfortable Court of Hesse-Darmstadt probably felt itself quite as far removed from the orderliness, power and

CUMMINGS, *Daily Express*

Change behind the Iron Curtain:
It's Simply a Matter of Armbands

fanatical nationalism of Prussian Potsdam as does today provincial Bonn from subeastern Berlin-Pankow. And, up to 1957, the rulers of East Germany shared a common fear with the erstwhile Grand Duke of Hesse — that of becoming a dependency of the "other," larger and more powerful Germany which might be prepared to back with force its claim to represent and to lead the whole German people. By 1959 this fear of the Ulbricht-Grotewohl regime in Berlin-Pankow had receded into the background. For the division of Germany had become more absolute and the independent existence of the East German State was an inescapable fact.

It is possible, on a short trip into East Germany, to gain useful general impressions of its lagging living standards, human reticences under the worst (because it is the most foreign) dictatorship in Eastern Europe, and the overall grayness of life there. But East Germans will not talk readily with strangers. They have reasons enough to be careful. To learn how deep the division of Germany is becoming, it is easier and more profitable to hear what a West German has to say who goes regularly to East Germany, who stays a reasonable length of time there, who has family and friends from whom he can learn.

A West German whom I know, but for obvious reasons cannot name, spent more than a month in East Germany in the spring of 1959 with his parents and their circle of friends in the town in which he was born and in which he had spent his life until 1950. These were the most vital impressions which he brought back to West Germany:

People were less ready to talk to him about any important subject. Their old refrain — that they were longing for the day of German reunification and for the more normal, more pleasant life which it would bring — had been repeated year after year. It seemed that they had got tired of repeating it any longer — or they simply did not believe that reunification was still a practical possibility. These East German relatives and friends were even slightly embarrassed if he brought up political topics. It seemed to him — and for the first year since 1950 — that he was unable to learn anything from them save that they had accepted the "System" and were no longer ready to rebel, in word or thought, against it. A contagious apathy had spread through the people of East Germany.

East German citizens were inclined to talk to this revenant about "our Republic" (the phrase was absolutely new to him, and he had been in East Germany only nine months earlier). For the first time, these manifest non-Communists talked about "our Grotewohl," and drew attention to the tour which the East German Prime Minister was making in the Middle East and Asia. They talked — and to this West German observer this seemed wildly incongruous — of "our Socialist achievements." A year before, this had been one of the most obvious, most ridiculed catch-phrases of the Communist regime. It had raised a restrained horse-laugh in plenty of East German family circles.

Another line of East German conversation was new to this very unsuspecting, very surprised young man — who had, in his day, fled from Saxony for his life, and who took a grave and calculated risk in coming back each year to his old home. This was as follows: The West Germans were the fat kine of Pharaoh's dream. And why? Because they had been given immense financial and economic aid by the Western world, because the American Secretary of State, Mr. George Marshall, had worked out a plan to put West Germany on its feet again, because the West Germans got off lightly and with a handshake full of dollar bills. . . . What, on the other hand, had happened to the East Germans? These particular East Germans had no hesitation in explaining: They had paid gigantic reparations to the Soviet Union, were still paying them. They had been harnessed to the economic donkey-engine of the Communist bloc, had worked desperately hard, and had seen much of the fruits of their labors dissipated by Communist-ideological mismanagement. Yet they were succeeding! The East German standard of living was rising and food rationing was abolished in 1958. By their discipline, self-sacrifice and instinct for survival the East Germans had

made their "German Democratic Republic" into the most important economic unit of the Communist bloc — against all the
odds! What had West Germans to show to compare with THIS
performance? And why was it that West Germans scrupulously
avoided mention or recognition of what their East German cousins had achieved?

There was a final, deeply disturbing process of thought that
my West German friend found in his 1959 five-week visit to his
native Saxony. This was that East Germans believed that West
Germans were no longer interested in them, had written them
off. This suspicion was based on reality. In 1957 roughly 23,000
East Germans sought refuge each month in West Germany. One
in twelve of them subsequently returned to East Germany. In
1959, only 12,000 East Germans fled each month to West Germany. And one in four was returning to his East German home.
Why? Because, of course, he found that life was not quite as easy
as he had expected in the "Golden West." He was not automati-
cally given a first-class job and set on the road to becoming a
millionaire. He even had great difficulty in finding a single room,
usually without running water, for fifty marks a month, or one
third of the rental of a four-room, modernized flat. He lacked
friends and he was homesick. Here he was in a quandary; the
East German authorities would simply not give him a special
"permit of residence" to visit his own family. Instead they were
liable to prosecute and imprison him for *Republikflucht* — flight
from the Republic — if he showed his nose in his home town.
The tighter East German regulations had come in at the end of
1957, and they came to stay.

But, most of all, East Germans who "chose freedom" were appalled by the lack of interest taken in them and their views when
they came to West Germany. It requires a big and bold decision
to leave family, friends, belongings, home and all its associations.
But it becomes doubly depressing when no West German even
wants to hear how and why so big a decision came to be taken.
West Germans are simply — too busy. And East German refugees
retort: "At home we were taught to reason in materialistic terms,

but we let our lives be guided by ideals — service to factory, to fellow workers and the State, the sacrifice of private interest for the public welfare. In West Germany people are taught to venerate fine ideals like democracy and freedom, but their lives are ruled by purely selfish materialism."

The increasingly deep division of Germany is the product of deliberate Soviet policy and timely Soviet economic progress. By 1953, for instance, Soviet aims had disclosed themselves in the cold, naked light of the Cold War. But these aims seemed to imply the dooming of East Germany to the position not so much of a satellite as of a slave. The June 17, 1953, rising in East Germany was directed against economic debasement far more than against Communist tyranny and foreign rule. Very few West Germans understood this; they continued to believe that the rising was a tremendous blow for political freedom. Six years later it became abundantly clear that they had been wrong; East Germany had not gained any fresh measure of political freedom, but it was attaining a reasonable degree of economic progress. And the East Germans were becoming — if not content — at least increasingly resigned to the one, solid and indisputable fact of the division of their country and their own incorporation in an expanding, ever more prosperous Eastern bloc.

A brief note of recapitulation may be necessary.

The Western Powers occupied Germany in 1945 in a spirit of "no revenge, but no more wars." Each Western occupying power brought its own ideas, and very often there was a conflict of ideas among its own representatives. What Germans, with a woolly-headed stupidity which is almost unbelievable, have never understood is that democracies do not relish the business of occupation and have no ready-made formula for saving the soul of the country which they have to occupy. (What a difference in comparison with the German Occupation of France in 1940, which Hitler decided would force the French people into the "New European Order." Or in comparison with the German Occupation of Holland, which was designed quite simply to grind down Dutch resistance until the war had been won. Or in comparison with the

German Occupation of Poland, which was the first stage in the decimation of a Slav people and its replacement by German colonizers who were intended to rule for that full interregnum of the "Thousand-Year Reich"!)

The Soviet Union occupied its zone of Germany with a very exact plan, which bore no relation to the interests of the Allied Powers as a whole or to those of the German people. Three teams moved into eastern Germany behind the Red Army; diplomats to deal with the Western Powers, political propagandists to prepare the ground for the erection of an independent East German State, and economic specialists to remove industrial equipment to the Soviet Union. As opposed to the other occupation powers the Russians had one big advantage — a ready-made Communist Party cadre, which could act as their intermediary. Four political parties were formed within a few weeks, dismantling began in earnest before a Four-Power dismantling program had even been discussed, 213 key industrial plants were confiscated and put under Soviet management, the uranium mines were opened up for the production of ores for Soviet nuclear development.

It appeared to be incidental, but was in fact organically necessary from the Soviet point of view to reform the whole East German social system. Basic industries were nationalized, all big and medium-sized landed estates were split up, Communist-controlled trade union and youth movements were founded. With a unique mixture of political ballyhoo and flattery, spies and secret police, concentration camps and crooked justice, the Russians proceeded to organize their zone on lines which barely promised survival but which have turned out to be brilliantly successful. Western observers proved so gullible that one distinguished British writer, Basil Davidson, was able to record:

> By August 1947 . . . the Russians had done two things: they had heavily penalized [Nazi] activists and still more important, they had changed the structure of their zone by dividing up the big estates, transferring a large part of industry to public ownership and exacting reparations. They had also fostered the emergence of political parties and

139

mass organizations in which ex-Nazis and people with Nazi sentiments might slowly learn — and on the elementary level that was necessary for them — the practice and principles of social equality and self-government.

It may seem incredible in retrospect that a first-class journalist should have had so little understanding of Soviet motives. But this was nothing exceptional four years after the war.

It is necessary to trace out the complex, outwardly drab but revealing story of the tightening Soviet control of the eastern zone of Germany. Soviet rule could not fail to be highly unpopular — for one reason more than any other: up to 1953 the Russians took out of East Germany 17,600 million dollars in reparations. This was 7600 million more than the Soviet Union had demanded at the Potsdam Conference! East Germany was bled white — during a period in which this entailed no grave political risk, but only continuous political manipulation and a calculated reliance on the pro-Russian sentiments which lingered on in many Western countries after the war.

The 1953 rising in East Germany marks a turning point in that story. Again more than a word of explanation is necessary. The East German Government which was established in 1949 was headed by Otto Grotewohl. This was a concession to the Social Democratic forces which had combined with the Communist Party — under Russian orders — to form the Socialist Unity Party in 1946. The choice of Grotewohl was held to make it easier, too, for the puppet Liberal Democratic and Christian Democratic parties to collaborate with the regime. But the real ruler of East Germany — as became quickly apparent — was to be Walter Ulbricht, a Moscow-trained Communist with a record of undeviating loyalty to the Soviet Communist Party. In the first four years of the East German Government's existence Ulbricht was in effect acting as overseer of Soviet interests — primarily the extraction of reparations in bulk and out of current production and the gearing of East German industry to produce what the Soviet Union needed most of all for postwar reconstruction. It was for this reason that Ulbricht embarked on the so-called "tough course" in 1951. His orders from Moscow were at all costs to increase heavy industrial production, to launch the large-scale development program in the uranium mines, and to restrict consumption in East Germany to a minimum.

In 1951 Ulbricht launched his first Five Year Plan, designed to raise production by 92 per cent above the 1950 level. This was a Soviet requirement, and Ulbricht did not hesitate to use every possible repressive method in order to reach his target. Workers were given collective wage agreements which reduced the trade unions to the status of an auxiliary arm of the Communist State; workers were set "production norms" on the Stakhanovite model and penalties were prescribed for their nonfulfillment; women were mobilized on a huge scale for industry; agricultural co-operatives were formed, not primarily for political motives but in order to wrest a higher output from the generally unfertile farming soil of East Germany.

The tough terms of the Five Year Plan made it inadvisable to allow free contact to be maintained with West Germany. Early in 1952 steps were taken to close the interzonal frontier running through the middle of Germany. On the very frontier itself a twenty-yard-wide "death zone" was established, often entailing ploughing up strips of ground or cutting rides through woods. East German frontier guards — immensely reinforced, armed with automatic weapons and very often stationed in watchtowers — were instructed to fire on sight on anyone entering the death zone. Behind it a three-mile-wide "restricted zone" was cleared of "unreliable" inhabitants. Open roads running into West Berlin from East Germany were reduced from 227 to 50. No free passage was offered to West Berliners wanting to enter East Germany (they used to make their day trips primarily to buy fruits and vegetables, to make excursions or to visit graves of relatives — since all big Berlin cemeteries lie outside the city boundaries). Telephone and tram connections between West and East Berlin were cut (they were still cut in 1960).

In the late summer of 1952 the Socialist Unity Party held its second Congress, in Leipzig. Its aim was the "consolidation" of the East German State. The strength of the People's Police was to be raised from 70,000 to 100,000 and President Pieck called on its members to follow the example of the Red Army in "mastering the technique of defense on land, in the sea and in the air." East German rearmament was henceforward to be open and unashamed. Behind the front-line forces two types of militia were to be set up — the armed and para-military "factory guards" (only in the planning stage up to the end of 1953) and the "Association for Sports and Technics," which gave its members training in the use of rifle, machine gun and grenades, and in infantry tactics. A major campaign began to popularize the monolithic "Free German Youth," which included the appointment of a twenty-four-year-old Minister of Education and a number of Lord Mayors between the ages of nineteen and twenty-five. A governmental purge took place, resulting in the arrest of Georg Dertinger, the Minister of Foreign Affairs, and Karl Hamann, Minister of Food, and their imprisonment for fifteen and ten years respectively. The object of this was, quite simply, to concentrate political power yet further in the hands of the Socialist Unity Party.

Stalin died on March 6, 1953, and Soviet policies in the satellite states went into the melting-pot. Vladimir Semeonov, the former political adviser to the Soviet military administration in East Germany, was sent out to East Berlin to examine the possibilities of a "new course," which would woo the East Germans and wean them from ingrained desires to return to the Western fold and be reunited with their more prosperous cousins in West Germany. In April came a reversal of policy in Moscow, and Semeonov was recalled there. But on May 28 he returned to Berlin as Soviet High Commissioner. He was confronted by an explosive situation. Work norms (production quotas) had been raised by a minimum of 10 per cent and by an overall 15 per cent. On June 5, before Semeonov had a chance of reintroducing his "new course," the first reductions of wages in conformity with the new norms took place and were made retroactive to June 1. Semeonov acted with promptitude. On June 9 the Socialist Unity Party admitted "errors," including the tightness of food rationing, the confiscation of farms, the persecution of independent tradesmen, the condemning in their absence of people who had fled to West Germany and the undue restriction of travel. On June 10 the Prime Minister, Otto Grotewohl, announced the restoration of normal relations between State and Church. Religious teaching in the schools could be resumed, Church property be restored, Church youth groups allowed to organize, and around fifty churchmen were released from prison.

But the higher work norms remained, and this alone ensured the failure of Semeonov's program. On June 14 the East German Government confirmed that the norms would not be altered. On June 16 the building workers in East Berlin's Stalinallee went on strike and marched to the government buildings in order to demonstrate in front of them. They called not only for a reduction of norms but also for free and secret elections. The news of the Stalinallee workers' act of defiance spread like wildfire over East Germany that evening, for three out of four East Germans with radios tuned in to West Berlin and West German stations. The revolution began in earnest next morning.

The June 17, 1953, East German revolution is an epic of courage, common sense and solidarity in the face of Communist repression. It was a popular movement, beginning with building workers and carried on by their colleagues in the coal mines and the factories — the very people whom the Communist Government was by way of representing in that mythical "Workers' and Farmers' State." It was a spontaneous movement; for it was given no encouragement from the West and people like the Federal Minister for All-German Affairs, Jakob Kaiser, even urged the East Germans to do nothing which could endanger their personal safety. The movement spread over the whole of East Germany; in nearly three quarters of it martial law was proclaimed, and Soviet troops had to be called in to restore order in every town with more than 50,000 inhabitants, save Plauen in Saxony.

In the days immediately following the rising I met and talked with East Germans who had been forced to seek refuge in West Berlin from the vengeance of the Ulbricht regime and its uniformed bullies of the People's Police. The story of one town illustrates what happened in the rest of East Germany on June 17. This is how the rising took place in the Saxonian town of Bitterfeld, sixty miles south of Berlin:

Bitterfeld was a town of 60,000 inhabitants, and around 16,000 of them worked in three large chemical plants. In these plants animated talk about the Stalinallee demonstration began at the very beginning of the early morning shift on June 17. By nine o'clock the workers had formed deputations which took lists of demands to their managements — for lower work norms, higher and guaranteed rates of pay, better food in their canteens, more pay for overtime. By ten o'clock workers, now in telephonic communication between one factory and another, decided to march into the middle of the town to demonstrate. Big columns, thousands strong, converged on the Youth Square, where over 20,000 people were already assembled.

In Youth Square the car of the Director of Police, Nossek, was overturned. Posters of Stalin, Pieck and Ulbricht were torn down. The town-hall and post-office were occupied by the demonstrators, and the civil jail was opened and its 260 political prisoners released. The demonstrators carried banners demanding the removal of all Socialist Unity Party and Free German Youth leaders and officials. Outside the State-owned stores, the *Handelsorganisation*, the Communist manager, Rueger, was recognized and killed. In the early afternoon the demonstrators raided beer and sausage stalls, but left money for everything that they took. The whole town was now in their hands.

In the late afternoon the first Red Army tanks appeared, rumbling purposefully through the streets and taking up their positions on Youth Square and at other key points in the town. They were followed by Soviet infantry and squads of the People's Police. House-to-house searches began, and in the course of them 280 people were arrested. On the next day the Mayor of the Wolfen suburb of Bitterfeld, Hartmann, was tried by summary court-martial and shot. Three factories and one coal mine held out until June 20, and only called their strike off when promises were made that no more reprisals would be taken. The rising was at an end, broken by the Red Army.

The Bitterfeld story was repeated all over East Germany. Everywhere huge crowds marched into town centers and took over all key public buildings. Offices of the Socialist Unity Party and the Free German Youth were burned down, civil jails were opened and emptied, committees of "public safety" were formed and drew up lists of demands which were forwarded to Berlin in the belief that the Revolution had succeeded there too. The "civil" People's Police often showed sympathy with the demonstrators and joined them; the para-military People's Police "in barracks" on more than one occasion refused to fire on unarmed crowds, but there was no act of mutiny — already, after four years, they were tolerably reliable servants of the East German regime.

The June 17, 1953, rising underlined one lesson which the West for so long failed to learn during the Cold War. On the diplomatic level, Western action has to be prompt and decisive. Although the Stalinallee workers were demonstrating by midday on June 16, the Allied Commandants in West Berlin did not send their unadventurously worded protest to the Soviet Commandant against the use of military force in East Berlin until the late evening of June 18. On June 17 the Allied Commandants and members of their staffs went down to the sector boundary and peered into East Berlin like so many dim-witted tourists. The sector boundary had been sealed off, but Allied minor officials were still going to the Four Power Air Safety Center and Combined Travel Board offices in East Berlin. The Allied Commandants had a perfect right to demand ingress to East Berlin and an immediate conference with the Soviet Commandant. Yet even on the afternoon of June 18, British and American officials were maintaining that the situation was "not clear" and that it was not even sure that East Berlin had been sealed off. The only "encouragement" from the West for the people of East Germany was the broadcast warning them not to do anything violent which might endanger lives. This was the measure of Western preparedness for a diplomatic initiative in the Cold War and for any concrete implementation of the often-repeated American thesis of "rolling back Communism."

The rising had many consequences, some of which seemed to conflict with one another. There were, for instance, immediate reprisals. At least 42 death sentences were carried out after the rising ended, and around 25,000 arrests were made. Hundreds of people were given prison sentences. While control of East Germany's frontiers was tightened and the overall number of refugees escaping to West Germany reduced, 467 members of the People's Police deserted in June alone — by far the highest number in any single month.

On the other hand, there were equally immediate concessions. On June 22 the East German Government announced that the lower production norms of two months earlier would be restored, that rates of pay would revert to April levels, that old-age and widows' pensions would be increased, and that more consumer goods would come onto the market. Cuts of electric current for domestic households were officially abolished; workers were told that time spent away from the factories on account of ill-health would no longer result in the cancellation of holidays; the Government would spend seventy million marks on "hygiene" and would divert six hundred million marks from investment in heavy industry to a special "social housing" program.

To offset these concessions, another governmental purge was carried out in July. Max Fechner, a former Social Democrat and Minister of Justice, was dismissed. His post was given to "Red" Hilde Benjamin, whose Jewish husband had been murdered by the Nazis, who had escaped from them with her own life by a miracle, and who was committed to serving a Communist regime with a unique blend of hatred for her tormentors and devotion to their liquidators. Dismissed too were Rudolf Herrnstadt, the editor of the Socialist Unity Party paper, *Neues Deutschland,* and regarded as the possible successor to Ulbricht, and Wilhelm Zaisser, the old-guard Communist and Spanish Civil War veteran who had organized and led the People's Police. Recruiting for the People's Police was stepped up and the force was put under the command of Ernst Wollweber, a former Communist sabotage expert who had worked boldly and bravely against the Nazis, and who — more important — had never fallen foul of Ulbricht in the process.

More significant still — production norms were again raised, in September. There were brushes between workers and the People's Police. There were a few sitdown strikes in the factories. But the Ulbricht policy of "whippings and lollipops" paid off. The East Germans were never to be quite so hard-pressed again, but their emotions were caught on the rebound. Sorely tried, frightened by their failure to win freedom at a single throw, prepared to be mollified by the vague and dishonest promise of an early abolition of food-rationing, the people of East Germany were herded into the post-1953 era, which has a continuity lacking before. This continuity is represented by the steadfast efforts ever since 1953 of both the Soviet and East German regimes to make East Germany into a pseudo-sovereign, fully committed satellite member of the Communist bloc. For the 1953 rising taught the Russians two lessons — they had tried to force too much out of East Germans who still felt themselves bound to their West German cousins by historical and sentimental ties; and they would only reduce their risks in East Germany if they built it up into a solid, going concern.

It was not enough to cut the East Germans off from contact with West Germany; they had to be given some hope for their future in isolation. So in August, 1953, the Soviet Government announced that it would return the last thirty-three of the key industrial plants which had been put under Soviet management and ownership seven years before. In only one company would the Soviet Union retain a proprietary interest — the Wismuth A.G., which employed 110,000 uranium-ore miners and which was for a decade to satisfy 35 per cent of the Soviet Union's uranium requirements. In September 1953 the East German Government was allowed to draw on People's Police stocks of grain, potatoes and other foodstuffs in order to deal with growing food shortages. In December 1953 all East German Ministries were told to show more initiative and imagination in meeting the wishes of the community. There was to be more food, tobacco and cosmetics; more attention was to be paid to "style and cut" of workers' clothing; a "war against waste" (collection of worn-out clothes, scraps of food, waste paper and so forth, based on the Nazi model) would remedy a number of shortages; the East German Government was even encouraged to organize its first dim gesture of sovereignty. It sent a note to the West German Government proposing the cancellation of all reparations and the limitation of costs of occupation paid by both German Governments to 5 per cent of their annual budgets. The note was not answered; it was not intended to be. But the East German people gained, for the first time, an impression that its own Government might actually look after its interests.

It is a mistake to imagine that the Communist world organizes its affairs with diabolical cunning and inevitable success. The Russians inspired distrust and hatred by the gross bestialities of the first few months of their occupation of East Germany. They permitted free elections in Berlin at the end of 1946, and tolerably free elections in their zone of occupation, in the mistaken belief that they would "work out" successfully for the Communist cause. Instead, an overwhelming majority of the Berliners rejected Communism and roughly half of the terrorized East Germans did likewise. The Russians were insatiable in their demand for reparations and very nearly lost all East Germany for good and all as a result in 1953. Only then did the common sense of Semeonov and his school assert itself, in face of the medievally minded agents of Soviet imperialism in postwar Germany — the glum, brutal General Sokolovsky, Soviet Commander-in-Chief in Germany during the Berlin blockade; his thumbscrew political adjutant, Colonel Tulpanov; the pseudo-paternal, peasant-minded General Kotikov, who commanded for four years in Berlin.

Since 1953 the Russians have worked with real skill in order to incorporate East Germany into the Communist bloc as a fully fledged, economically and strategically valuable satellite member. However much West Germans may hate and dread the thought, East Germany has gained an existence of its own which could guarantee its indefinite survival as a separate state.

Postwar life in Eastern Germany was drab. Hence the appeal of the Ulbricht regime to youth. What was important about the Free German Youth (F.D.J.) was not just its uniforms, medals, march-music and march-discipline. While Germany's defeat in war had brought an apotheosis of frustration in its train, East German leaders told members of the F.D.J. that the future lay with THEM, that they could rebuild what Hitler (and the bomber-planes of the Western Powers) had shattered. Postwar East German society was in a state of total disintegration. More even than in West Germany, it had depended so much on a land-owning class, the Army and the civil service that every one of its props had been up-ended.

Members of the F.D.J. to whom I have spoken are insistent on one point. Once a member of the organization, it is difficult not to be grateful to it. The F.D.J. inculcated the belief that the sons of farmers and workers should have preference in securing places at the universities. They have, and by 1959 they constituted roughly 70 per cent of the university population. The F.D.J. organized the only holidays worth having, with the best food, hotels, sports facilities on the Baltic coast and the lakes of Mecklenburg, in the mountains and forests of Saxony and Thuringia. The F.D.J. cells were set up in the factories in the works councils, in every publicly owned firm of consequence. The F.D.J. drafted its members into the People's Police as leaders and instructors, and later into the armed forces. F.D.J. members have admitted quite openly to me that both mass emotion and reasoned self-interest have been successfully used as weapons by their organization in order to secure both conformity and enthusiasm — "We were not merely given more of every material thing than other people, we were given more hope."

The F.D.J. has some reasons for pride. It can point out that 90 per cent of East German University students in 1959 received grants of 130 to 180 marks a month (only 10 per cent of West German students received help on this scale), that young East Germans at the universities have better living conditions and meals than their West German contemporaries, that their organization has been able to invite 70,000 West German children each year for free holidays in East Germany, that since 1955 they have been sending "discussion teams" to West Germany to argue the merits of "People's Democracy."

Russian backing of the Free German Youth movement has been one of the most potent means of consolidating a separate East Germany. Of course, more liberal Soviet political and economic policies towards East Germany have played their part too. Up to 1955 it was fashionable for Western newspapermen to write annual accounts of "impending economic collapse" in East Germany. Such stories had some justification. There was a chronic shortage of electricity. Food-rationing continued. (Albania was the only other European country with rationing, and East German meat and fat rations were often not honored.) Failures in agricultural planning led at one time to nearly one million acres lying fallow and to an increasing exodus of farmers to West Germany. In 1954 subsidies to agriculture were reduced by 1600 million marks, while expenditure on the People's Police and State Security Services was increased by 2200 million marks (these two organizations absorbed 10,000 million marks out of the 36,000 million mark budget that year). Consumer goods were deficient in quality and too few were being produced. There was a growing labor-shortage, due to the flow of refugees to the west, a static birth rate, the increase of para-military forces and the employment of over 100,000 uranium miners who were working exclusively for the Soviet Union.

But by 1956 the economic tide had already turned in East Germany, even though for three years afterwards it did not run strongly. A small table of results published in 1956 shows this.

	Planned Increase (1950 = 100)	Actual Increase
Steel	313	250
Iron Ore	910	400
Machinery	215	300
Textiles	367	250
Fats	214	500
Meat and Fish	212	250

The first Five Year Plan, which ended in 1956, fell only 10 per cent short of targets which had been deliberately set high. Against the much publicized failures were such facts as a 65 per cent increase in lignite production — East Germany's main source of fuel — and the success of the so-called *Schwerpunkt-Programm,* under which certain branches of industry were given priority. The progress of such firms as Leuna Chemicals, Schopkau Buna and Zeiss Optics was indisputable.

The East German economy, moreover, had been intimately linked with that of the Soviet Union and its satellites. East Germany's foreign trade increased by 180 per cent during the Five Year Plan. The dominating feature was the machinery needed by the Communist countries. In 1950 machinery accounted for only 32 per cent of exports, in 1955 for 60 per cent and in 1960 (planned) 68 per cent. Three quarters of all East German exports flow to the Communist bloc, and nearly four fifths of those to the Soviet Union and China consist of machinery. East Germany is becoming the workshop of the Communist bloc.

In 1949 the Soviet Union organized the "Council for Mutual Economic Aid" (Comecon), which was designed to co-ordinate the economic policies of the different Communist bloc countries. Comecon's interest in East Germany dates specifically from the institution of the Seven Year Plan at the end of 1957 — until a year before, at least, East Germany had been regarded as a "special case" and primarily as a source of reparations in kind to the Soviet Union. Comecon gave East Germany the following tasks:

It must more than double chemical production by 1965. In the Communist bloc it will become, next to the Soviet Union, the biggest producer of petrochemicals, potash, calcined soda and plastics (Comecon intends to raise Communist bloc production of plastics from 350,000 tons in 1958 to 6 million tons in 1975). The Soviet Union will help the East German chemicals program by building an oil pipeline from the Ukraine to Schwedt, two miles west of the Oder, by 1963. In 1965 the pipeline should be bringing 4.8 million tons of crude oil into East Germany annually.

At least 9000 million marks are to be invested in the East German chemicals industry by 1965, and Comecon's "Permanent Commission for Chemistry" has its seat in East Berlin.

East Germany is to become the principal producer of nickel and zinc in the Communist bloc. The main center of these industries will be at St. Egidien, near Chemnitz. The nickel plant which will be built there will cost 160 million marks and is to be completed by 1963. East Germany will remain the biggest Communist producer of lignite products. These will be increasingly used for specialized purposes, while East Germany's fuel requirements will be increasingly met by imported hard coal from Poland and Czechoslovakia.

The Communist bloc is short of shipping, and East Germany has a surprisingly big role to play here too. It will concentrate on building ships of between 5000 and 15,000 tons, while smaller ships are built on the Black Sea and ships of over 15,000 tons in the Baltic ports of Poland and the Soviet Union. East Germany will also build sugar and cement factories for the bloc and will develop its specialized skills in precision instruments and optics, turbines and tractors, locomotives, rolling stock and nuclear power. The first East German nuclear power plant was scheduled to be in operation by the end of 1960 and the second by 1965.

The economic buildup of East Germany has been more obvious than the political — at least up to the two Geneva Conferences of 1959. For the Soviet Union earlier affected to regard both German states as "provisional" and did not have a high degree of confidence in the powers of survival of the East German regime. In 1952, after all, the Soviet Union (in its note of March 10 to the Western Powers) was still asking for a German peace treaty, German reunification, the withdrawal of all foreign troops from German soil within one year and the military neutralization of a united Germany. And at the Berlin Conference of January and February 1954 the Soviet Union repeated its chief demand, the military neutralization of a united Germany, while insisting that provisional regimes in both parts of Germany should prepare elections for an all-German constituent assembly.

Was this Soviet offer — amounting to reunification in return for military neutralization — serious? Six years later Dr. Adenauer's critics were still sure that it was. They believed that a unique chance was missed — because the Western Powers did not realize how ready the Russians were to get rid of a part of Europe which was giving them so much trouble. But the opposite view is that Western agreement to this deal would still not have secured free All-German elections, but would only have led on to Soviet conditions for the form which reunification would take. It is not possible to say which view was right. What is sure is that a great many West Germans were upset by the failure in the Berlin Conference to come to grips with the German problem. At the end of it, less than 10,000 West Berliners assembled in order to demand German reunification; and in Bonn 3000 students marched through the streets of the Federal capital as a protest against the Berlin fiasco.

From 1955 onwards the Soviet Union has steadily pursued a policy of bolstering up East German prestige and consolidating East German independence. In May 1955 East Germany was a signatory of the Warsaw Pact Treaty, although the East German armed forces were not immediately to be integrated under Marshal Rokossovski's command. In July 1955 Khrushchev and Marshal Bulganin visited East Berlin and reached "full agreement" over the need to evolve a system of European security which would include both German States. In September the East German State was given control over its own frontiers and internal communications. In 1956 East German leaders visited Moscow and obtained promises of Soviet economic aid and of a cut-down of support-costs for the Red Army divisions in Germany. In July of that year support-costs were limited to a figure of 800 million marks and the East German military contingent to the Warsaw Pact was fixed at 80,000 men.

Khrushchev was again in Eastern Germany in 1957, and full East German sovereignty was proclaimed on September 20. Three weeks later Yugoslavia became the first state outside the Communist bloc to recognize the East German Republic. "Satellite solidarity" was underlined by the visit of the first secretary of the Polish Communist Party, Vladimir Gomulka, to East Berlin and by a Polish-Czech-East German conference which tabled demands for the end of West German rearmament, the recognition of the Oder-Neisse Line frontier, and the maintenance of the "defensive" Warsaw Pact Treaty. In 1958 Khrushchev proposed the handing-over of Soviet responsibilities in Berlin, and, on its lines of communication with the West, to the East German Republic. He encouraged the East German Government to send notes to the Western Powers in September, proposing talks on the preparation of a German Peace Treaty, and the establishment of an All-German Commission to work out steps towards German reunification. He allowed another East German Government purge (Schirdewan, Öllsner, Wollweber). The Soviet Union stated explicitly that the only road to reunification lay through the formation of a "Confederation" of two equally entitled German States.

That, in barest outline and prosaic terms, was the course taken by the Soviet Union in "building up" the East German Republic as a sovereign, independent state. How should this policy be interpreted?

It is fairly obvious that East Germany is economically valuable to the Communist bloc. In the past it has suffered from the deliberate depressing of living standards in order to extract immense reparations, and from the same sort of extravagant muddles in planning which have been perpetrated in most Communist countries. Both reparations and muddles are things of the past. The satellite states will continue from now on to mirror the immense economic strides forward made by the Soviet Union. There are solid economic reasons for the Soviet Union's wanting to keep Germany divided and retain its eastern half in its own economic orbit.

Political reasons are even more operative. In the first place both Poland and Czechoslovakia are best pleased by the continuing division of Germany. West Germans are blissfully — almost criminally — unaware of the feelings of the peoples of these countries, which the Nazis attacked, absorbed and ter-

rorized in the most brutal manner. (One former Silesian landowner told me, in all good faith, that Germans and Poles "got
on very well together." Political parties like the Free Democrats
and Social Democrats have equally naïvely assumed that the
resumption of diplomatic relations with Poland and Czechoslovakia would result in compromise agreements over the Oder-
Neisse territories and the Sudetenland which would be perfectly
agreeable to everybody.) Poles and Czechs may, individually,
have forgiven Germany for what was done to them between
1938 and 1945; but they and their governments have not for one
moment ceased to look on a united Germany as a potential
menace.

The division of Germany is synonymous with the solidarity of
the Satellite bloc. And the Russians themselves have no reason to
relish the reunification of the one nation which could carry out a
"conventional" conquest of their country. They will never forget
that the German panzers pushed to within ten miles of Moscow.
They will scarcely overlook Hitler's statement, "I should deem it
a crime if I sacrificed the blood of a quarter of a million men
merely for the conquest of natural riches to be exploited in a
capitalistic way. The goal of *Ostpolitik* is to open up an area of
settlement for one hundred million Germans." A new German
Army backed by the Western Powers could, with time, become
an immensely greater danger than Hitler's hordes. For one reason, the combination of American technical genius and German
basic fighting ability is the only one which the Soviet Union has
cause to fear. For another, this combination would bring the
creed of democratic freedom in its train — whereas the Nazis
brought cruelty and repression, and ruthless plans for carving up
the Soviet Union.

Finally, a military occupation of Russia could only take place
with the aid of German man power. One German ex-officer once
told me how two Russians whom he took prisoner in the Ukraine
remained with him as camp-followers and servants. Both of them
were ready to fight for him against their own countrymen; one of
them saved his life. "All they required," he told me, "was decent,
just treatment. If Hitler's policy, too, had been based on this,

nothing could have stopped Nazi Germany from liquidating the Soviet Union and destroying Soviet Communism." I believe him.

East Germany is strategically valuable to the Soviet Union. Its western frontier is within thirty miles of Hamburg and the mouth of the Elbe, and within sixty miles of the right-angle turn of the Rhine at Mainz. Strategic and political reasons combine to make Berlin so important to East Germany and to the whole Communist bloc. The annexation of Berlin by the East German Republic would ease communications, eliminate Allied garrisons, remove the one big listening-post behind the Iron Curtain, stultify the hopes of all those East Germans who still see in an independent Berlin the symbol of freedom and the hope of reunification. The editor of *Die Welt*, Hans Zehrer, wrote in 1959 that "He who has Berlin has Germany, and he who has Germany has far more." The phrase is portentous, but the road to eventual Soviet domination in the whole of Germany could lead through Berlin. Its forfeit to the East German Republic would be attributed by thinking Germans to Western weakness, by unthinking Germans to Western treachery. With Berlin, East Germany could become a springboard for the Communist advance to the Rhine, even to the English Channel.

What, then, of German reunification? For the theme remains vastly important, even if actual reunification has seemed from 1945 to 1960 unattainable. It is important because there will always be tension in Europe as long as Germany remains divided. The Germans will see to that, but so will the Russians. For their idea of coexistence with the West is not of an armistice established along static lines but of a state of nominal peace in which Communist pressure is never relaxed for a moment.

On October 1, 1958, the West German Bundestag held a session in West Berlin in order to refocus public and world attention on the problem of reunification. The Bundestag used the occasion to protest against the continuing repression of the East Germans and the restriction of their free movement westward, to repeat its demand for a Four-Power standing committee to examine the German question, and to confirm its promise to be sole guarantor of German democracy until the day of reunification. But in spite of the stirring strains of Beethoven's Egmont Overture and the reappearance on top of the Brandenburg Gate of the assertive Quadriga of Victory (female Germania figure, and chariot drawn by four horses), the Bundestag statement sounded flat and stale. For it contained nothing new and it is doubtful whether any new idea can conceivably come out of a West Germany which is hypnotized by its "Economic Miracle" and the joys and marvels of a rising living standard.

A real national desire in West Germany for reunification did not exist up to 1960. Several million "Brandenburg Gate medals" were sold at the beginning of 1959 for prices ranging from two and a half cents to one dollar. But when the families of (theoretically) politically aware Bonn citizens were asked to volunteer to take poor Berlin children for a fortnight's free holiday, just a dozen offered to do so. The population of Bonn is 120,000. Bonn democracy, one German politician declared in a biting attack, consisted of fancy decorations and ribbons of merit worn at pompous "Press Balls" which only a few of the best-paid journalists could afford to attend; of weekly illustrated journals which pack their columns with stories and pictures of princely weddings; of eternal cocktail parties and receptions, frock coats and top hats, moral and intellectual frustration and political apathy. Bonn democracy, in his view, has no spiritual content.

While the Bundestag was making its rhetorical declaration, Walter Ulbricht was laying down the terms on which the Communist bloc would permit reunification. The Confederation of two equally entitled states was only the first of these. The Federal Republic would have to withdraw from NATO and its government would have to abolish conscription. The West German political parties, civil service, armed forces and Government should be purged of "Fascist" elements. Land-reform should be carried out and all estates of over two hundred acres split up. Basic industries should be nationalized. Industrial and banking "cartels" should be dispersed and a purge of "industrial reactionaries" carried out. Finally, the works-council law should be revoked and replaced by the East German system of contractual relationship between the workers and the State. The "social achievements of the German Democratic Republic"—the favorite topic for the braggings of Ulbricht and his fellows — would not merely be preserved there; they would be extended to the whole of Germany.

West Germans have been too prone in the past to dismiss Ulbricht's pronouncements as mere propaganda, designed to bolster or inflate Communist prestige. This is a mistake. There is no evidence that Ulbricht ever made an important pronouncement save with the certainty of Soviet backing. His statements have been dictated by Moscow. Only occasionally has propaganda been their sole purpose. This man, with his goatee-beard, his sallow gray-green complexion, his high-pitched, hating voice, and his cold, pitiless eyes, is the embodiment of the evils of Communist dictatorship. During a lifetime of service to Moscow Bolshevik-imperialism, Ulbricht has shown no sign of any human feeling. He has both plotted and ordered political murder; he has acted with unbridled ruthlessness against his enemies and his own party colleagues (he has never had a friend). "Comrade Cell," as his own associates know him, has never shown a single pang of compunction; he has been the perfect tool for unscrupulous masters and the admirably efficient executor of their policies. It may sound fanciful, but he could well be a direct emanation of the Devil in person.

In June, 1959, the *Frankfurter Allgemeine Zeitung* published long letters from two East Germans who, naturally, remained anonymous. They gave exactly opposite views on whether the people of East Germany could remain mentally independent in face of endless, nagging Communist pressure. The first writer believed that there was still real "human solidarity" among the many who had not inwardly accepted Communist ideology; the second believed that resistance was being broken down and would vanish. The first writer thought that most East Germans had not ceased to hope for reunification; the second, that the waning of hope had produced almost universal resignation to the rule of the Ulbricht-Grotewohl regime.

On the whole, the second writer may be nearer to the truth than the first. The imposition of severe restrictions on travel at the end of 1957 meant that the number of East Germans visiting West Germany dropped by 40 per cent in 1958. A year later half as many refugees as before were escaping to the West. Millions of East German children were writing letters to small Soviet citizens, and their incurably sentimental parents were beginning to find something "nice" about it. Thousands more children sent letters of greeting to Khrushchev when he arrived in East Germany in March 1959. In the schools twelve-year-olds were learning the names of forty to fifty towns in the satellite states, but not a single Western capital city. They were being rigorously grounded in the Russian Revolution, but they had never heard of Frederick the Great. The human mind, like the human body, can accustom itself to a radically new diet; and it will not dimly remember the old.

Straws in the wind? Or signs of the times? It is not easy to judge, for the greatest danger of all about the German situation is its unpredictability. But this chapter must be concluded with two thoughts: the division of Germany suits the Soviet Union very well; and the East German Republic is of considerable value to the Communist bloc. This was made plain at the "phony" Berlin Congress in 1954; it was underlined at the Geneva Conferences of 1959. When Humpty Dumpty fell off the wall, all the King's horses and all the King's men could not put Humpty together again. The same thing has probably happened to Germany.

And these two thoughts lead on, in turn, to a footnote on Western policies in Germany. It would be easy — as inveterate "German-haters" have made plain in all Western countries — to shrug off the problem of German division and to reiterate the obvious truism that it is the result of Hitler's war. Yet this would ignore the fact that — in Mr. George Kennan's words — "Germany sits at the fulcrum of world power, as between the Russians and the Western world." How easy to abandon a satellite East Germany to its apparently eternal twilight of the soul! How easy—and how futile! In Germany the Cold War has proved that the West cannot entrench in illusory positions: free, all-German elections, the right of a unified Germany to belong to NATO, the inevitable eventual victory of democratic freedom. It has proved that it is nonsensical to leave the initiative to the Russians, to relax diplomatic pressure in order to let the Russians "save face," to wait patiently for a Russian "Anti-Communist Revolution" and the consequent dissolution of "satellite Europe."

The leading West German Free Democrat, Thomas Dehler, coined the phrase "Our German impatience, which is holy." It is a phrase redolent of German overstatement. German impatience, for reunification in freedom, must be modified in the interest of the West as a whole. But the West must not ignore it. For reunification will benefit the West in the long run. It can be brought about, not by fortuitous circumstances, but by diplomatic intelligence, flexibility and finesse. And every day that passes without the evolution of a Western initiative binds the East German Republic more closely into the Communist bloc.

-7-

Two German Armies

War is the highest summit of human achievement; it is
the natural, the final stage in the historical development of
humanity.
— GENERAL VON SEECKT (Founder of the post-1918
Reichswehr)

No quarter will be given, no prisoners taken. As a thousand years ago the Huns under King Attila made a name
for themselves which tradition and legend have kept alive
to this day, so may your deeds in China make such a name
for Germans that never for a thousand years will a China-
man dare look at a German.
— KAISER WILHELM II, in a message to the troops of the
German expedition to Peking in 1900

When a German officer comes on parade, every man on
the barrack square should tremble in his shoes.
— GERMAN CAVALRY OFFICER to General J. H. Morgan,
a British member of the post-1918 Allied Control
Commission

No recruit is any good until he's been knocked about.
—PRINZ VON HOHENLOHE, former German Prime
Minister

ON August 21, 1959, ex-General Hasso von Manteuffel was
sentenced by a Düsseldorf court to one and a half year's imprisonment for the illegal execution, in January 1944, of a nineteen-
year-old German soldier suspected of having shown cowardice
in the face of the enemy. On the same day hundreds of thirty-
seven-year-old reservists of the "1922 class" staged protest meetings in various parts of Germany against being registered for

CUMMINGS, *Daily Ex[...]*

M. Schumann (French Prime Minister) to Dean Acheson and
Anthony Eden: "I Don't Know What Effect He'll Have on the
Enemy, but — by Heaven! — He Frightens Me!"

possible temporary enlistment, during the 1959 autumn maneuvers of the Bundeswehr. The two events were not directly connected, yet they had this in common — both were manifestations of the psychological difficulty of building up a new army in Western Germany after the good name of the German soldier had been sullied in Hitler's war.

The Manteuffel case aptly symbolized the German tragedy during the Nazi era. In January 1944, von Manteuffel was in command of the 7th Armored Division in the Ukraine. His division was on the extreme left of the sector of the Russian front held by Marshal Erich von Manstein's Army Corps. Round the town of Shepetovka, held by von Manteuffel's troops, the Red Army launched one bitter attack after another. In the town were thousands of German wounded awaiting rail transport to Rumania. Not for this reason alone was von Manteuffel committed to a last-ditch defense; Marshal von Manstein told the Düsseldorf court that the whole southern sector of the front depended on the 7th Armored Division. If it retreated, the Soviet forces would have had a unique chance of rolling up the left flank of his Army Corps, cutting it off from the remainder of the German armies and forcing it back in isolation towards the Black Sea coast.

No better man could have been found for a desperate defense than von Manteuffel. He had won a reputation for unrivaled dash in the earlier stages of the Russian campaign, and in North Africa (he was later to lead the armored spearheads in the Ardennes offensive of December 1944, which penetrated almost to Dinant on the river Meuse and threatened to prolong the war in Europe by another six months). Von Manteuffel was popular with his troops, although a strict disciplinarian who expected his men to be as unsparing of themselves and as courageous as he was himself. The German front held at Shepetovka; Marshal Manstein's Army remained intact.

But on a night in January 1944 an incident occurred which von Manteuffel could hardly have guessed would wreck his life fifteen years later. A report was brought to him that a regimental commander intended to shoot for cowardice two soldiers who had "lain low" during a Russian raid on the front line in which the N.C.O. in charge of their post was captured. Von Manteuffel sent a message countermanding the shooting order. He immediately convened a court-martial to try the two men. The court-martial found one man not guilty, and the second, a nineteen-year-old soldier from Vienna whose name has disappeared from history, of dereliction of duty only. He was sentenced to two years' imprisonment.

Von Manteuffel studied the report of the court-martial's findings, and decided that its verdict was wrong. He ordered the soldier's execution, thirty-six hours after his alleged crime was committed. He had the soldier in, to speak to him personally in his own defense. But the soldier was either too stupid or too stunned to say anything at all. In the Düsseldorf courtroom, fifteen years later, von Manteuffel admitted that he was "astonished" at the young man's docility and evident composure. He was taken out of the divisional commander's office and shot. Admirably efficient with tanks, cannons, machine and burp guns and grenades, the average German soldier was rarely a good rifle shot. This particular squad's shooting would have disgraced the rawest recruit in the American or British armies. The condemned man eventually had to be "finished off" on the ground, in the welter of his blood and bowels.

There was a perfectly legitimate defense open to von Manteuffel before the Düsseldorf court. He had overruled the findings of a legally convened court-martial because he had believed the man guilty of cowardice and felt that the military situation was so serious that an example had to be made of him. Although he should, in theory, have sent the man back to a base area to be retried, von Manteuffel could well have pleaded the exigencies of a situation in which transport was not available even for seriously wounded men. As a commander in the field he had the power of life or death over his men. He only exercised it on this single occasion and he sought to justify it with the reflection: "After that there was not a single case of desertion to the enemy in my division, and not a single case of serious indiscipline."

Unfortunately for Manteuffel this single execution was recalled during the trial of the bullying martinet and fervent Nazi, Marshal Ferdinand Schoerner, a year previously. Schoerner was charged with the same offense, of ordering a summary execution, and he was sent to prison for it. His defense counsel pleaded Hitler's "Fuehrer Command Number Seven" as justification. This command was issued in 1943 and gave all commanders the right to have men shot, on the spot, for indiscipline and failure to carry out orders. But the emphasis of the "Fuehrer Command" was on the words "on the spot," in the assumption that an acute emergency existed. Schoerner was sent to jail because no acute emergency was found to have existed; von Manteuffel was sentenced for the same reason. His mistake had been to engage a defense counsel whose long experience in defending real war criminals had led him into the habit of producing the least likely explanations for his client's actions and of fatally assuming that the sins of a whole nation could conveniently be blamed on its cremated Fuehrer.

If Schoerner could be jailed, then why not von Manteuffel? This was the immediate reaction of plenty of German citizens. But the cases were in fact very different in essence, however similar they happened to be juridically. Schoerner was feared and hated by his men, and one of them struck him in the face in public after he had reappeared from a Soviet prison-camp long years after the end of the war. Von Manteuffel was respected and liked. Nor was he a believer in that code of "terror in war" subscribed to by Kaiser Wilhelm II and plenty of other Prussians, long before Hitler came to power. In North Africa he instructed his men not to carry out Hitler's order for the murder of the soldiers of the British commandos and long-range desert groups who pounced on German headquarters and base installations. On the Elbe, in 1945, he organized the surrender of 200,000 men to the American forces, so that they should not fall into Russian hands. Von Manteuffel tried to represent that Prussian ideal of selfless service and "knightliness in war" which has been slurred-over by the excesses of a minority of his countrymen.

Even more important, von Manteuffel became a "model" citizen of the 1949 Federal Republic. From 1953 to 1957 he sat in the Bundestag as one of the most enlightened members of the Free Democratic Party. When that party's right-wing radicals quarreled with the Federal Government, von Manteuffel was one of the sixteen Bundestag members who formed the Free People's Party, later joining the German Party and staying in the Government fold. From 1957 to the end of 1958 he was German Party chairman in the Rhineland. For more than two years he sat on the Bundestag Defense Committee, helping to organize the new West German armed forces along democratic lines. In the ex-soldiers' associations his voice was loudest and most authoritative in demanding allegiance to the Federal Republic and loyalty to the Western democracies.

Changing his career, of necessity, at more than fifty years of age, he worked up to become a director of the light-engineering firm of Bauer und Schaurte in Neuss. While other ex-generals fulminated against the West and dabbled in the politics of neo-Nazi parties, von Manteuffel turned himself into a solid and sensible supporter of Western civilization. Yet nothing could save him from his own past; just as nothing could save the German people from theirs.

Of course the thirty-seven-year-old reservists who were protesting, in August 1959, against being called up for maneuvers were not primarily actuated by disgust over the Manteuffel case. Most of them, no doubt, were leading humdrum, comfortable lives and were not disposed to be disturbed during their holidays, or during a holiday period when it was easy enough to earn good overtime pay. "Their" war was over so long ago, and they had plenty of reasons for wanting to forget it. Some of them had been roughly treated, at first, as prisoners of war (the American Army's record in this respect was not an invariably good one); others had seen their commanding officers tried as war criminals.

The old German trait of believing the wildest sort of story reasserted itself. A senior civil servant in Bonn explained to me the reluctance of the thirty-seven-year-olds in terms of a "true story" of what the British did to all the senior officers of Admiral Doenitz's staff when the German surrender took place at Flensburg in May 1945. "The British stripped them all naked and herded them onto a big lawn in front of Doenitz's headquarters," he told me. "Then they assembled a horde of Western war correspondents and cameramen. This was the reason for this disgraceful incident."

"And why was it, then," I asked, "that no photograph of these naked admirals and generals ever appeared in a Western newspaper?"

My informant brooded over this for a time: "Ah, well," he said, "I can only suppose that even newspaper correspondents had some decent feelings left!"

The Manteuffel case has been only one of many which has had an undeniable psychological effect on West German rearmament. There was, for instance, the Ramcke case of February 1959. Ex-General Bernhard Ramcke commanded the "Green Devils" of the German Parachutist Division, who fought with brilliant success in Crete, Italy and France. In 1944 Hitler made one of his many tactical blunders by leaving these crack troops in the fortress of Brest, cut off and doomed to eventual surrender. From mid-July until mid-September the Green Devils defended Brest, and Ramcke only surrendered when 10,000 men of the garrison had died and further resistance was useless.

In February 1959 Ramcke brought an action in a Hamburg court against a playwright, Erich Kuby, and the program manager of the Northwest German Radio Corporation, Ruediger Proske. Ramcke claimed that he had been libeled by references to him in a radio play written by Kuby, called "The End of the Fortress of Brest." Kuby had served under Ramcke. His play was based on the fairly simple thought that war is purposeless as well as terrible. In Brest he had been appalled by what he considered was a senseless sacrifice of human beings. He did not consider that the defense of Brest had tied down large numbers of Allied troops who could have been used against the main German forces in the West, nor the fact that these German forces were already withdrawing beyond the German frontier before Ramcke surrendered.

Ramcke found three passages in Kuby's play offensive. Ramcke's defense of Brest was described as "The first great hour in the military career of this man, which brought death to Brest and to 10,000 German soldiers." The second passage read: "Was he [Ramcke] a swine?" And the commentator's answer was, "Well, he was just a paid hack." The third passage suggested that Ramcke had deserted the burning fortress, in order to land on the Crozon Peninsula opposite and await the hour of his capture and the award of the "Iron Cross with Brilliants" by Hitler.

Ramcke maintained that he had defended Brest as steadfastly as a good commander should have done. He had denied the use of this vital naval base to the Allied warships and transports. Men of his command mostly gave evidence on his behalf, but Ramcke had at least one unpleasant surprise during the trial. One witness, a former private soldier, was asked to identify him, and Ramcke gave the man a hard, tight and, in intention, encouraging smile. The witness said very slowly: "I think the Herr General would not smile, if he realized how many wives and mothers mourned their dead of Brest. Nor would he smile if he had listened to the cries of the wounded and dying on that last night before the fortress fell."

Ex-General Ramcke smiled no more during the hearing of the case.

For that matter, he did not smile at the end of it. Playwright Kuby and program manager Proske were found not guilty of libel, on the grounds that no proof of "intention to libel" had been shown. This was a travesty of legal argumentation. Libel is libel, whatever intention lies behind it. The Hamburg court evaded the only issue on which it was entitled to give judgment.

Another incident during the same year of 1959 rubbed home the lesson of psychological difficulty which has hamstrung the rearmament of Western Germany in defense of Western democracy. In February 1959, the London County Council decided, by 59 votes to 58, to grant licenses for the exhibition in London of the film *Operation Teutonic Sword*. This was a documentary, produced by the Communist-controlled, East German Peoples-owned film corporation and violently attacking General Hans Speidel, the German commander of NATO Land Forces in Europe.

The film suggested, blatantly, that General Speidel had been a fanatical supporter of the Nazi regime. In reality, he had been

Field Marshal Rommel's chief of staff and second in command in North Africa, and had shared that brilliant general's aversion for the Nazi hierarchy. After Rommel was forced to commit suicide by the Nazis (in order to save his family from persecution), Speidel was arrested by them. He was lucky to survive the war and the Nazi era. The East German film accused him of having played a leading part in the murder in Marseilles, five years before the war, of the King of Yugoslavia and the French Foreign Minister, Léon Barthou. It was perfectly true that Speidel was German Military Attaché in Paris at the time. This was "good enough" for the East German propagandists. It was much more important to them that he was the principal link between the armies of Federal Germany and the rest of the Western Alliance in 1959. Their film was not a distortion of the truth; it was a deliberate lie, conceived in the sole interest of Communism. They have never produced one shred of proof that Speidel — or, for that matter, the Nazi Government — was in any way connected with the "double murder" of Marseilles.

There is nothing particularly surprising and certainly nothing new about propaganda films. The Germans themselves produced such epics as *S. A. Mann Brandt* and *Hitler-Boy Quex* in the Nazi era. The basic German sense of publicity was not newly hatched out by Hitler's foul-mouthed propaganda chief, Josef Goebbels. In 1916 the Germans had struck a medal to commemorate the sinking of the passenger liner, the *Lusitania*. On one side of the medal was a grinning skeleton, gloating above the heads of the agonized drowning and the face-up, floating corpses; on the other side was the inscription: TO HIM WHO DISREGARDED OUR WARNING.

And after the terrible massacre of Belgian civilians at Dinant, during the First World War, the German press actually found fit to report that affair. The reason? A small Belgian girl had been found quite unhurt among a heap of murdered Belgians. She had been given chocolate by the German soldiery, who had fired their final volley and were no longer under orders to murder defenseless people. According to the official German report, the small girl had been "quite happy." The whole massacre began to redound to the credit of German *Kultur* and the German Empire.

Yet the horrors perpetrated by pre-Nazi Germans provide no excuse for the fatuous idiocy of the London County Council. Its members argued that General Speidel could take legal action, if he felt that he had been libeled. But action against whom? General Speidel had no desire to damage the British distributors of the Communist East German film. He knew that this would only stir up feeling against the West German Republic. And he could not sue the East German DEFA film company in a British court with the slightest hope of getting damages. The members of the London County Council knew all this perfectly well. Yet they allowed a film to be shown which had only one constructive purpose — to disrupt the Western alliance and slander a German who was playing a leading and an honorable part in it. This incident is a perfect illustration of the hazards — for a German — of putting on uniform again.

For that matter, the psychological heritage of the Second World War could hardly have been more clearly illustrated than during General (later President) Eisenhower's visit to Frankfurt in 1951. Six years earlier Eisenhower had refused to shake hands with General Jodl (later executed as a war criminal) when the latter had surrendered at Rheims. Years afterwards he referred to him, in his memoirs, as an "evil conspirator." In Frankfurt he had to meet Generals Heusinger and Speidel, who had been selected to play key roles in the rearmament of Western Germany. It was at first rumored he would not see them. The meeting was described by Mr. Charles Thayer in his book *The Unquiet Germans* in somewhat idyllic terms:

> As I brought forward the two German ex-Generals, the big Ike smile wreathed his round face and a large hand shot out to greet them. With that gesture at least two of his former adversaries were thoroughly cleansed of their resentment of the general who had refused to receive them.

"Thoroughly cleansed . . ."? What sublime foolishness! Germans have unnaturally long memories. And, in any event, Generals Speidel and Heusinger were no simpletons who imagined that a "big Ike smile" — nor even the "befitting" statement which Eisenhower made on the next day on the honorable and soldierly qualities of the German soldier — would solve their problems. Speidel and Heusinger had decided to believe in and belong to the West, and even a painful gaucherie on Eisenhower's part would not have made them change their minds. The dilemma of their former enemy and present-day ally may even have faintly amused them. For he had been so obviously primed to make the right sort of gesture in the interest of the Western alliance; while they had been studying the same problem for years.

It has often seemed to me that the psychological problems of West German rearmament have been much more interesting than the practical. In October 1954 a student of Bonn University said to me, "You Allies did a good job in demilitarizing the German soldier — rather too good a job from the point of view of your present-day policies. You taught him about the misdeeds of the German Army. You razed our armaments industries to the ground, while the Russians went on using the Junker works at Dessau and building motor-torpedo boats at Rostock and Stralsund. You made it clear that armies were bad things of themselves and you made the name of the Wehrmacht stink. But what, after all, did that name mean? It meant 'defensive forces,' and those are just what you are asking us to produce today." A member of the Federal Defense Ministry was equally blunt: "You rounded up the whole German Army in 1945," he said, "and you did terrible things to the German soldier. Now you need him again. You made a bogy out of the German General Staff, yet you must have someone to command the German army-to-be."

The psychological difficulties of the Germans over rearmament were illustrated by the silent, preoccupied 1956 audiences who trooped out from showings of the prewar film of Erich Maria Remarque's *All Quiet on the Western Front*. They were illustrated by the triumph of Hellmut Kirst's book and film *0815* — the numerals belonged to an outdated German machine gun, and in the soldiers' dictionary came to represent the idea of useless, outdated military routine. *0815* was not a particularly good book, but it was a best-seller. For it preached the futility of war against a backdrop in which a young, independent-minded German soldier continually outwitted a gross, bullying Prussian drill-sergeant. It had all been done before — bully Plazek was merely a replica of bully Himmelstoss of *All Quiet*. But he became very much better known in the no-more-war, we've-burned-our-fingers-too-often atmosphere of post-1945 Germany.

The Social Democrats opposed West German rearmament because they were afraid that it would inevitably bring the rebirth of a military caste in its train. The younger generation opposed rearmament because it was liable to interfere with their studies and their careers. The women opposed it because they remembered only the horrors of war, and nothing of its comradeship and sense of patriotic and manly fulfillment. The German nationalists opposed it because they could never forget Germany's military humiliation by victors whom, in a military sense, they despised. The Communists opposed it because they were instructed to do so by Moscow; the keenest apostles of German unity — in the political parties, in the Evangelical Churches, in social debating societies and industrial get-togethers — because they were afraid that it would put off rather than advance the day of reunification.

The Free Democrats opposed it because they were angling for the ex-soldier vote. One of their especial grievances was that the Allies had insisted on the unconditional surrender of Hitler's Germany. This issue has produced only barren and futile arguments. Yet it is quite certain that no good could have come out of a peace negotiated with a German people still corroded with Nazi doctrine; the German case against unconditional surrender utterly fails to take this into account. Then there were always the ex-soldiers themselves, with their claims of unethical treatment by the victors and unjust designation of their leaders as war criminals. In 1954 the Liberal students' weekly summed up the most widely held view: "The citizen has a right to defend his homeland, but soldiers are a necessary evil and nothing more than that."

The course of West German rearmament was, in the event,

bound to be uneven and full of hesitations and contradictions. In the summer of 1950 Dr. Adenauer was already inviting regular visits from military advisers, including the ex-generals Speidel, Geyr von Schweppenburg and Count Schwerin. In September 1950, the NATO Council proposed a limited West German rearmament. In October, the French Government put forward the Pleven Plan for the creation of German "combat-teams," and the British Labor Government reluctantly admitted that, in view of the danger of Soviet aggression, "it seems only fair and reasonable to us that the people of Western Germany should help in their own defense."

In February 1951 the Paris Conference began work on the basis of the Pleven Plan. Out of its deliberations was born the idea of a European Defense Community, in which German units would be integrated. The E.D.C. was eventually rejected by the French National Assembly on August 30, 1954. The build-up of Communist conventional forces, the rearming of East Germany, Soviet political aggression in other parts of the world, and Soviet progress in the nuclear field then combined to induce the Western Powers to take the only logical alternative action left open to them — in fact, to invite West Germany to become, first, a member of the Brussels Pact, and then of NATO.

Meanwhile there had been plenty of indications of German feelings on the subject of their own rearmament. Ex-soldiers divided sharply into two groups. Dr. Adenauer's advisers, and ex-generals like von Manteuffel, Blumentritt, Mahlmann and Cruewell, preached the need for a German contribution to the Western alliance and for the creation of a new, more democratic German military tradition. These were men with no illusions about the difficulties ahead, but with a surprising and commendable readiness to bury their own personal and professional resentments. One ex-general, the Wehrmacht's radio commentator von Dittmar, told me: "We do not want to be regarded ever again as battling robots. The old General Staff will not, in any event, come back to power. We want to be citizens of a united Europe and fulfill our obligations to that ideal by helping to defend it."

But there were plenty of dissenting voices among the ex-generals. Heinz Guderian, for instance, produced his violent book, *So Geht es Nicht* [*This Won't Do*]. In it he attacked almost every phase of Allied policy in Germany, but most of all treatment of war criminals and prisoners of war. The pages of this book were instinct with the ingrained German beliefs that France was "decadent," that the British were middle-class shopkeepers, and the Americans merely military beneficiaries of their advanced industrial techniques. Guderian thought nothing of victor-nations who had won the war only because "a vast superiority in forces enabled the German Reich to be overcome." His conclusion was that the Allies would only recruit "a handful of unemployed" in Germany.

Ex-General Ramcke came out in violent opposition to a German contribution to the West. In a speech in Verden to five hundred former members of the Waffen S.S., in October 1952, he asked: "Who are the real war criminals? They are those who made the Versailles Treaty, those who dropped bombs on Dresden. . . . They are not the German front-line soldier." Ex-General Otto Remer took the same line in one inflammatory speech after another on behalf of the radical, neo-Nazi "Socialist Reichs Party." At a press-luncheon ex-General Hans Friessner told foreign correspondents that the Germans went to war in 1939 in order to "preserve Europe from the Bolshevik flood," and that the actual cause of war breaking out was the brutal treatment of German nationals in Poland. He called the 1944 conspiracy against Hitler "an attempt to murder our Supreme Commander behind the front line," and advised against any German rearmament until "the good name of the German soldier has been cleared."

Ex-Major and wartime air ace Hans Rudel wrote to a Düsseldorf paper in praise of the swastika, and even so responsible a paper as the Hamburg *Die Zeit* produced fantastic views in its article "Injustice in Landsberg" (the American prison for German war criminals). One of the objects of *Die Zeit's* solicitude was General Oskar Schroeder, who had "only been medical chief for the Luftwaffe." In reality, Schroeder took part in some of the grisliest of all German medical experiments on human beings. Men were subjected to high-altitude decompression-tests, which resulted "in the victim literally exploding, like a deep-sea fish suddenly brought to the surface."

What of the general public's attitude towards rearmament? Long after the protests of the ex-generals had begun to die down, it remained lukewarm. In the early stages of the rearmament controversy it was hostile. In Bonn University students voted 335 to 150 against rearmament of any kind at the end of 1950. More than 70 per cent of them said that they would never again, under any circumstances, put on uniform. A year and a half later one public opinion survey showed that only 34 per cent of the people of Western Germany favored rearmament within the Western alliance; 46 per cent definitely opposed it. By October 1953 the proportions had hardly changed at all; and enthusiasm was most absent from the 30-to-50 age group whose members had fought in the war. Only by mid-1954 did this so-called *Ohne Mich* ("Leave me out of it") attitude of mind begin to wane. By then a great many ex-soldiers had been mollified by the release of war criminals and by complimentary expressions of faith in the good sense and fighting qualities of the German soldier. From being the most outspoken opponents of rearmament, the ex-soldiers became its most reasoned and balanced supporters.

Doubts about the nature of a new German Army began to die down. The "shadow" Defense Ministry led by Herr Theodor Blank was responsible for this. Herr Blank, himself a middle-of-the-road trade-unionist and the reverse of the jack-booted militarist of German tradition, installed a group of young "reformers" in the organizational departments of the shadow Defense Ministry. Led by such men as Graf Baudissin, Graf Kielmansegg and Herr de la Maizière, the reformers planned for the reduction of drill, the elimination of the goose-step and the jack boot, the destruction of the old *Kommiss-geist* of the overdisciplined Reichswehr and its replacement by the concept of the "citizen soldier" who could attend political meetings, stand for Parliament, walk out in civilian clothes and restrict saluting to what would be considered reasonable in any Western army.

Behind these superficial innovations was a more subtle thought. This was that the soldier must be given as much responsibility as possible. He must learn to think, reason, act — not merely react to orders. The new form of military discipline was to be based on self-discipline.

Some of the changes may have seemed obscure, pernickety or even misplaced. But Count Baudissin and his aides were intent on teaching the new German soldier that he must not live in isolation from the rest of the community, and that he would be treated as a human being and not an automaton. When the first 101 officers and men of the *Bundeswehr* were given their uniforms in November 1955, and were commissioned in a barracks-garage in Bonn, they looked something like cinema-commissionaires or the old-fashioned London hotel hall-porter. Their baggy uniforms have since been changed. So have their first-issue rubber-soled boots. They have been given back their medals. But these are superficials. Apart from the new, milder spirit which has been introduced into the armed forces, there is today a non-political, part-civilian committee which confirms the appointments of senior officers, a liaison officer representing the interests of the soldiers in the Bundestag, and an all-party Bundestag Defense Committee to check the overall management of the armed forces. The German soldier, whether he is a volunteer "regular" or a conscript serving his one year, is sure of Parliamentary and public interest and understanding. And he is aware of the political reasons for rearmament — the desire for Western military security, and the need for a minimum of military backing for policies, which include "legitimate" political objects such as German reunification and a German Peace Treaty.

In the circumstances it was not surprising that the weight of opposition to rearmament shifted from the general public to the political arena. The collapse of plans for the European Defense Community gave the Social Democrats their chance to become unbridled critics of rearmament. Those plans collapsed because

176

they required too much of the French — who still distrusted Germany, were militarily committed in Indo-China and Algeria, and were suffering from general political paralysis. This last factor was the most operative, for French governments and parliaments were chronically unable to make up their minds. Under the European Defense Agreement there would have been no German divisions; the Social Democrats used the revised plans to make German divisions available to NATO as justification for claiming that rearmament would impede German reunification and must therefore be opposed.

In 1955 the Social Democrats and the trade-unions launched an anti-rearmament campaign in the Frankfurt St. Paul's Church. They hoped to weld all the elements of the *Ohne Mich* movement into an organized political force which would sweep Dr. Adenauer and the C.D.U. out of power. The St. Paul's Church campaign fizzled out after three months — because it was badly run; because the Adenauer Government was popular; most of all, because Germans were too busy with their own affairs to oppose rearmament.

In 1957, fifteen German scientists, all members of the Max Planck Institute in Göttingen, issued a solemn warning against the arming of the *Bundeswehr* with nuclear weapons. They infuriated Dr. Adenauer by adding that "a small country like the Federal Republic can make its best contribution to European stability and world peace by renouncing all nuclear weapons." For the Chancellor considered that this was a political and military issue, and he told the scientists so very bluntly when they sent a deputation to Bonn to meet him. A few weeks later, Albert Schweitzer issued a more universal warning against nuclear weapons from Lambaréné. The Social Democrats were so enchanted that they put up a huge poster of Dr. Schweitzer on their headquarters offices in Bonn and kept it there for the next three years.

But it took the Social Democrats nearly a year to evolve their next destructive move against rearmament, the anti-atom-death campaign of March 1958. The trade-unions supported it and threatened a general strike. Herr Ollenhauer announced that a nuclear war would create "an all-German cemetery." Dr. Adenauer countered by pointing out that there was no intention of West Germany's manufacturing or possessing nuclear weapons and that the most that would be given to the Bundeswehr would be "nuclear tactical weapons," which were "only a projection of conventional artillery." One C.D.U. paper published a cartoon showing the German Michel armed with an umbrella and confronting the Russian bear and its bagful of atom bombs.

Once again the campaign flopped. Once again it was badly managed. Some of the scientists had second thoughts and one of them, Professor Carl von Weizsaecker, began to expound the view that it was necessary "to live with the bomb." Dr. Adenauer's solid arguments in favor of parallel progress in conventional as well as nuclear disarmament began to have effect. Most important of all, rearmament as such was no longer unpopular with the German people. They had become used to the idea, and Gallup polls showed that only one German in four had concrete objections to it. In 1958 there was a flutter of excitement over the stationing of rocket units in different parts of the Rhineland and Westphalia. In Dortmund there were demonstrations against the billeting of a British rocket regiment near the town's airfield. In the Teutoburger Forest there were protests against a launching-site for "Matadors," but only because the local tourist association thought that it might keep custom away.

Thus the *Bundeswehr*, even with its complement of "Nikes" and "Matadors," had come to be accepted as a part of the German sector of the Cold War. With some justifiable pride the Federal Defense Minister, Franz-Josef Strauss, claimed in 1959 that the Bundeswehr had the lowest desertion rate of any army in Europe. The proportion of conscientious objectors in West Germany worked out at 4.5 per thousand. Brawls between ordinary citizens and troops — although the latter frequently wore uniforms off duty — no longer took place. Communist propaganda had no effect on the public or on the troops themselves (the latter are showered with Communist magazines, leaflets, forged call-up papers, orders, and letters from their wives to spurious boy friends). Even the easily roused German farmers gave up cursing armed forces taking part in maneuvers and churning up their fields with their heavy tanks.

One reason for the *Bundeswehr's* relative popularity was its inconspicuous functioning. At the end of 1955 some excitement was caused when four former colonels who had worked in the shadow Defense Ministry of Herr Blank were rejected for permanent commissions by the special selection committee. Early in 1957 some *Bundeswehr* recruits were drowned on the river Iller during exercises in the field. In the same year a General Müller-Hillebrand came into personal conflict with Herr Strauss by refusing to promote one of the Minister's assistants in the Defense Ministry. There were some scandals over cases of bribery of officials of the *Bundeswehr's* commissariat department at Coblenz, and periodic bickering with the Western Powers over barracks and maneuvering grounds. This all added up to very little; by and large, the *Bundeswehr's* affairs were being managed with tact and understanding.

The plans of Count Baudissin and his friends for the new type of "democratic army" were largely being realized. The "citizen soldiers," who did not have to spend far too much time drilling and saluting, who did not have to wear uniforms off duty, gained in self-respect and self-confidence what they may have lost in clockwork efficiency. Many soldiers, indeed, complained that discipline was too lax and drill too infrequent, that they were in fact being trained as part of a democratic army in spite of themselves. But even they could not ignore the immensely better relations between officers and men, the sense of freedom and the lack of constriction, the burgeoning of a new tradition in place of the outworn legends of the Officers Corps and the soldiers' "corpse obedience."

The *Bundeswehr* has been helped, finally, by the purely defensive philosophy of the successive Adenauer Governments. NATO's role is defensive, and its task has been to make Europe a safer place to live in. It has been loyally supported by men like Adenauer, Strauss and Blank. Its vital role has been underlined by Communist aggression in Korea, Hungary, Tibet. The *Bundes-*

wehr is dependent on the Federal Republic's Western allies. This has not generally been regarded as a slight, but as a fresh bond with the Western alliance. It has made Germans feel more like Europeans.

Attitudes in the Western world towards West German rearmament have involved one supreme paradox. Its most vocal opponents — left-wing intellectuals, pacifists, "professional German-haters" like the Beaverbrook press in Britain and the "Prevent World War III" group in America — have been agog with the dangers of a rebirth of German militarism. But they have generally, astonishingly, perhaps deliberately, ignored East German rearmament. Yet it is in East Germany that militarism is being reborn, and not in the West German Federal Republic.

In the West — in spite of hesitations, confusions and occasional excess of zeal — steady efforts have been made to create a "citizen army" along conventional Western democratic lines. In the East, the German armed forces have readily admitted high-ranking ex-Nazi officers to their ranks, reintroduced the jack boot and the goose step, and followed the example of Hitler's Waffen S.S. in giving soldiers political indoctrination. In East Germany, moreover, the Nazi and Russian Communist ideal of the soldier as the servant of the Party has found full expression. The basis of that ideal has been the creation of a ruthless armed elite.

East German rearmament is not only more dangerous to European peace than West German rearmament; it is much older. In July 1948 the Russians ordered the raising of para-military *Bereitschaften* in the five *Länder* of their zone. These alert-squads were to be called the *Kasernierte Volkspolizei*, or "People's Police in Barracks" (the civil People's Police had existed since 1945), and they were put under the command of a former Nazi officer, Hermann Rentsch. A year later the *Bereitschaften*, still armed mainly with rifles and machine guns only, were increased to a strength of 48,000 and were given a new commander, Wilhelm Zaisser, an old-guard Communist who had led the International Brigade in the Spanish Civil War under the pseudonym of "General Gomez" (he was to become Minister of State Security in 1950). The individual alert-squads were raised in strength from 250 to 1200 men and received their first light tanks and artillery. Four training schools were established, and the first purge of the new force was carried out in the summer of 1949.

In 1950 East German rearmament progressed a big stage further, at a time when only four Western divisions in the Federal Republic confronted twenty-five divisions of the Red Army in East Germany, and when no plans for raising a West German army existed. General Zaisser increased the Police in Barracks to 55,000 men, began the organization of an "air police" which produced the cadres for the future East German air force, and increased the training schools from four to seventeen. Another old-guard Communist and Spanish War veteran, Karl Heinz Hoffmann, took over military training.

All pretense of these para-military forces being some kind of police was vanishing. In 1951 the *Bereitschaften* received medium as well as light tanks, howitzers and antitank and antiaircraft guns. The "air police" received their first, somewhat outdated Yak fighters from the Soviet Union, and the newly-organized "sea police" their first minesweepers. To each *Bereitschaft* was attached a senior Red Army officer and three Soviet assistants. Out of a dozen of the *Bereitschaften*, moreover, the first five mechanized East German regiments were formed, organized exactly on the Soviet model. The fiction that the para-military forces were primarily for "frontier duties" could no longer be sustained, but in 1952 units of the *Bereitschaften* were in fact used to seal off the interzonal frontier after the signing of the Bonn and Paris Agreements.

In the meantime the Western Powers had, indubitably, decided to rearm West Germany. As is now known, this was primarily an American decision, and the principal reason for it was the example given by the Korean War of the sort of "local aggression" which could be carried out by the Communist bloc in Europe too. As is now known, too, Dr. Adenauer would have been content with a "frontier police force" of the same type and strength as the East German *Bereitschaften*. The British Government supported this view; the French Government was, as has been usual in its attitude to German problems since 1945, guarded and deliberately noncommittal. The decision to rearm West Germany certainly inspired the Soviet Union to push ahead its plans to rearm East Germany, even if it did not originate those plans.

Soviet policies are often more pragmatic, more empirical, than they are credited with being. The original purpose of rearming East Germany was to produce a display of force necessary for the holding-down of the Soviet zone and the consolidation of Communism there. The Russians have never felt at home in their zone of Germany. They could never — as the British and the Americans did — garrison towns like Hamburg and Munich with skeleton brigades. Originally they left in their zone what they considered to be adequate forces to hold it down, rather than a potential striking force to conquer West Europe. They supplemented these forces with an East German army which could be turned from a shadow into a fact — if and when the Communist satellite bloc was able to stand on its own feet.

The Russians had another reason for creating an East German army. They wanted someone to do their dirty work for them. The *Bereitschaften* were an ideal complement to the Red Army. Their existence meant that the Red Army could withdraw to its wired-in compounds outside the big towns and to the depths of the Gardelegen Forest and other training areas. Soviet planners may even have foreseen the East German rising of June 17, 1953, when the *Bereitschaften* displayed surprisingly good discipline, and — unlike the civil units of the People's Police — consistently refused to make common cause with the insurgents. Soviet planners almost certainly remembered that unkind but trenchant saying: "Give a Prussian a gun and tell him to shoot his grandmother and he will . . . shoot his grandmother." The essence of the *Bereitschaften* was that they were an elite. The Russians were perfectly justified in believing that they could be used against their own fellow citizens. This was one of the reasons why they were raised, trained, ideologically schooled.

The year 1953 was a key one in the history of East German rearmament. The *Bereitschaften* increased to a total strength of around 110,000. More important, they reorganized into strategically based military commands. Army Group North, consisting of three motorized divisions, was centered on the Mecklenburg town of Pasewalk. Army Group South — also with three divisions — began to take shape round its headquarters at Leipzig. A seventh division was in process of formation, as a "strategic reserve" for use in and around Berlin, at Potsdam. The army units of the *Bereitschaften* absorbed around 90,000 men; the naval and air force units another 20,000. At the very end of 1953 the East German armed forces were given new teeth — 45 Yak fighters, around 350 Josef Stalin T.34 tanks, another 1200 armored vehicles of various kinds.

They obtained, too, a first-class fighting soldier as Chief of Staff. General Vincenz Muller was a former member of Hitler's General Staff, who rose to the rank of Lieutenant General, commanded the 12th Army Corps in Russia, and was awarded the Knights' Cross. Here was no Communist saboteur, no guerrilla chieftain from Catalonia or the Basque provinces, but one of Hitler's paladins — highly trained, versatile, efficient. Muller, like Count Einsiedel and so many others, had signed on with the Committee for a Free Germany in Russia after capture by the Red Army. But ideals probably played little part in this decision. Like so many other German officers, Muller saw the Russo-German link-up as the natural medium for the soldierly profession to take its due place in society. That place was the "honorable" one of a ruthless striking force in the service of a dictatorship.

The East German armed forces — and this is yet another sign of their Hitlerian origins — had to be given a mythology. Visitors to West Germany may sometimes be surprised by the monstrous Hermann Memorial in the Teutoburger Forest and the almost equally top-heavy *Germania Denkmal* at Bingen — the one commemorating an obscure tribal chieftain who did the Germans almost irremediable harm by repelling the forces of Roman civilization, and the other a meaningless effigy. But they are both still objects of great veneration. The East German armed forces were given Tauroggen, when the Prussian Count Yorck von Wartenburg raised the standard of revolt against Napoleon; and Dresden, where at the Battle of the Nations the forces of eastern Europe smashed the French Emperor. They were given the military traditions of Scharnhorst and of the "great," first Moltke, the Bismarckian dogma of "keeping the lines open to St. Petersburg," and — of course — the Rapallo and Ribbentrop-Molotov pacts.

Mythology has to be brought up to date. At the end of 1953 the Russians brought Field Marshal Paulus back to Germany from the *dacha* outside Moscow in which he had been living in semi-retirement. On October 31, he published a statement calling on all Germans to work for friendship with the Soviet Union "and other peace-loving peoples." But he quickly shot his bolt. As the man whom Hitler had specially decorated for his vain resistance in Stalingrad and who had then sadly surrendered to the enemy, Paulus belonged to no tradition other than that of the professional soldier who had been asked to do the impossible. The Russians quickly decided that they could not use him profitably. He was a failure. They turned to the more truculent General von Seydlitz, composing a "Seydlitz March" in his honor, but they reluctantly decided in 1955 to send him home to West Germany. Two dozen other ex-generals accompanied him, dressed in new suits which were fitted in Moscow before they left and so overfed during the last few weeks that one S.S. general, Uhlmann, died of a heart attack before he was able to see the sacred soil of the Fatherland once more. Von Seydlitz had failed the Russians. It may have been in recognition of this fact that he was greeted at the returned prisoners of war transit-camp of Friedland in West Germany with cases of beer and Coca-Cola, and such improbable gifts as baby clothes.

Perhaps mythology was not so very important, after all, in an East German police state which was run on strictly ideological lines. The *Bereitschaften,* which were technically a volunteer body, could draw on the younger generation. By 1955 the Free German Youth had three million members. It included two out of every three young East Germans. It supplied virtually all the recruits for the *Bereitschaften,* and they were all politically indoctrinated and mostly political fanatics. Here was the perfect basis for the cadre army. The Free German Youth could, in time, provide all replacements for the 8000 officers and 12,000 N.C.O.'s. It could ensure a reasonably high morale — desertions from 1952 to 1956 were only just over 2400, more than 65 per cent of the deserters were under twenty-one years old, and most of these had not completed their first year's service.

The Free German Youth carried out recruiting and searched out the best material. It is not surprising that the training of the East German armed forces has since 1955 been tough and successful. At the end of 1957, it was even possible to dispense with the services of the two Red Army officers (*Sovietniks*) still attached to each East German regiment. The especial links between the East German armed forces and the Soviet Union were reduced to training courses for East German officers and senior N.C.O.'s in Leningrad and Saratov, Russian technical advice and arms-shipments, and the East German staffs at the various levels of command in the Warsaw Pact organization. This was not a sign simply of relaxing Russian control, but rather of the growing independence and reliability of the East German armed forces. This, in turn, underlined the progress of East Germany towards statehood.

It is interesting to recall that in 1955 the East German target for its armed forces was believed to be 300,000 men under arms by the beginning of 1957. This target may or may not have been attainable, but for practical purposes it was too high.

In the first place, even conventional arms were costly and it was quickly clear that the 500,000-strong West German army which was first envisaged would never materialize. The East German sights could be lowered correspondingly.

In the second place, the 300,000 figure was soon found to be too high because of the shortage of labor in East Germany. The population was declining and the bulk of the refugees to West Germany were people of working age (78 per cent of those who fled between 1953 and 1959 belonged to the 18-50 age-group).

Between 1955 and 1957, indeed, the East German Government

reduced the strength of the armed forces from 110,000 to 95,000. At the same time it pushed ahead the organization of two new para-military organizations, the *Betriebsgruppen,* or armed factory-guards, and the "Societies for Sports and Technics." The former received rifles and machine guns, grenades and grenade-throwers, antiaircraft weapons and motorized transport. The "Sports and Technics" were trained in the use of infantry weapons and in infantry exercises in the field. The estimated strengths of the two organizations reached 300,000 and 650,000 respectively by the end of 1959. These were not forces which could be readily converted into front-line troops in the field. Their ostensible purpose was to deal with civil disturbance — but they could equally be used to promote it. They trained in their spare time and cost the State next to nothing. They became one of the most useful if scraggy sinews of the shoddy East German totalitarian state.

How reliable are the East German armed forces? They are well-armed by the Russians and this will remain so as long as East Germany is a Communist satellite state. The proportion of Free German Youth members must grow, and must develop the spirit of devotion to "People's Socialism." But the ex-Nazi element is strong. In 1957, 30 per cent of the army staff officers had served in Hitler's Wehrmacht; so had 17 out of 30 Generals. Yet their loyalty to the East German regime was unquestioned; all that they had had to do was to deny Hitler and his works. This was not as hard as might be imagined; for Hitler was dead, and his works were in abeyance.

A German ex-officer summed up the differences between the East and West German armies to me in these words: "Both are going to be well-trained, because their respective backers want it that way. But the East Germans have been given a military tradition which they can more easily understand. Both armies must pay for most of their weapons. But the East Germans will not waste time arguing about theirs; they will merely be equipped by the Russians. Both armies will be reluctant to fire on fellow Germans. But the East Germans have already had practice in doing this, in June 1953. The West Germans are being trained to take part in the defense of the West, but the East Germans are just being trained to carry out orders. West Germans are being taught that they have no traditional foes; East Germans are being filled brimful with vitriolic invective directed against 'Western and NATO militarists and warmongers.' They are learning that they are the 'new Prussians,' standing guard against the decadent, plutocratic but acquisitive West. It is they who will recapture a composite Germanic spirit of aggression and blind obedience; and it is they who may constitute a danger to the peace of Central Europe."

What are the long-term implications of German rearmament — in both German states? It is easy at least to draw some conclusions about West German rearmament. It will not lead to the Army again becoming an independent power in the State. Just before the First World War, the elderly out-of-work who was masquerading as the "Captain of Koepenick" was able to tell the Lord Mayor whom he had gratuitously arrested that "as a Prussian officer" he had "absolute powers" over the civil administration. And the Lord Mayor believed him. Just after the First World War a Social Democratic Minister of Defense, Gustav Noske, came smartly to attention when an unemployed ex-general addressed him. The unnatural independence of the army ended with those Prussian traditions which were outworn, and which died when Prussia itself ceased to exist.

The good Prussian traditions — hard work, efficiency, sobriety and absolute loyalty — will never die. The bad ones have to, and will be forgotten. As a prisoner-of-war, a friend of mine was once temporarily imprisoned in the fortress of Graudenz. From his cell-window he watched German soldiers on "punishment fatigue" in the barrack-square below. Their daily drill was to double round the square, carrying huge bags of cement on their backs. When they fell down, they were kicked until they got up. When they continued to lie on the ground, N.C.O.'s jumped on their stomachs. Then they usually got up again. This sort of sadism is, happily, a thing of the past.

A West German army need never become, like the Reichswehr, the instrument of duplicity and aggression. "Hitler," John Wheeler-Bennett wrote in his *Nemesis of Power*, "offered glory, freedom; a national resurgence and an expanded army; promotion, hope . . ." But Hitler was not unique. In the 1920's General von Seeckt planned deliberately for the war which he regarded as inevitable, rearmed illegally and trained his officers in Russia, connived with Gustav Stresemann in breaking the Treaty of Versailles which his own Government had signed. He boasted of having created a "Socialist-free" force which could be used with utter ruthlessness. Pre-1914, Marshal Ludendorff was preaching "the divinity of war." A hundred and fifty years earlier Frederick the Great was saying: "I snatch what I want at the start; I can always find German pedants to prove my right to it after I have taken it." By contrast, the men of the *Bundeswehr* are being brought up to believe that the only just war is a defensive war, and that the soldier, like the community, should believe in the rule of law.

A West German army need never become dominant in Western Europe. What was the position, for instance, at the beginning of 1960? True, there were ten West German divisions against a rather nominal twelve other NATO divisions in the Federal Republic. But nuclear warheads for their guided missiles remained in American hands, and the Federal Government had contracted never to produce or purchase nuclear weapons. True, the West Germans were expressing their personal wants more readily than in the past. But what were these wants? They boiled down to greater standardization of NATO weapons and a concrete plan for defending Schleswig-Holstein and the approaches to Denmark against an eastern aggressor. German wants were dictated by objective reasoning; NATO has always needed plenty of that. The advance in modern military technology makes it virtually impossible for any Western European country to become dominant even in the restricted Western European area.

A West German army need never be an object of ridicule. A period of confusion and anarchy of mind is over. That period was well illustrated by the story of the German General who had just returned from Russia. He wanted to know about his old comrades — Admiral Doenitz, for instance. "He is in Spandau jail," he was told. "Why Spandau?" he asked. Because Doenitz was a major war criminal. "I see," said the General. "And what about Speidel?" He was in Paris, was the answer. "In jail?" asked the General. No, at NATO headquarters. "Panzer-Meyer, then?" He was in Canada. "With NATO, I assume?" said the General. No, in jail. "Well, what about General Heusinger, where is he?" In Bonn, was the answer. "And in jail, too?" No, he was the new German Chief of Staff.

"In that case," said the General just back from Russia, "I shall leave now and book myself a room in a cozy lunatic asylum. For if what I have heard is true, I am stark, staring mad!"

Confusion and anarchy of mind were increased by the contradictions of war crimes, war guilt, the aftermath of an era of successful Nazi propaganda and the absence of any clear Western "doctrine" to put in its place. But the *Bundeswehr* has developed into a solid fact. As the Germans learn increasingly about their military past, they should be correspondingly less worried about it. In time the armed forces will be regarded quite simply as a valuable and integral part of the community. Nor should they be bedeviled by a new stab-in-the-back legend. It was a Social Democrat Reichs-President, Friedrich Ebert, who greeted the returning troops in 1919 with the words: "I salute you, who have returned unvanquished from the field of battle." In 1945 the Nazi armies were ground into the dust, and few Germans could have ever believed that the men of the resistance to Hitler were responsible for their defeat. The old legend of German invincibility was an eternal incitement to military aggression. That legend is dead.

The East German Army has been given a new and equally dangerous legend: that of the invincibility of the Red Army. While West Germany has discarded party-cracker mottoes, East Germany has been given a string of new and fatuous ones. *Der ruhmreiche Rote Armee*[1] is one of the worst of them. East German rearmament, moreover, is one of the biggest obstacles to German

[1] *Ruhmreiche* means "glorious."

reunification. How can one envisage the scrapping of the People's Army, with its Russian tanks, cannon and howitzers, of the Factory Guards and the Societies of Sports and Technics, with their ideological training and injections of Communist beliefs? Is East German rearmament something which would be quietly discarded, in the unlikely event of an East-West agreement over Germany? I think not. The Soviet planners have envisaged the East German regular and para-military forces as the guarantors of continuing East German independence and Communist survival there. That is the sense of the Khrushchev "offer" of a confederation of two equally-entitled German States. Still held fast in the grip of its Moscow-trained political leaders and its military elite, East Germany would be the steppingstone for an eventual Communist advance to the industrial riches of the Ruhr and the strategic boundary of the Rhine.

Such is the desire for security in this nuclear age that it is difficult to envisage agreement on a substantial reduction of the East and West German armed forces. The most positive effort in this direction was made in the spring of 1959 by the British Prime Minister, Mr. Harold Macmillan. In order to reduce tension in Europe he proposed the demarcation of "zones of limited and equalized armaments" in both Western and Eastern Germany. Such zones could be, for instance, 100 kilometers wide on either side of the German interzonal frontier. A 200-kilometer-wide "combined zone" would, if arms in it were controlled and inspected, provide against surprise attack from either East or West. More important, its creation would readjust the balance of conventional forces in the West's favor. For in mid-1959 there were only a half-dozen NATO divisions in the hundred-kilometer-wide West German zone; there were roughly twenty in the corresponding East German zone.

The Macmillan plan therefore had a chance of giving the West the diplomatic initiative in Central Europe. For its key was "equalization" of strength. Soviet objections could be answered by pointing out that it was precisely the Russians who maintained that NATO was aggressive and was planning to attack the "peace-loving" states of the Communist bloc. In addition, a system of arms limitation and inspection would genuinely have made the planning of a war in Europe more improbable. But Dr. Adenauer rejected the Macmillan plan out-of-hand. Was this merely because of his deep-rooted suspicion of British motives in Europe? Or because of his persistent doctrine that NATO forces must continue to be built up in strength until the Soviet Union makes political concessions in Central Europe? Either way, it is a poor prospect for political settlement in Europe. Either way, it suggests that two German armies are to become permanent features of the military scene. And even though West Germany has created a new and democratic army, which will never again be big enough to dominate Europe, this means that final peace in Europe is as far off as ever.

CUMMINGS, *Daily Express*

"Careful Not to Tread on Your Partner's Toes,
Harold! She's Very Sensitive . . ."

- 8 -

Architect of the New Germany

DR. ADENAUER (CDU): "I am fully aware that the Social Democratic Party contains many valuable people . . ."

DR. ARNDT (Social Democrat): "It is not for you to pass judgment on that!"

DR. ADENAUER: "Believe me, Herr Arndt, I was not referring to you."

— Excerpt from a Bundestag debate, January 11, 1952

Never tell a lie, not even in politics. For you will never be able to remember all the things that you have said.

— KONRAD ADENAUER to Dr. Paul Otto

My wish is that sometime in the future, when mankind looks beyond the clouds and dust of our times, it may be said of me that I did my duty.

— KONRAD ADENAUER to a friend

BEFORE the days of serious and often stormy discussion which followed the Soviet ultimatum to Berlin of November 27, 1958, an event of some importance took place which practically nobody noticed. The Allensbacher *Institut für Demoskopie*, which conducts periodic public-opinion polls, asked a cross-section of the West German population what man had ever done most for Germany. A poll on the same question had been held as long before as 1952. Then, Dr. Konrad Adenauer, although already a highly successful Federal Chancellor for three years past, scored 3 per cent of the votes. One of his nearest rivals was Adolf Hitler, with 2 per cent. Goethe and Beethoven did conspicuously better, but the first Chancellor of the German Empire, Bismarck, easily headed the poll with 36 per cent of the votes.

In the course of the next few years the vote for Bismarck wavered between 27 per cent and 32 per cent; that for Adenauer rose to 9 per cent in 1953, to 17 per cent in 1955 and to 24 per cent in 1956. But in 1958 he overhauled Bismarck at last, with a 26 per cent against a 23 per cent vote.

This was a remarkable tribute to the Federal Chancellor. Generations of Germans have grown up in the almost religious belief that Bismarck was by far the greatest man in German history. Germans are notoriously slow to change their views. Konrad Adenauer had won — could only have won — his place by his undeviating, unresting service to his country and his people over a ten-year period which has, not unnaturally, come to be called "the Adenauer era."

"The Adenauer Story" is a long one — but utterly relevant to the story of Germany today. It has a romance of its own, for it is the story — unlikely as this may sound to those who have savored the Chancellor's Olympian calm and disdain — of a hicktown boy who has made good.

For seventy years Adenauer's story was one of decent mediocrity. He was born on January 5, 1876. His parents were of middle-class stock, and his father — a secretary at the Cologne District Court — gave him a stern and deeply religious upbringing. His mother, Helene Scharfenberg, was the daughter of a bank clerk. Konrad Adenauer was a dutiful and hard-working son, who made few friends and successfully concealed the sharp Cologne wit which peeped out ever more frequently as years and greatness came upon him.

With the greatest difficulty, his father scraped together enough money to send him to the university, where he studied law, first at Freiburg, then at Bonn. The family economies on his behalf were well repaid. He became an apprentice clerk to a Cologne lawyer, opened his own practice in 1902, and in the following year earned 6000 marks — only $900 by the exchange-rates of that time, but a fair income for those days. Surprisingly, he married — for he seemed to be a cold fish — and by Emma Weyer had three children. Surprisingly, too, he wore a mustache. It was his only concession to Imperial Germany, which he did not much care for — the Empire of obedience, riches and arrogance, of pan-Germanism, the Navy League and the goose step, of Treitschke's creed of the desirability of war and of Lissauer's Hymn of Hate against England.

"The German house," the English historian, G. P. Gooch, wrote, "was blocked with medieval lumber." Konrad Adenauer seemed singularly unaware of the fact. He became a city councillor of Cologne in 1906, then an Assistant Judge. He had already developed his remoteness from all human beings other than members of his own family. It was this trait which enabled him to ignore the grosser manifestations of an era of German history in which the glorious and the grotesque, the fine and the fouled, mingled in the sort of witches' caldron which the Germans periodically have created for themselves ever since the Thirty Years' War broke the continuity of the chain of German enlightenment and undemanding courage.

"Germany," Prince von Bülow wrote in 1913, "is like a well-tended garden." Konrad Adenauer, indeed, had already become an accomplished amateur gardener, and it may have been a contributory factor to his apparent disinterest in the warning signs of the disasters which loomed ahead for his country — the fumbling aggressiveness of the German Foreign Office, the sheer irrresponsibility of Kaiser Wilhelm II, the dreary incapacity of the dynasty of marionettes who served him: Hohenlohe, Caprivi, von Bülow, Bethmann-Hollweg. Adenauer, at any rate, did not dedicate himself to Imperial Germany, unlike his later colleague and enemy, Gustav Stresemann, who proclaimed that "the land on every foot of which German blood has flowed is hallowed" and demanded that "Belgium shall be joined to the old home — Germany." Adenauer still had a part to play in the First World War. He took over the Cologne Food Office, which was responsible for the rations of 600,000 people. Unexpectedly he showed an inventive streak, introduced "Cologne bread" (made with a percentage of maize and potato flour) and "Cologne sausage" (soya basis, but still edible).

In 1917 he was nearly killed in a car crash, and expert surgery gave him his "new face," with its high Mongolian cheekbones and stretched parchment skin. In 1917 he became Lord Mayor of Cologne and in 1919 had his first brush with the British Military Occupation. He was asked to post up notices requiring all male Germans to raise their hats to British officers. He refused, politely but crushingly.

In the same year he married for the second time. By Gussi Zinsser, who died in 1948, he had four children. In 1919, too, he dabbled with Rhineland separatism. France was trying to organize a separate Rhineland State and Adenauer expressed the view that "we cannot resist France's demands" (curiously, he was to say the same thing about the Saar issue in 1945-1955, and on each occasion he was proved wrong). But the separatist movement collapsed, killed by kindness and by British unwillingness to allow constitutional changes. The Rhineland issue brought Adenauer into conflict with Gustav Stresemann, ostensibly because he wanted to withdraw Government subsidies from the Ruhr, but more probably because Stresemann represented Protestant, "pagan" Prussia.

Adenauer's achievements between 1919 and 1933 were not startling. In 1926 he was given the chance of forming a Reich Government — on the grounds that he commanded the support of the solid Catholic Center Party and was too obscure to offend anyone. His efforts failed, almost certainly because Stresemann was blocking them. Adenauer gave Cologne its own electricity supply, its Green Belt and a new bridge (the city councillors wanted to build a different bridge, but Adenauer overrode them with that easy domination which he was so often to exercise later in life). The climax — and apparent termination — of his active career came in 1933, when he refused to have swastika flags flown on the bridges for Hitler's visit to Cologne. He refused to meet Hitler personally, and was dismissed from the mayoralty in March.

He was already fifty-seven and was to spend the next eleven years in total retirement from public affairs and in periodic fear for his life. He sought refuge at the Abbey of Maria Laachs, was twice arrested by the Gestapo and narrowly escaped being murdered by the Nazis. Yet he had refused to join the resistance to

Hitler, for he was a man with a rigid code of behavior who could only see his duty when it ran in an orthodox groove. His fortitude was impressive — "We are all in God's hands," he said, when the Gestapo forced the information as to where he was hiding out of his wife. But at the end of the war he was a worn, frail and obviously old man. The American Occupation authorities "rediscovered" him and made him Lord Mayor of Cologne for the second time in his life — probably believing that they could get a year or two's work out of him.

He lasted only six months. In October, 1945, a British General visited Cologne and remarked angrily that it was a disgrace that mountains of rubble still blocked most of the city's roads. General Templer was so badly briefed that he did not know that Cologne had been 75 per cent destroyed by Allied bombing against 60 per cent for the large towns of the neighboring Ruhr. Someone, Templer suggested, should be thrown out on his ear and another German found who would get on with the job. The conducting officer, a Brigadier Barraclough, had already had differences with Adenauer over the felling for firewood of trees in the Cologne parks. He dismissed Adenauer, who left his Cologne offices with two folders, "Dismissal by the Nazis" and "Dismissal by the Liberators." Brigadier Barraclough returned later to Britain, where he received a decoration from a grateful country.

Germans with grievances are like dogs with bones — they may bury them, temporarily, but always somewhere handy, where they can be easily dug up. On each of the first three occasions on which I heard Adenauer talk to a small circle of people he recounted the story of his dismissal by the British (by then he had added the somewhat improbable piece of embroidery of a Union Jack, which he had kept hidden in his home in order to fly on the "day of liberation").

By treating Dr. Adenauer with such lack of courtesy and wisdom the British authorities unintentionally launched him on his real, postdated political career. A friend, Dr. Leo Schwering, had organized the Cologne branch of the Christian Democratic Union, the party which was intended to be the rallying-point of conservatives and middle-of-the-road "non-socialists." Adenauer joined it and represented it at the British zonal party-conference in Herford.

The chairman of the conference, Dr. Holzapfel, arrived late. Adenauer took the chair, with the words "As the oldest person here, I assume that this chair is for me." He progressed to the leadership of the C.D.U., first in the British zone, then in the whole country. Dr. Holzapfel was to be relegated to the post of first Federal German ambassador to Berne — and was to prove not an outstandingly successful ambassador at that.

In September 1948, Adenauer became chairman of the Parliamentary Council which sat in Bonn in order to draw up a Federal Constitution, choose a capital (Bonn, which was so conveniently close to Adenauer's own home across the river Rhine at Rhoendorf) and prepare for the first West German elections. In September, 1949, Adenauer became Federal Chancellor — by a majority of a single vote, which he unashamedly admitted was his own. He formed the first West German Government, with 202 out of 402 seats in the Federal Parliament (Bundestag).

How had Adenauer risen, in a brief three years, from the obscurity of a municipal mayoralty to the political leadership of a country of close on fifty million inhabitants? Obviously, one reason was the lack of competition. The ex-Nazis were temporarily in disgrace. Their most active opponents were dead. The Social Democrats were condemned to the opposition benches in the Bundestag — partly because they entrusted their leadership to the ailing, cranky Kurt Schumacher; partly because they were identified with the British Laborites, who were embarked on a thoroughly unsuccessful essay in government at home in London; and partly because the most prominent Social Democrats who survived the Nazi era were exiles back from London, Stockholm and Switzerland, rubber-stamped plainly if untruthfully with the word "re-export."

But Adenauer had acquired a new depth of character in the years of persecution, poverty and postwar hunger. A friend remarked of him, "He is like one of those narrow-necked earthenware jars in which the Italians store their olives. He's full of olives but one can only get them out singly and with great trouble." Adenauer was adept in canalizing emotions, ideals and energy into reserves on which he could draw in due course. In those postwar years of graded wretchedness he moved and spoke with a natural restraint, while his fellow politicians indulged in hysterics over dismantling, de-Nazification and food shortages. He was one of the few who did not search frenziedly for extra food or get prematurely tipsy at the first "mixed" cocktail parties of occupiers and occupied. He refused to complain about physical discomforts, and he showed a steely insistence in getting on with the tasks of political organization. He preserved his dignity. How few other Germans did!

Work and responsibility probably combined to make Adenauer a younger, healthier man, in spite of a weak chest and bronchial tendencies which are legacies of a lifetime spent in the humid, airless climate of the lower Rhine valley. Work and responsibility certainly gave him chances which he never previously possessed of developing a taste for power. Before the 1949 election he announced, "We must win power now. And we must remain in power for at least eight years. If we can do that, we shall have placed Germany firmly on a road along which she can move in safety." A taste for power brought an ability to compromise with the past. It was strictly rational, if near-Machiavellian in concept, that the leader of the C.D.U. in the Protestant *Land* of Württemberg had to go through three de-Nazification trials before he gained a free run in politics, and that one quarter of the first thousand C.D.U. members in the Hansa-State of Hamburg were former members of the Nazi Party.

Adenauer's first task, which began even before he became Chancellor, was to give a firm and distinct political line to his party. Humanitarians and liberal progressives had flocked to the C.D.U. in the first years. It was they who carried through the party councils the so-called "Ahlen Program" which foresaw a fused and classless society, in which basic industries would be put under a system of public control, and the ideal of service to the State would be synthesized with the earthier concept of private material gain.

With the cynicism which he finds no difficulty in marrying with the ideal of patriotic service, Adenauer realized that the left-wingers in the C.D.U. were not practical men. Karl Arnold dreamed of a near-perfect society which has existed nowhere since the days of the Greek City States; Jakob Kaiser hoped for a unique German reunion, in which traditionally hidebound Prussia would contribute the most radical social and economic ideas. Conservatism was to be represented not only by Cabinet members — like Ludwig Erhard, Minister of Economics, or Fritz Schaeffer, Minister of Finance, or Robert Lehr, Minister of the Interior. Behind the C.D.U. stood the Cologne banker, Robert Pferdemenges; the multiple company-director, Hermann Abs; the President of the West German Federation of Industry, Fritz Berg; the President of the Bank of the German *Länder* (the bank of issue), Hermann Vocke. Here were the true props of the prosperity which Adenauer intended to make his first contribution to the West German community. He selected his own teams in Parliament and outside it.

Adenauer's second task was to find allies outside his own country. Looking through that erratic, patchwork record of German statesmanship since the fall of Bismarck in 1890, one is conscious of one overwhelming national failing. German statesmen invariably contrived to forget that loyal and solid friends are a prerequisite of sustained success. This forgetfulness was only in part the product of an arrogance which sprang out of Bismarck's three successful wars, the foundation of the Empire and an a-social structure based on moneymakers, militarists and a blindly conservative class of large landowners. It sprang, too, from a Teutonic inability to see anybody else's point of view.

Bismarck calculated ruthlessly, but always knew that he must have allies in the diplomatic field in order to manipulate the European balance of power. His 1863 convention with Russia safeguarded Prussia's eastern frontier. He divided Austria from France by playing on their rival aspirations in Italy. He exploited

Napoleon III's vague plan to annex Belgium in order to keep France and England apart. He never went to war, never emerged from war, without allies.

Bismarck's diplomacy was a brilliant essay in *Realpolitik;* the story of his successors is one of misplaced finesse and misused talent. By the turn of the century Germany had begun to command a wealth of admiration, but no affection at all. The dynamic Kaiser dominated his Ministers of State. Caprivi, Chancellor from 1890 to 1894, toyed with the idea of alliance with France and England and fell because his liberal home policies were out of step with the jack-booted stamp of soldiers and Junkers. His successor, Prince Hohenlohe, was obsessed with hatred of France and would have liked to come to terms with England. But he let the reins of power slip into the clumsy fist of Kaiser Wilhelm and looked on helplessly while the Kaiser insulted his uncle, the Prince of Wales and future King Edward VII of England, and frightened British statesmen out of their wits by discoursing on the merits of a German-built and run Berlin-Baghdad railway.

The Kaiser frightened England into permanent alliance with France by his animosity at the time of the Boer War, and encouraged Prince von Bülow, who took Hohenlohe's place, to look east. Intrigues with Czar Nicholas were fruitless, for "Nicky" regarded "Willy" as the most dangerous and compromising sort of ally. From 1909 Theobald von Bethmann-Hollweg saw the Empire into its final stage of disgrace and red ruin. His eight years in office coincided with the fateful flowering of those Germanic mirages — the Prussian-run domain stretching from the Kiel Canal to the Black Sea, the union of the two "fighting races," the Teutons and the Turks, on the Bosporus, and a German "Raj" in India and tropical Africa.

The Kaiser's advisers would have accepted allies without looking for them; the statesmen of the Weimar Republic were ready to look but doomed never to find. Walter Rathenau allowed himself to be talked into signing the Treaty of Rapallo with the Soviet Union in April 1922 by Ugo von Maltzan, the head of the Eastern Section of the German Foreign Office (von

Maltzan later said, "I had to force my way into Rathenau's bedroom in order to explain that he must sign at once, and I pretty well had to rape him before he did"). France and Britain were frightened out of the budding alliance with a democratic Germany, and Rathenau was murdered, ironically enough by young men who considered him to be "too accommodating" to the same Western Powers whom he had just antagonized.

Gustav Stresemann was the only man after Rathenau who had a chance of saving Germany from the nationalists who lay in wait for her hour of weakness, for Heinrich Brüning came too late on the scene to do more than fight a delaying action against Hitler's followers. As Foreign Minister from 1923 to 1929 Stresemann faced a task similar to that which confronted Adenauer twenty-two years later. Parts of Germany were under military occupation. The French had just marched into the Ruhr and blockaded industrial production. The currency was in the grip of a monstrous inflation, and a huge load of reparations hung over the head of the Reich Treasury. German hopes were pinned on this stocky, bulletheaded man, whose memory is today enshrined in the soft "Stresemann" hat to which he lent his name.

The German "story" was that Stresemann died brokenhearted because the Allies would not make the concessions which would have crowned his policies with success and forced back Nazism. But the German "story" is, too often, a product of wishful thinking. In 1919, for instance, the Allies were accused of imposing a "hunger blockade" after the war ended. The result of this "hunger blockade" was that the death rate among German civilians dropped from 24.8 per thousand in 1918 to 15.6 per thousand in 1919. In 1924 the Allies were accused of wanting to wreck the currency. In fact, the Dawes Plan helped to stabilize the financial situation and to defeat the Nazis and nationalists in the November elections. In 1925 the Allies were accused of holding down Germany by force; but the Locarno Pact had just provided for the first stages of the evacuation of Germany by foreign troops. In 1926 a "respectable" Germany was admitted into the League of Nations, and in 1927 direct Allied control over German armaments was abolished. In 1929 the Young Plan brought fresh financial aid, and agreements were made for the total withdrawal of Allied garrisons by June, 1930. All this happened during Stresemann's stewardship, and in the same period Germany received over 25,000 million gold marks in loans and paid out under 8000 million in reparations.

It may be more important to remember that Stresemann watched the intrigues of the German General Staff with Soviet Russia complacently, that he negotiated with Russia for a prospective fourth partition of Poland, and that he discussed with the industrialist, Hugo Stinnes, the potential advantages of a Russo-German economic bloc. "Germany's policy," he said once, "may be two-sided, but it is not double-faced." Who was to believe that? Stresemann made the same elementary mistake as Rathenau: he scared his potential Western friends and foreshadowed the disastrous Ribbentrop-Molotov Pact of 1939.

These examples of German statesmanship must have convinced Adenauer that real friends were a necessity for Germany. He had not, after all, been a young man when the Empire collapsed in the foyers of the smart Spa hotels which sheltered the Kaiser and his courtiers in 1918. He was virtually a contemporary of Rathenau and Stresemann. And in 1949 there were additional considerations to guide him. Germany was totally disarmed, impoverished and divided. Even her western half was not yet a sovereign state, and her eastern half was condemned to progress by stages towards the status of a Communist satellite.

Adenauer set out to bind West Germany indissolubly into the West's community of nations. The Cold War gave him a unique opportunity of doing this — for otherwise the hatred aroused by Nazi excesses would have taken years longer to overcome. The Cold War made immensely more cogent the arguments in favor of building up the West German economy and granting the Federal Republic sovereignty. The Cold War suggested a certain way in which West Germany could reestablish herself. In his ludicrous apologia, the former German Secretary of State for Foreign Affairs, Ernst von Weizsaecker, once suggested that the other European powers tried persistently to create a political vacuum in Germany. For "political vacuum" read "military vacuum" — this was Adenauer's thought. Western disarmament had almost denuded West Germany of troops; but just on the far side of the Iron Curtain were twenty-five Red Army divisions, a striking force which could reach the Rhine in two days of war. West German rearmament was to be the price paid for sovereignty and equality, and at the same time the guarantee of West German safety. Adenauer paid it gladly.

The Cold War put Adenauer on the same path that the Western Powers were bound to tread — that of consolidating the West German state politically, economically and spiritually, and incorporating it into a western defense system and a western Europe in process of unification. The milestones along this path were the Petersberg Agreement (which converted the Allied Military Government into a High Commission administering under the terms of the Occupation Statute); the entry of West Germany into the Schumann Plan coal-and-steel community and the council of Europe; the Bonn and Paris agreements, which conferred sovereignty and the right to rearm; and German entry into NATO.

These agreements brought three immense advantages — advantages which no German in 1945 could have dreamt would be gained in under twenty years. The Federal Republic became an equal partner in a Western alliance headed by the United States; all German differences with her western neighbors were settled amicably; and the beginnings of a Franco-German entente fulfilled Adenauer's own dearest wish. The man who said "You can smell Prussia as soon as you cross the Elbe" was first and foremost a West European. The re-emergence in federal form of Charlemagne's Empire (which, significantly enough, ended on the Elbe) would enable him to die happy. But it was clear, even by 1955, that he was the man most responsible for breathing life into the great ideal of European Union.

How did Adenauer achieve all of his objectives save German reunification? In the first place he was a resolute and skillful negotiator. Sir Ivone Kirkpatrick, the British High Commissioner at the time, once introduced him to Field-Marshal Lord Montgomery. "Does this chap give you much trouble?" asked Montgomery, robustly jovial, holding Kirkpatrick's coat lapel. "Not half as much as I intend to give him," was Adenauer's answer. He meant it.

The people of Cologne are notoriously free and easy in their ways; Adenauer is the exact opposite, a throwback to some Roman ancestor who administered in Colonia while the legions held the outpost-lines against the barbarians. Every paragraph of the complex Petersberg and Bonn agreements was subjected to Adenauer's searching scrutiny and criticism. The minutes of the High Commissioners' meetings with the Chancellor show that it was frequently they, and not the German — dealing from a position of inferiority — who lost patience and gave tricks away.

In the second place, Adenauer exerted an absolute authority over his own advisers. The story that at Cabinet meetings he munches a bar of chocolate (no smoking allowed!), and, when the bar is finished, so is the Cabinet meeting, is not apocryphal. Federal Ministers have explained how Adenauer has a habit of telling them their own troubles first and how he exercises his gift for "polite interruption." The habit of authority dates back to his sixteen years' tenure of the mayoralty of Cologne. In those days a mayor was something of a potentate. Long years as mayor gave Adenauer his habit of making "lonely decisions" and of governing by experts. When he was seriously ill in the fall of 1955 his sole confidant was Hans Globke, his Secretary of State in the Chancellery and author of the commentary to the infamous Nuremberg racial decrees of the Nazis. Like Holstein, the gray eminence of the pre-1914 Wilhelmstrasse, Globke has a molelike capacity for working in the dark, private world of his own office. When he wanted economic advice, Adenauer went to Robert Pferdemenges, the Cologne banker. His "moral tutor" was Cardinal Frings of Cologne, and his publicity expert was burly Ernst Bach, who acquired the requisite ruthlessness in the Freikorps of the 1920's. A clever man can govern best through experts and civil servants; but it is questionable whether this has been a boon to German democracy.

With no knowledge of economics, Adenauer wisely gave a free hand in these to the portly, cigar-puffing Professor Ludwig Erhard. Erhard combined liberal trade policies with an astonishing flair for timing. He understood the German psychology. So he liberalized imports, reduced tariffs, lowered taxation and offered fresh incentives at every favorable moment. His cheap-import policy held prices steady and kept down the cost of living. He applied the needed "credit squeeze" before — and not, as in Britain, after — an economic recession began to make itself felt. Hard work may have been the core of the "German Economic Miracle," but Erhard crusted it with his genius.

Both Erhard and Adenauer understood that prosperity was by far the best ticket on which to fight Federal elections. Election posters in 1953 and 1957 were often inscribed with columns of figures showing how much quicker the cost of living had risen in countries other than Germany. In good time for the 1957 election, the Federal Government introduced a national pensions scheme which will cost at least 6000 million dollars a year by 1985 and which was an immense advance on any system in a major European State.

The achievement of his objectives has been helped by Adenauer's mastery in the Bundestag. German members of Parliament have a tremendous preoccupation with their own affairs. During debates they talk about them, often loudly, and allow their attention to be diverted only in order to catcall at some political opponent. They read newspapers ostentatiously when political opponents are speaking, or busy themselves with files of work or correspondence. Once I heard a speaker, who was an East German refugee, say "Let me tell you a little about what refugees are still suffering today . . ." He told the Bundestag, in some detail. But hardly a member was listening, and the Chamber was emptying while he was making an impassioned plea to those with the goods of this world to give a little more time and thought to families who came across the Iron Curtain frontier with not much more than the clothes on their backs.

Adenauer has been one of the few men, in ten years of the Bundestag's life, who has commanded invariable attention.

When he rises to speak there is always an immediate hush. Famous orators usually have a fire and fervor in their persons or their words. Adenauer has none. But he speaks to the point, sticks to the point and never wastes a word. His speeches have a Roman clarity of diction, a Roman economy of emotion, an utterly Roman logic and precision. The force of his arguments is masked by a deceptive moderation of tone and gesture, by a deceptive gentleness and rhythm. He has an easy way with interrupters. (Heinz Renner, of the Communist Party: "The Chancellor has forgotten! He's seventy-four, at least, or seventy-five." Adenauer: "Herr Renner has a good heart, but no head — for figures.") Each Adenauer speech is a perfect précis in the German language. Each speech is an occasion.

The Chancellor has been helped by his political opponents. The Social Democrats, in spite of honorable intentions and many good men in their ranks, failed at the first three Federal elections. It is fashionable but specious to suggest that this was due to the death of Kurt Schumacher. On his successor, Erich Ollenhauer, descended Schumacher's mantle, and there can be little doubt that it smothered him. But Schumacher had, long before his death in 1952, put his party in the political wilderness by his ironic, erratic, rhetorical handling of the task of opposition. He laid down the line of consistent negation, of obstruction of every agreement with the Allies, of every arrangement with the other members of the European community. He produced no clear alternative to the Federal Government's policies of economic retrenchment and discreet diplomatic progress. Ollenhauer was not a big enough man to modify the precepts of a predecessor who was virtually canonized by his party. This, along with a refusal to shed the Marxist label until 1959, has been chiefly responsible for the persistent failure of postwar German Social Democracy.

Dr. Adenauer's other chief opponents, the Free Democrats, suffered from bad leadership and internal chaos. Too late they discarded the errant, windy Dr. Thomas Dehler and took on as Chairman shrewd old Reinhold Maier; too late they discovered that their right and left wings were drifting far apart. As long as the C.D.U. remained intact, the Free Democrats faced an insoluble problem. A right-wing F.D.P. would quickly lose its soul to the reactionaries who lurk in the wings of the German political stage; a genuinely liberal F.D.P. would be crushed between the upper and nether millstones of Social Democracy and the C.D.U.

Adenauer governed by self-control. During the first ten years of the Bundestag, he lost his head only once and his temper twice. The first happened when he was on the verge of his dangerous attack of pneumonia in 1955; he had a straight black-out. Each loss of temper was caused by the Saar problem, for each time he was accused of sacrificing the national interest for love of France. At one banquet he allowed himself to be carried away sufficiently to criticize his own invaluable Ministers of Economics and Finance.

When France finally rejected the European Defense Agreement, Adenauer sent for the correspondent of *The Times* of London and talked to him in terms which were the reverse of diplomatic: "I can fairly claim that we had replaced the old concept of narrow nationalism with the European Idea. If this European Idea is to be wrecked by France, will that not mean a return in Germany to a narrow nationalism? . . . And if Germany is rebuffed by the West and wooed by the East, do you not think that the new nationalism will look to the Soviet Union? That is a great danger."

Of course it was not — at least, in a foreseeable future. But it may be that Adenauer's words were weighed more carefully than at first seemed likely. For the effect of his outburst was to spur the British Government into action and to open the way to German entry — with the connivance of a shamefaced France — into NATO.

Wit is the saving grace of mankind, and it is wit which has given Adenauer his balance and tranquillity. In 1957 he holidayed on Lake Como, embarked one day with members of his family and Chancellery officials, and was caught in a storm. It was really rough, but Adenauer's only reference to the heavy pitching of the small boat was: "This boat is pretty well-sprung, I should say." In 1957, too, the Cabinet was perturbed to hear that the British Government was considering withdrawing a part of

the British Rhine Army from German soil. Adenauer's only remark was, "Anyway, it should make it easier to fight to the last
Englishman." Two of his favorite sayings are, "Politics are not always conducive to Christianity" and, "Success in politics is the
result of being able to stay seated longer than the other fellow."
Adenauer has something of a small-town Pascal about him.

Adenauer would himself probably admit that he owes more to
application than to wit. One of his own sayings is, "Do not be
diverted from a job until you have finished it — not even if a
cannon goes off at your elbow." His application is the result of
rigorous routine which is broken only in order to fulfill a yet more
demanding emergency program. Adenauer sleeps for little more
than five hours, rises punctually at six o'clock. His "best moment
of the day" is around seven, when he opens the door of his
Rhoendorf home, watches the daylight play over the Rhine
valley and, if it is summer, sniffs the scent of the roses he has
himself planted and tended. He may actually telephone members of his staff at seven o'clock, in order to confirm details of
the day's work.

The fifty-three steps down from his front door to the road take
him into his black Mercedes 300 and the chauffeur whom he
continually urges to drive a little faster. Ahead of Adenauer is a
ten-hour working day, which he interrupts twice — for a frugal
lunch and for a fifty-minute walk round the three kilometers of
paths of his Palais Schaumburg (the park was laid out by Adenauer himself after being reduced to a desert by 1949, and is
patrolled by policemen who are versed in classics of their calling
— such as *The Workings of a Criminal's Mind,* by former Hamburg Inspector Kosyra of Criminal Police). This devotion to fresh
air — in addition to restraint in eating and drinking, no smoking,
a good heart and a Yoga-like conservation of energy — helps
Adenauer to stay young. On his eighty-fourth birthday he went
through a day of celebrations which would have daunted any of
his fourteen grandchildren. (Yet at fifty-five his application for a
life insurance policy was turned down. He was considered too
delicate!)

Outside interests play their part in Adenauer's life. He has his garden, and he is a strong walker when on holiday. He loves music, especially Schubert and Haydn. He reads detective stories for relaxation, with a preference for English and American. He will always find time to see something for the first time. In the heat of an international conference and a Mediterranean summer he had to see the Roman Forum during his luncheon interval. He does not note but watches a Rhineland sunset, fading in its pastel shades of blue, pink and buff over the hills of the Eifel. He appreciates a glass of good wine and knows more than enough about the German vintages and growths. (By an unfortunate chance, Adenauer was given *Liebfraumilch* at the first banquet which he attended on his first visit to London. *Liebfraumilch* is a generic name for wines of no particular charm or quality which are grown in the Rhine-Hesse. And Adenauer had just sent the British Prime Minister a dozen bottles of Maximin Gruenhauser Beerenauslese 1947, one of the finest and most aristocratic wines of a very fine year!)

Adenauer is happiest of all in his own little vineyard, among his own flowers. The man who stays so close to the soil must have patience, skill and humor — qualities which make a statesman.

Every man has his failings. Adenauer is no exception. He is free with his own caustic brand of criticism. He was easily provoked into a frantic vendetta by Dr. Thomas Dehler, then chairman of the Free Democratic Party. He made harsh jests at a public banquet in Cologne about his Ministers of Economics and Finance, suggesting that they did not know their jobs (Adenauer himself had virtually no knowledge of either subject). He complained about his Foreign Minister, Heinrich von Brentano, while in close proximity to a microphone of the West German Radio Network which had been left tuned-in. He did the same thing in 1959, this time to the Minister for All-German Affairs, Herr Lemmer. When the Berlin Crisis of November, 1958, was provoked by Soviet threats, Adenauer went up to Berlin in order to make a "no quarter" election speech directed against the Social Democratic Lord Mayor, Willy Brandt, who was playing the major role in maintaining the morale and courage of the Berliners. On the day following, Adenauer failed even to pay Brandt a courtesy-call.

Like all authoritarians he will not brook argument. At a private dinner party I was given personal proof of this. Over the coffee and brandy Adenauer talked freely, brilliantly, to the small circle of journalists who had been invited to meet him and learn something of the real background to his policy. It was an off-the-record press conference of the most valuable kind.

In one of his anti-British moods, he claimed that the British bore a major responsibility for the war by "not stopping Hitler." If they had refused to be polite to Hitler, he maintained, the German people would have risen against the dictator and ended his reign. I was daring enough to suggest that Britain did not bear the major responsibility for the war, and that Germany did.

"You were only a very young man at the period of which I am talking," was his prompt answer.

"Just who would have risen against Hitler, then?" I asked.

"Consider my own Catholic Center Party," said Adenauer. "We never gave up our struggle against Hitler; we never gave in."

"But," said the correspondent of the *Christian Science Monitor,* "isn't it a fact that your own Catholic Center Party voted to a man in favor of the Enabling Act which gave Hitler the powers of a dictator?"

There was a strained pause, followed by an organized buzz of conversational camouflage. Adenauer was pink with annoyance. I was not asked to dinner again. It was a revealing episode.

"Dr. Adenauer," one observer of the Chancellor's moods wrote, "has more supporters than he has opponents; but he has more enemies than friends." In spite of his little touches of humanity, he has remained remote from the normal human being, curbing all spontaneity of emotion and sentiment. It takes something very special to touch his heart and make him admit the fact. Such an occasion occurred in December, 1958, when he decided to round-off his visit to Berlin by driving through the working-class quarters of the city. He was given a tremendous welcome. To his Minister for All-German Affairs, Ernst Lemmer, he remarked, "They have made me feel that they really are my own people."

It may be possible for a man to impress his personality too firmly on the history of his country. Critics have demanded that he should decentralize authority and let departments make their own decisions. "The sad thing," one West German newspaper wrote, "is that Dr. Adenauer has more understanding of daily duties and political tactics than of long-term constitutional evolution and the principles which should underlie it." A Göttingen Professor, Werner Weber, maintained that Adenauer's authority was so absolute that existing German democracy was his creation and would not survive his departure. The Frankfurter *Allgemeine Zeitung* has coined the phrases "Chancellor Democracy" and "the Chancellor Regiment," in reference to the respectable camarilla which has served him and Germany so well.

The writer and dramatist Erich Kuby produced one of the most biting criticisms of the Chancellor's place in this "Chancellor Democracy," in an electioneering pamphlet of September, 1957. To Kuby — an artist, an ecstatic but essentially "difficult" member of society — Adenauer was sheer anathema. Kuby could not abide his bland self-satisfaction, his dull rationalism, his small-town sentiments and bourgeois, limited lust for power. Kuby, burning himself out with his zest for life, resented the phenomenon of the dry octogenarian, "who produced not a single constructive political thought in fifty years of public life" — unless the consolidation in the Western alliance of a "Rump Germany" which ends fifty miles short of Goethe's Weimar should be regarded as such.

With a flash of prescience, Kuby discovered a trait in common between Adenauer and Bismarck. Neither could brook the idea of his ever being succeeded or replaced. (This trait, for that matter, is probably the only one that Adenauer has in common with Hitler.)

To Adenauer's failings must be added his failures. He failed over the Saar, for he misjudged the strength of French diplomacy on the one hand, and the strength of the national feelings of the Saarlanders on the other. He was ready to sign away the Saar when it was not necessary, and give its people a "Saar Statute" which would have left the area as a "European enclave."

He failed to settle the question of his successor at the correct tactical and logical moment. On April 7, 1959, he announced that he would run as C.D.U. candidate for the Federal Presidency. His election as President would have been certain and he would therefore have relinquished the Chancellorship in September. But on June 5 he announced that he would stay Chancellor after all.

There were, Adenauer explained, "good" reasons for his reversal of his previous decision. The American Secretary of State, Mr. John Foster Dulles, had died in the meantime. The world situation had not improved. The Russian threat to Berlin — uttered in November 1958 — still remained. Dr. Adenauer told the Cabinet, the executive of the Christian Democratic Party and its parliamentary group, that his new decision was "unalterable." After the Cabinet meeting, a Chancellery official was asked if anything else had transpired at it. "Of course not," was the answer. "Naturally, there was no discussion." The official did not even see anything funny in his own remark.

The real reasons for Adenauer's change of plan were very different from those that he gave. He had discovered that the Federal Constitution could not be "reinterpreted" in order to give the President a bigger voice in the government of the country (in April, Adenauer instructed officials to look into the possibilities of this "reinterpretation"). He had also discovered that he could not force his own choice as new Chancellor, the Finance Minister Dr. Franz Etzel, on his Christian Democratic Party. A new Chancellor would have to be given the support of a majority in the Bundestag, but the party wanted Professor Ludwig Erhard, Minister of Economics, in the post. Adenauer found that he could not win the bitter tug-of-war with the party, which lasted for nearly two months. He decided not to lose it either. By remaining Chancellor he bewildered the electorate, flung the party into a state of temporary chaos, and treated the office of President as a mere pawn in political huckstering of the worst kind. At the first *Land* election after these events — in Bremen, in October 1959 — the C.D.U. vote was halved.

Adenauer failed to establish genuinely good relations with the British Conservative Governments of Churchill, Eden and Macmillan, which were really anxious to be on the best of terms with Western Germany. He was aggrieved by the Macmillan visit to Moscow in the spring of 1959 (which led to the Khrushchev visit to Washington). He rejected the Macmillan plan for a zone of limited and equalized armaments in Central Europe without even studying it (he admitted as much). He attacked British policies in a series of newspaper and radio interviews in June. After he had given five, his Press Chief, Felix von Eckardt, returned from Geneva and put a stop to the nonsense. Von Eckardt is one of the very few Germans to whom Adenauer has been known to listen. He canceled the further nine interviews which had been arranged.

In the fall, Adenauer accused the British Conservative Government of supporting the Rapacki plan for a nuclear-free zone in Europe. When the British Government denied that it had ever supported the Rapacki Plan, Adenauer claimed that the British Conservative Party did. The Conservative Party was fighting the British general election at the time. It could scarcely be blamed for resenting this ill-aimed stab in the back. Only five days before the British Election, Adenauer said that Mr. Macmillan would drop his plans for a zone of equalized armaments as soon as the election was over. The sense of his words was plain: Mr. Macmillan's plans were a kind of electioneering stunt. Yet the alternative to a Conservative victory was the return to power of a British Labor Party, which really did support the Rapacki plan! Although his London visit in November 1959 established a slightly friendlier atmosphere, Englishmen can hardly be expected to forget such antics in a hurry.

He failed to establish satisfactory relations with the Soviet Union. In September 1955 he returned from Moscow much as Disraeli had from Berlin in 1878 — preaching "peace with honor." In fact, he granted the diplomatic relations so earnestly sought by the Soviet Union in order to stratify the political *status quo* in Central Europe and to carry on a policy of peaceful co-existence with both German states. In return, he obtained the repatriation of around twelve thousand German prisoners of war. But the Red Cross, if left to get on with the negotiations which it had already begun, would probably have got the prisoners home. And, in fact, a number of them were war criminals who were to prove a grave embarrassment to Western Germany.

Adenauer disobeyed his own instincts by going to Moscow at all, and in private he showed none of the elation reserved for the Bundestag and the press. He told an American diplomat, "First of all, I managed to free a hundred thousand German prisoners of war. Second, I learned that the Kremlin leaders are firmly convinced that Communism under Moscow leadership will one day rule the world. And third . . . I could see on the faces of the men I met that they had lost their souls. . . . Such a regime is fatal to mankind." This was the language of despondency and foreboding.

Both were justified. Adenauer's own precept, "It is less important to have the right, than to be in the right" had little application to the task of treating with the Soviet Union. Might, not right, was the basis of Soviet policy towards Germany, and it very quickly became apparent that the Soviet leaders had established diplomatic relations with an Adenauer government in the confident expectation that a man of seventy-nine could not last much longer in office. Two successive Soviet ambassadors in Bonn, Valerian Zorin and Vladimir Smirnov, canvassed the opposition parties in Bonn and the industrialists in the Ruhr. With considerable skill they played on the weaknesses of the Social Democrats and on the foibles of the Free Democrats, as well as on the worries of the Ruhr bosses over the incipient American recession.

So cleverly did Zorin and Smirnov play their disruptive diplomatic game that journalists of Western countries blamed Adenauer for "cold-shouldering" them. Smirnov made bland statements to the press, which indicated his belief that the Chancellor was a liar. It must have been aggravating for a deeply religious man to find himself being bested by atheists whom he regarded as the agents of the Devil. On top of that, the Russians did not return home German civilians who had been deported in the early years after the war, but demanded a separate package-deal for them. This involved the signing of a trade agreement which was immensely favorable to the Soviet Union. In return for surplus Russian oil and wheat, West Germany undertook to send to Russia light and heavy engineering products, including integrated steel plants.

Even more distressing for Adenauer was persistent Soviet blocking of any progress towards German reunification. It is a dogma in West Germany, not only that reunification is necessary but that reunification is certain. No politician can indicate the contrary — it would be fatal to him. In his Yale University speech in June 1956, Adenauer sounded a note of false confidence: a new phase in the struggle between East and West had begun, and peaceful coexistence was a purely tactical Soviet demand. Stalin's successors had not accepted the right of the free world to live in its own way, and the West must remain supremely watchful and must continue to distrust Soviet aims. "We Germans," Adenauer said then, "want no eastern adventure. Our Government will therefore continue to pursue its straightforward policy, which will lead to reunification." It was an unjustifiably bold promise.

Adenauer has been accused of inflexibility over the issue of reunification and a final settlement of the German question. These are the terms in which he described his policy to me early in 1959:

The Soviet Union was still intent on penetrating further into western Europe, and the long-term Communist aim was still the domination of the whole of Europe. Communist tactics were varied in order to match changes in the situation in Europe — typical was Khrushchev's switch from the political to the economic field, and his new plan for a Soviet economic policy which would make association with the East more attractive than political and military pressure ever had done.

The Western Powers, Dr. Adenauer went on, must be wary and united, and must continue to press for a global solution of East-West differences. Only in this way could the German problem be solved. On no account should the West allow itself to be hustled into the type of "German Confederation" which the Russians were proposing — "The Soviet Union would then contrive to show that the West Germans are the troublemakers and are ready to block reunification on Russian terms. The Soviet Union would play on German susceptibilities and exploit German impatience." Adenauer added, "And I am afraid we cannot trust all of our own people."

On no account, Adenauer said, should the Western Powers be driven into making concessions over a broader field by the Soviet threat to Berlin — "There will not be a war over Berlin, for the Russians do not want war. So we must keep our nerve. Mine is all right, but I have the feeling that the nerves of some of my friends are not too good. And on no account should we give way over Berlin itself. That would have a shattering effect on German and world opinion."

In this same spirit of firmness pushed to the borderline of effrontery Adenauer opposed military disengagement in Europe, opposed any reduction of NATO forces which could point the way to an eventual American withdrawal from Europe, opposed any nuclear-free zone of the sort recommended by the Polish Foreign Minister, Adam Rapacki. He insisted on free All-German elections as a preliminary to reunification and the signing of a peace treaty, and coined the phrase which his allies adopted: "No concessions without counter-concessions."

Adenauer's attitude towards the Soviet proposals for a German peace treaty, talks between the German states, and the formation of a confederation which would perpetuate the division of Germany, were implicit in his broadcast to the people of West Germany on January 13, 1959. These were his comments on the Soviet proposals:

According to the Soviet draft, the present partition of Germany was to be maintained, and Berlin (under the terms of the Soviet plan for making West Berlin a "free city") was to constitute a third, separate part of Germany.

Germany was to be rendered defenseless. Her treaties of alliance with the free nations of the West were to be canceled.

The European economic organizations were to be destroyed (this was assuming that Germany was detached economically, as well as militarily, from the West).

The Communist system of government, as it exists in East Germany, was to be introduced by stages into West Germany too.

Dr. Adenauer's summing-up was that the Soviet Union was intent on "frustrating the economic and political union of the free peoples of the West, because only in this way can the Soviet Union achieve the world-domination which she desires."

Whether this view is right or wrong, the future alone will show. Whether Adenauer's simple, but crystal-clear concept of counteraction was correct, will remain a matter of endless debate in the meantime. He sponsored the creation of the twelve-division-strong West German Army, its equipment with nuclear weapons and its subordination to overall NATO requirements. He set his face steadfastly against the only obvious "horse-deal" — the guaranteeing of military neutrality of a united Germany, in return for genuine and free reunification. Dr. Adenauer owes loyalty to the West as a whole, as well as to his own country. Does he emphasize the first to the detriment of the second? If so, his Allies should be the last people in the world to reproach him.

Ten years of rule have given Adenauer an astonishing record: three Federal elections won by wide margins; steadily increasing material prosperity; a growing confidence on the part of the Germans in the West and in themselves; the foundation and consolidation of a democratic order which has a real chance of survival.

The most important lesson of all which Adenauer learned and applied was how to make and keep good friends. "During the ten years which the Federal German Republic completes today," he said in his broadcast to the German People on September 20, 1959. "We have stood side by side with the free peoples. We have stood there because of our own deep convictions, and by doing so we have served the well-being of the German people and the freedom and peace of the world." What other German achieved this during the last seventy years? Bülow and Bethmann-Hollweg dabbled recklessly with the intricate mosaic of European feelings. Stresemann and Rathenau looked for allies, but in too many directions. Brüning was faced with the emptying hourglass of internal German politics. None of them had the time or the inclination to find out that friends are made once, and lost once.

The "Wandering Jew" was said to be accursed. But I sometimes feel inclined to back his chances of dishonest survival or decent extinction against those of the errant German. It is the outstanding peculiarity of the German that he is compounded of much dullness and more unpredictability, of persistence and hysteria. Churchill called Adenauer "the greatest German since Bismarck." Only "since"? Bismarck was, indeed, by far the more typical of his race. He has been pictured "weeping with rage" — a very German habit — and sitting with his head clutched in his hands, muttering "I think we are all going mad." He is quoted as saying that he could "think clearly only in a forest," and that "Hate, as a spur in life, is no less indispensable than love." He allied political genius with this sort of tipsy philosophy, and his epileptic energy became the symbol of German success.

How different is Adenauer — that suburban Rhinelander who never saw Paris, Washington or London until he was seventy-five years old, who reasoned without passion and who cast aside German dynamism in favor of Roman logic! Bismarck contributed very much to Germany, and very little to civilization. Adenauer has remained a good German, while working consciously for a free world which is civilized.

Adenauer had an appeal for defeated, frustrated Germans which Bismarck could never have had. He was simply, religiously, but naturally, paternal and patriarchal — not least by virtue of a score of direct descendants. He made himself a "father of his people" by shouldering their burdens and acting as their protector. This near-paragon of domestic virtue and middle-class common sense was the appropriate symbol of the postwar era in Germany. For during that era Germans wanted to learn how to enjoy life in an orthodox groove. As Professor Heuss said to me once: "We need time to relax, to think, time even for a little honest enjoyment. And we shall be a real community when the outside world helps Germans to make a pleasure out of their industriousness." A sound and sensible philosophy! Too often in the past the Germans have organized themselves for suicides as spectacular and futile as that of the Gadarene swine.

In the Tiergarten, Berlin's Hyde Park, there was once a leafy walk lined with the statues of some of Germany's greatest men. It was called the *Siegesallee*, or "Victory Avenue." After the Russian capture of the city, the trees were felled for firewood. Sometimes the statues got in the way and were rudely toppled from their pedestals. Many had already suffered in the fighting. Here, a mortar bomb had decapitated a Prussian general; there, small-arms fire had lopped off a Junker nose, and a random shell had blown a corpulent Crown Prince to pieces. For four years the gaunt, crumbling and generally unrecognizable figures continued to stand in gloomy isolation along the weed-covered road. Then a gardener was set to work; the rubble of the past was carted away, and young trees were planted in its place.

Even so has Germany lost her old stone gods of War, Might and Glory. For those grim figures were not just a part of Germany; they *were* Germany. And in that gardener's patient, purposeful performance I see a replica, in miniature, of that of Konrad Adenauer, who has planted and tended the first tender shoots of German democracy in the uncertain springtime of the post-Nazi era.

The Shutter in the Brain

A neo-Fascist-Europe is not inevitable. But it is more than a bogy, it is a danger. . . . There exists, unhappily, a profound inner relation between anti-Bolshevism and Fascism.
— WALTER DIRKS, editor of the *Frankfurter Herfte,*
1948

While entering the offices of the occupation authorities in Bonn, Dr. Ingleday, undersecretary of the Ministry of Labor for Rheinland-Pfalz, said "Heil Hitler." He later admitted that . . . apart from this, he had sworn at a British officer and expressed sympathy for National Socialism.
— *Tagesspiegel,* West Berlin, 1948

ONE of the least comfortable heritages of the Nazi era is a psychological chain-reaction which is almost sure to go on for a long, long time. Here is a single, short human story to illustrate this.

In May 1945 the spearheads of the Red Army reached the little town of Malchin in Mecklenburg. Many of the townspeople fled to meadows just to the west of the town to escape the artillery barrage which heralded the entry of the Soviet troops into the town. There all sort of pitiful scenes took place. For stories of rape, violence and murder had flown ahead of the Red Army ever since it reached German territory in East Prussia months earlier. Some of the inhabitants of Malchin fled into the woods; others prepared for a further exodus to the west. Some families split up, others decided that it was better to die.

The father of one of the latter was a forty-two-year-old member of the Nazi Party. He had a wife and two sons, aged fourteen

SZEWCZUK, *Die W*

Sprouting in the German Springtime

and thirteen. His wife asked him to shoot the two boys first, then her and finally himself. He agreed. He shot the three people he loved most in the world and found that there was no bullet left for himself. He had by mistake taken a friend's revolver from the hiding place where both of them kept their weapons. His own had been fully loaded.

The Russians were very close by now, and he failed to think out an alternative method of committing suicide. He was captured, and sentenced to twelve years' imprisonment as a member of the S.A. He returned to Germany in 1957, and in January 1959 a Hanover court declared him not guilty of murder or manslaughter. If what he did was a crime, he had certainly paid for it times over.

Crime and punishment become no more than relative terms when a case like this is shrugged off with little surprise by those who read about it. Germans could be excused if some of them pulled down a shutter over a section of their brains, deliberately forgot. For very often they need to forget very badly. A German lawyer once told me how his daughter tried to escape across the river Elbe in May 1945, and how the Russians caught her on the riverbank. She was raped eighteen times, then they let her go. And another German, a chauffeur, told me how one of his kidneys was smashed and destroyed by Nazi jack boots in the Neuengamme concentration camp. Stories like theirs illustrate how barren are the concepts of collective guilt and collective punishment. The German people has punished itself.

One of the most remarkable examples of a private psychological chain-reaction was that of Dr. Otto John, who became head of the West German security services ("Office for the Protection of the Federal Constitution") in 1950, who vanished into East Germany on July 20, 1954, and who subsequently escaped back into West Germany, and was tried for treason and sentenced to four years' imprisonment by the Federal High Court in Karlsruhe. This case perfectly represents the difficulty of reconciling the German past with the postwar German present, and the consequent uncertainty of the German future. Otto John himself had a phrase which he was very fond of using in 1953 and 1954: "Whatever things look like, nothing has really been settled." The phrase is equally true in 1960; it may turn out to be still applicable twenty years afterwards.

Otto John was born in Marburg in 1909, the son of a senior civil servant and stanch "Kaiser-true" monarchist. He grew quickly to a fair height of nearly six feet, to good looks, and to an independence of mind unusual in a German. He went through school in Wiesbaden and studied for the law; he was instantly shocked and infuriated by the Nazis when they came to power. "If they can dictate to us how we pray," he remarked when Nazi prayers were introduced to schools, "they will control our whole lives soon enough." In 1937 he became a junior legal adviser to Lufthansa German Airlines. He was already in touch with opponents of the Nazi regime, but was so disgusted by it that he wanted to get a job abroad from Lufthansa.

In Berlin, where he first worked for Lufthansa, Otto John quickly made friends with such men as Klaus and Dietrich Bonhoeffer, zealous Protestants whose loathing for Nazism was founded on religious belief, and their relative, Hans von Dohanyi, who worked for the Reich Ministry of Justice. This group of civilians had misty ideas of kidnapping Hitler and having him certified as a lunatic by Klaus and Dietrich's father, Professor Karl Bonhoeffer, who was a doctor. They established contact with Hitler's opponents among the German generals (von Hammerstein-Equord, Beck, Witzleben) and in the secret service (Admiral Canaris, General Oster). They considered the possibility of a royalist restoration, with the obvious candidate Prince ("Call me Mister") Louis Ferdinand, the son of the former Crown Prince, who had worked at the Ford Motor Works in Detroit and acquired more knowledge of democracy than all of his forbears together.

John and his friends extended the field of their plotting — if such a word can be used in conjunction with the attempted overthrow of a tyrant and mass-murderer. They made friends with the opponents of the Nazis among former Socialist and Liberal politicians, in the Foreign Office, the Prussian aristocracy and the churches. They knew of the March 1943 and November 1943 plots to kill Hitler (in the first a bomb was successfully placed in Hitler's private aircraft but failed to explode; in the second a young officer with hand-grenades strapped under his own great-coat was prevented from blowing the Führer and himself into oblivion only by Hitler's failure to arrive at a parade). Latterly they all lived in daily danger of their lives, and two of them, von Dohanyi and Dietrich Bonhoeffer, were arrested in April 1943. They were fully implicated in the main plot to kill Hitler on July 20, 1944.

John has described his own part on that final day in a memo-randum which was of considerable value to the author of the best account of the Resistance to Hitler, Mr. John Wheeler-Bennett, in *The Nemesis of Power*. John went to the old Defense Ministry in the Bendler Strasse in order to see whether he could be a *liaison* between the generals and the political wing under Popitz and Gördeler. He left the Bendler Strasse after the attempt on Hitler's life had failed, when — unknown to him — the attempt of the generals to seize power was already in process of failing. By one stroke of luck, he was not caught by the "Hitler-true" troops led by General Remer to "recapture" the Defense Minis-try; by another, he was not at the house of ex-Minister of State Johannes Popitz when the latter was arrested on July 21. With the vague thought that there might still be something for him to do, he stayed on in Berlin until July 24, then boarded the Lufthansa plane for Madrid and was smuggled by British agents into Portugal.

John agreed to work for the BBC, believing that it was his duty as a good German to bring the war to an end. Only after the end of the war did he learn that his younger brother, Hans, had been murdered by the Nazis. This may be the reason why John agreed to help with the interrogation of German war crimi-nals and to assist the British prosecution in the trial of Field-Marshal Erich von Manstein. In 1949 he married a British sub-ject, Mrs. Lucie Mankiewitz, who was ten years older than him-self. In 1950 he applied for the post of head of the security services of the newly created Federal Republic. He was not the candidate of the British Occupation authorities, but of the Federal Minister of the Interior, Dr. Robert Lehr. In spite of this being made plain, the West German press never afterwards ceased to assert the contrary. The British, certainly, made no secret of the fact that they approved of John's candidacy, and they had indeed advanced objections against other, manifestly unsuitable candidates whose names had previously been put forward.

It is questionable whether any man who has worked for his country's enemies — however honorable his motives — can ever re-establish himself in his own country. Otto John was hardly given a fair chance to do so. He had enemies in the apparatus of government: Hans Globke, the "gray eminence" of the Federal Chancellery; Gerhard Schroeder, the ex-Nazi who was to become John's direct superior as the second Federal Minister of the Interior; Theodore Oberländer, the Federal Minister for Refugees and a former member of the S.S. He had a rival and a more dangerous potential enemy in Colonel Reinhard Gehlen, head of the separate counter-intelligence service organized under American aegis in the Pullach garden-suburb of Munich. He was not popular with the Federal Chancellor, who was once reported to have remarked "I don't care for that man" and who saw him personally just twice in four years. He was disliked by all those survivors of the Nazi regime whose careers had been founded on the ideals of functional loyalty or emotional hero-worship.

Otto John had a scar on his mind — an honorable scar. Almost all of those friends who had fought with him against the Nazis were dead — summarily executed in the courtyard of the Bendler Strasse, hunted down and tortured, garroted and strangled slowly to death on meathooks. Their struggle had been hopeless — as one of them, Berthold Graf von Stauffenburg had summed it up, "The worst thing is knowing that we cannot succeed, and yet that we have to do it, for our country and for our children." The expectancy of failure haunts the pages of Otto John's own memorandum on July 20, 1944. And among his dead friends was his only and beloved brother, Hans.

To serve the German State — even a new German State —

was bound to be difficult for a man who had suffered like John, and who felt an unjustified but understandable embarrassment over having survived his friends. He was bound to be painfully conscious of the surviving smug and successful progeny of an evil regime against which he had fought and failed; he was liable to be hypersensitive to their influence, real or imagined, on an infant German democracy. Moreover, in the four years during which he managed the West German security office, ex-Nazis were conspicuously active and very far from being unsuccessful.

In June 1950 a West German newspaper published a cartoon which showed the chairman at a board meeting addressing a candidate for promotion in the company: "What's really fantastic about this fellow is that he was never a Nazi! We've got to get rid of fellows like that. Why, his party membership card was a forgery!" The joke was apt. Not only were ex-Nazis back in positions of authority in industry, in the law and in education; they had returned to the one field which should by rights have been out of bounds to them, that of politics. Between December 1949 and June 1950, twenty-three ex-Nazis joined the Federal Ministry of Economics alone. They included such trusties as Gerhard Rauschenbach, Otto Pallsch and Hans Grotjan, party members from 1933-1945, all of them Storm Troopers and one of them a *Sturmführer,* all of them holders of high Nazi decorations.

In the personnel section of the *Auswärtiges Amt* (the Federal Foreign Office) Dr. Haas announced in 1950 that "only" 14 out of the last 31 recruits were ex-Nazis. Two years later, in March 1952, it was found that 39 out of 49 senior officials in the *Auswärtiges Amt* were ex-Nazis. The Refugee Ministry of Dr. Theodor Oberländer was busily finding jobs for the Minister's former associates in the S.S. and S.A. At the beginning of 1950 the Minister for *Länder* Affairs, Herr Hellwege, appointed as head of the cultural affairs section of his ministry a Dr. Ehrich, who had joined the Nazi Party in 1932 and became *Landesgruppenleiter* in Italy. This went far beyond the limits of the contention that "small" Nazis could be trusted again in politics; Ehrich belonged to the category of high-ranking Nazi administrators who were jokingly known as "the Golden Pheasants."

The steady infiltration into the political arena of ex-Nazis disturbed many people besides Otto John. But he became obsessed by it. Foreigners who had merely fought against Nazi Germany and for their own countries must have seemed agonizingly complacent to him. Why, he asked legitimately, did Dr. Adenauer choose four of Hitler's supporters for his 1953 Cabinet? Why were ex-Nazis left in such profusion in the civil service, the law, the press, the schools — the professions which exercised so tremendous an influence on the formative life of the community? Why were they accepted so readily by the political parties? The epic case here was the election to the Bundestag of a man calling himself Dr. Franz Richter, who sat for two years in the ranks of the reactionary Reichs Party. Only then did it transpire that he was Fritz Rössler, the former Nazi *Gauleiter* of Saxony!

These were the sort of events which developed John's suspicions into a phobia. They are only a few, selected at random, out of very many:

In November, 1950, talk of German rearmament brought the reappearance in public and in print of a whole crop of ex-generals. Years earlier Count Blücher von Wahlstatt had written in his book, *Know Your Germans,* that the first in the field of postwar German apologists would be the ex-generals — "They will pay each other and their enemies compliments. It is sweeter to have conquered an outstandingly clever enemy than an outstandingly stupid one." How right he was! Ex-General von Dittmar began to fill columns of the daily press; ex-General von Manteuffel became one of the most popular public speakers in West Germany; ex-General Count von Schwerin became a confidential adviser of the Federal Government; ex-General Guderian published two books. An organization of ex-officers called the *Bruderschaft* (Brotherhood) began to become active. It was a veiled conspiracy against the democratic state. Its leaders were an interesting assortment of anti-Communists and Russian agents

— the classic mold which best suits the obscure but objective policies and plannings of the Kremlin.

Late in 1950, too, appeared *Germany's Fateful Years,* the literary effort of ex-Admiral Kurt Assmann. The book would not be worth mentioning save for the fact that it was widely read and offered the German people one of the most convenient of all alibis for their part in World War II. Assmann maintained that Hitler "tried, honestly and consistently, to follow the road from Berlin to London"; that he "accepted the British Empire and only wanted living space for the overpopulated Reich in the underpopulated and fertile territories of eastern Europe"; that a German victory in Europe would have brought an era of universal happiness — for Hitler would sooner or later have died, and the "healthy and reasonable elements" of the German population would have overcome the Nazis. This atrocious nonsense excited wide interest, and practically no trenchant criticism.

In April 1951 the Schleswig-Holstein *Land* elections brought the smaller right-wing political parties into the picture. Karl Meissner's "German Block" and Herbert Muenchow's "German Right Party" dressed up their followers in black breeches, white shirts and jack boots. At their meetings the Hitler salute was given, referred to as the *Deutsche Gruss* (German greeting). The first verse of the old national anthem was sung again, with that same frightening fervor which had once enabled young S.S. men to trample their victims to death without especially noticing the blood and entrails.

In April 1951 a fourteen-year-old schoolgirl was "put in Coventry" by her classmates because her father had been executed after the July 20, 1944, plot against Hitler.

In the same month, the right-wing Socialist Reichs Party joined in the Lower Saxony *Land* elections. Led by ex-General Otto Remer, whose troops had crushed the July 20 plot, this party captured 11 per cent of the votes cast and 16 seats in the *Land* Parliament. One of its members, Hans Festge, said that there had been only one gas oven in all of the German concentration camps (for sanitary use!) and that others had been brought in by the Americans in 1945, in order to pin guilt on Germany. Another member said that the pictures of the concentration camps were forgeries, and that the corpses shown in them were wax dummies.

In August 1951 the former members of the Waffen S.S. completed preparations for forming their own "association." Ex-Generals Gille and Hausser were the moving spirits. Gille had already formed an association for the S.S. Viking Division (Scandinavian and East European mercenaries of the Nazis, who fought under German leaders), and Hausser had organized the men of the Hitler *Leibstandarte* (bodyguard) regiments. The purposes of a Waffen S.S. association (it was to be called the HIAG) were to promote comradely get-togethers, to provide legal aid for war criminals and suspects, and to "clear the fair name of the fighting S.S."

In August 1951 the Federal Government had to order an inquiry into the personnel policy of the *Auswärtiges Amt*. The inquiry showed that 134 members of the A.A. had belonged to the Nazi Party and 138 had served in the convicted war criminal Joachim Ribbentrop's foreign office. Yet one member of the A.A. told me that any further examination of the problem of who should run West Germany's diplomacy was now out of date — "a line should be drawn through the past," he said.

In 1952 the following associations were formed in Western Germany:

Bund für Wahrheit und Recht, an association of former leading members of the S.S. and Nazi Party.

Hilfsgemeinschaft ehemaliger Waffen SS Angehöriger (HIAG), described above.

Reichsorden und Reichsjugend, a blackshirted, uniformed group formed at Bückeburg in Lower Saxony.

Vereinigung ehemaliger Internierter in Moosburg, a group of ex-S.S. and other political suspects formed in Munich.

Neu-Soziale Demokratischer Arbeiter Party (NSDAP), a similar group in Berlin.

Kameradschaftsverband ehemaliger internierten National-sozialisten, a similar group in Hesse.

Bewegung Reich, a right-wing group, in Dortmund.

National Sammlungsbewegung, a similar organization, in Detmold.

There were at least a dozen other suspect organizations formed in the same year. These were the sort of things that their leading members said:

Herbert Muenchow: "The war was not Hitler's fault. We lost the war because we were betrayed. Adenauer had his son made a priest so that he should not serve at the front."

Former Lord Mayor of Frankfurt Krebs: "Look at democracy! It's like a fur filled with lice. But front-line soldiers know what to do with lice; you crack them with your fingernails until the blood spurts! That's what we have to do with democrats."

August Haussleiter (speaking in Bonn!): "The time has come for us to chase out of their offices all the criminals who moved into them after 1945."

In October 1952 the Waffen S.S. staged their first big public rally in the town of Verden. Schools, shops and post offices closed on Saturday, October 24, in order to ensure a good turn-out. Hotels and bars were given permission to stay open all night. The Lord Mayor and the town councilors instructed the townspeople to decorate their houses with flowers and flags, and themselves welcomed veterans of the S.S. in the market place. Ex-General Bernhard Ramcke addressed four thousand former members of the S.S. and told them that citizens of the Western Powers should be tried for war crimes — for perfecting the atom bomb, and for "smashing our beautiful city of Dresden."

In October 1952 Walter Huppenkothen was tried by a Munich court for his part in the murder of Admiral Canaris and other members of the resistance to Hitler at Flossenburg concentration camp in April 1945. Huppenkothen had organized the summary court which sentenced these men to death by slow strangulation. Admiral Canaris is believed to have been, in effect, executed twice. He was revived after being virtually dead, and was then garroted a second time. He had been tortured intermittently for nine months. (In all, 61,000 people died or were murdered at Flossenburg camp.)

When Huppenkothen came into court he was greeted by a hum of approval which went round the public galleries. The onlookers remained reasonably restrained during the first few days of the trial, but when his counsel, Dr. Alfred Seidle, beat on his desk in fury while asserting that the court was prejudiced against his client, loud applause broke out and clapping lasted for minutes before order could be restored. The court was suitably awed. On November 5, it pronounced Huppenkothen not guilty. It found that he had ordered death sentences but not officially confirmed them; this meant that Hitler must have sent "secret orders" for them to be carried out. It decided that Canaris and his friends were proven traitors in any case. And its view was that the court convened by Huppenkothen had "acted according to established legal procedures." Such bare-faced casuistry was exceptional even for a German court.

In January 1953 the leaders of the "Naumann conspiracy" were arrested. In February the German authorities pounced on a similar organization called the *Deutsche Freikorps*. Four prominent ex-Nazis, including the former *Gauleiter* of Hamburg, Frauenfeld, were arrested. Like the Naumann group, the Freikorps called itself a "sworn and dedicated society," and its nominal head was the Luftwaffe Major and air ace, Rudel, who lived in the Argentine but who made frequent clandestine trips to Germany.

A few days before the arrests, Dr. Adenauer said publicly that there was no danger of a Nazi resurgence; and the Minister of the Interior, Dr. Robert Lehr, scoffed at any right-wing political danger. He told me personally that the Nazis had "gone into permanent retirement." Here was an amazing paradox. Otto John was personally concerned with the rounding-up of the *Gauleiter* group cadets. Yet the head of the government he served, and the minister to whom he was personally responsible, disapproved of his actions and attempted to disown them. In retrospect, it can be safely said that the right-wing menace was not as serious as it appeared to be at the time. But German democracy was only half-fledged in 1953. Otto John was rendering it a useful service.

Typical of the uncertain mood of the German people at the time was the affair of the "Hamelin graves" in March, 1954. The German press in Lower Saxony "discovered" evidence of "secret" mass executions of "innocent" German citizens carried out by the British after the end of the war. These people were "so-called" war criminals, and the British authorities were subjected to all sorts of accusations. The *Hannoversche Allgemeine Zeitung* wrote that "gruesome executions" had taken place in which "the innocent were struck down along with the guilty." Other papers asserted that the British had refused to give information about their "victims" and that they ensured that "no honor was paid to the dead." The *Cellische Zeitung* wrote: "We will state quite clearly: these victims of conquerors' justice were refused even the due of a revolting murderer — in fact, a decent burial. The hiding of corpses and their destruction with chemicals are methods which have nothing to do with Western culture. Failure to inform relatives and the destruction of the lists of the dead are hideous crimes against humanity."

What were the true facts? The British authorities had executed 202 people who were convicted of revolting war crimes. They included such people as Josef Kramer ("the Beast of Belsen") and Irma Greise (the "Woman with the Whip"), who had maltreated and murdered. All of them had been tried publicly and executed after the public announcement of each sentence. In answer to questions, the British authorities had invariably supplied all details about the sentences, as well as times and dates of execution. The place of burial had not been kept "secret," but had been handed over to the German authorities.

Only a month after the last-mentioned revealing incident I had a long talk with Otto John. I knew that he was a worried man. In the previous year he had carried out mass arrests of members of a Communist underground, the so-called "Vulkan" spy ring. Around forty people were arrested. They were under the orders of the East German Government and the Soviet Control Commission in East Berlin. Their activities — the collection of military, political and economic information — had been co-ordinated by a cover-organization, "The Institute of Economic Studies." The spy ring had been active since 1951, and its members were chosen by the East German Minister of State Security, Wilhelm Zaisser, and the Deputy Minister of Foreign Affairs, Anton Ackerman. They were trained at a spy school at Forst-Zinna, in Saxony.

John had not approved of the orders which he had to carry out. He treated a Communist spy ring as a "foreign" organization, believed that he should watch it, infiltrate it, and not act prematurely. But he had plenty of other worries. His security-office was kept short of funds. Gehlen's counterintelligence service was spreading its tentacles into countries of the West, particularly France, and John disapproved of watching Germany's allies. The June 1953 rising inflamed his suspicions that Gehlen's men were acting in many cases as *agents provocateurs* and risking the lives of East German workers for political ends. His first boss, Robert Lehr, was succeeded in the fall of 1953 by the ex-Nazi Gerhard Schroeder — tough, keen but personally unfriendly to him.

And there was the strong tide of neo-Nazi feeling running. John told me that he was frightened by the re-emergence of glib nationalists in the German press, by the complacency of German government leaders and of the "Bonn hierarchy," by the audacity of ex-Nazis. (A few days before our talk the Nazi Lord Mayor of Hönningen, a village almost on Bonn's doorstep, was re-elected. He had sentenced three officers to death in 1944 for failing to blow up the Remagen bridge across the Rhine, which the Americans captured.) John used his phrase, "A great deal is perhaps being done in Germany, but nothing is being settled." Specifically, he meant that too little was being done to root out Nazism in the Federal Republic, and nothing was being done to reunify Germany.

In May, John was in the United States, and he came back to Germany more alarmed than ever. During his stay he had met people who talked with what seemed to him an appalling lack of discretion, and with astonishing cold-bloodedness. The theorists of a "preventive war" against the Soviet Union frankly horrified him. For they talked openly about launching nuclear war, without making allowance for the feelings of a man who knew that retribution would hit his own comparatively defenseless country first of all. To friends, John made no secret of his belief that some Americans were in a dangerous mood, and that the risk of war had become very great indeed.

What should a man of Otto John's standing have done in the circumstances? He carried no weight with Dr. Adenauer, who blamed him for failure to have all the men of the Vulkan spy ring imprisoned (this was actually the job of the Public Prosecutor). He was disliked by Gerhard Schroeder, who early in July 1954 was tactless enough to tell a group of German journalists that he was going to get rid of John (his own and his country's servant!). He could not publicize his views, and he believed that Europe was drifting into war.

On July 20, Otto John had what he imagined to be confirmation of his own worst fears. He went up to Berlin to attend the memorial service for the dead of the German resistance — "his" dead, as he saw it; and the image of his brother Hans was probably a lively one on that tenth anniversary of the attempt on Hitler's life. The service took place in the Dahlem parish church of Dr. Dibelius, Bishop of Berlin and Brandenburg. The preacher, who shall be nameless, felt constrained to make "Thou shalt not kill" the text of his sermon. No doubt he meant to point a Christian moral. He only succeeded in infuriating members of the congregation that day. There is nothing beautiful about assassination; but neither is there beauty in giving a moral lecture to men who had tried to rid their country of the most grotesque tyrant since Caligula.

There were reported to have been smug ex-Nazis in the congregation. Otto John was seen to be weeping when he came out of church. He will no longer talk openly about what he saw, heard and felt that day. At all events, he got through the rest of the day; he told his wife that he would be out meeting a friend that evening, and he was put down by his official chauffeur, Fritz Wussow, at 7:30 P.M. at the doors of the Maison de France — the French restaurant-bookshop and cultural-center on the Kurfurstendamm.

Perhaps half an hour later, John called on an acquaintance, Dr. Wolfgang Wohlgemueth, whose consulting rooms (unlike so many German doctors he really did belong to the medical profession) were close by at 175 Uhland Strasse. Wohlgemueth was a curious friend for a man like John. He was popular with women (John was shy with them, in spite of his good looks). He was a brilliant conversationalist and social butterfly (John liked to talk seriously). He was a familiar figure in Berlin's night clubs and flamboyant social circles; and he was a "drawing-room Bolshevik," who liked to chatter about the decent, bourgeois virtues of Communism. He was, in fact, one of the men whom John ought to have watched. Instead, he was one of the men to whom John liked to listen.

The attraction of opposites drew John to Wohlgemueth, like a drab moth to a candle-flame. The ostensible reason for this particular visit was to ask Wohlgemueth's help in regulating the pension claim of a mutual acquaintance. Whether this was the real reason or not, Otto John was driven in Dr. Wolfgang Wohlgemueth's car, later that night, to the Soviet sector. He did not return; and on July 23 the East German Government announced that he had "sought refuge in the German Democratic Republic." It is also known that he took no belongings at all with him, no official documents, nothing which could have been of the slightest interest to either the East Germans or the Russians. His disappearance was inexplicable; it has remained inexplicable ever since.

In Bonn the Federal Government tried at first to assume that nothing had happened to him. But on the night of July 23, he broadcast from East Germany in the following terms: "Germany is in danger of being rent asunder forever through the dispute between East and West; striking action is needed in order to summon all Germans to initiate the reunification of Germany. For this reason I have taken a resolute step on July 20, and have established contact with the Germans in the East. In the German Federal Republic I have been deprived of the basis of political activity. . . . Prudent and politically experienced men have confirmed to me in recent conversations that German policies are in a blind alley." The trend of what he had to say was definite enough, but his voice was shaky and slow. Even on July 26, the Federal Minister of the Interior, Dr. Schroeder, was announcing that John had either been kidnapped or "enticed and outwitted." On August 6, he offered a reward of half a million marks for anyone who produced the solution of his disappearance.

On July 26, John broadcast again from East Berlin. He had in the meantime been accused of being a babbler, drunkard, a homosexual and an inefficient. As far as babbling went, his office was better run than most West German ministries, and there had been no single serious scandal in it. He certainly drank, and sometimes a lot — but he was not a drunkard. He had no record at all as a homosexual, in a country in which there are plenty of homosexuals, some of them in high places. He was not outstandingly efficient, by German standards, but that would not be regarded as a crime in other countries. His second broadcast was certainly colored by salmon-pink indignation. He claimed that American foreign policy was one-sided and dangerous, that Dr. Adenauer was pursuing a purely inflexible and unproductive line of policy (Mr. George Kennan accused the Chancellor of the same thing four years later), and that he had followed the dictates of his conscience in "going East."

On August 11 John presided at a press conference in East Berlin. He told 300 German and foreign press correspondents that he had gone to East Berlin of his own free will, that American diplomacy was paving the way for a third world war, that West German remilitarization was under way.

He explained his distrust of anti-Communism — "The British have grasped the fact that Communism cannot simply be eliminated, but the Americans cannot or will not understand this." At another point he said, "It became clear to me while I was in America that Germany was being forced to provide soldiers for an American crusade against Communism."

He referred, at first in short clipped sentences, to the return of the Nazis in West Germany. He reeled off a list of them — Professor Oberländer, heading the Federal Ministry of Refugees; Ernst Achenbach, sitting in the inner councils of the Free Democratic Party; Werner Naumann, the neo-Nazi conspirator; Dr. Paul Leverkuehn, the "reformed" President of the "reforming" Europa-Union; Otto Abetz, the tricky, socialite ex-Nazi ex-Ambassador to Vichy France. He referred to the former generals who had made their virulent, premature come-backs: Ramcke, von Manstein, Kesselring. He castigated the counterintelligence service of his rival, Gehlen.

He played down the part of Wolfgang Wohlgemueth, who was "only an intermediary." He denied that he was a Communist, and described himself as "a liberal, which I have always been." He explained his departure from West Germany in the words: "Everything suddenly crystallized in my brain — I knew what I had to do." And he explained his choice of East Germany for his "base" with "One must work in one's own country — one cannot do political work in a foreign country." (But that was, of course, just what he had to try to do.)

The "John Episode" had various repercussions. The Social Democrats called for Schroeder's head. They argued that he should have kept a check on his subordinate — which was utterly beside the point. They should have cited Schroeder's monumental lack of tact in talking openly about dismissing a man who had, at least until then, been loyal to him. Pained and harassed, Schroeder told a jeering Bundestag on September 16 what little he knew. John had not been a homosexual or drunkard. He had never belonged to a Communist organization. (It was a fascinating commentary that the Gehlen organization was able to vouch for this. The Germans have in the past been addicted to setting rival intelligence services to watch each other.) John had betrayed no official secrets, not even while in East Germany. He did not even have a bank account in Switzerland! (This was something with which a great many influential Germans had provided themselves during the Korean War.)

Dr. Gerhard Schroeder did not offer to resign (seven years later he was still Minister of the Interior). If ever an occasion called for an admission of ministerial responsibility, this was it. His alibi was that the affair was "a national catastrophe, which hits all of us equally" and "a piece of enemy action in the Cold War." The principle of ministerial responsibility is not practiced. in Bonn. Schroeder at least set out to clear up the mess promptly and with his usual efficiency. He received a 228 to 123 vote of confidence in the Bundestag.

The second effect of the "John Episode" was a surge of anti-British feeling. The old, disproved story that the British had forced John's appointment was raked up again. John's work for the BBC was remembered, or rather misremembered, and he was written about again and again as a "former British secret-service agent." One paper published a cartoon showing John Bull pointing at Otto John and saying, "Give him a good job! He's a good German, because he's betrayed his Fatherland!"

The survivors of the Resistance to Hitler came in for their share of recrimination. The right-wing press had vicious things to say about people who "proved themselves twice over to be traitors to their country." The Federal Minister for All-German Affairs, Jakob Kaiser, was bitterly assailed in the press. (The only reason was that he, too, had struggled against Hitler.) The episode gave fresh impetus to the second "stab in the back" legend. After the First World War the mutinying sailors at Kiel and the workers out on strike in Berlin were blamed for Germany's military defeat; in 1945, evidently, the people responsible were John and his fellows. It was a convenient tale, which accorded well with the consecutive conventional German descriptions of the end of the war. At first it was called, blankly, *die Niederlage* (defeat). Then it became *der Zusammenbruch* (collapse). And then *die Überrollung* (the process of being overwhelmed by superior numbers). Now, *der Dolchstoss* (stab in the back) — as in 1918.

John's supposed defection may have affected the reasoning

powers of the Federal President, the venerable and respected Professor Theodor Heuss. On November 7, 1954, the four Great Powers released the aged and ailing Baron Konstantin von Neurath from the major war criminals' jail at Spandau, in West Berlin. Von Neurath had been "Protector" of the dependency of Bohemia-Moravia, created by Hitler after the rape of Czechoslovakia. Perhaps he was unlucky to have been classified as a "major" rather than a "minor" war criminal; the shocking massacre of Lidice, at least, was after his day. But this thought hardly excuses Professor Heuss's telegram to him: WITH PLEASURE AND SATISFACTION I HAVE LEARNED ON MY RETURN FROM A SHORT JOURNEY THAT THE NEWS OF THE LAST FEW DAYS HAS BEEN CONFIRMED, AND THAT YOUR MARTYRDOM OF THESE RECENT YEARS HAS NOW BEEN ENDED.

The British and American press seized on that word "martyrdom." After making due allowances for German feelings, it still seemed inappropriate to place Neurath in a bracket with Saint Peter and Saint Paul. Heuss then made things much worse by issuing an idiotic statement to the effect that there was a difference between the words *Martyrertum* and *Martyrtum*, and he had used the one which merely implied "passive" suffering. With the enthusiasm of the short-sighted detective, a British newspaperman looked up the two words in Cassell's most voluminous dictionary. He found that they meant the same thing.

Nor did it help matters when a Federal Government official suggested that the President's words had really referred to Neurath's ear trouble and failing eyesight. For, whether in Spandau or his Württemberg home, these afflictions remained with him. Professor Heuss's sympathy was, in any case, not an isolated gesture. Dr. Adenauer sent von Neurath a more discreet telegram, and the head of the Federal administrative office in Berlin, Herr Vockel, met him personally at the gates of Spandau, presented him with a bouquet of yellow roses (usually reserved for film stars and divas) and put an official car at his disposal.

How different was to be the experience of Otto John, when he eventually surfaced again in the Western world! In the meantime he had lapsed into almost complete obscurity. First he was taken to an isolated village in the Caucasus and interrogated ceaselessly by the Soviet security service for eight weeks there. He was then placed, under guard, in a villa on the Zeuthener Lake, just east of Berlin. In December 1954 John took up his residence at this villa, and started work on a book entitled *I Choose Germany,* for which he was to receive 30,000 East Marks and a retainer of 3000 marks a month. He wrote one or two newspaper articles, and gave talks for the Communist-controlled National Front.

Already John's ideas were beginning to change. There had been no rush of young West Germans to get into uniform and train for an eastward crusade at the dictates of President Eisenhower. The neo-Nazi political parties were losing votes all the time, and one of their leaders, the anti-Semite Wolfgang Hedler, had been dragged out of the Bundestag by Social Democrats and thrown on his head in the street outside. Already the bellicose words of some hothead in the Pentagon seemed half a lifetime away. And in the political sense, things were not getting worse but better in West Germany. Ex-General Kesselring, indeed, led his Stahlhelm supporters in a torchlight procession through the streets of Goslar; and in Hamburg the man who had helped to murder a Foreign Minister, Walter Rathenau, more than thirty years before, was working on a film-script of his victim's life. But Germany was quieting down, and Walter Huppenkothen had even been sentenced at last to the imprisonment which he so richly deserved.

John began to think of escape, wrote to his wife for a pair of stout walking shoes which he had used on a holiday in Switzerland, smuggled messages to the Ministry of Justice in Bonn and was informed that he could return "without risk" and would only need to "answer a few questions." He rehearsed his escape from the building of the Humboldt University in East Berlin, where he was giving a series of talks, and actually carried it out on December 12, 1955. He slipped out of a side door, after "losing" his permanent escort in the crowd of students, got into the car of a Danish journalist, Hendrik Bonde-Henriksen, and was driven by him into West Berlin. There he handed himself over to the Federal authorities, was put on the plane for Cologne and submitted to "voluntary confinement" while his case was investigated.

On December 23, John was formally arrested and moved in secret to Mannheim jail, where he was held incommunicado. A West German Government spokesman facetiously remarked that he was being held "because he may be afraid of being kidnaped again." Asked whether it was then admitted that John had been kidnaped on July 20, 1954, the spokesman said he had made "an unfortunate slip of the tongue." But he agreed that John was not being granted bail. He might escape to a foreign country, since he had many friends abroad, "particularly in England." This was another "unfortunate slip of the tongue," for the implication was that the British would not extradite him if he arrived at Lucie John's Hampstead flat.

In Cologne, where she put a new flat, close to the university, in order for him, Lucie John told me that her husband's escape should be regarded as a "gain for the West." "I always knew in my heart that he did not go over of his own free will," she said. "Now I know this for a fact. There were four good reasons why he could never put himself at the disposal of a totalitarian regime. He fought against Nazism as a member of the Resistance. He dealt firmly with Communist plotters in his job as head of the West German security service. He was religious. And he was a Westerner in thought and deed."

Lucie John told me the story which her husband later repeated to me. This, according to Otto John, was what happened on the night of July 20, 1954.

He called at Wohlgemueth's consulting-rooms in the Uhland Strasse at around 8:20 P.M. He wanted to discuss the question of a disability pension for a friend with him. Wohlgemueth gave him a cup of coffee which must have been drugged. He felt sleepy but agreed to drive home with Wohlgemueth. He remembered saying, "For God's sake don't drive so fast, Wowo, or we'll have a smash." Then he blacked out.

He came-to in a darkened room in Soviet headquarters at Karlshorst. He must have vomited, for his jacket had been pressed but was still showing stains which had not been there before. He was interrogated forcefully, then told that he had better make a statement on the East German Radio to say that he was not going back to the West. He believed that this offered a better chance of finding a way out than if he refused to "co-operate" and was subjected to "truth drugs" and torture which could break him down. From then on, he had acted under duress but with as much circumspection as possible. He betrayed no worthwhile secrets, paid only lip service to Communist propaganda campaigns, and escaped as soon as he had a fair chance to do so.

John told his wife this story in December 1955. By an interesting coincidence a former Communist official, Robert Bialek, who had fled to the West in 1953, disappeared on February 4, 1956, in West Berlin. A workman found him in West Berlin lying senseless on the floor of a lavatory in a Wilmersdorf flat belonging to a former East German People's Policeman called Drzewiecki. The workman had helped Drzewiecki and another man (subsequently identified as the People's Police Inspector for the East Berlin borough of Rummelsburg) to put Bialek into a car. That was the last seen in West Berlin of Bialek and indeed of the East German agent Drzewiecki and the East German Police Inspector Hellwig. John's story, in fact, might have been true.

The State Prosecutor came to a different conclusion after holding John incommunicado in a series of jails for eleven months. He was tried by the Karlsruhe High Court on November 11, and sentenced on December 23, 1956, to four years' imprisonment. In a strange summing-up, the court gave six main reasons for its verdict. He had not shown "sufficient horror" over his alleged betrayal by Wohlgemueth; he had written letters to his wife saying he went over of his own free will; he could not have stood up at a big press conference if the East Germans had not been sure of his co-operation; and he had told a visitor to Weimar who met him there that he had gone willingly to East Berlin.

These first four reasons were of doubtful validity. John, for instance, could hardly have written in different terms to his wife or told the truth to a stranger whom he met in Weimar. But the two most compelling reasons given by the court for pronouncing John guilty of treason were even less credible. One witness, a Fräulein Sievers, had been in a Halle jail at the time of John's disappearance. East German officials asked her questions there about John's "known character." They told her nothing, but the Karlsruhe court assumed that she would not have been interrogated had John not gone across of his own free will! It would be hard to think of a more fatuous legal *non sequitur*. In addition, the court held that Wohlgemueth was not a kidnaper, because he came back to his West Berlin consulting room during the night of July 20-21 and took away some documents. But the Russians or East Germans could well have instructed him to do this. And if he had a clear conscience, why did he not remain in West Berlin in order to tell the true story of John's disappearance?

These were not the only curiosities of the John case. The President of the High Court, Dr. Geier, said that he was "not a criminal in the eyes of the law." Yet he sentenced him to four years' imprisonment, when the Public Prosecutor had asked for a sentence of only two years. The probable length of his sentence had been discussed with an appalling lack of discretion beforehand. While he was under arrest, John was examined by a psychoanalyst whom the prosecution had instructed to produce a "character report" — a document which was likely to prejudice the court (it probably did). A principal charge pressed against John was that he had "betrayed false State secrets" — in fact, that he had "betrayed" a nonexistent secret codicil to the European Defense Agreement. A secret codicil would have been contrary to the Federal Constitution, and it hardly became the High Court to treat this "revelation" as an indictable offense.

Finally, a special Parliamentary Commission was formed in 1955 to examine the John case. Six months after he was sentenced, it found that "final clarification is as yet impossible."

The curiosities of the John case were thrown into even sharper relief when Wolfgang Wohlgemueth was in due course brought to trial before the same High Court. Wohlgemueth could not keep away from West Berlin, although he knew well enough that the police were on the look-out for him. He paid one clandestine visit too many, and was caught by them on February

12, 1958. The bright lights of the Kurfurstendamm may have been his undoing, but a near-miraculous reprieve was in store for him. On December 18, 1958, Wohlgemueth was found not guilty of treasonable connections by the High Court. He was embraced by friends and handed bouquets of red and white carnations.

While John was refused bail, Wohlgemueth was granted it. His friends, however, were not in England but on the other side of the Iron Curtain. John, whether drugged or not, did not know where he was going on the night of July 20, 1954. But Wohlgemueth did. He drove him there, and the High Court itself announced that his contact man was a leading member of the Communist-controlled Socialist Unity Party, Franz Dahlem. The court ruled that Wohlgemueth was not a "free agent" while in East Berlin; it ruled that Otto John was, although he was demonstrably under guard and could produce witnesses. The prosecution treated John toughly; it characterized Wohlgemueth as "only a subordinate" and "not a Communist, but sometimes liked to talk of himself as being one."

The court saw nothing significant in the fact that Wohlgemueth wanted the post of chief doctor at East Berlin's Charité Hospital. This post could only be given to him by the Communist authorities. The court felt that his desire for this plum job was "simple ambition." Was it? A job of that kind had other interesting possibilities. One need only recall the beneficial influence exerted over Heinrich Himmler by his masseur, Felix Kersten, during the war. A surgeon has unique opportunities for extracting confidences and, by an interesting coincidence, Wohlgemueth had worked as chief-assistant to the sinister Dr. Theodor Morell, the quack injection expert who treated Adolf Hitler. Finally, the court ruled out a mass of evidence given about Wohlgemueth's political leanings and casual statements. It seemed to be intent on finding him not guilty, for it had ruled two years before that Otto John's guilt rested on the fact that he had gone over willingly. The court had no intention of proving itself wrong.

The John and Wohlgemueth cases were not the only ones of their kind. An employee of the Federal Ministry of Defense went over to East Berlin, apparently of his free will, but escaped when he found he was going to be kept there. The Federal Minister of Finance, Dr. Fritz Schaeffer, suddenly visualized himself as the savior of German unity and went across the sector boundary of Berlin at the beginning of 1956. He wanted to see the Soviet Ambassador, but he found himself instead closeted with the East German Minister of Defense, Vinzenz Mueller. Minister Schaeffer went to considerable lengths in order to avoid admitting what he had done, and it took the threat of a Parliamentary inquiry to pin him down.

Treasonable connections were imputed to Dr. Viktor Agartz, a leading West German trade-unionist who allowed his economic news service to be partially financed by the East Germans. As it happens, the East German authorities level the same accusation against all East German citizens who accept the ten marks' "travel-money" offered to them in the Federal Republic by the Government. When questioned about his political motives, Agartz said that he wanted all-German talks, and believed in the military neutralization of a united Germany. (So did the American diplomat, George Kennan.) Agartz talked about a synthesis between East German Communism and West German Social Democracy, and the faces of his judges grew stony. But those same judges were assuredly among the millions who praised the East German, Dr. Wolfgang Harich, who went to prison for wanting the same political synthesis as Dr. Agartz.

Only a short time before Otto John's return and arrest, the Federal Government proclaimed that it was the inalienable right of every German to move freely between the two parts of his country. Such a pronouncement evidently meant exactly nothing.

Was Otto John wrong — rather than foolish — to venture into East Berlin, give way to threats there, and come to an unsound compromise while searching for a road to German reunification? For this is probably what happened. While he was worrying about West German democracy, the Federal regime was young and by no means as solidly based as it became after ten years of Adenauer rule. And even in November 1956, while John was being tried, I find that I made these notes:

"Otto Brauetigam, who decided that Jews in the wartime occupied territories should be killed 'regardless of the economic consequences,' is back in the *Auswärtiges Amt*."

"General Lothar Rendulic, who strung-up alleged deserters in the last days of the war, is contributing regularly to a Free Democratic weekly."

"General Kurt (Panzer) Meyer, of the S.S., who was imprisoned for his part in the murder of prisoners-of-war, has been given a new car, a house and a civic reception on release."

"Konstantin Hierl, who said that land reclamation was 'too honorable a service' for concentration camp prisoners, was eulogized when he died."

And in 1959 a Munich publicist estimated that at least forty dangerous war criminals were still at large. The Ministry of Justice in *Land* Baden-Württemberg found that there were sixty-one judges and other senior legal officers in this one corner of Germany who had served on Nazi summary and special courts. The same *Land* found that it was still employing 152 former full-time members of the Gestapo.

Hag-ridden Otto John may have been, moving in a nightmare in which he was forever seeing the faces of the tormentors of his dead brother and friends, obsessed with hatred of the forces which Hitler mobilized and which live on, burrowing like weevils into the body of the state. Hag-ridden and haunted, he may have lost his head and — because of the severity of his punishment — his soul as well. But Otto John's tragedy is an intrinsic part of the German tragedy provoked by Hitler. Human frustrations as bitter as his will endure as long as the German problem remains unsolved. And for so long, too, there will be Germans who will ask themselves where their loyalties ultimately lie — to a "set-piece" Western alliance, which happens to include Rump Germany, or to an ideal of unity for which any sacrifice should not be too great. Implicit in this choice is the stress imposed on every thinking German by the unnatural division of his country. The stress was too great for Otto John, when he chose the sleep-walkers' path to East Berlin and to dire disgrace.

10

The German Conscience

What sort of woman does a good German most like to possess? A blonde? Not really, A brunette, then? No! Then what? — An Aryan grandmother.
— GENERAL J. H. MORGAN, *Assize of Arms*

The non-Nordic man occupies an intermediate position between the Nordics and the animals, just about next to the anthropoid ape. He is therefore not a complete man. Better and more apt is the designation: subhuman.
— HERMANN GAUCH, *Neue Grundlagen zur
Rassenforschung*, 1935

I have five million reasons why I do not want to go to Germany.
— SIR LEWIS NAMIER, Professor of Modern History at
Oxford University

I N November 1937 I was walking down the Türkenstrasse in Munich late one night with two friends. We came to a corner and found there, hung on the wall at head height, one of the so-called *Stürmerkasten.* These were boxes roughly two feet square with wooden frames and with a pane of glass over the salacious, anti-Semitic cartoons of Julius Streicher's infamous paper *Der Stürmer.* We stopped to look at them by the light of a street lamp, disgusted in advance but morbidly interested all the same.

The first cartoon showed a German "Aryan" girl being fondled revoltingly by a Jewish doctor. The next was devoted to the conventional theme of the chamber pot on head, which Germans never failed to find funny (it is interesting that jokes to do with chamber pots or lavatory seats and chains and flushes have not

ErichAndres, Hamburg-Altona

Young Germany Brings Flowers for Anne Frank
to Belsen's Mass-burial Place, 1957

been anywhere near so popular since 1945). These were the sort of pictures one expected to see, and we were in no way surprised by their crude vulgarity.

But the third cartoon we looked at showed Mr. (later Sir) Anthony Eden in a lavatorial setting. All three of us were British, and this picture aroused a militant spirit in us. There were no stones in the Türkenstrasse, no loose bricks or other missiles. After some thought we smashed the *Stürmerkasten* with our big, heavy house keys (we were all living with German families) and removed ourselves quickly as lights came on in several houses.

Two days later the Munich papers announced an outrage in the Türkenstrasse, where "Government and Party property" had been wantonly destroyed. All Jewish families living within three streets of the place had therefore been handsomely fined. We went to the corner on the Türkenstrasse, chalked up THIS WAS DONE BY ENGLISHMEN, NOT BY JEWS alongside the empty and battered box. But we guessed that it would do no good; Germans would think this a "Jewish trick" to shift the blame onto somebody else.

A petty incident, of course, in comparison with the horror of the *Kristall-Nacht*, then only a year off, and of the unbelievable atrocities perpetrated by the Germans against the Jews from then on. Yet it was fairly typical, as typical as the apathy of the German public towards what they could not help notice was happening. A whole nation was in the process of being inured to Hitler's "final solution" for European Jewry — its extermination.

One of the most usual mistakes made about anti-Semitism in Germany is to suppose that it was invented by Hitler. This is also a popular explanation among the Germans themselves. Hitler can be blamed for everything which went wrong or which was of itself demonstrably wrong — for the attacks on Czechoslovakia and Poland, the organization of the war on two fronts which he originally set out to avoid, for persecutions and ultimate defeat (at this stage almost every German is likely to remark, "Of course, he did build the Autobahns"). Anti-Semitism in Germany, however, is obviously as old as the history of German Jewry. But the vital impetus was given to it by that spirit of rabid racial arrogance born in Bismarck's Germany out of three brilliantly successful wars and the foundation of the German Empire. Anti-Semitism was the inevitable adjunct of pan-Germanism.

One of the real evangelists of Nazi racialism died only in 1954 at the age of eighty and in complete obscurity. Adolf Lanz — he called himself "Dr. Georg Adolf Josef Lancz von Liebenfels" — was a defrocked Roman Catholic priest who left the Church hurriedly in 1899 after an affair with a woman. As a priest he worked in the Abbey of Heiligenkreuz near Vienna, where he spent much time in contemplation of the tomb of Duke Heinrich the Cruel ("der Grausam"), son of Leopold VI of Austria. The tomb shows the Duke with his foot on a small, dark subhuman representing the Devil.

At Heiligenkreuz Adolf Lanz had a dream in which Knights Templars of the twelfth century appeared to him and told him what his task was to be. This was to propagate the "gospel" that the world is divided into two races engaged in a struggle to the death: on the one hand the blond Aryans represent the Forces of Light and could lead mankind back into an earthly Garden of Eden; on the other the dark, malign subhumans (specifically including the Jews) represent the Forces of Darkness. It is the mission of the Aryans to fetter and even liquidate them.

In 1905 Lanz founded a monthly journal called *Ostara*. Its third number was entitled "An Easter Message on the Mastery of the European Races." These were the Nordics. And the "subject-races" included the dark-skinned peoples of the Mediterranean littoral, as well as "Asiatics," Jews and "subhuman ape people." Up to 1914 about seventy numbers of *Ostara* were published, and the following were a few of the means which the paper recommended for making the dream of the Aryan world come true:

Abolition of the freedom of the press. This was necessary, Lanz pointed out, because the Aryans were in a minority. The Nazis started out from exactly the same premise.

Organization of human stud-farms. Lanz maintained that the Aryan birth rate had to be stimulated. Hitler established stud-farms by his *Lebensborn* experiment, in which S.S. men were coupled with blue-eyed, blonde volunteers of the right physique and blood-groups. Their babies were "gifts to the Führer."

Prostitution as a means of polluting the subhumans. Contraceptives were to be encouraged for subhumans, so that their birth rate would fall.

Sterilization and castration. Both were carried out by the Nazis.

Mass deportations and mass liquidations. Lanz wrote that all "inferior" races should be "banished to the jungle and live there with their gorilla and mandrill cousins."

Typical of Lanz's mystic, inverted-erotic trend of thought was his veneration of Fremiet's statue, *Geraubt,* which depicted a blonde girl struggling in the grasp of a gorilla. To Lanz the gorilla typified subhumanity; the rape of the girl symbolized the masochistic abasement of the "Aryan race." Some of the drawings in *Ostara* were copied meticulously by Streicher's *Stürmer.* Lanz selected the swastika as his emblem and hoisted a swastika flag on the tower of the ruined Werfenstein Castle in Austria in 1907. At about the same time he introduced "Heil" as the conventional greeting. And around 1909 Hitler began buying *Ostara* at a tobacconist's shop in Vienna's Felberstrasse and discussing its contents with his down-at-heels cronies in the café of the *Goldener Kugel.*

Lanz's repugnant ideas must have been immensely attractive to Hitler — socially and sexually frustrated and often out of work. But Lanz's "New Order of the Knights Templars" (the renegade priest used to dress up as its First Prior) was only one of many similar societies which burgeoned during that era of German material prosperity and spiritual decline. Writers like Marr, Ammer, Lagarde and Lange founded their own "racialist" groups in the same period. It is very likely that the Bismarckian-Wilhelminian era has left more binding habits and traditions behind it than the interlude of Nazi rule. This in turn suggests that there was no valid reason at all why German anti-Semitism should have perished with Hitler in the ruins of the Reich Chancellery, or even in the P.O.W. cages and in the jails for war criminals, where the most venomous of his followers were very properly shut up. Nor did that happen.

Certainly, anti-Semitism was slow to show its head again in postwar Germany. The reasons for this, however, were not moral but material. The tracking-down of Nazis, which was bound to develop some of the attributes of a witch hunt, was carried out in the face of extreme difficulties. Whatever is said to the contrary today, the Nazis constituted something like an elite. The most damaging thing about the German community was that — with honorable exceptions — it did not merely tolerate Nazism but subscribed freely to it. After the war the elite of the Nazi movement itself, the S.S., organized a sort of freemasonry. They smuggled some of their members out of the country. They gave others forged passports and new names. They met S.S. criminals returning from Russian P.O.W. camps and told them where to seek legal advice. They organized their own tracing service. All the while there were a great many "wanted men" in Germany. It paid them, and their friends, to lie low.

Any open admission of anti-Semitism was tantamount to inviting an inquiry into one's antecedents by Allied as well as by German authorities. Under the cold compress of Allied occupation Germans remained the greatest conformists in the civilized world. Anti-Semitism had been pronounced wrong; very well, it *was* wrong. Those who wanted to indulge in it had to find discreet methods. In 1947 the desecration of Jewish cemeteries began. The police did nothing about it; except in one case, the Allied authorities did not know what to do. At a little village near Trier the French military authorities mustered all grown men and put them to work repairing the damage. There was never any trouble in that area after that.

In April 1950, the weekly Jewish paper, *Allgemeine,* in Düsseldorf, received leaflets through the post telling all Jews to get out of Germany (there were only 20,000 survivors out of the prewar Jewish community of 670,000). The Federal Chancellor, Konrad Adenauer, received an anonymous letter which termed the Nazi campaign to exterminate the Jews a failure, because some Jews had been left alive, and which appealed for "a new leader to free Germany from the Jewish yoke."

In the same month a half-Jewish witness at the trial in Hamburg of Veit Harlan — who produced the film *Jew Suess* for the Nazis — was physically threatened by well-dressed, prosperous and ostensibly respectable citizens. Yet there had been only one outstanding, public statement of anti-Semitism up to that time. This was made by a Rendsburg bank clerk and member of the right-wing "German Party" in Schleswig-Holstein, Wolfgang Hedler. He proclaimed the responsibility of France and Britain for the war, the "blood guilt" of the men who resisted Hitler, and the "treachery" of the Jews in bringing about Germany's defeat. "The only doubt in my mind," he said at a public meeting, "is whether the gas chamber was the most effective way of getting rid of the Jews." Hedler was later ejected from his seat in the Federal Parliament in Bonn.

Two years later anti-Semitic manifestations were still not on the increase. In Föhrenwald camp, south of Munich, certainly, there was a shocking incident when the Bavarian police staged a raid in the belief that there was black-market traffic among the Jewish displaced persons there. Lorry loads of police drove into the camp with sirens screaming. The Jews, almost all of whom had lost relatives and even all of their families in the concentration camps, feared some gross repetition of their sufferings. Jewish women lay down on the road in front of the lorries and refused to move. Some of them were pregnant. The men formed up in order to prevent the police entering their huts. Jews were beaten, kicked, and cursed in such terms as "Stinking Yids!" and "We'll put you in the gas ovens yet!"

The incident was revealing, since it showed what lurked just beneath the survace — even in the minds of the guardians of the law. But in 1952 the Federal Government signed a debts agreement with Israel, by which it undertook to provide 3000 million marks' worth of goods as their German contribution to resettling half a million Jews in Israel. And in the same year there were no anti-Jewish demonstrations at the Munich trial of Philipp Auerbach, the former head of the Restitutions Claims Office in Bavaria. Auerbach had misapplied government funds, partly in order to get something done quickly for the many Jews who had lost everything, and partly because he was a dictatorial and arrogant man who refused to take advice. One sum of 250,000 marks had been distributed among one hundred and eleven claimants who were never subsequently traced. Auerbach, a Jew who had spent the war years in Ausschwitz and Buchenwald concentration camps, refused to account for the money.

With lamentable spinelessness the American authorities failed to put Auerbach before a military court and dismiss him for inefficiency. Instead, a German court, in which an ex-Nazi, Dr. Mulzer, presided, sentenced Auerbach to two-and-a-half years' imprisonment. On August 16, 1952, he committed suicide in the Josefinum Hospital, where he had retired a year earlier with diabetes and kidney trouble.

A Bavarian whom I met on the next day remarked, "A pity the swine didn't do himself in a lot sooner." Anti-Semites were beginning to pluck up courage. A year later a writer, George Mikes, described his conversation with one of the most stupidly wrong-minded of them: "The German girl student told me that she did not like the Jews very much. Did she perhaps hate them? Yes, she did. Did she know many Jews? No, not very many. Did she know one at all? Well, no, as a matter of fact, none. And had she ever seen a Jew? Not to the best of her knowledge."

Mikes described, too, how everyone he met in Munich declaimed against the Jewish "ghetto black-market" in the Moehlstrasse. He went to the Moehlstrasse, but could find no trace of it. It had, as it happened, ceased to exist. But there never had been anything very strange about it. In the burst of sympathy for the survivors among Hitler's victims more food and tobacco parcels were sent from America, Britain and elsewhere than were strictly needed. The Jews bartered much of their contents, and undoubtedly made quick profits. Who should grudge them these? They had lost everything they had ever possessed. And, for that matter, flourishing black markets existed in every railway-station square in Germany. The Moehlstrasse market was an object of self-righteous distaste only because it was Jewish.

The Jews and others whom the Nazis persecuted had plenty of their own grounds for grievance. In 1954, two exceptionally courageous German journalists, Helmut Hammerschmidt and Michael Mansfeld, produced a short radio program describing the different treatment accorded to ex-Nazis who had been in state service and Nazi persecutees. The financial compensation of the ex-Nazis was assured by a law passed in 1951. It was quickly given a detailed supplement, nine implementary ordinances and one hundred and twenty administrative instructions. Compensation for victims of Nazism was provided for only in 1953, and by a law which, in the course of one year, was given no supplement, no administrative instructions and only one implementary order.

The law for the ex-Nazis laid down instructions for the distribution of quotas among claimants. The law for Nazi persecutees did not. The law for the ex-Nazis provided state assistance for all who had suffered any loss of livelihood. The law for Nazi persecutees laid down that claimants must be more than 50 per cent disabled for work. The law for the ex-Nazis debarred only proved war criminals, and Gestapo officials still serving in May 1945. The law for the Nazi persecutees debarred anyone who had committed a crime or breach of the peace (this included resisting arrest by the Gestapo!). An ex-Nazi official's widow was entitled to the pension which her husband would have drawn at the age of sixty-five. A Jewish merchant's widow was entitled to the minimum disability pension which her husband would have drawn at thirty-five or forty, his age when the Nazis murdered him.

Hammerschmidt and Mansfeld estimated that more than half the Jews who had sought refuge in the United States had already died there without securing one cent of compensation, that it was taking more than four years for a claimant to get even a small part-payment, and that the whole business of compensation of the victims of the Nazis would take twenty years. History will show that their predictions were not wide of the mark.

History may prove, too, that whole classes of Hitler's victims will have deliberately been debarred from the compensation to which they were entitled. The outstanding example of this was provided by the so-called "Persecutees on grounds of nationality," mainly Poles and Yugoslavs who did not return to their Communist-controlled homelands. For twelve years after the war cases multiplied of German law courts who refused to pay compensation to people who had been imprisoned in the worst of the concentration camps and shockingly maltreated there, who had lost limbs and livelihood as well as all their possessions and many of their relatives. German law courts are more casuistic than the Jesuits. Polish priests who protested against Nazi barbarity were ruled to have "opposed the German military occupation." Polish boys who worked for the Underground were declared to have committed acts of sabotage. Polish and Yugoslav schoolteachers who would not pass on Nazi ideology to their children were ruled to have incited civil disobedience to the occupying power. Up to 1959 thousands of "national persecutees" received no compensation whatever.

By 1954 the Jewish community had grown only to around 24,-000. Its average age was the astonishingly high one of fifty-four. Not a single Jewish marriage had taken place in two years in the city of Bremen (population 400,000). Of 250 Jews in Hannover only 13 were in the "marriage-bracket," between the ages of twenty and thirty. There were only 150 Jews at German universities and technical colleges. Their very inconspicuousness was one reason for the apparent absence of serious anti-Semitism. But a B'nai B'rith team from New York found no basic lessening of anti-Semitism, no readiness to evaluate the German past, and, instead, that significant German amalgam, "a haunting feeling of shame, accompanied by a deep sense of their own rectitude as psychological compensation."

In 1954 and 1955, desecrations of Jewish cemeteries were on the increase; but no single arrest was made on account of them and the police always claimed they were the work of "children playing" (one of their "games," in that case, being to carry off and then smash tombstones weighing four hundred pounds). A Hannover court ruled that tombstones from one Jewish cemetery could be used as building material, as the cemetery was "in a poor state" and was "no longer an object of piety."

In Berlin people were battered by uniformed thugs and told to "go back to the concentration camps" when they failed to stand up to sing the (officially forbidden) first verse of the old national anthem at a German Party meeting. Abusive letters to Berlin Jews announced that, "We are back again! Berlin will soon be rid of her Jews. Our hour has struck!" And the head of the Jewish old people's home in Berlin received this: "Germany will be purged of the Jews once more! Target date for the operation, February 27, 1956." Large sections of the Christian Democratic and Free Democratic Government parties opposed ratification of the Israeli Debt Agreement in Parliament, and it was only passed because one hundred and fifty Opposition Social Democrats supported the government. In an interview given to the paper *Die Welt*, Dr. Adenauer said that the German people had overcome the hatred of the Jews engendered by the Nazis. But a public opinion Gallup Poll showed that 55 per cent of those asked were friendly to the Jews; 22 per cent were "neutral" and 22 per cent were still "unfriendly." Had the proportion of the "unfriendly" ever been any larger?

It was probably in the realization that an acute psychological problem was not solved by the passage of a mere ten years that the Federal President, Professor Theodor Heuss, sent a message to the German people in which he urged them never to forget the sense of "collective shame" which they should feel for the deeds committed in their name by the Nazis. He urged, too, "moral" as well as material restitution, and his words carried so much weight that in a period of a few weeks the Jewish *Allgemeine* had letters from more than three hundred young Germans who wanted to go to Israel to learn about the country and work for nothing for their hosts there. Others offered to join Israel's armed forces if she were attacked by her Arab neighbors. One former S.S. man became an Israeli citizen.

Yet there were unhappy signs that anti-Semitism was far from dead or even decaying. Not only the ex-generals, with their excuses and accusations, were back in the literary field: they were being joined by far more sinister relics of the Nazi past. At the beautiful little village of Leoni on the Starnberger See near Munich, the Druffel Verlag publishing house was founded by Helmut Sündermann, former deputy press chief in Josef Goebbel's Nazi Propaganda Ministry. These were some of the books which Sündermann published:

Old Enemy — What Now? by Helmut Sündermann — a violent attack on Britain.

Smile . . . and Conceal Your Tears by Julius Lippert, former Nazi Burgomaster of Berlin, who compared Hitler's services to Germany with those of Disraeli to England.

England — Nuremberg — Spandau by Ilse Hess, wife of the imprisoned major war criminal, Rudolf Hess. A defense of her husband's politics and ideas.

Supreme Beings by the Prince of Schaumburg-Lippe, a former high-ranking S.S. officer. An account of the S.S., extolling them.

Between London and Moscow by Ilse Hess, which includes an account of her and her friends celebrating Hitler's birthdays since his death.

The Druffel Verlag was in no way unique. Under Leonhard Schlüter the Göttinger Verlagsanstalt was beginning to publish books by Franz von Papen, who saw Hitler into power and served him faithfully as Ambassador to Ankara even after the Nazis had murdered his personal secretary, and by Friedrich Grimm, the most unrepentant apologist of the Nazi regime. In his *Politische Justiz, die Krankheit unserer Zeit,* Grimm wrote that the purging of so-called democratic politicians in 1933 was a mild and reasonable affair which could in no way be compared with the terrible things done by the Allies in 1945. The staged trial of the alleged perpetrators of the 1934 Reichstag fire was, in his view, conducted judicially and correctly. The concentration camps had been properly run as soon as the State took them over and organized them. The murders of German statesmen who tried to fulfill the terms of the Treaty of Versailles were justified.

> I cannot imagine [Grimm wrote] that in a war in which all weapons were so fully developed, that of propaganda — that weapon of spiritual poison — would be neglected. What is more, I know that it was not! In the last months before the collapse [of 1945] I read foreign newspapers every day. They carried reports of German atrocity which

were invented by a central office. They were about one area after another which was occupied, France today, Norway tomorrow, then Belgium, Denmark, Holland, Greece, Yugoslavia and Czechoslovakia. At first the talk was of hundreds of dead in the concentration camps, then — as each country came up for its turn — thousands, tens of thousands, hundreds of thousands. Then I said to myself: Will this inflation of numbers actually move into millions? I looked at yet another leaflet. Yes, it was millions all right!

Under former S.S.-Führer Waldemar Schütz the Plesse Verlag published the works of Alfred Rosenberg, Hitler's crackpot Reich Commissar for the occupied eastern territories in Poland, Russia and the Baltic States, and of S.S. generals like Paul Hausser. The Abend Verlag in Wuppertal brought out books accusing the Allies of war crimes; the Strunk Verlag in Düsseldorf published blatant anti-Semitic propaganda; former S.S. men found ready publishers in Lüneburg, Stuttgart, Hannover. The growing volume of anti-Semitic weeklies and periodicals was heralded by the imported *Der Weg* from the Argentine. Failure to ban this journal led to the appearance of violently anti-Semitic and neo-Nazi papers like *Anklage, Nation Europa*, the *Ring, Das Fanal, Reichsruf*, the *Deutsche Freiheit* of former S.A. man Otto Strasser, and the *Volkswarte* of the Ludendorff circle.

Anti-Semitism was creeping back into the ordinary habits of the German people. At a diplomatic dinner party in Bonn I was surprised to find myself the recipient of a tirade against the Jews from a middle-aged lady bedizened with jewelry. The wife of a high-ranking government official, she informed me that the Jews had brought their troubles on themselves, "by making gross and unfair profits out of the First World War and the inflation." Her armory of ornaments suggested that she herself had not fared badly, this time, from the Second World War and currency reform. The biggest profiteers from the 1923 inflation, in any case, were the Ruhr industrialists, who redeemed their debts with worthless Reichsmarks, and the German Treasury. "In the years following the war," wrote Count Blücher, "Germany gave an exhibition of sustained inflation, which arose from the State's practice of meeting its requirements with Treasury Bills which were discounted by the Central Bank. In other words, the State covered its expenses with the printing press."

In a discussion group organized by the Evangelical Academy at Loccum, the following figures were given as evidence of the failure of the German people to address itself to the Jewish problem. Of a large number of people questioned, 28 per cent said they did not believe the usual figures given of the number of Jews exterminated by the Nazis. Over 30 per cent admitted that they regarded the Jews as "different" and "did not care for them." Worst of all, 88 per cent said they did not want to hear about the Jews at all.

Typical of this last attitude was the story of the fifteen-year-old boy who wanted to take a history book out of a Frankfurt public library. He wanted something about the recent past. The librarian showed him five different books about the concentration camps; he recommended *The Gates Open*, by Derrick Sington, the story of the relief of Belsen by the British forces.

The boy took the book home and brought it back a few days later. "What, finished it already?" the librarian asked him. "No, as a matter of fact, I didn't read it." "But why ever not?"

The boy was embarrassed. "Well, my father saw the book. He told me that I should not read it. He said that it was bound to be absurdly exaggerated. And it was not the right book at all for a boy who was barely at school in 1945. He said that books like that ought to be banned, as they really poisoned the air itself."

Miss Sue Ryder, a British girl who has done untold good helping displaced persons still regarded as third-class citizens of a rank-conscious Germany, told me how she once went to look at the sites of two of the first Nazi concentration camps, in Friesland. At first she could not find them and could get no answer at all from the surly villagers in a beer hall at Esterwegen. When she persisted with her questions, they told her that there had never been a concentration camp near there at all. When she told them that this was nonsense, the villagers became violently hostile. "People were only put into camps like that," they shouted at her, "because they were antisocial and the scum of Europe! Hitler began the task of building the New Order in Europe in the right way — he liquidated the undesirables! They were far better dead."

It would be difficult to think of a more revealing incident than one which occurred during the Federal election campaign of 1957. A young writer suggested that Erich Ollenhauer, Chairman of the Social Democratic Party, was a Jew. The mistake was not unnatural. Although Jews do not conform strictly to any given physical type, Herr Ollenhauer has often been thought to be one. His party has done more than any other to secure redress and material compensation for the Jews whom Hitler persecuted. Yet Herr Ollenhauer gave instructions for the young man to be sued for "defamation"! It was not easy to explain later that Herr Ollenhauer did not personally regard being called a Jew as defamation: but he considered that his "accuser" had intended it to appear as such.

Ollenhauer is a comfortable, friendly man who suffered from Nazi persecution himself and who was forced to emigrate to Britain. His action can be put down, at least in part, to the average German's infallible gift for saying or doing something childishly irresponsible or wrong-minded at some time or other. But his action showed, too, that he was no potential prophet of German-Jewish reconciliation. Nor is Dr. Adenauer, with his intense parochial Catholicism and innate lack of emotion. Nor has any man risen from the front political rank to take up a task which would help to bring sanity and peace of mind to the German people. For the Federal President, Theodor Heuss, it was only one of many obligations. It has been left to a man of humbler political origins and attributes to crusade for recognition of the sins of the past and for the promise of enlightenment in the future.

I first met Erich Lueth in the early, darkest days of the post-Nazi era. As Chief of the Press Office of the City and Land of Hamburg he faced a daunting task. He was overworked, underfed and his city was in ruins. I was struck at that first meeting by the resolution and kindliness of the man. With his slow, childlike smile, his soft, thoughtful speech and his intense interest in every human problem, Erich Lueth was the epitome of the best

German virtues (and they have many). Lueth was born in Hamburg in 1902. At seventeen he was known as a rebellious character, by stern Wilhelminian standards. He organized and edited a clandestine, liberal-minded school magazine which, unbelievably, was considered an illegal activity in 1918. He was expelled from the Hamburg-Eppendorf high school as a result, just eight days before he should have taken his *Abitur,* or final examination.

Lueth became a journalist, joined the *Jungdemokraten,* a liberal youth group, and was for a short time its Hamburg chairman. In 1927 he was a member of the Hamburg *Land* Parliament, but as his party drifted steadily and in conformity with the general trend in Germany to the right, so Lueth moved leftwards. His break with his party came over the Weimar Republic's naval rearmament program. Who should blame him for opposing the building of Battle Cruiser A? The Tirpitz naval program before 1914 had been solely directed against Britain, and it could not have been clear against what other country Battle Cruiser A might be used.

Lueth was working for the liberal *Hamburg Anzeiger* when the Nazis came into power in 1933. He lasted only a few weeks, before being forbidden to take any further part in "publicistic activity." He took jobs in retail-trading associations and as "blurb writer" for a firm which made sewing machines in Kaiserslautern. His brother, Herbert, was taken away to a concentration camp and he himself twice narrowly escaped arrest by the Gestapo. But he was lucky. On the first occasion he had moved house and had sensibly registered his new home in the maiden name of his wife (whom he married in 1930). On the second occasion his name was deleted from a black list of anti-Nazi journalists by some anonymous friend.

In 1943, Lueth was drafted into the army, in spite of extreme nearsightedness. Within a few days of the end of the war he was nearly in serious trouble for demanding that the Hitler salute (right arm raised at full length at an angle of forty-five degrees) should be abolished. The war ended just in time for him, taking him to an American P.O.W. camp, where he edited the *Ghedi Lagerpost* with a circulation of 10,000. Within eighteen months he was press chief to the first postwar Lord Mayor of Hamburg, Rudolf Petersen.

Like many other Germans, Erich Lueth was horrified by the anti-Semitism of the Nazis; unlike all but a few, he tried to find out exactly what had been done to the Jews. As a prisoner of war he wrote a book *Abkehr vom Militarismus*, which set out in print his detestation of the Prussian militaristic tradition. But he wanted to do something constructive too. In the early post-war years he made friends with such people as Rudolf Küstermeier, the editor of *Die Welt;* Dr. Gertrud Luckner, a leading member of the Roman Catholic relief society *Caritas;* Professor Franz Boehm, a member of the Bundestag; Hermann Maass, an evangelical clergyman. These were men who, like Lueth, believed that something had to be done to bring about a true reconciliation between the Germans and the Jews, and that otherwise the German people would relapse into their easy way of believing what they found convenient and rewriting their history in the comfortable legend of German innocence and highmindedness.

In 1951 this group of people, with backing from a great many others, launched the campaign for "Peace with Israel." A series of leaflets were widely distributed throughout Western Germany; long articles went into the *Telegraf,* the *Neue Zeitung* and *Die Welt;* the Northwest German Radio put on a half-hour discussion of the theme. Big meetings were organized with the help of the newly formed Society for Christian-Jewish Cooperation and at one of them, in Berlin, Willy Brandt (later Lord Mayor) and Erich Lueth spoke before an audience of over two thousand. Money was collected and was given freely, for Jewish charitable organizations, for the planting of olive and citrus trees in Israel, for the tending of Jewish cemeteries.

The campaign did not come a moment too soon. Spiritual apathy and the frantic quest for material gain were becoming the dominant features of German thinking and living. From Italy the poet Hermann Hesse wrote to Lueth, "Peace with Israel — this was something that had to be said. And yet there can be no doubt that this is the voice of only a tiny minority." And the former Chief Rabbi of Berlin, Leo Baeck, told a Danish journalist, "I have loved Germany so much that my heart could break. Not just its people, its language, and its culture but its very landscape. Nowhere else are the fields so green, nowhere is the air so sweet. . . . But returning here I said to myself: No longer is this my country. It has become completely foreign to me. My Germany has gone forever. . . ." The new Germany must have seemed a spiritual desert to him, in which human feelings were restricted to grief suffered in bitter silence and resentment which boiled just beneath this troubled surface.

The ideas of the campaigners for "Peace with Israel" were simple enough. All Germans should be informed of the facts of the Nazi persecutions. They should be given figures too. Accordingly, one of the first of the leaflets set out the grisly tally — of 8,295,-000 Jews once living in the parts of Europe which were occupied by the Germans, 6,093,000, or 73 per cent, died; over 90 per cent of the German Jews died, and over 80 per cent of the Jews of five other countries. Germans had to learn, too, what was being done in Israel and how Israel could be helped by them. Above all, German youth had to be brought into contact with Jewish youth, for in their mutual understanding lay the real hope for the future.

The first result achieved by Lueth and his friends was that the Federal Chancellor made a government statement on the Jewish question. "At last," as the group remarked in its pamphlet, "reconciliation with Israel." For the first two years of its existence there had been no government statement on the problem which involved the greatest stain on the German national character. The reaction to "Peace with Israel" among German youth was immediate. Subscriptions and letters poured in. A typical one came from Franz Ansprenger, in Berlin: "I hope this letter is one of a pile. I only want to say how glad I am about your action. I hope soon to work actively in your cause. You must propose new and practical steps which will help to an understanding with the Jews and in which we little people can help."

From Jerusalem came this letter: "Seven years in a German concentration camp and typhus, which robbed me of my eyesight and hearing after release, have not deafened me to your appeal. I cannot speak for Israel, nor for a single one of those who have suffered, but there is even less justification for me to stay silent on my own account. Five years have gone by, but not for my beloved dead for whom there is no time factor. Today, and every day of my life, they are dying afresh. But in every respect . . . I give back peace to Germany."

Three out of every hundred letters written to Lueth and his group were negative. Writers complained that Jews were securing compensation for their war losses but "decent" East German refugees were not; that the numbers of Jews murdered by the Nazis were exaggerated; that Germany owed the State of Israel nothing; that stories of Nazi persecutions were "impossible" because Germans were honest, kind, good. Most of these critical letters were anonymous.

Erich Lueth is cast in the image of Mr. Valiant-for-Truth, of Bunyan's *Pilgrim's Progress*. His work was only beginning. In 1953 he paid his first visit to Israel, aware of the delicacy with which he had to deal with the feelings of those he met of the 70,000 German immigrants to Israel and the 350,000 other Europeans to whom Germany and Germans conjured up only horror or hatred. He traveled incognito under the name of Julius Bermann, inwardly ashamed of doing so but knowing it was necessary. With him went four other Germans. Their prevailing impression was that German-Israeli relations had to be fostered with the greatest tact, and not pressed ahead too fast. "We had to avoid opening old wounds, when so many could not yet have found peace of mind," Lueth told me. He knew that the memories of other peoples are much longer than those of his own countrymen, with their easy phrases about "letting bygones be bygones" and "drawing a line through the past."

Lueth and his friends went again in 1955, openly this time, learning Jewish views, bearing with harsh criticism, fully aware that they would not reap immediate success. They were asked a great many questions, nearly all of them roughly phrased. More than once they were told that a true reconciliation between Germans and Jews was impossible. Lueth was not discouraged. He went back to Israel in 1956 and 1958. He began to call it his "second homeland." He made endless friends — a remarkable achievement even for this man, who radiates basic goodness and understanding.

In Germany Lueth led thousands of schoolchildren to the mass graves of the Nazis' victims at Belsen. He organized parties to visit Israel, helped his friend Küstermaier to settle in Jerusalem as correspondent of the German News Agency, D.P.A. He urged quicker compensation to the survivors of the concentration camps, launched a long legal case (which he won) against the ex-Nazi film producer, Veit Harlan, organized meetings between German and Israeli children, wrote endless articles, and talked, talked, talked. . . .

His greatest enemy was German forgetfulness; but in 1957 an unexpected ally came to his aid in the shape of the book and play, *The Diary of Anne Frank*. The story of the sixteen-year-old Jewish girl who lived in hiding in an Amsterdam attic with her family and who died in Belsen, after being caught by the Nazis, touched the Germans on their weakest spot, their sentimentality. The story is terribly moving in its suggestion of terror lurking always a few yards away from the hiding Jews, in its prolonged pathos and sense of doom. Theatre audiences all over Germany watched the play in strained silence, left at the end like school children filing away from the grave of a dead playmate. Many wept openly. On the tenth anniversary of the relief of Belsen, and the first such anniversary after the showing of the play, five thousand children took part in the pilgrimage to the mass graves and laid flowers on them. One boy said, "These graves are as much a part of our history as the works of Goethe and Beethoven."

Some observers talked about an "Anne Frank movement" — so marked were the feeling aroused by her story. But men like Lueth knew that a wave of sentiment may be only temporary. It was significant that German pity was expended on the young girl, not on her companions. A 1958 public opinion poll showed that two thirds of the population thought the figure of five to six million Jews murdered by the Nazis too high, and 37 per cent talked of gross exaggeration. Among countryfolk only 60 per cent thought that marriage between a Jew and a Christian could be happy. Older people were especially unwilling to shed their anti-Jewish prejudices. Some parents prevailed on schoolteachers not to allow children from their classes to go to Belsen. The reason given was that it was "morbid" to do so.

The process of compensation still lagged, and by the beginning of 1958 only about 40 per cent of all claims lodged had been examined. But there were far more disturbing signs than this that anti-Jewish feeling was still very much alive in Germany. In 1958 and early in 1959 cases of anti-Semitic utterances and incidents multiplied. Here are just a very few of them:

An Offenburg schoolmaster, Ludwig Zind, said that too few Jews were gassed and that Hitler's anti-Jewish policies were amply justified. He was sentenced to one year's imprisonment, but appealed. When his appeal was rejected, Zind was not in court but actually on his way to the United Arab Republic, where he joined forces with other ex-Nazis working for President Nasser and against Israel. There is every reason to suspect that Zind was smuggled out of Germany by members of the S.S.

In New York the sixty-five-year-old German Consul, Hans von Saucken, had to be suspended from his post for making flagrantly anti-Semitic statements.

In Hamburg a timber merchant, Friedrich Nieland, and a printer, Adolf Heimberg, were sued for writing and publishing a pamphlet "How many more World (Money) Wars must the Nations lose?" In it Nieland maintained that the extermination of six million Jews was organized by "international Jewry" and that no Jew should be allowed to occupy any position of trust or authority. Nieland and Heimberg were found not guilty of spreading ideas which were dangerous to German democracy, and Hamburg's Social Democratic Lord Mayor, Herr Max Brauer, traveled post-haste to Bonn to consult Dr. Adenauer. The result was an amendment to the legal code and the subsequent confiscation of the Nieland pamphlet.

In Düsseldorf swastikas appeared on the walls and the three doors of the new Jewish synagogue; the old one was burned down in 1938. The police arrested one former Communist and imputed this act of vandalism to "Communist agitators." Members of the Jewish community recalled about this time that 176 out of 1700 Jewish cemeteries in Germany have been desecrated during the last ten years.

In the village of Köppern, near Frankfurt, a Jew, Kurt Sumpf, was repeatedly and publicly insulted and threatened in the small café which he and his wife ran. On one occasion his wife was physically assaulted and half-strangled; on another, shots were fired through the windows of their house. His nine-year-old son was jeered at by his schoolfellows because he was a "Jewish brat." The village policeman, like his other assailants, used anti-Semitic language and told him that his café would be closed down if he could not keep order in it. The Sumpf family moved to Frankfurt, with the intention of emigrating later. Only one of their assailants was sent to prison, in October 1959.

In Marburg violently anti-Semitic leaflets were distributed in and around the university. The writer called for the ejection of Jews from Palestine and claimed that "the Communist and Capitalist worlds have given Palestine to the Jews in return for their part in causing the downfall of Germany."

In Munich a cardboard swastika was sent to the Bavarian Youth Ring, which had appealed for money in order to build a youth hostel in Israel to be named after Anne Frank. A spokesman of the Youth Ring admitted that this was a part of "the current wave of anti-Semitism."

In Lübeck the schoolmaster, Lothar Stielau, told his pupils that the Diary of Anne Frank was a forgery, that she and others had exploited Germany's defeat. He was suspended from his post by the Minister of Education of *Land* Schleswig-Holstein.

In Frankfurt the state attorney, Otto Schweinsberger, was accused of repeatedly making anti-Semitic statements. His passport was confiscated when it was found that a place on a plane from

Munich to Cairo was booked in his name and a room in a Cairo hotel reserved for him.

In Herford the tradesman, Carl Krumsiek, was charged with committing a breach of the peace in a restaurant. He told other guests that Hitler was quite right to send the Jews to the gas chambers, and that all surviving Jews should be killed either by shooting or poisoning.

Yet another public opinion survey revealed that out of over 1200 people questioned 23 per cent were openly anti-Semitic, 15 per cent were slightly anti-Semitic, 41 per cent considered themselves to be "tolerant," 15 per cent were neutral, and 6 per cent pro-Jewish. When asked what caused anti-Semitism, 53 per cent opted for "the characteristics of the Jews" and 12 per cent for the Jewish religion. Only 30 per cent agreed that the principal reason was anti-Semitic propaganda.

In Frankfurt the office of the World Jewish Congress received abusive anti-Semitic letters. One letter contained these passages: "One day we shall break every bone in the body of the Jewish bastard who denounced Professor Zind. As for the rest of you Jewish rabble, see to it that you get out of our Germany as quickly as possible! Otherwise you will share the same fate. You arrived here in a caftan, dirty and lousy, and you have cheated and robbed us of millions. Out with the Jews! Perish Judah!"

In Bonn the Social Democratic party published a list of prominent ex-Nazis who in October 1958 were receiving pensions which were often twelve times as large as those of the people whom they had persecuted. There was Dr. Ernst Lautz, a former attorney general, who sent dozens of innocent people to their deaths, drawing a pension of $420 a month for seven years. There was former S.S. man Dr. Ernst Gritzbach, former personal assistant to Hermann Göring, drawing a pension of $320 a month and, for at least three years, earning around $6500 a year in addition as an employee of the Stinnes industrial group. There was Erich Raeder, former Grand Admiral and a convicted war criminal, with a pension of $550 a month; and Walter Schroeder, a former

S.S. brigade leader and Police President of Lübeck, with a pension of $300 a month.

During most of the period in which these men drew their pensions the average old-age or disability pension was around $22 a month. This is what the victims of the Nazis were qualified to draw.

In Bonn the Federal Chancellor told a British television-team early in 1959 that anti-Semitism had virtually ceased to exist in Germany, that acts of vandalism on Jewish property were the work of Communist "agents," and that openly anti-Semitic expressions were used by only a few "loutish" members of society. This statement was utterly disproved by the desecration of the Cologne synagogue on Christmas Day, 1959, and the sequence of anti-Semitic incidents which then took place.

Anti-Semitism is, after all, only a part of German race-consciousness. Individual Germans have told me, with complete certainty and guilelessness, that Poles are "barbarians" (then they are called "Polacks"), Czechs are "dishonest," Austrians are "tricky," and Russians "Tartars" and "Mongols." Farther to the West, the British are "hypocrites," the French "decadent," and even the Swiss Spiessbürgers — by which is meant a sort of dreary Central European Babbitt.

"Our pride," Alfred Rosenberg wrote in 1937, "is the pride of race." That race surrenders itself to phobias even about its own subdivisions. A Bavarian newspaper editor told me in all seriousness that Prussians were "swine," and George Mikes recounted the story of the Bavarian car dealers who had to dismiss efficient and honest agents, "because these men offered automobiles for sale in the Silesian dialect and people refused to buy them." But sectional hatreds do not compare with hatred of the foreigner as such. When Veit Harlan came back into business with a new film in 1957, entitled "Different from You and Me," the principal character was a young and blameless German who was perverted by homosexual "foreigners," ruined by a villain with the Slav name of Boris, and first led astray by "foreign abstract art."

A Jew whom I have known for some time past came back in 1952 to his home town, Berlin. He had been an exile in Africa since the Nazis came to power. He had purposely waited a long time till after the end of the war and the foundation of a new German democratic state. "I wanted to be sure," he explained. "I meant to stay a long time, perhaps settle in Germany for good. But I shall go back to Africa again." His friends, he found, had not changed. Those who had joined the Nazi Party were perfectly prepared to explain it away. The Nazi experiment had been a "mistake." No more experiments of that kind, thank you! At the same time, they considered that it had been much harder for them, as Germans, than for him, a Jew, to know what to do.

"Nothing has really been settled," the Jew said. "But I am afraid that anti-Semitism is not dead. For it cannot really be dead until it has been replaced by a real understanding of what happened in the past. Instead, the past is simply put into the backs of people's minds, docketed, and left there. And the Germans have not had an economic setback since 1949. Wait until one comes along; then see who they blame, and who they listen to."

One is reminded of the words of Count Kurt Blücher: "The historians will maintain that the compulsory course of German history, started by Luther or Caesar, had from time immemorial predestined them to turn on the gas taps in order to murder millions."

Laws will be passed in order to stifle outbreaks of anti-Semitic feeling. The press, the radio, even the film industry, will try to help. Men who were nurtured on Nazi doctrine will gradually disappear from government service, will die out elsewhere in the community. But there may still not be a positive attitude on the part of the mass of the population towards the Jewish problem. For Germans will continue to be encouraged to forget their country's past — on the grounds that it is too terrible to live with, and that people's "nerves" have suffered too much already. That is why Erich Lueth must go on with his self-appointed task — a sturdy, infinitely courageous crusader and a living testimony of mankind's reason to trust the Germans to "find themselves" in the long run.

During a memorable hour I listened to Lueth tell the story of the *Reichs Kristall* night of November 9, 1938. He described the columns of smoke rising from the burning synagogues; the pillaging of Jewish shops when the mob smashed windows and grabbed the goods they wanted — in silence; the embarrassed inactivity of the police who watched this organized robbery; the terrible constraint of all those who watched too and hated themselves for not protesting. I listened to Lueth tell how one thing more than all others affected him while in Israel — on the bare arms of women working in the fields he could still see the tattooed numbers of their former concentration camps.

I listened to him say: "Never let your sons and daughters be deceived by that trite saying, Leave the grass to grow over these things. Germans unborn must not inherit the blindness and the cowardice of our generation." Mr. Valiant-for-Truth has a long and difficult road ahead of him. But never were men like Erich Lueth more needed by their country. For their problem is to set the German conscience at rest — by setting it first to work.

11

Money Is Power

> With us there is no diversion of talent into the field of politics, as in other countries. Neither the rich nor the more gifted members of the middle class are withdrawn from economic life to devote themselves to politics.
> — WERNER SOMBART, the economist, writing in 1903

> The history of the use of I.G. Farben trust by the Nazi reads like a detective story. Defeat of the Nazi armies will have to be followed by the eradication of these weapons of economic warfare.
> — FRANKLIN ROOSEVELT, writing in 1944

> I fear German tractors more than German tanks.
> — SIR IVONE KIRKPATRICK, British High Commissioner in Germany, 1950-1953

IN December 1958 a little two-year-old child was dying in the Rhineland town of Kleve. Ulrich Fittkau had a straitened and deficient aorta, which meant that his heart could not pump enough blood through his body to keep it warm. He needed a new aorta and nothing else could save his life.

The Mayo clinic, of Rochester, Minnesota, specialized in the tricky operation of giving patients a plastic aorta. No German clinic had anything like the same experience of this particular operation. Ulrich Fittkau's parents in any case were too poor even to call in a German specialist — his father was a "white-collar" clerk earning barely eighty-five dollars a month (once upon a time it was considered a great privilege to be an *Angestellte* in Germany; today it means a life sentence to genteel penury). A German specialist would have been shockingly expensive, but the

Cummings

GREAT GREAT GRANDPA KRUPP

GREAT GRANDPA KRUPP

GRANDPA KRUPP

BERTHA KR...

FATHER KRUPP

ALFRED KRUPP

"The Third Reich will last a thousand years!"

CUMMINGS, *Daily Ex*

"But KRUPP Will Last a Thousand Years."

costs of sending their only son to Minnesota were, to this poor family, simply staggering. They would have come to at least five thousand dollars or roughly five years' wages of the father.

The American businessmen's club in Düsseldorf heard of the Fittkau case. (It is, perhaps, significant that it required a foreign organization to take some initiative in the matter.) The club approached the United States Air Force, which agreed to fly baby Ulrich free to America. This left a four-thousand-dollar bill to be met. The members of the American club circularized their German business acquaintances. The whole sum of money (and a surplus) was subscribed in two weeks.

Baby Ulrich was sent to Minnesota. As it happened, the story did not have a happy ending, for the little boy died after the operation had been performed, apparently successfully. But it caused a minor sensation in the Ruhr. For not only had the rich men of the Ruhr contributed the money readily; they even asked in many cases that their names should not be mentioned or put down on a subscription list. The "Ruhr Barons" have not been noted at any time for generosity, and certainly not for generosity which remains anonymous. (In 1959 one of the rich businessmen's clubs in Düsseldorf was asked for a contribution to charity, offered $150. Düsseldorf's bankrupt artists raised $2600.)

These Ruhr Barons, indeed, have remained a class apart from the remainder of society. An American who becomes very rich gives money to a foundation, perhaps establishes his own. He may well go into politics, or he will interest himself in art, form a famous collection and leave it to a grateful nation. The British millionaire will very often buy a country house, involve himself in the affairs of the neighborhood, sit on county councils and the boards of charitable societies, mix with the landed class, perhaps move into one or other of the British Houses of Parliament.

Rich Germans practically never do any of these things. In the Ruhr they follow a particular pattern. They build themselves expensive but sadly tawdry villas on the outskirts of Düsseldorf, Mulheim, Duisburg, and surround them with high walls surmounted with the jagged glass which generally graces the fences of penitentiaries. (One Ruhr businessman has boasted that his front door is modeled on one of the gates of Alcatraz.) In their villas, generally miracles of bad taste, "Ruhr Baronial" or "Gelsenkirchen Gothic," the Ruhr Barons remain entirely cut off from the outside world. The next-door neighbor — unless he happens to be one of their own kind — the local Lord Mayor, the pastor and the priest, the tradesmen, and the townspeople might, for all they care, be natives of the Congo. They even look down on the landed class, whose members they regard as deplorable dodos in an age of economic progress, a hapless remnant clinging desperately to the vestiges of their estates. Utterly divorced from society, this class of big industrialists has a better right than any other to be regarded as antisocial.

In a social sense its past record is wretched, and in some respects criminal. In others, it could offer excuses. The Germans pushed their industrial revolution through at breakneck speed, in a space of about sixty years. The German industrialist was excluded from political power in the class-conscious, Prussian-dominated Germany of Bismarck, the Kaiser and the Weimar Republic. His concentration on economic power became single-minded, all-absorbing, remorseless. It is understandable, even if it is not excusable, that the industrialists treated economics as a power factor. They built up cartels on a huge scale (in proportion to overall national wealth) in order to fix prices, ensure high profits and move ahead into the next stage of expansion. The earlier cartels were "vertical" — entailing control of the means of production in a single industry. Coal was wedded with iron ore and steel, chemicals with lignite, heavy engineering with shipbuilding. But the biggest family trusts of all — Krupp, Stinnes, Flick — developed their vast interest "horizontally" too. They bought or built plants of other industries, town property, tramways, distributing and trading firms.

They linked themselves with the big commercial banks which helped to finance them; they exchanged and shared directors. It is hardly surprising to find, even before 1914, a periodical, *Die Bank,* worrying over this process of "rationalization" through the concentration of power. "Other banks," it wrote, "will follow the same path and in time the three hundred men who today govern

Germany economically will be reduced to fifty, to twenty-five, or even fewer. One fine morning we shall wake up in surprise to see nothing but trusts before our eyes, and to find ourselves faced with the necessity of substituting state-monopolies for private monopolies." In 1960, German bankers follow that same path — in their search for a streamlined economy.

The big industrialists became even more powerful after the First World War. For the 1923 inflation and the German end of the 1929 world economic crisis wrecked the smaller, independent undertakings and left the field to the big trusts. Marxist historians have even suggested that the big industrialists encouraged inflation, in order to pay off their debts with valueless Reichsmarks. This scarcely seems likely, for inflation brought unemployment and falling production, which in turn interfered with profit-making. But they certainly set out to benefit from it as far as possible and to complete the process of concentration. This was the decade — 1920-1930 — in which AEG and Siemens Schuckert acquired control of four fifths of the electrical industry, I.G. Farben of half the chemical industry, and UFA of the whole of German film production and marketing. Of steel production 95 per cent, along with 65 per cent of hard-coal production, fell into the hands of eight combines. Of these the Vereinigte Stahlwerke alone controlled 47 per cent of steel production and over 30 per cent of hard-coal production.

The big industrialists were generally completely amoral. The Krupps had sold arms to Napoleon — whom they were far too canny to regard as the liberator of their country — and to the Russian Czars, with a fine disregard for German national interests. Another steel family, the Roechlings, helped the French Government to build the Maginot Line. In 1923 Hugo Stinnes paid a call on a general of the French Army of Occupation, Degoutte, and asked for armed help to break the trade-unions and reintroduce a ten-hour working day. But generally the big industrialists stood to gain most by wholehearted support of their own government. If this support was in pursuit of illegal objectives, so much the better. The government would pay more for their help.

Thus the Ruhr Barons gave ready support to clandestine German rearmament between the wars, which was contrary to the disarmament clauses of the Treaty of Versailles. Gustav Krupp was later to boast, "After the assumption of power by Hitler, I had the satisfaction of being able to report to the Führer that Krupps stood ready after a short warming-up period to begin the rearmament of the German people without any gaps in experience." Krupp began collaborating with the *Reichswehr* (the post-1919 German Army which was officially limited to 100,000 men) in 1922. Designs for tanks had been worked out by 1926, which may help to explain the astonishing superiority of the German Tiger and Panther tanks until the closing stages of the Second World War. There seems little doubt that Gustav Stresemann, foreign minister for ten years before Hitler came to power, was privy to the activities of Krupp and other firms. The victorious Allies were later to reproach themselves bitterly with having allowed Krupp to retain over half of its 20,000 machines. As General J. H. Morgan wrote in his bitter book, *Assize at Arms*, "Germany was left with every lathe that turned a shell."

It is often supposed that industrialists have more to gain from peace than war. For war may mean re-tooling in order to produce arms, and it may bring the disorganization which springs from diversion of labor and enemy action. This was the case for many American and British firms during the Second World War. But German industrialists looked at matters in a very different light. The steelmen had their eyes firmly fixed on the iron-ore deposits of Lorraine, on the coal-mines of the Liége basin, on the comparatively small but tremendously prosperous steel industry of Luxembourg. The giant chemical trust of I.G. Farben, formed in 1925, had even brighter visions of what final German victory could mean. In the West it would bring control of the French and Belgian chemical industries, and the stifling of competition by restricting the construction of new plants to Germany. In the East it would bring a link-up with Russian oil-resources and an infinite reservoir of cheap labor.

With some justice the Nuremberg indictment, when German industrial leaders were tried by Allied tribunals, read:

I.G. Farben marched with the *Wehrmacht* and played a major role in Germany's program for acquisition by conquest. It used its expert technical knowledge and resources to plunder and exploit the chemical and related industries of Europe, to enrich itself from unlawful acquisitions, to strengthen the German war machine and to ensure the subjugation of the conquered territories to the German economy. To that end it conceived, initiated and prepared plans for the acquisition — with the aid of German military force — of the chemical industries of Austria, Czechoslovakia, Poland, Norway, France, Russia and other countries.

Banking is regarded in most countries of the West as the height of bourgeois respectability. The alliance of the big commercial banks of Germany with the coal, steel and chemical cartels ensured the stifling of genuinely free competition. The big banks financed German rearmament with their eyes open. In 1943 a director of the Dresdner Bank wrote that he had heard a "very flattering ditty" from a client. It was:

> Who marches behind the leading tank?
> It is Dr. Rasche, of the Dresdner Bank!

Would this have been regarded as "flattering" in any other country of the West?

The big industrialists backed pan-Germanism and the Navy League — with its plans for the biggest fleet of ironclads in the world — before 1914. They backed Hitler, after a period of understandable hesitation. The banker, Baron Kurt Schroeder, called "the midwife of Nazism," used the deposits of the Stein Bank to finance the equipping of the blackshirted S.S. He helped to secure the support of men like Gustav Krupp, Fritz Thyssen (author of *I Paid Hitler*) and Emil Kirdorf. Industrial managers such as Hans Guenther Sohl (Vereinigte Stahlwerke), Wilhelm Zangen (Mannesmann), and Hermann Reusch (Gütehoffnungshütte) were imprisoned by the Allies in 1945 because of the active help they had given the Nazis. Baron von Schnitzler, of the I.G. Farben, contributed an estimated forty thousand dollars a year into a Nazi Party "special bank account"; he was in no way unique.

German industry, with the collaboration of the Reich Government, organized the artificial German economic expansion in the Balkans, so brilliantly described by Paul Einzig in his book, *Bloodless Invasion.* This expansion was based on the so-called "clearinghouse agreements" between Germany and individual Balkan countries. Under these agreements, clearinghouses were set up reciprocally in both Germany and the Balkan country in question. German importers paid money into the German clearinghouse account, and German exporters drew money out of it. The converse happened in the Balkan country.

In order to save dollars and sterling, Germany ordered large quantities of Balkan raw materials. But no German goods were at first available in return. German exports were earning more valuable currencies for the purchase of "strategic" goods needed for Hitler's rearmament program. When the Balkan countries became desperate for imports, in order to satisfy the Balkan creditors of their clearinghouse accounts, Germany exported surplus goods which could not be marketed elsewhere. By 1938 Yugoslavia had imported enough aspirins to cover her needs for the next ten years. Balkan governments found themselves forced to accept second-hand armaments — which in turn assisted the modernization of Hitler's armies.

The Germans even cheated on the system which they themselves had approved. German exporters were instructed to offer good credit terms and sell on the installment system. Balkan clearinghouse accounts once more became drained of money needed to pay their own exporters, and Balkan governments once more became inclined to encourage purchase of any and every German surplus-product on offer. The profitability of this business enabled the Nazi Government to offer immensely favorable exchange rates to Rumanian exporters — 39 lei to the mark. This, in turn, gave Germany the principal share in the purchase of Rumanian oil — another vital fact of the Nazi rearmament drive, based on government-organized near-robbery.

Industrialists conventionally look for quick and easy profits. German industrialists were no exception. But it is not usual for industry to be encouraged by government to indulge in crooked dealing. That the Nazi Government did this is beyond question, and this is the root of postwar doubts about German commercial probity. The Nazis knew that they could work on men who belonged to a tradition of complete ruthlessness. This tradition was conveniently discarded after 1945 — even though many of the men who belonged to it returned to positions of power. What the tradition really meant could be shown by a score of examples. Let one speak for the rest — that of the Krupp coal, steel and engineering combine. (Krupp has the additional virtue of being the best-known or most notorious firm in Germany.)

Friedrich Krupp founded the firm at the beginning of the nineteenth century in Essen. In 1812 he tried to move his steel file and tooling shop to the left bank of the Rhine, in order to pick up fat French arms contracts. Twenty years later Krupp began to make guns, and in 1844 offered the first cast-steel barrel to the Prussian state. During the next thirty years the family firm bought up coal and iron-ore mines, and in 1870 Krupp siege-guns battered Paris. The family biographer, Wilhelm Berdrow, describes with sickening sentimentality the arrival of these guns on the heights of Montmartre: "The Prussian grenadiers pressed around them on the march. They fondled the guns as one pets a horse, and admonished them to behave gallantly and strike the mark. They gave evidence of a childlike, tender affection."

In 1902 the head of the family, Friedrich Krupp the second, died without a male heir. Four years later his daughter Bertha married Gustav von Bohlen, a counsellor of the German Embassy in Constantinople. Kaiser Wilhelm II, the Emperor of Germany, had counted Friedrich as one of his personal friends, and walked behind his coffin at his pompous funeral. He permitted — or instructed — Gustav to take the name of Krupp. In 1909, Gustav became chairman of the firm. In the same year Krupp produced its fifty-thousandth cannon. Only a year before, it had entered a sinister form of war production when it launched the first German submarine from its Kiel shipyard.

The First World War was grist for the Krupp steel mills. During its course the firm made profits of more than four hundred million marks. Its biggest field gun — named with characteristic Ruhr lack of taste "Big Bertha" — smashed the defenses of Liége and was intended to be used against Paris and London. Has any other country in the world named weapons of appalling destruction after its women?

But a lost war is bad business for armaments firms. The Allied Disarmament Commission managed to dismantle or destroy nearly half of Krupp's twenty thousand machines. French troops moved into the Ruhr, and by an act of culpable folly fired into a crowd of Krupp workmen, killing thirteen. Simple workmen have little to do with the launching of world wars. On the other hand, the French put Gustav Krupp von Bohlen in prison. With their usual maddening lack of logic, Germans remember only the massacre.

In theory, Germany disarmed in 1919; in practice it did nothing of the sort. Krupp went on designing and even producing guns. Although the firm's employ declined from 110,000 to 48,000 by 1924, Gustav was already boasting that he was "duping" the Allied Disarmament Commission. He had managed to preserve seventy-eight big machines in "Shop No. 10" at the Essen Gusstahlwerke, machines with heavy lathes which planed, milled and rifled field-guns. A promise to dismantle forty-seven of them was never carried out. Nor should a single firm bear the stigma of national dishonesty. Krupp followed the example set by the ostensibly peaceable and democratic Reich Government. (It was this government which refused to surrender the Spandau School of Design's blueprints of weapons of every kind, on the ground that they had been "lost." Can this be believed? History teaches that the Germans never lose anything and will hang on with incredible tenacity, and a sort of crazy orderliness, even to dangerous and incriminating documents.)

Within a few years Gustav was helping to finance Hitler and the Nazi Party at a time when their success was far from assured. Gustav's son, Alfried, who became head of the firm after the Second World War, has suggested that his father did this merely in order to preserve the family business and that refusal to help Hitler would have resulted in the Nazis seizing the firm after coming into power. This could — just — be true. But Gustav volunteered the information that he was ready to make arms again on a big scale; he played an important part in the meeting of Nazi-minded industrialists at Hermann Göring's Berlin house in February, 1933; and he took the lead after that meeting in collecting 3 million marks for the Nazis. It has been estimated that he "invested" twelve million marks in all in the Nazi cause. His performance was equivalent to offering allegiance to Lucifer, in case he should gain control over mankind.

Krupp was certain to be singled out for Allied animosity in 1945. It was not merely that Krupp built its biggest gun of all, the 80 centimeter railway-gun, Mighty Gustav; that Krupp designed the Tiger tank which remained supreme up to 1944; that Krupp churned out field guns, antitank and antiaircraft guns and howitzers. The firm employed 55,000 displaced persons, 18,000 prisoners of war and 6000 inmates of concentration camps, who were leased as a part of the "Extermination through Work" program. It overworked and underfed them, and barely troubled to pay them at all. It treated them as un-German animals, it employed hundreds of young women, shaved their heads to the shape of a cross, worked them to death.

Krupp directors have since maintained that they could not "help" doing all this, that refusal to use available slave-labor would have "meant trouble," and that workers "had" to be put into arms factories and exposed to murderously effective Allied bombing. Yet Krupp, of all firms, could have risked a protest to Hitler. In 1943 the Nazi State had done something unparalleled: it signed an "agreement" with the firm. This took the form of a "law," the "Lex Krupp," of November 12, 1943. "Over a period of 132 years," its text ran, "the firm of Friedrich Krupp . . . has rendered outstanding services, unique of their kind, to the armed forces of the German People." For this reason, the document continues, "it is the wish of the Führer, Adolf Hitler, that the owner of the Krupp family property be empowered, with this property, to set up a family business with special arrangements as to succession."

The "special arrangements" were that the Krupp family would

not be subject to inheritance duty, that the share capital and the headship of the firm would stay in the hands of a single man, and that taxation affairs would be settled between him and the Reich Minister of Finance. Hitler signed this amazing document personally; its object was to put Krupp outside the ordinary law of the land, and to make him the sworn ally as well as the servant of the State.

The Krupps were proud, with the feudal virtues of responsibility, absolute honesty and fairness to their own German workers, the *Kruppianer*. They were reared in an atmosphere of Prussian hardness, mixed with asceticism. "Strong as Krupp steel," was a German idiom; the Krupps were as resilient as the steel they made. In 1945 they needed to be.

Sentence of death was pronounced on the family firm of Krupp in 1945 by a bespectacled British chartered-accountant, Mr. Douglas Fowles, who had been appointed Allied "administrator" of the firm. In the brash, outsize nineteenth-century palace of the Krupp family, the Villa Hügel, Fowles told the assembled Krupp directors: "The firm of Krupp is simply going to cease to exist. We are not going to make the same mistakes that we made after the First World War." This sounded like the sober truth. The Gusstahlwerke in the heart of Essen had already been reduced to a gigantic ruin by fifty-five raids of Allied bombers. The Russians had occupied two Krupp factories in their zone of Germany, torn them to pieces and shipped the component parts to Magnitogorsk, Semipalatinsk and other burgeoning industrial centers of the Soviet Union. The most up-to-date Krupp plant of all, the Essen-Borbeck steel rolling-mill, had been earmarked as reparations and was likewise being shipped to Russia. Krupp shipyards and steel plants lay idle, awaiting dismantling; Krupp coal-mines worked at 20 per cent of capacity and under Allied control.

In 1945 Gustav Krupp von Bohlen was dying. He was semi-paralyzed and did not speak for five years before his death in 1950. His son and heir, Alfried, was arrested, tried by a war crimes tribunal in Nuremberg, and sent to jail as a "substitute" for his father. His jail sentence was to run ten years; his property was confiscated. Nine of his fellow directors went to prison too.

The trial, before an American court, had farcical elements about it. Ethically it was absurd to try a shy, well-mannered young man (he was thirty-five, but suffered from the retarded mental development which springs from parental over-disciplining) in the place of his father. The British Prosecutor at Nuremberg remarked, "This is not a game, in which a substitute can be provided for a player who is ill." Alfried was not allowed to brief the counsel of his choice, the American lawyer Earl Carroll. Evidence was used against him which was not made available to the defense counsel whom he was forced to accept, Dr. Otto Kranzbühler. Confiscation of property was almost certainly illegal, for it was not ordered even in the cases of the dependents of Hitler's paladins, Göring and Ribbentrop.

The tide began to turn for Krupp on April 10, 1949. On that day the American Military Governor, General Lucius Clay, modified the order for the confiscation of Alfried Krupp's property. General Clay did not do this out of love for the Krupp family. He had been warned that the Russians were preparing to claim one quarter of all Krupp property in western Germany. General Clay now ordered that Zone Commanders should implement the confiscation order on their own responsibility. The Zone Commanders hung back; they had always doubted the legality of the American court's judgment. They did not confiscate. The Russians, as it happened, did not claim.

The next act in the process of rehabilitating the Krupp firm was likewise the work of the head of the American administration. In January 1951 the U. S. High Commissioner — for Germany was no longer under military government — decided to release Alfried Krupp and repeal the order confiscating his property. Mr. John McCloy declared, in explanation, that confiscation of property was "repugnant to our American concepts of justice," and that he could find "no personal guilt in defendant Krupp to distinguish him above all others sentenced by the Nuremberg courts." Mr. McCloy had to iron out a monumental muddle; in a most confused way — for Krupp properties were not even in the American Zone, and Mr. McCloy forgot to consult his British and French allies — he fulfilled his task.

Alfried Krupp was still shy, courtly and remote from his fellow beings. During his six years in jail he had occupied himself, typically, in the prison-chapel, for which he carved ornaments and fashioned altar-rails, working with the wood and iron which had made his family notorious. He refused, when he came out, to complain, and told avid reporters, "War, and the aftermath of war, always bring grievous suffering. What has happened to industrialists in Germany and elsewhere is now a thing of the past." This may have been trite, but it was not hypocrisy. He stated publicly that he would never make arms again. This was a point of policy. He made immediate inquiries into the fates of thousands of Krupp pensioners. This was the best kind of industrial feudalism. He surveyed the tortured ruins of his family empire and asked the workers' spokesman, "Tell me, Herr Waldeck, can we build again?" "We can and we will," was the answer. "We are still *Kruppianer.*"

Alfried had to wait until March 4, 1953, before the Western Powers published their master plan for the dismemberment of the Krupp combine. These were its details.

Alfried was instructed to sell his coal and steel holdings within five years — although a "special commission" would consider time-extensions if a "fair" price were not offered. The coal and steel companies were placed under trustee-managers who were acceptable to both Krupp and the Allies. Their sale was to be carried out by a banking-syndicate headed by the Rhein-Ruhr (later Dresdner) Bank.

One engineering plant, Capito and Klein, was transferred to Alfried's sister Irmgard, with an additional eight million marks from the sale of coal interests. His nephew, Arnold, was to receive eight million marks; and his brothers Berthold and Harald and his sister Waldtraut, eleven million marks each. Under a written agreement Alfried undertook never to re-enter the coal and steel industries in Germany. (Nothing was laid down about the making of arms.)

The purpose of the agreement was to destroy Krupp as an "undue concentration of economic power." The same thing was being done to the other big coal and steel trusts, to the chemical industry, and to the banks, under Allied Law No. 75. It is not possible here to go into the details of this immense undertaking. An outline must suffice. I.G. Farben, for instance, was split into three main "successor-companies" and two smaller ones. The "Big Three" commercial banks were split into nine regionally-based successors. The principal coal and steel trusts were divided into twenty "unit companies," and the biggest of the old trusts, the Vereinigte Stahlwerke, effectively ceased to exist. The official Allied purpose in implementing Law No. 75 was always the same — to leave compact, viable firms in existence which would provide a solid basis for fair and competitive German heavy industry and finance.

German critics have since maintained that the purpose of the law — as with Allied dismantling of German industry and the successive limitations placed on steel production — was to reduce German economic power and place Germany in a weak competitive position vis-à-vis other countries of the West. Of course, there was an element of truth in this. It would have been surprising if French and British industrialists, whose undertakings had been damaged or dislocated by Hitler's war, had not been anxious to curtail that unresting German creative urge which would now be concentrated in the economic field. The German cartels, they argued, had proved themselves to be the instruments of an overweening, unbalanced economic ambition. They had sought not to develop but to dominate. They had been guilty of every unfair trading practice which had ever been invented. (One example is indicative. In 1926 Germany joined the International Steel Cartel. This laid down quotas for its members. Germany deliberately exceeded its quota and paid the fines imposed without a murmur. But the German steel industry continued to expand capacity, then demanded an increased quota and threatened withdrawal from the Cartel. The net result was that penalties on overproduction were cut, and German output increased by four million tons during the first two years of the

Cartel's existence. French output meanwhile remained stationary.)

When the Allied plan for the "deconcentration" of Krupp was announced there were howls of rage all over Germany. Yet it was at once obvious that the plan was full of flaws. Alfried was left in sole control of holdings with an estimated value of one hundred and forty million dollars. (He tried to laugh this off by saying that "people are apt to put in one or two zeros too many when they talk about my fortune"; but his assets were certainly worth more than eight hundred million by 1960.) His family lawyers at once made it clear that they regarded the promise not to re-enter the German coal and steel industries as illegal. The Federal Government was obviously embarrassed by it. And who was to decide, anyway, what was a "fair" price for the Krupp coal and steel firms? For that matter, would any other firm have either the cash or the courage to make an offer? Cash was in short supply, and there is honor even among thieves.

The Allied plan, moreover, came years too late. The process of "deconcentration" was already in the act of being reversed. In November 1953 the German Iron and Steel Federation decided that "vertical" trusts — controlling coal, iron ore and steel-making — should be reconstituted. In December 1954 the Schuman Plan High Authority in Luxembourg gave the Mannesmann steel trust in Düsseldorf permission to reconstitute itself. Within three years this trust was producing seven million tons of coal and nearly two million tons of steel a year. It was a good deal more powerful than before the war.

In January 1955 the Gütehoffnungshütte coal and steel trust re-formed. In May 1955 the Hoesch syndicate announced that it would reabsorb its old coal mines. Two of the components of the Vereinigte Stahlwerke, Huettenwerke Phoenix and the Rheinische Roehrenwerke, combined as the Phoenix-Rheinrohr firm a year later. Of the incredibly complicated Allied deconcentration program only two acts continued to withstand the test of time. The I.G. Farben chemical and the Vereinigte Stahlwerke steel trusts had not regrouped.

In the meantime there had been another turning-point in the

history of Krupp. On September 22, 1952, Alfried signed on as "General Manager" Berthold Beitz, a thirty-nine-year-old businessman with no connection with the Ruhr. Beitz had a short but brilliant record in banking and insurance. Breezy-mannered, modern in outlook and a dandy, Beitz was the exact antithesis to the shy, introspective Alfried Krupp. One friend called him "the born cutter of red tape." Another explained his role in the words, "Beitz is introducing Krupp to the twentieth century." Beitz quickly became the driving force behind the firm's continuing recovery and expansion.

He believed that the Krupp empire must be maintained intact. He saw to it that this happened. Following the 1953 agreement, only one Krupp property had, up to 1959, been sold. This was the Emscher-Lippe coal mine. The cash paid for it (22 million marks, or five million dollars) was immediately and more profitably invested in an engineering plant. Buyers did not come forward for the Hannover-Hannibal and Konstantin the Great coal mines, or for the Rossenray and Rheinberg coal fields, with proved reserves of more than five hundred million tons, or for the Rheinhausen steelworks, with an annual output of around two million tons. Beitz was confident that these properties would never be sold. "Without coal, iron and steel," he declared, "we are deprived of long-term investment. The resulting atmosphere of insecurity hamstrings our entire organization and, incidentally, West German industry as a whole." Because of the Allied "agreement," Beitz argued, it was not possible to exploit the Rossenray reserves. The Hannibal mine had not been able to build and finance the nitrogen plant which it needed.

"It is ludicrous to enforce a must-sell order," Beitz declared. "I do not believe that the American State Department wants it. I know the Bonn Government is against it. It is not just our problem, for it affects German public opinion as a whole."

The American State Department and German public opinion were real clues to Beitz's purposeful campaign to preserve the Krupp family inheritance. Why should the United States — still pouring millions of dollars into the Old World — sponsor what looked like an economic absurdity? Why should German public opinion tolerate it? Beitz coined a useful slogan: "We must all row our hardest for the West. But there is no point in tying the arms of one of your best oarsmen."

Beitz began to pay frequent visits to Washington. He wanted a visa for Alfried Krupp (who got one in 1958). More important, Beitz wanted to interest the American Government in new Krupp plans. The most spectacular was the so-called "Krupp Point Four and a Half Program" for the underdeveloped countries. Its essential details were: the formation of German and, if necessary, international consortia in order to finance capital investment in these countries; the tenders put forward by these consortia to be strictly competitive and involving fair profits; additional financing to come from the World Bank and the United States Export-Import Bank; initial concentration of interest on the Middle East, Africa and Southeast Asia.

Krupp would be ready to join and lead consortia, place its technical knowledge and good will at the disposal of the United States Government, map out programs based on its already great experience. Beitz's work between 1954 and 1957 offered a fine basis for future planning. Krupp was building a two-hundred-million-dollar steel plant at Rourkela in India, an eighty-million-dollar steel plant in Pakistan, a twenty-million-dollar nickel-smelting plant in Greece, a bridge over the Nile at Cairo, factories, docks, harbors, cement and chemical plants in Iran, Iraq, Siam, Afghanistan. The Federal Government had already subscribed over fifty-five million dollars to these projects.

The slogan of the "Point Four and a Half Program" was devised by the firm's intelligent American public-relations adviser. He was only one living proof of Beitz's increasing interest in a close tie-up with America. Beitz began to be seen even more often in Washington. He gave his sales-booklets an increasingly transatlantic flavor. "Old Man Cheops had no labor-problem when he built his pyramid. Nor will you, if you move your materials, mountains, molehills by Krupp giant tipping-truck."

"Good relations" were furthered in other directions and other ways. Alfried traveled more himself as time went on, visited Asian and Middle East countries as the honored guest of their governments. He sent more and more teams of industrial and financial experts to the underdeveloped countries, selling their expert advice for fat fees. One such team was flown out post-haste to Karachi when the Russians offered to build three steel mills for Pakistan at a low cost. Another dashed to Cairo when Colonel Nasser received a Russian offer for both the Cairo bridge and the Aswan dam. These German teams brought a comfortable line of political talk with them — they were representatives of a "non-colonial power," with the best kind of interests in the "trade, not aid" American concept.

In West Germany Alfried had become the Federal Government's unofficial "industrial ambassador." His father had only been Kaiser Wilhelm's gunsmith. In the unedifying, neoclassic barn of the Villa Hügel, on the outskirts of Essen, Alfried entertained the Negus of Ethiopia, the Shah of Iran, the heads or foreign ministers of numerous other states. Even members of the hierarchy of France's Fourth Republic were able to find their taste in ladies' fashions a suitable excuse for ingratiating themselves with the most powerful family of the old German industrial oligarchy. Guest-of-honor at mannequin shows was the French Ambassador in Bonn, M. André François Poncet, whose previous services to his country had included the issue of unheeded warnings about the true character of Hitler and the vain attempt after 1945 to annex by stealth the prosperous steel and coal area of the German Saar.

It was an interesting experience to attend the "diplomatic ball" which Alfried Krupp gave in the Villa Hügel early in 1956. Among the guests were one hundred Western diplomatists and their wives, who were brought up from Bonn in a special train, given a conducted tour round Krupp plants in and around Essen, and paid off with fancy gifts made from Krupp steel accompanied by brochures listing the Krupp properties which were due to be sold under the agreement with the Western Powers. The diplomatists and the rest were served with frothy German champagne ("Sekt") and a discreetly chosen 1953 Moselle. Balding bachelors were guided round the floor by dance-hostesses who had been specially flown in from Vienna. Among the curious touches were the reception of the guests — they had the option of shaking hands with Alfried and his wife Vera, or of moving straight into the champagne bar (were there some who did not like the idea of shaking hands with a "war criminal"?); and private cars were delivered to their owners at the end of the function, driven up to the hall door by liveried flunkeys, car tanks filled brimful of Krupp gasoline.

The "diplomatic ball" was a part of the Krupp campaign to retain the firm's coal and steel holdings, in spite of the agreement to sell them. The disposal of the Emscher-Lippe coal mine had served a dual purpose — it gave apparent evidence of "good faith" in fulfilling the agreement and it provided working capital at a time when Krupp was going through its first postwar phase of dynamic expansion. In December 1956 the Konstantin the Great coal mine was sold too, but this was a very different kind of transaction. It was bought for 37.5 million marks (nine million dollars) by the Bochumer Verein steel firm, which resold some of the shares but retained a 52 per cent interest in it.

The Bochumer Verein firm made high-vacuum steel and its plant capacity was roughly 1.5 million tons of steel a year. At the time of the purchase of the Konstantin coal mine, the firm had just patented a brilliantly successful process of casting big steel blocks in a vacuum (absence of air means absence of flaws, and an immensely quicker and more efficient casting process). It owned few coal-mining interests and the purchase of Konstantin made good sense in one respect, in that it helped re-establish the vertical trust of the classic Ruhr type. But in another respect it was a surprise, for the Bochumer Verein had suffered more than most big Ruhr firms from war damage and postwar dismantling, and was notoriously short of capital.

In fact, the transaction had been planned by Krupp and his associates with considerable forethought. A large share had been bought late in 1954 in the Bochumer Verein by a close personal friend of Alfried Krupp, the Swedish industrialist Dr. Axel Wenner-Gren. It was the first time that Dr. Wenner-Gren, whose field of speculative interest was far-flung, had interested himself in a major steel firm. It was supposed that he had bought, initially, a 20 per cent to 25 per cent share in the Bochumer Verein. In reality he had bought a 40 per cent to 42 per cent share, and in the course of the next eighteen months he bought privately and on the open market until he controlled a majority holding in the firm. The Bochumer Verein shares were placed in the hands of VIGAU, the "Vermoegens Verwaltung," a "cover" holding company which administered Dr. Wenner-Gren's other financial interests in Germany.

In February 1958 it became known that Dr. Wenner-Gren was preparing to transfer his controlling share in the Bochumer Verein to Krupp. It also became known that Krupp's own Rheinhausen steel company (which he had agreed to sell in 1953, but which he fully intended all along to retain) had bought a 27 per cent share in the Bochumer Verein. Undercover control had been completed. Krupp openly sent Dr. Karl Hundhausen, a member of his own board of directors, to be managing director of Rheinhausen (the announcement was made three days before the Federal Election of September 15, 1957, so that it should pass unnoticed) and the head offices of Rheinhausen were moved, in January 1958, from the banks of the Rhine in Duisburg to Essen, Krupp's headquarters.

At the end of 1958, Krupp appealed to the European Coal and Steel High Authority in Luxembourg for permission to merge the Bochumer Verein with the Rheinhausen company. Permission was readily granted.

In my own files is a letter from the Coal and Steel High Authority dated September 1954. It points out that mergers were being allowed between German steel firms which did not "disturb the balance" of the industry and which were in no case creating combines with a steel capacity of more than two-and-a-half million tons a year. The Bochumer Verein-Rheinhausen merger gave Krupp a capacity of roughly four million tons a year — or one million tons more than the next-biggest single steel firm in Germany at that time, the Dortmund-Hörder Hütten-Verein. It gave Krupp's just double its prewar steel capacity.

It was significant that Krupp merged the Bochumer Verein

company with Rheinhausen, although the latter was still due to be sold by March 1959 — which allowed five years from the signing of the Krupp agreement, plus one year's automatic extension because no buyer had come forward. This was a mark of Krupp's complete confidence that Rheinhausen would never be sold at all. Every possible step was being taken to ensure this. In America the State Department, as well as individual Senators and members of the House of Representatives, were canvassed for this purpose. In West Germany the active sympathy of the Federal Government was enlisted. In July, 1957, the Federal Government asked the Western Powers to reverse the Krupp agreement. Its appeal was backed by a vigorous West German press campaign. Its arguments were straightforward — the agreement was "out of date"; it represented a forced sale by a free and independent German subject; it was not practicable, since no buyers for the Krupp properties could be found; it was a leftover of the Morgenthau Plan and the era of Allied economic oppression in Germany.

In March 1959 Alfried Krupp appealed personally for the repeal of the sales agreement. He said, "I think that we have been very patient, but I believe that the time has now come when we must have the situation clarified. For we wish only to enjoy the same conditions as other big combines in the new European Common Market." He gave three reasons for his view that Krupp should remain intact; past history had always shown that the living standard was highest where big industrial concentrations exist; the trend towards bigger concentrations is generally considered rational; and German combines are still much smaller than American.

The position of Krupp in 1959 showed just how futile Allied efforts to break up this outstanding concentration of economic power had proved. The firm employed 93,000 workers in its engineering and manufacturing plants. Sales in 1958 totaled 3.44 billion marks (820 million dollars). This figure did not include the 720 million mark (170 million dollars) sales of the Bochumer Verein. Exports amounted to 130 million dollars, and a limitless field has been opened up by the firm's pioneering work in the underdeveloped countries. In spite of the recession in the German steel industry, Krupp sales were roughly 50 million higher than in 1957. This single firm, owned by a single man, controlled 16 per cent of Germany's total steel capacity, and 6 per cent of its coal. In rough terms, it was 70 per cent to 80 per cent larger than before the war.

The reconcentration of Krupp was part of the general pattern of German industrial expansion. At the end of 1958 two of the largest components of the defunct Vereinigte Stahlwerke, August Thyssen and Phoenix-Rheinrohr, proposed to merge. Naturally, the approval of the High Authority of the European Coal and Steel Community in Luxembourg was taken for granted. The new combine's annual steel capacity of 5.5 million tons was more than double what the High Authority originally envisaged as a suitable maximum for a single firm. If this merger were to go through, three firms would control nearly 50 per cent of total German steel production.

About a month before the plans for this biggest of all German mergers leaked out, the Mannesmann steel company in Düsseldorf announced that it would unite six subsidiaries with the parent company. Mannesmann, admittedly, had around 66,000 shareholders, and one in six of its 72,000 workers owned shares in the company. The Trade-Unions protested strongly, but without avail.

A private industrial empire of a different kind which had reconstructed itself was that of Friedrich Flick, one of Hitler's financial backers who was imprisoned by the Allies as a war criminal after 1945. Flick provided a textbook example of what the Nazis had intended to do with Europe if they had won the war. During the course of it, he grabbed iron-ore mines in French Lorraine, the Virog wagon factory in Latvia, the Rombacher steelworks in the Saar, and the Aciéries de Rombas in the French department of the Moselle. He founded a coal trading-company, the "Union Société Charbonnière" in Brussels, and was believed to have salted away large sums of money in France and Belgium. This list gives an idea of Flick's far-flung holdings in 1959:

A 50 per cent to 100 per cent interest in: Ravene steel, Berlin; Metallhuette, Lübeck; Maschinenbau, Kiel; Roeschling steel, Wetzlar; Monopol coal-mining, Kamen; Maximilianhuette steel, Sulzbach; Auto-Union, Düsseldorf; Kraus Maffei lorries, Munich; Lauchhammer steel, Düsseldorf; Bunderus steel, Wetzlar.

A 25 per cent to 50 per cent interest in: Deutscher Eisenhandel, Berlin; Hessische coal-mining, Wetzlar; Feldmuehle paper, Düsseldorf; Société Metallurgique, Hainaut-Sambre, Belgium; Daimler Benz cars, Stuttgart.

A 15 per cent to 25 per cent interest in: Dynamit AG chemicals, Troisdorf; and Société des Aciéries steel, Chatillon, France.

Friedrich Flick has organized this "diversified" industrial empire, partly because he has always been an exponent of the "horizontal" type of trust, partly because the Allies sought to force him out of the coal-mining and steel-making industries. He is probably the most ruthless German industrialist of all, and in 1960 he maneuvered himself into control of both Feldmuehle and Dynamil-Nobel. He paid off minority shareholders at below-market price. Other similar empires have been built up since the war, but they are not strictly relevant to the story of the Ruhr, the heart and hub of European as well as German industry. The Ruhr, primarily, means coal, steel, chemicals. Here, then, are the operative details of its structure in 1959.

The Allies have utterly failed to break up what they considered to be "undue concentrations of economic power" in the Ruhr. Their program would have needed twenty years to implement. Before the war eight trusts controlled between them 94 per cent of German steel production and 51 per cent of hard-coal production. In 1959, after a decade of complicated Allied tinkering, eight trusts controlled 78 per cent of steel and roughly 40 per cent of coal production. Six of these trusts are prewar survivors: the two others are former components of the Vereinigte Stahlwerke. Only one name has vanished from the prewar list, that of Otto Wolff. This firm has not reabsorbed its old manufacturing and mining interests and has remained a coal and steel-trading company, as envisaged by Allied deconcentration legislation. It is ironic that the only absentee from the list of the mighty was the only firm among them which had Jewish managerial participation.

The Allies believed in 1945 that the German chemical industry had, in effect, been reduced to a monopoly of the immense I.G. Farben trust. They planned to split it up into at least eighty independent companies, then reduced the proposed number to thirty. In the event, just *five* successor companies were created, but over 90 per cent of I.G. Farben interests in West Germany are today in the hands of the three "young giants" — Farben Bayer of Leverkusen, Farbenwerke Hoechst, and Badische Anilin of Ludwigshafen. These three firms divide up fields of specialized interest, even dovetail production of different colors of dyes, cooperate with one another in all essential planning. They are independent of one another; but they can hardly be called strictly competitive.

The tendency of German trusts to spread "horizontally" has reasserted itself. Thyssen, Krupp and Rheinstahl are building ships; Flick purchased a big interest in Daimler-Benz (producing the range of Mercedes cars); entered the field of plastics in 1958; Krupp has embarked into nuclear-power and aircraft-production; Mannesmann is interesting itself in plastics; the richest of all the "new millionaires," Rudolf Oetker, controls breweries, shipyards, hotels, banks, insurance-companies, paper-mills, film-companies, aircraft-firms, chemicals, light and heavy engineering plants — in addition to the family pudding-powder business in Bielefeld on which he based his empire.

The Allied deconcentration programs were actuated by the belief that Germans were cartel-minded and that cartels dominated the German industrial scene. All deconcentration was useless, it was thought, unless strong and effective anti-cartel legislation were forced on the Germans. And what happened? The Federal Government (although the Minister of Economics, Ludwig Erhard, is a genuine disciple of free competition) provided for the formation of cartels in times of economic crisis, in order to boost exports, in order to carry out a necessary rationalization of industry. I listened to Professor Erhard giving an exposition on the anti-cartel law in Essen to the Federation of German Industries. He adopted a pleading tone when asking its members to trust him. This was quite understandable. That assembly of sober gentlemen, mostly bull-necked and with comfortably filled waistcoats, represented the orderliness, inventiveness and ruthless energy of the real rulers of present-day Germany.

One of West Germany's most successful businessmen, Hermann Abs — Chairman of the Deutsche Bank and of a dozen other firms and corporations — said in mid-1959 that there would be no further moves towards cartelization in West Germany or, for that matter, in the other Common Market countries. He believed that the existing industrial structure had come to stay, and that it would guarantee full and fair competition and an ever-strengthening economy. Herr Abs, and many like him, are satisfied that heavy industry is now on the right basis.

Some facts speak in favor of his views.

Many of the old names of the Ruhr barons have dropped out of active business. Baron Kurt von Schroeder, Albert Voegler and Ernst Poensgen did not survive the war. The Thyssens, Kloeckners and Haniels no longer administer their mighty interests. At all events that chilling figure, the "Herr Dr. Direktor" of prewar days, is no more — resplendent in cutaway coat, often monocled and manicured, hidden in the plush fastnesses of his inner office from the gaze of his thousands of workers, conventionally depicted with an outsize cigar in his mouth and cold, predatory eyes dominating his stony, supercilious face. In control today are men of the "General Manager" class, like Wilhelm Zangen (Mannesmann), Hermann Reusch (Gütehoffnungshütte), Hans Günther Sohl (Thyssens), Berthold Beitz (Krupp). Some of these General Managers belonged to the prewar era, but they have been dying out since 1945. General Managers do not in any case found dynasties.

The departure of so many of the Ruhr elite and of its families from active affairs means that the old processes of concentration and cartelization will operate on a purely material basis. Economic expediency has become the sole criterion; the old urge for power of the Ruhr oligarchy has at least diminished in effect. The survivors of that oligarchy have certainly learned from bitter experience. Take the case of Alfried Krupp. He shuns ostentation, lives in a glorified bungalow, refuses to have neon signs on the head office buildings in Essen. He is all for the West. "It is my opinion," he told one questioner, "that co-coperation with the West is the only wise policy, for it helps to preserve world peace." Alfried Krupp has not allowed success to go to his head. "Do not overrate the German Economic Miracle," he told his workers. "We must not be proud or presumptuous about it, for we are not yet over the hill."

Yet it would be true to say that something like a "restoration" has occurred in the Ruhr. There are many reasons for this. The trade unions are not strong — in spite of their massive membership of six and a half million. The granting of a right of co-determination to the workers in the coal and steel industries (the workers elect half the members of the advisory boards, as well as a "Labor Director") has been a useful sop, without weakening management. The big firms have helped to secure industrial peace by giving "fringe benefits" (good canteens, shower baths, locker rooms, sports fields) of a far higher standard than anywhere else in Europe save Sweden. The urge to produce, and to expand production, has been rooted in the individual worker's determination to earn for himself all those comforts of which he was totally or partially deprived from 1929 to 1949. It is hard for workers who are successful to remain militant Marxists. This has been by far the most potent reason for the astonishing freedom from strikes enjoyed by the Ruhr since the war.

There is nothing economically weak about the structure of Ruhr heavy industry. The functioning of the European Common Market will bring increased concentration. The renaissance of the capital market — dating from 1956 — will make large-scale capital investment easier as time goes by. The steady growth of demand overseas will be a continual spur to increased output. The absence of an armaments industry has already given West

Germany special advantages in exploiting these markets. Only five years after the end of the war, James Stewart Martin wrote in his book, *All Honorable Men:* "What was emerging was a European economy dominated from a central hub of German heavy industry, with an outer ring of satellite states supplying food, raw materials and light industrial products." Fifteen years after the war this development was anchored in European history.

Of course there are dangers ahead. Some people, who have observed the German scene closely, believe that the immense and restless energies of an industrious people will be concentrated on the goal of economic domination of the whole of the Old World. Others fear that the Ruhr industrialists will — if and when it suits them — "turn East," in order to secure the biggest profits of all as the workshop of the Communist bloc. Others, again, see in the "Ruhr Restoration" the beginning of a new era of exploitation of the worker, and in April 1959 the trade-union weekly, *Welt der Arbeit*, uttered a trenchant warning against "those enemies in the Ruhr of working-class freedom and independence."

Or, again, there is the possibility of European cartels, under German leadership — a possibility which Berthold Beitz, for instance, has already clearly envisaged. With the advent of the European common market in 1959, fears became acute in Britain that the "cartel-minded Continentals" would group themselves under German leadership, would seek to dominate the European market and, protected at home, would undersell their competitors in the other markets of the world. The very profitability of European cartels could bring American capital pouring into them.

I see a different danger, and it is best illustrated by a story. Rosemarie Nitribitt was, in 1958, the most famous and expensive prostitute in Frankfurt. Her favors were sought particularly by the richest of the rich, who needed her chaff, baby talk and "understanding." They gladly paid upwards of five hundred dollars for an evening in her company. Then blackmail intruded into the picture, although the police could not make up their minds whether the blackmail was exercised by Rosemarie herself or by someone who "looked over" her interesting address book.

Rosemarie was murdered; the police, after interviewing dozens of the tycoons of German industry, arrested only an obscure pimp on grounds that were flimsy and may well have been faked. The Munich dramatist, Erich Kuby, wrote a film script of the Nitribitt story. *Das Mädchen Rosemarie* was about the most successful German film since the war. It depicted the twentieth-century conquistadors of the German industrial world as gross, unattractive figures, and their wives as hopelessly humdrum, socially self-conscious women who run early to fat. Kuby's picture of these people was an arresting one. It reaffirmed that the barons of industry had remained amoral, lacking in taste and moderation, and had remained, above all, divorced from the rest of society. Here, then, is the most serious danger inherent in this powerful class of industrialist: it has still not fused with the rest of the community, and it retains the peculiar arrogance which springs from social isolation. As long as that remains so, the immense power of the Ruhr could be once again misapplied. And that power is greater than before, and is still concentrated in the hands of a very few.

LANCASTER, *Daily Express*

"Watch That Right Arm, Siegfried!"

-12-

The Lunatic Fringe

Politics are once more being paraded on the streets and brought into the sphere of the tub-thumper. The chaotic state of German liberalism is due to three things: the nationalism built up on Bismarck's bayonets, the blaming of the Treaty of Versailles on European Liberals, and Allied failure after 1956 to promote a Liberal Party in Germany.
— VICE-CHANCELLOR FRANZ BLÜCHER, in a private interview, March 1956

The spirit of Germany today is the spirit of a people who have repudiated the tyranny and the brutality of the Nazi rule.
— DR. JAMES CONANT, former United States High Commissioner in Germany, in a lecture to the University of Minnesota

Why not once again be good National Socialists? For the *Boehme Zeitung* has always supported national revolution in Germany.
— *Boehme Zeitung*, Lower Saxony, 1949

I N the very first interview which I had with Dr. Kurt Schumacher, the first postwar leader of the Social Democratic Party, I asked him what the "new Germany" most needed, in order to establish itself, make its way as a modern democracy. He screwed his already tortured features into an expression of immense concentration. "Stability" was his answer, eventually.

What, I persisted, was needed to create this stability? Schumacher's face began to take on the ambiguity of an unexplained oracle. Was it, I suggested, something like the two-party political system which exists in America and Britain? He nodded sagely

— Yes, it was, would be, something of the kind. Of course, he added with unconscious irony, it was difficult for his Social Democrats to visualize what "second" party could arise.

Indeed, a two-party system was not a likelihood, even when the Federal Republic was born in 1949 and Schumacher's Social Democrats had become unpleasantly aware of the challenge posed by the interdenominational Christian Democratic Union. Intense material prosperity was not envisaged at the first Federal Election, of September 1949. Then, certainly, fourteen million Germans voted for the Christian Democratic and Social Democratic parties. But nearly three million votes went to the Free Democrats, who have since moved steadily to the right and away from classic German liberalism. Another four million votes went to parties of the "Right" with a fairly obvious nationalist flavor. Three million Germans did not vote. Some were debarred from doing so, as "major Nazis," but the great mass of them did not vote because they did not like democratic parties. Over and above groups which were professedly or potentially antidemocratic, nearly a million and a half votes were cast for the Communists.

The ex-Nazi vote was destined throughout that first prosperous decade of the Federal Republic's existence to remain a constant but "hidden" factor in West German politics. It was at first neither discreet nor safe to profess Nazi beliefs or sympathies. Even after political amnesties it remained unfashionable. Yet German politicians cast loving eyes at the ex-Nazi vote, aware of its attractions if it could be mobilized *en bloc*.

The ex-Nazi was only one kind of "floating voter." Here, for instance, is the case of a personal friend — a most respectable, anti-Nazi refugee from the now Polish-occupied city of Danzig. He was never a Socialist, and so could not vote for a Social Democratic Party, which clung to Marxist dogma like a drunkard clinging to an empty bottle. He did not believe in the association of the Christian ethic with a single political party. Therefore he did not join the Christian Democratic Party. He looked round for a safe haven for someone with progressive, humanitarian ideas and a keen desire to take a part in the political life of the "new" Germany.

He joined the Free Democrats, and was happy with them for a time. But the emergence in 1954-1955 of young right-wing radicals in the party, purging its apparatus in the Ruhr and other parts of Germany, disgusted him. He left the party, drifted disconsolate and unattached. Then came the split in the ranks of the Free Democrats, and he joined the smaller offshoot, the Free People's Party. But the tide was by then running strongly towards a two-party system, and the new group lacked organizers and funds. It merged with the more obviously conservative and right-wing German Party. My friend from Danzig lasted only a short time with this semi-respectable raggle-taggle. He became, at last, a Christian Democrat — but not by conviction. It seemed to him that there was no good alternative to government by the party of Dr. Adenauer.

This man was a refugee, but would have nothing to do with "refugee politics," by which is meant primarily the linking of the refugees' claims to their old homes with their allegiance to a political party. Yet by 1959 there were nearly twelve million refugees, or people of refugee blood, in West Germany. Since the BHE refugee party could never obtain outright majorities in any constituency, the refugees became the biggest floating vote of all.

Ex-Nazis, refugees, right-wing Nationalists, Liberals and moderate Conservatives with no political home — here was the sort of amorphous mass of voters which a second Hitler would have regarded as the most promising possible material for a new assault on democratic order and freedom. More than one putative "second Hitler" appeared during the first years of the Federal Republic. The failure of such people after 1949 to capture at least a decent proportion of the eight million unattached votes was due to three reasons — the Western Powers were still occupying Germany and had plenary powers; economic reconstruction was an all-absorbing and hugely successful undertaking; and Nazism was mistrusted because it had brought a national catastrophe.

This last was a much more important consideration than the

high-flown thought of Dr. James Conant, former U. S. High Commissioner in Germany, that the German people had "repudiated Nazi tyranny and brutality." Most Germans have not given Nazi tyranny and brutality much thought; if they have, they regard them as matters of secondary importance. This is not to level an accusation against them, but to state a fact. Germans have had too many other things to think about since 1945.

But if a Nazi revival was never likely in the postwar period, one of the essential origins of Nazism probably remained a German characteristic. Worship of the spirit of opportunism runs like a red thread through the history of Germany since the days of Bismarck. Opportunism which paid off was the personal characteristic which induced "Bismarck worship." Opportunism remained the essence of German political thinking after Bismarck's fall — but was no longer backed by Bismarck's flair and sense of timing. It led to the tragic wrong-mindedness of men like Holstein and Admiral Tirpitz. Holstein dabbled with the idea of alliance with Russia "to secure us from the English lust for war." Tirpitz expressed his political creed with the words, "The sympathy of our intellectuals for Western civilization is to blame for our misfortunes. Its glib utilitarian, capitalistic mass civilization is less profitable to the German character than the perverse idealism of the Russians." German opportunism prompted one member of the German foreign office, Kiderlen-Waechter, to say, "A four months' press campaign is enough to convince the German people of any idiocy."

Opportunism produced the pre-1914 Schlieffen Plan and the violation of Belgian neutrality, the 1922 Treaty of Rappallo and the forfeit of Western trust, the 1939 Ribbentrop-Molotov Pact and the setting of the stage for World War II. More recently it produced that astonishing phenomenon — the organization by Red Army Commissars of Prussian officers into an expeditionary force of politically proselytizing mercenaries. The story of this experiment in manipulating men's minds has been told in his book, *Shadow of Stalingrad,* by Count Heinrich von Einsiedel, a young man of noble family, ultra-conservative upbringing and considerable charm and ability. This is what Einsiedel could feel about Communism only a few months after being shot down and captured by the Russians: "I could see no power and no ideas which had a more positive, a more realistic conception of the future. Perhaps the Church? Perhaps democracy? But had they been able to alter or prevent the catastrophes which had swept across the world? Was there any sign that they would be able to do anything now? I saw none."

A good and intelligible concept, in fact, ceased to be worthwhile because it had failed to eliminate the factor of brute force. From this strange appraisal it was only one step to volunteer one's personal assistance to Lucifer. But, of course, there had to be "historical justification"; and so Einsiedel wrote, "We have a great example in our history. One hundred and thirty years ago, when German troops were still fighting on Russian territory, the very best Germans, Von Stein, Clausewitz, Arndt and Yorck, called upon the conscience of the German people to fight for freedom, addressing them from Russia above the heads of their treacherous leaders."

It was this German gift for drawing imbecile "historical parallels" that enabled men like Edmund Hoffmeister (who had taken part in the extreme right-wing Kapp Putsch aimed at overthrowing the democratic Weimar Republic) and Vinzenz Müller (former adjutant to General von Schleicher) to offer their services to Stalin. Müller and men like him — Homann, Lenski, Rentsch, Korfes, Lattmann — were to build up the East German People's Police and armed forces under Soviet direction, and make them into the most potent instruments of Communist tyranny in East Germany.

It is interesting to note how the German instinct for opportunism operates in reverse. Two years before the war the Nazi city fathers of the Ruhr town of Düsseldorf built a model homes exhibition on its northern outskirts, admirably designed and planned, and admirably placed close to the Rhine. After the exhibition had stayed open to the public for a few weeks, the friends of the Nazi Party — including the local *Gauleiter* — moved into its two hundred houses. Its streets were named after the "heroes" of the Nazi movement and the settlement as a whole was called the

"Schlageter Siedlung," after the young man who fought against the French occupation of the Ruhr in 1923.

In the closing days of the war American troops advanced to the outskirts of Düsseldorf and prepared to lay down an artillery barrage. From Stockum — the part of the town which contains the Schlageter Siedlung — five worthy citizens set off with white flags for the American front line. There they explained that there would be no resistance in Stockum if the Americans would treat it as an "open city."

There was no artillery barrage and a great many lives were saved. But when the five men got back they were met by a small detachment of S.S. who had heard all about their "mission." Before the Americans arrived, the five men were strung up and garroted on the little green in the middle of the Schlageter Siedlung. When its streets were renamed after the war, the names of the five men were among those used. I lived for seven years in the Siedlung and I never met a German who knew their story. To so many Germans martyrdom and failure are synonymous.

Sometimes the events of ten years ago seem very close indeed, sometimes very far off. The latter applies when recalling the many signs of a still lively German spirit of opportunism during the first years of the Federal Republic's life. The first of those signs was the organization of the semisecret society of the "Brotherhood." In 1950 the "Brotherhood" leaped suddenly into the news headlines.

Its founder members were a sinister crew. Chief among them were Alfred Franke-Griecsch and Ernst Achenbach, the former a son-in-law of Gregor Strasser — the rival for the leadership of the Nazi Party whom Hitler had murdered — the latter a smooth-tongued Essen lawyer who had served under the Nazis' wartime "ambassador" to Paris, Otto Abetz. The German General Staff was represented by Beck-Broichstetter and Stauffenberg, a cousin of the hero of the Resistance to Hitler. The Nazi Party was represented too, by former *Gauleiters* Kaufmann and Lauterbacher. But the spirit of the group was nationalist and opportunist, rather than Nazi.

Its earliest members were S.S. and army officers who decided to organize for "the completion of the National-Socialist revolution" while they were still in British and American prisoner of war camps. "We lived like monks there," Franke-Grieksch told me, "and we really had time for thought." The purpose of the organization was to establish itself on a nonpolitical, nationwide basis. "We have men of proved efficiency," Franke-Grieksch said, "who will take over control of every phase of German administration when the time comes"; and, "We have our agents and our liaison officers everywhere." The Brotherhood quickly established powerful "cells" in Hamburg, Lübeck, Kiel, Bielefeld and Düsseldorf. Its members met in mock-romantic surroundings — the Teutoburger Forest; Till Eulenspiegel's home, the town of Moelln, on the silver-sandy shores of the Baltic; and in the glum wastes of the Luneburg Heath. There they held discussions in the open, in the light of campfires. There is something in the German character which revels in the pleasures of the overgrown Boy Scout.

Franke-Grieksch, with his glittering eye of the "Ancient Mariner" and his steely, untruthful smile, explained the aims of the Brotherhood fairly fully to me. Europe was to become a "real third force" and would be "independent of Moscow and New York." Germany would cease to be a "glacis," a springboard for American military-planning, and would become the core of a new neutral bloc. For practical reasons, German eyes would turn East and away from a Western alliance "which crusades for an outworn democratic faith." The Soviet Union would give German skill and industry illimitable chances of expansion. At home, Germans would be divided into citizens and helots, re-grouped "by rank and degree, by achievement and worth." Political parties were being infiltrated and would be "taken over" in due course.

Franke-Grieksch made his plans sound frighteningly feasible, even though he projected his words to an unseen audience, and directed his stony stare on the obscure future of the Aryan Race. The Brotherhood, he made plain to me, was the natural focus of the ex-army officer, war cripple, jobless, discarded Nazi, violent Nationalist and submerged Strasserite. Behind it were the dynamics of the German character — the fierce desire to launch a better belief than democracy, the deep-rooted faith in Germany's destiny, the sad yearning for the comradeship of other nations than those who have merely been bullied into alliance in the past.

The Brotherhood ceased to be a potential force when Franke-Grieksch sought his true spiritual home in East Germany, after quarreling with both Stauffenberg and Beck-Broichstetter and disrupting the upper strata of his organization. But it had played its part already in sowing the seeds of latter-day German nationalism, and there were other claimants in the field for the leadership of all those Germans who regarded democracy as feeble and futile.

Chief among them was the Socialist Reichs Party, founded by two unrepentant ex-Nazis, Fritz Dorls and ex-General Otto Remer. Dorls was that type of German who combines organizational genius with a love of subterranean activity and complete political ruthlessness. Remer was to be the vote-catcher. He had scotched the Resistance to Hitler by marching the men of the Grossdeutschland Division to the old Reich Defense Ministry in the Bendler Strasse and arresting the "conspirators" on July 20, 1944. Seven years later he and Dorls fought the *Land* Lower Saxony election on what was virtually a straight Nazi ticket. They rejected the Federal structure and constitution of West Germany. They called the Bonn Government the "lickspittle of the Western Powers," and the black, red and gold Federal flag "the banner of defeat and of all those who crawl to conquerors." They ridiculed democratic government as weak and "un-German," and called for rule by experts. Remer was the epitome of Nazi virility. His lean jaw had a wolfish strength. His eye glared; his voice rasped; he spat his words out. Remer dressed up his strong-arm squads in jack boots and riding breeches and planned their conversion into a *Reichsfront* or *corps d'élite* of the same pattern as the S.S. He demanded the creation of a Youth Front and a Labor Front, again on Nazi lines. He demanded the re-establishment of "the honor of the German soldier," the release of all war criminals, the rehabilitation of ex-Nazis, the condemnation of the men of the Resistance (pitfully few had survived), whom he called "those blackguards, who betrayed their country."

One of his followers, Hans Bormann, called the men who had been imprisoned by the Nazis "the scum of the earth who are having a fine old time today," and contrasted them with those members of the Nazi Party — "fine, honorable fellows" — whom the Allies interned in 1945. Another follower, Hans Festge, stated on oath there had only been one concentration camp in Germany, which had done an excellent job cremating prisoners who had died of old age. Yet another, Heinz Richter, declared that Presidents Truman and Eisenhower and Generals Clay and MacArthur should be tried as war criminals. He called the British diplomat Sir Robert Vansittart "the prince of liars," and Sir Winston Churchill "the damnedest dictator of all."

Other party spokesmen told election audiences that the Americans had thrust pieces of glowing wood under the fingernails of their prisoners in order to extract confessions from them. The German war criminals in Landsberg jail had been led several times to the scaffold in order to give American women the chance to photograph them. The Americans had "appointed tribunals exclusively composed of Jews in order to ensure the award of the death sentence." Another S.R.P. speaker, Werner Baentsch, said that the British gave their political prisoners a daily dose of arsenic in their bread in order to make them sterile; "this was a part of the Morgenthau Plan."

The S.R.P. polled nearly 400,000 votes in 1951 in economically backward *Land* Lower Saxony, comprising 11 per cent of the electorate there. That so many people could be found to vote for a party blatantly Nazi was surprising enough. It was even more significant that the S.R.P. meetings were invariably the best-attended and aroused the most spontaneous enthusiasm. When the Federal Government sent off the Minister of the Interior, Dr. Robert Lehr, to find out how serious the situation was, Lower Saxony garage proprietors refused to service his official car. Armed bodyguards simply pushed the local police out of their way when "the Party" marched through the streets of the hick towns of the Luneburg Heath to the stirring strains of *Preussens Gloria* and the *Badenweiler Marsch*.

Of course, this part of Germany is the poorest and most politically backward in the whole of western Europe. It has always been a breeding ground for rabid nationalism. It was the one area where something of the "Werewolf" spirit, which Hitler had wanted to foster, persisted, and where shots were occasionally fired uncomfortably close to members of the occupation forces. Beer hall meetings which I attended in the villages were packed by massed rows of clodhoppers who sat in sullen silence until the speaker of the day arrived. They had no cheer, no conversation, even for each other. Lower Saxony was refugee-infested into the bargain, with some of the worst of all the hutted camps. It was probably the darkest corner of the moral and spiritual backwoods of Germany.

That the S.R.P. did not prosper was mostly due to the energetic action of the Federal Government. After a second success in the *Land* elections in Bremen, the S.R.P. was banned. Remer was sued before the Brunswick criminal court, in March 1952, for slandering the men of the Resistance, and was sentenced to three months' imprisonment. (The judge who imposed the sentence received nearly fifty threatening letters in the course of a few weeks — a typical specimen was, "The gallows and the meat-hooks are waiting for you, you pig-dog.") Remer fled to Egypt, and the S.R.P. disappeared — for the time being — from the political scene.

Alfred Franke-Grieksch had told me that the "life of the S.R.P. can be timed with a stop watch." The sense of this somewhat cryptic remark now became apparent. A neo-Nazi party which might have had some chance of success in 1949 had much less in 1951. The economic revival of West Germany was gathering impetus and there were increasingly fewer Germans whose Nazi sentiments were so strong that they were ready to support policies which were openly hostile to the Western Allies and which advocated an uneasy German neutrality between East and West. And in 1951, as in 1949, the Western Allies were in a position to control events. This and the twin watchwords of postwar German democracy — security and a full stomach — doomed the S.R.P.

The same factors doomed the party's successor, the Deutsche Reichs Party. The D.R.P. appealed to the same electorate and "inherited" 30 per cent of the S.R.P. members. Its only concession to democracy was that it did not campaign openly against the Federal Constitution. Dorls and Remer vanished from the political stage and their places were taken by Adolf von Thadden — a typically upstanding, outspoken and muddleheaded ex-member of the Hitler Youth — and Wilhelm Meinberg, a former S.S. Gruppenführer. But while the S.R.P. had collected 400,000 votes in Lower Saxony, the D.R.P. was able to muster only 300,000 in the whole of West Germany in the 1953 Federal election. In 1957 von Thadden was still campaigning in a Federal election, with the dedication born out of arrested mental development and a sense of injury at the failure of the German people to recognize his talents. The total poll increased in 1957 from twenty-eight to thirty-one million; the D.R.P. vote rose by only twelve thousand. Its share of the poll dropped from 1.1 to 1.0 per cent.

Hitler founded the Nazi Party with a handful of followers. He built it up into a gigantic and gross monolith. Inevitably there were plenty of unrepentant ex-Nazis left in Germany after the war. One of them — a small, sandy-haired man wearing his badge of a Hitler mustache with bravado — walked into my office one day and announced, "I am a Nazi." "Well, sit down," I told him. I offered him a cigarette.

"Why do you do this?" he asked me.

"To put you at your ease."

"But why do you want to do that?"

"In order to find out why you came to see me."

"I only came to see you to tell you that I was still a Nazi!"

"How interesting."

He cogitated. "Perhaps what was really in my mind was to show that not all Germans desert a cause to which they have sworn their service. Thank you for the cigarette." He walked out of my office and out of my life again.

Here was the right kind of material for men like Dorls, Remer, von Thadden and the other "Leaders" of the dozens of crackpot right-wing political organizations in obscure corners of the Federal Republic. But they were incapable of mobilizing it into a movement. Something was missing; and other, far more clever men were already considering very seriously what that something might be. Their conclusions were identical — it was possible to draw on only a small, hard core of unrepentant ex-Nazis by appealing to their youthful ideals and their unreasoning contempt for democracy. It was necessary to delve further back into the German past than Hitler's 1923 Munich Putsch in order to find a clue to the essential, vital German characteristic. Why has Bismarck been worshiped as the greatest German of all time? The easy answer would seem to be "Because he united Germany." This is only a half truth. Bismarck's method was at least as important as his achievement. He united Germany by means of a unique blend of ruthlessness and shrewdness. His brand of opportunism has been an object of German veneration ever since.

Even while Dorls and Remer were trumpeting their defiance of the Western Powers and the "bureaucrats of Bonn," two groups were forming whose members recognized that the creed of opportunism could still swing the German people away from "decadent" democracy. One group believed in applying the creed of opportunism skillfully, and at first secretly; the second group believed in preaching it openly in order to build up a following. In plush offices and luxury flats in Düsseldorf and Hamburg, members of the first group were meeting clandestinely, drawing up their "master plan." Scattered far more widely over West Germany were other equally small groups of disaffected politicians, looking for the mouthpieces of the neutralist movement which, they believed, could enable the German people to play off East against West and again make Germany great.

Simply because the orthodox neutralists decided to operate in the open, their movement was the less important of the two. In 1949 they found their first mouthpiece in the person of Herr Rudolf Nadolny, the former German Ambassador to Moscow. I paid a call on Herr Nadolny at that time. By a curious coincidence he lived in a villa within a few hundred yards of Dr. Adenauer's Rhöndorf home. The two men could, had they wished, have semaphored a plan for German reunification to each other from their front steps.

Nadolny had a finely molded head and an idiot-ingenious manner. He impressed me chiefly as a well-meaning, woolly-minded man with a wealth of historical and technical knowledge and no idea at all as to how to apply it — in fact, a fairly typical German diplomat of the pre-Hitler era. To him the European political arena was a sort of monster chessboard on which moves could be planned with an utterly irresponsible flair and an equally misguided finesse. He belonged to that school of German diplomats who cannot discuss a problem without pulling out a map (generally out-of-date and therefore inapplicable) in order to illustrate their geopolitical arguments. He had some rather fine old maps which, he explained, enabled him to plan his new policy for Germany; and a wealth of Russian literature which, equally, made it perfectly simple for him to read the Russian mind. In the course of an hour's conversation he convinced me that his plan (briefly, the creation of a neutral Germany within its 1939 frontiers which would be a "bridge between East and West") was impracticable, and that his knowledge of Russian character had most to do with the Russia of Anna Karenina and the Battle of Borodino.

Nadolny's writings betrayed an increasing senility of mind, and the neutralists turned to Dr. Josef Wirth, the Reichs Chancellor at the time of the Treaty of Rapallo. Wirth demanded the creation of an all-German Council to work out steps towards German reunification, the dissolution of the Federal Ministry for All-German Affairs of Herr Jakob Kaiser, and the West's agreement to the military neutralization of the whole of Germany. His *Bund der Deutschen* was organized at the end of 1951 as a political but "nonparty" body. Wirth told me that he would seek to "affiliate" his movement with sections of the Evangelical Churches (he was thinking primarily of the pacifist group headed by the former submarine commander and anti-Nazi, Pastor Ludwig Niemöller), with parts of the Catholic Center Party — a declining political force, owing to the drift of its members into the C.D.U. — and with ex-Minister of the Interior Gustav Heinemann's "Society for European Peace."

Wirth, like Nadolny, was too old and too muddleheaded to lead a neutralist crusade. Gustav Heinemann should have been a very different matter. He was Minister of the Interior for the first two years of Dr. Adenauer's first Federal Government, and resigned only when it became plain that West German rearmament was going to take place. He retired to Essen, his home town, in which he already had a flourishing legal practice, and formed his "Peace League." This organization established "cells" all over West Germany, which were still in being years later and which offered a permanent basis for a future German pacifist movement.

In November 1952 Heinemann decided to enter the political lists and formed the "All-German People's Party." He had the support of half-a-dozen members of the Bundestag, and his two chief lieutenants were Frau Helene Wessel, formerly of the Center Party, and Herr Bodensteiner, of the C.D.U. (for a pacifist, a man surprisingly free and capable with his fists; he was one of two members of the Bundestag who took part in the only stand-up fight in the Bundeshaus). The new party opposed rearmament and should have been able to draw on the large section of the community which answered the call to arms with the phrase *Ohne mich* — "without me." The party advocated the formation of a "German Commission" composed of delegates of the occupying powers and of the two German Parliaments. This commission should work out an all-German electoral law and organize all-German elections. The Four Powers should prepare a German peace-treaty, and the elected all-German assembly should endorse it. The stage would be set for the institution of an independent, militarily neutral German Republic.

Heinemann's plans sounded remarkably good, on paper. They were less compelling coming from his own mouth, for he is a colorless, cold man who finds it hard to give vivid expression to his very real convictions. "I do not intend to bring Communists or Nazis into this movement," he told me. "But I believe the right Germans can be found in the East as well as West to make reunification possible. Germans have been too interested in the question of who caused the division of their country. The real problem is what should be done about it, and quickly. If Germany is reunited, it should not be aligned with any group of powers."

The All-German People's Party polled only 318,000 votes (1.2 per cent of all cast) at the 1953 election, in spite of Heinemann's clear-cut ideas and the support of the Wirth group. By 1957 Heinemann had given up the struggle and had joined the Social Democrats. Not surprisingly, the All-German People's Party, standing on its own now, failed wretchedly in the 1957 Federal Election. It polled a mere 60,000 votes. Political neutralism, on a party level, had been beaten by the German people's desire for the security offered by firm alliance with the West, and by the German electorate's preoccupation with material gain. The neutralist parties had no particular domestic policies to offer.

Political neutralism had its next, even briefer fling in 1954 and 1955. Two famous names from the German past suddenly reappeared in the headlines: those of Dr. Hermann Rauschning, the former President of the Danzig Senate and Hitler's first serious biographer, and of Dr. Heinrich Brüning, the last German Chancellor before the Brownshirts' John the Baptist — Herr von Papen — ushered the Nazis into power. These men were not opportunists so much as critics of Dr. Adenauer's foreign policy. They both believed that the Cold War had been "overdone," that the Federal Republic should open diplomatic relations with the Soviet Union, and that European politics should be freed from the pressure of overgrown armies and the atom bomb.

In long talks which I had with both men I came to the conclusion that they were both utterly sincere and that Heinrich Brüning was still young enough to play a big part on the political stage — if he wanted to (it transpired that he did not). Rauschning was obsessed with the dangers of the political *status quo*. He thought that the least shock could upset it, and he coined the phrase "The *status quo* provides only winter quarters for the next war." He thought that West German rearmament had become a policy for its own sake, in the mistaken notion that military integration with the West would lead to German unity. His own view was that it postponed reunification indefinitely; and what was bad for Germany was just as bad for Europe — "Europe cannot sit indefinitely on the muzzles of the atomic cannon of Russia and the United States."

Rauschning laid down seven points which "governed" the German situation. The West German military contribution was no longer essential to the Western Alliance (NATO was still emphatically disagreeing with this five years later). Western European Union was no longer as attractive to the Germans as All-European Union. The chief strategic value of Germany, to anyone, should be the land mass which it interposed between enemy powers. A stable, united Germany would be in the interests of everyone. A united Germany would reduce world tension. Germany could be controlled best by interlocking guarantees, and not by having its two parts bound into military alliances. Finally, undertakings of this kind would presuppose hard and fast guarantees, given by Germany to her neighbors.

It was a coincidence that Rauschning proposed that Brüning should head an all-German *Direktorium*," which would prepare All-German elections. For there was no shadow of collusion between the two men. Brüning had just returned from the United States, where he had spent twenty years, to take the Chair of Political Studies at Cologne University. He was keeping himself scrupulously clear of politics at this time — the end of 1954. Yet Brüning, as I subsequently found out in a talk with him, shared many of Rauschning's views. He believed that it was a mistake to place complete reliance on the United States to secure Germany's unity for her; he foresaw the extreme difficulties of three Western Allies ever organizing anything like a diplomatic initiative in the face of relentless Russian political pressure; he simply did not believe in the theory that the military and moral union of Europe would force the Russians to withdraw behind the Oder. Brüning called for Four-Power talks with German participation, for secret diplomacy in place of propaganda blast and counterblast, for diplomatic relations with Moscow, and a united Germany bound to both East and West by security guarantees.

It has always been one of Dr. Adenauer's failings that he never forgives or forgets a slight, real or imagined. Past disagreements with Brüning — mainly of a petty nature — still rankled. He attacked the ex-Chancellor with deliberate rancor, accused him of damaging Germany's good name. Brüning withdrew once more to America. He said sadly on leaving that it seemed that his country did not need him any more. But his country never had the chance to decide about this. Dr. Adenauer drove him out — possibly sensing that here was a potential rival of far greater character and caliber than any of his own Federal Ministers.

There was a sinister and unsavory background to the activities of Rauschning and Brüning, although only the former was in the the slightest degree implicated in it. A neutralist weekly had been founded in Düsseldorf, and Rauschning contributed largely to it. This was the *Rheinisch-Westfaelische Nachrichten,* which printed 35,000 copies a week and sold only 4000 of them. The rest were distributed free, and the paper was almost certainly financed with Russian money passed through Prague and the Locarno Verlag publishing house in Switzerland, which had co-operated with the Nazi Propaganda Minister, Josef Goebbels, during the war. The editor, Hermann Schaefer, had been publishing the neo-Nazi *Die Nation,* in Munich, up to the middle of 1954. As a political plotter, he seemed to base his code of behavior on that of Groucho Marx. His specialty was a rapid sequence of "Visky-Sodas" in the middle of the afternoon.

Schaefer's friends were preparing to launch two further neutralist newspapers, the *Neue Reich* and the *Rheinisch-Westfaelische Zeitung.* It is fairly sure that their failure to do so was due to Russian funds being withheld. Schaefer's early successes amounted only to the enlistment of Rauschning as leader-writer and the former member of the Defense Ministry, Colonel von Bonin, as defense correspondent, and the attraction of a number of ex-*Gauleiters* and other Nazi officials. Too late in the day he began to seek support in other quarters. The ex-officers of the Hans Seeckt Association imbibed with him and embraced his political ideas — chief among them being the East-West All-German talks desired by the Russians. Several score West German ex-officers met their East German counterparts in secret in

East Berlin and discussed a joint plan for asking ex-General Paulus, the defender of Stalingrad and one of the Russians' tools in the formation of the National Committee for a Free Germany, to "play the part of Hindenburg" — allow himself to be proposed as the first All-German President and take Germany out of all military alliances.

But the Russians had lost interest in Schaefer and his activities. Rauschning and von Bonin drifted off the staff of his paper. Schaefer shut up shop. On the surface, his failure seemed to be due to the withdrawal of financial backing. In reality, he failed because he did not explain clearly enough that neutralism and opportunism might be identical, in this instance and at this period of history. In fact, he failed to take the German character into account.

The open preaching of opportunism failed largely because it was done so halfheartedly. The alternative was to apply the principles of political opportunism in secret. A totally different group of enemies of the established order decided that this was the way in which West German democracy might be overthrown.

They were given their chance to do this as a result of the efforts of the "respectable" right-wing political parties to swallow and digest the ex-Nazi and ex-Nationalist vote.

The three nominally respectable right-wing parties were the Free Democratic Party, the Refugee Party, and the German Party. The Refugee Party obviously restricted its interest practically entirely to the refugees. The German Party had developed from the *Niedersaechsische Landespartei*, in the Hannover area. The Free Democrats, on the other hand, had aspirations to becoming a real "third force" in German politics. But here they were faced with a difficult problem. Although the F.D.P. called itself a liberal party, its leaders knew that there were very few liberals left in Germany. A solid core of liberal voters existed only in Württemberg, Hamburg and the Frankfurt area. The gap between the Social Democrats on the one hand, no longer militantly Marxist and on the lookout for middle-class voters, and the C.D.U. on the other, was far too small. The trend towards a two-party system was beginning to make itself felt and the Free Democrats felt a desperate need of some possibility of expansion. They needed room — to breathe.

At the end of 1952 the party chairman was Dr. Friedrich Middelhauve, one of the founders of the F.D.P. and a publisher in the Rhineland town of Opladen. Middelhauve believed that there was only one way in which the F.D.P. could become a real third force — it must attract the extreme right-wing vote. (This vote would never go to the Social Democrats and was not attracted to the bourgeois-clerical C.D.U.) Other right-wing parties would make their terms and come in too.

With a smug satisfaction in his own wiliness, Middelhauve drew up his "German Program," which he intended to have adopted at the Party Congress in Bad Ems in November. The program called for more centralized government, a cut-down of the *Länder* from eleven to five, the end of discrimination against ex-Nazis and the annestying of all political prisoners, a more independent foreign policy and the formation of a "National Front" of right-wing parties. In conversation with me Middlehauve freely admitted that liberalism meant nothing at all to him. "The age of liberalism in Germany is over," was one of his catch-phrases, and another was, "the mobilization of the ex-Nazis into the democratic fold."

"A National Front led by the F.D.P.," he told me, "will make for a healthier political climate in Germany. The Western Powers banned German Conservatism in 1945. That was a mistake. Today we are setting out to rally all conservative forces in the belief that a strong Conservative Party will be the backbone of a Germany which wants to play its full part in Western integration and Western defense." Quite unintentionally, Middelhauve was on the way to wrecking German liberalism and, incidentally, his own political career.

Full of bold but unoriginal ideas, he organized discussions with the B.H.E. and less reputable right-wing parties, such as Haussleiter's *Deutsche Gemeinschaft* and Meissner's *Deutscher Block*. He met ex-S.S. Generals Gille and Hausser, won promises of support from some Ruhr industrialists. But at the Bad Ems Congress he suffered a surprising reverse. The Württemberg liberals, led by Reinhold Maier, counterattacked with spirit. They demanded that the F.D.P. should remain a real liberal party and "the last bastion of spiritual and political freedom on German soil." Talk of the "politically wide-open spaces to the right which we must occupy" was scotched. Although some fierce declarations were made about war criminals, the bulk of the "German Program" was discarded.

Middelhauve went off in a huff — as it happened, to involve himself with much more dangerous people than his colleagues of the right-wing of the F.D.P. For in Düsseldorf and Hamburg a group of men were busy planning what turned out to be by far the most serious conspiracy against the West German State during the first ten years of its existence. The group was led by Dr. Werner Naumann, State Secretary in the Josef Goebbels Ministry of Propaganda, nominated in Hitler's will to be Goebbels's successor, and one of the last men to leave the ruins of the Reich Chancellery before Hitler committed suicide. Naumann had escaped with Martin Bormann from the Chancellery, made his way to western Germany, and lived so long there under assumed names that he never had to be de-Nazified. (Here was a special triumph of the S.S. "underground" which hid so many men after the war, or smuggled them to Spain, South America and Egypt.)

Naumann formed a small circle of men who were, in his own words, "dedicated" — dedicated to the ideal of single-minded service given to a new "Leader." One was Dr. Gustav Scheel, a former *Reichstudentenführer* and *Gauleiter* of Salzburg, nominated in Hitler's will to be future Minister of Culture, working in 1952 as a doctor in a Hamburg clinic. Another was Dr. Heinrich Haselmeyer, who took part in the 1923 Nazi Putsch in Munich, became head of the Nazi Students League in Hamburg, was one of the Nazis experts on "racial science" and sterlization of the unfit.

Yet another was Dr. Karl Scharping, a former leading official in Dr. Goebbels's Propaganda Ministry, who became a director of the Stern Verlag publishing house after the war, churning out cheap novelettes. There was Karl Bornemann, an ex-Nazi and member of the Brotherhood, who ran a news-service in Düsseldorf called the "Independent German Newspaper Service." There was Karl Kaufmann, a former *Gauleiter* of Hamburg and a member of the Brotherhood, and Wolfgang Diewerge, a contributor to the Nazi paper *Völkischer Beobachter* since 1926 and a veteran Nazi.

This "sworn and dedicated" group established links with the political parties and with Nazi cells abroad. Diewerge, conveniently, was Middelhauve's personal secretary. The link with the F.D.P. was strengthened through such people as Siegfried Zoglmann, editor of the Free Democratic weekly *Deutsche Zukunft;* Ernst Achenbach, a member of the party's foreign affairs committee; F.D.P. officials Brandt and Deumling, the former a personal assistant of Henlein, the Nazi Quisling in Czechoslovakia, and the latter an ex-*Obersturmführer* of the S.S. Then Naumann had other, less vital connections with the B.H.E. Refugee and German Parties. Nonparty friends included Hans Fritzsche, formerly Goebbels's chief commentator, ex-parachutist Otto Skorzeny in Spain, ex-air-ace Hans Rudel in the Argentine, and ex-S.S. man Johannes von Leers in Egypt.

There seems little doubt that the aim of the Naumann group was to infiltrate at least three political parties, of which the F.D.P. was by far the most important. The group intended to win over men who already sat in the Bundestag for the F.D.P., Refugee and German parties, and in the tiny groups on the extreme right of the house. This was to be done prior to the 1953 Federal Election. Through these men it should have been possible to recruit other party candidates. A year beforehand there seemed every prospect that the 1953 election would produce a close race between the two big parties, the C.D.U. and S.P.D. The Naumann group intended to mobilize at least forty parliamentarians who, as soon as the election was over, would be able to hold the balance in the Bundestag and even dictate the future course of German history. A subsequent "rally" of all right-wing parties would ensure that a "third force" would go into a future Federal Election on a straight Nazi ticket, with every chance of emerging as the most powerful single party. Instinct in these plans was a blind faith in "destiny." Naumann believed that the new Germany, like a phoenix, would rise out of the ashes of Hitler's Reichs-Chancellery.

It will never be clear what the Naumann group might have achieved. For on January 14, 1953, the British High Commissioner, Sir Ivone Kirkpatrick, decided to break up the conspiracy at what he considered to be the right tactical moment. Seven leaders were arrested on that night, and an eighth a few days later. Kirkpatrick, humorously secretive but astute and determined, knew that his action would be unpopular and temporarily damaging to British prestige. At the same time he was quite sure that it was the right action. His intelligence officers had been watching the Naumann group with the greatest attention. Compared with the "Boy Scouts" of the Brotherhood and the wild figures of the political lunatic-fringe, these men, they knew, were dangerous. Kirkpatrick, with wry humor, called them "A pirate gang, which intends to seize the ship by gaining control of the bridge, then board other ships and collect a nice little navy."

"I see no reason," Kirkpatrick told me, "why we should wait for these gentlemen to put into action all the plans which they have religiously committed to paper. Those plans speak for themselves and their purpose is, in their own words, to achieve those ideals for which they once stood and for which their comrades fell." The British intelligence officers collected thirty crates — four feet by three feet by two feet — from the houses and offices of the Naumann group. They contained all the evidence of the last plot during the Adenauer era which aimed, quite simply, at a Nazi restoration.

Because Naumann and his friends were being held in investigatory confinement, the British authorities would not publish details of their activities. When later this became possible, it was quite rightly considered that any further publicity would merely cause the Federal Government embarrassment. The Kirkpatrick White Paper on the conspiracy was put into cold storage. Naumann and his friends were duly released from jail — but the purpose of Kirkpatrick's action had been achieved. The German political parties had received their warning: they would not be easily infiltrated in the future.

The German secret service — the Office for the Protection of the Constitution, in Cologne — had been watching the Naumann group since May 1952. It was in no doubt about the nature of the group's activities. Dr. Adenauer readily admitted that the group was more dangerous than he had at first imagined. Enough information was passed out to the press to rub the lesson home. Yet a respectable paper like the *Frankfurter Allgemeine Zeitung* wrote that the arrested men were "merchants" and the British had obviously been afraid of trade competition. The *Deutsche Zunkunft* published banner headlines, GHETTOS FOR FORMER NAZIS?; and a paper in Lower Saxony said that the British had made the arrest in order to fill up their war criminals' jail at Werl. Other German papers wrote that the whole affair had been organized by Lord Norwich (formerly Alfred Duff-Cooper), or Lord Vansittart.

The German Party leaders, Joachim von Merkatz and Heinrich Hellwege, went puce with rage when asked questions at a press conference. Their consciences were none too good; they had themselves been dressing up party strong-arm squads in gray uniforms, black jack boots and black belts. These bullies in fancy dress had been manhandling people at political meetings with a vigor which must have commended their party to Naumann and his friends. The F.D.P. were gravely embarrassed, especially when it transpired that Ernst Achenbach had been acting as agent in order to try to purchase the newspaper *Die Welt*, which had the third largest circulation in Germany. And Dr. Adenauer's initial mood of understanding quickly changed to one of resentment. He hastened to assure the German people that the Naumann group had never posed a real threat to German democracy, although he agreed that Naumann's arrest may have been a justifiable precaution. He wanted no association with an incident which — when Naumann was released — looked tame.

Kirkpatrick shouldered the blame with little concern. He had been in Germany for years before the war as well as after it, and his knowledge of the German character was considerable. He knew that the Germans worshiped success. Had the Naumann group captured forty members of the Bundestag and then held one of the major parties to ransom, it would have had a unique chance of creating its planned national rally out of the millions of ex-Nazis and nationalists who had still not come to terms with democracy. With a certain shamefacedness the German authorities followed the lead which Kirkpatrick had given them. They proclaimed Naumann a "major Nazi offender" in August and banned him from any further political activity. This action wrecked the election chances of the German Reichs Party, which Naumann had joined only two months earlier. The German authorities also banned the "Free Corps Germany," an anti-Semitic and violently nationalistic successor to the Brotherhood, out of which Naumann intended to create his Stormtroopers.

Finally, a note of comedy was provided by the American High Commission which published, at a most inopportune moment, a public opinion survey on *The Germans and Nazism*. This survey showed that 44 per cent of those asked considered there was more good than bad in Nazism, and only 34 per cent were sure there was more bad than good. The survey, it appeared, was never meant to be published at all. For a short time the Americans were as unpopular as the British.

The S.R.P. and the D.R.P. worked in the political arena and failed. The Brotherhood and the Naumann group worked underground. They failed too. The neutralists were unable to make their appeal to German opportunism ring with sufficient force. In Düsseldorf a small group of Free Democrats watched these failures and drew their own conclusions. To them, as to Ernst Achenbach and Friedrich Middelhauve, it seemed obvious that the F.D.P. must build up a new core of supporters to the right of the established parties. It might be best to do this in collusion with the Refugee and German Parties; otherwise the F.D.P. could do it alone.

These young Free Democrats were, to a man, former members of the Hitler Youth. Some of them were Nazi Party members. Their leaders were Wolfgang Döring, Willi Weyer and Hermann Kohlhase. Only the last-named had a "party past"; he had been a member of the Nazi Party, the brownshirted stormtroopers, and the Waffen S.S., and had risen to the rank of *Hauptsturm-führer*. They co-opted men like Achenbach and Zoglmann, who had already been implicated with the Naumann group; and "elder statesmen" like Lothar Steuer, the former secretary to Hugenberg, who had helped Hitler into power, and Werner Best, the former Nazi Reich Commissar in German-occupied Denmark. All of these men had one thing in common — a profound contempt for the liberalism to which they paid lip-service.

The young men of the F.D.P., who became known as the "Young Turks," first purged the biggest and richest *Land* branch of the party, in North-Rhine Westphalia. The purge was carried out cleverly and ruthlessly, and genuine liberals were either thrust into the background or, if necessary, out of the party. The "Young Turks" next "captured" the party chairman, Dr. Thomas Dehler. His erratic verbosity had already brought the C.D.U.-F.D.P. coalition in the Federal Government to the point of dissolution. This suited the Young Turks' book; they believed that the F.D.P. would do better in opposition, and they shared Dehler's paranoic hatred of Adenauer. (Dehler was Minister of Justice from 1949 to 1953, but was given no Cabinet post in Dr. Adenauer's second government. He never got over this slight.)

The Young Turks next proceeded to overthrow the C.D.U. *Land* government of North-Rhine Westphalia in February 1956. This was an epic of political opportunism. They had no complaint against the *Land* Prime Minister, Karl Arnold. Instead they claimed that the C.D.U. in Bonn had forced them to act by putting forward a new electoral law which would finish the smaller parties. This was Dr. Goebbels's technique of the "Big Lie"; for the C.D.U. had dropped the electoral law before the Young Turks forced Arnold out of office. At all events, an S.P.D.-led *Land* government meant a reduction of the majority favorable to Adenauer in the Bundesrat, or Federal Upper House.

What the Young Turks offered their party and their supporters was absolute freedom for destructive criticism of the Federal Government, an incentive to organize the right-wing ex-Nazi and nationalist vote against the "Federal pigsty of Bonn," the chance of contracting out of the Western Alliance at a moment which they might consider opportune for Germany, and the prospect of a hugely increased vote at the 1957 Federal Election and genuine political power afterwards. Privately they admitted that they would get rid of Dehler when the time was ripe; he was no more than a captive kite which was to be released into outer space when his wild denunciations and frondes became a nuisance to them.

The Young Turks organized their campaign brilliantly. Its one flaw was its timing. An S.P.D.-led coalition came into power in Düsseldorf. It gave the Young Turks some practical experience in government; it gave them nothing else at all. Their action split the F.D.P. in the Bundestag, and 17 out of its 52 members there left the party and formed a new liberal group of their own. It forced the F.D.P. out of the Bonn government, and this left the Young Turks free to preach their "new" foreign policy of German military neutrality between East and West, a European security-pact, and overtures to the Soviet Union. This policy was intended to offer a short cut to German reunification.

NATO was to be nothing more than a means to achieving this end. The way had to be cleared for an independent German approach to Moscow; and, explaining this, Dehler asked rhetorically, "Can the price for the freedom of seventeen million East Germans ever be too high?" The sober reply of the Federal Foreign Minister, Heinrich von Brentano, "Our freedom is too high a price," passed unnoticed.

A lot of nonsense was circulating, at the time of the Young Turks' coup, about "a fresh wind blowing," "a role for Germany in Europe" and "a healthy sense of change and movement." There was in reality nothing fresh or healthy about the Young Turks. They bragged about their lack of political principles and their practice of political opportunism. They hit out venomously at "the frock-coated Bonn diplomacy," at "the American trick of withholding gifts for political purposes," at the French for plugging European Union and the British for staying out of it. Their threadbare panache made no impression on the sober German electorate. In the 1957 Federal Election the F.D.P. vote dropped from 9 per cent to 7 per cent; at the North-Rhine Westphalia *Land* Election next year a third of their supporters turned over to the Christian Democratic Party which they had forced out of power. Their malevolent attacks on Dr. Adenauer had no part in the Chancellor's decision to give up his post in April 1959.

For all their big words and promises, the Young Turks achieved nothing. Their story was in line with those of all other postwar exponents of opportunism. Was, in fact, something being "bred out" of the German character? Were peace and plenty producing — as Dr. Adenauer assured — a revolution in German thinking? I do not believe that this was necessarily the case.

Worship of opportunism has been limited and restrained by three factors. The first was the shattering experience of the Second World War. Bold, original solutions will not have their old appeal as long as Germans remember. And the ruins are still with them in 1960, admittedly no longer on the principal streets, but close behind them. Worship of opportunism has been limited by the ruthless pressure of Russian diplomacy. The Russians might have won the whole of Germany had they been prepared to offer friendship tempered by the obvious diplomatic consideration of detaching Germany from the West. Finally, political opportunists have had little popular appeal in an era of such plenty. Their real enemies have not been the dull but worthy members of the Bundestag and Federal Cabinets, but the new TV sets, washing-machines and Volkswagens which have flooded the home market, the rocketing indices of meat and fat consumption, the Ages of Food and Drink, Consumer Goods, and Travel.

One German friend asked me *"Haben wir es zu satt?"* — (Literally, "Are we too sated with the good things of life?") My answer was "Not yet. You will almost certainly be more sated before the old spiritual restlessness reasserts itself; but don't fool yourself that the old restlessness has been bred out by a short decade of good living."

Is that an unfair answer? I think not. In 1933 the Nazis had every chance of success, but not just because of the Treaty of Versailles, the burden of war debts, the loss of the old German colonies and the world economic crisis. The Nazis knew how to mobilize the frantic energy of a people which believed that it had not yet fulfilled itself. The cult of opportunism was their mentor and their tool. The German people is still aware that it has not fulfilled itself, and it is a question just how long the lessons of 1945 will stick in its brain.

There has been a period of productive quiet. It is an advantage that this period has given ordinary people time to learn the superficial values of material objects. It is not an advantage that the only liberal party in Germany has been wrecked by active young men who should have acquired some equivalent moral standards. Opportunism had itself little to offer during the first ten years of the West German State, but it may have a great deal more to offer in years to come. The West German honeymoon with democracy will turn into a happy marriage only when German dynamism has been harnessed to intelligible ideals. That ideals will be needed has been underlined by Khrushchev's caustic "War is unnecessary for the victory of Communism — peaceful competition is enough." Lack of ideals must make Germany doubly vulnerable to the Communist challenge.

-13-

The Problem Unsolved

> God once promised Abraham that he would not destroy
> Sodom if there were but ten just men in it. I hope God
> will not destroy Germany.
> > — HENNING VON TRESCKOW, member of the
> > Resistance to Hitler

> Woe to us Germans if we try to suppress this [Nazi] part
> of our history! The future of a people which, in the New
> Testament sense, is hardened against parts of its past his-
> tory would be unimaginable.
> > — FREIHERR AXEL VON DEM BUSSCHE in the foreword
> > to the German edition of John Wheeler-Bennett's
> > *Nemesis of Power*

> I have only one Fatherland, and that is Germany. To
> Germany alone, and not to any one part of it, I am devoted
> with all my soul . . . My creed is unity.
> > — FREIHERR VON STEIN — a worker for Germany's
> > liberation from Napoleon

ON Christmas Day, 1959, two twenty-five-year-old citizens of
Cologne daubed swastikas and anti-Semitic slogans on the walls
of the newly rebuilt Cologne synagogue. Their action, which
aroused anger, horror and disgust, but also a certain measure of
petulance and mistaken sentiment, unloosed a chain-reaction in
West Germany and other countries. Within a few weeks there
were over four hundred anti-Semitic incidents of one kind and
another in Western Germany. Buildings were smeared with
swastikas; there were clandestine rallies of Nazi-type youth-
groups; a few individual Jews were threatened and insulted.

The baker's assistant Arnold Strunk, and the shopkeeper's

KOHLER, *Frankfurter Allgemeine*

"It All Began Twenty Years Ago . . ."

clerk Paul Josef Schönen were tried by the Cologne *Land* Court on February 5. Their trial revealed little that was not already known. They were both members of the extreme right-wing German Reichs Party. But their party had not told them to sally out at dead of night with pots of paint and discarded tooth-brushes. They were both petty criminals, with past convictions for fraud and theft. They were antisocial types, who might well have been expected to do something disgraceful at any time. But their crime was a curious one — for both Strunk and Schönen had been only eleven years old when Hitler died. Not only had they no personal experience of Nazism; they had no personal memories of a period when Nazism might have suggested other things to the German people than war, destruction and death. They had gleaned their total knowledge of Nazism from loose talk with Reichs Party cronies, and from the memoirs of S.S. Generals and former leading Nazis.

The reactions of the German people to the Cologne outrage were prompt, for at least three reasons. It had happened in the early hours of Christmas Day. Germans are highly sentimental; Christmas Day is not just a religious and a family festival; it is axiomatic that it is a time when there is only good will among men. Ten months earlier the daubing of the Düsseldorf synagogue with swastikas attracted little attention. The police took so little interest that a year later their investigations had produced only the arrest, as a suspect, of one out-of-work member of the banned Communist Party.

In the second place, many Germans rightly guessed that the Cologne synagogue incident would earn Germany hard words abroad. It was this thought which induced Dr. Adenauer to make the highly suspect suggestion that the outrages were part of a deep-laid plot. No evidence was ever forthcoming to show that such a plot existed. The Cologne court which tried Strunk and Schönen discovered nothing of the kind. Neither the Communist-controlled Socialist Unity Party in East Germany nor the Fascist International — which has co-ordinated cells in Cairo, Lausanne, Malmö, Madrid and a score of other places in Europe and outside it — bore any responsibility. Yet the West German Government went on plugging the convenient alibi of a "plot from out-side." This was unwise, and stupid.

Finally, Germans were upset by the Cologne synagogue inci-dent because they were shaken, suddenly and violently, out of their special, West German beauty-sleep. The sense of that beauty-sleep was material prosperity. It had already, fleetingly, been disturbed by a most mundane dream: the President of the Federal Bank, Karl Blessing, had warned against the dangers of inflation; the upward thrust of the stock markets had been ar-rested. For once, a Federal Budget could not be balanced. The unions threatened major wage-claims. And all at once thrifty, confident citizens foresaw a check to their patient, purposeful planning for personal remuneration. Could it even be that the D. Mark — so long a-sailing, like the Man in the Moon, on a backcloth of silver and gold — was in danger? The thought was horrific.

But it was only a bad dream, after all, for Karl Blessing has-tened to say so on the eleventh of January, 1960. The anti-Semitic outrages, on the other hand, were reality.

Of course, the fifty-four million West Germans must be given greater credit than that of merely showing signs of alarm because their own self-interest was at stake: plenty of Germans were really scandalized. For the latter, the time factor must have seemed the worst feature of the case. Something which had died fifteen years before was trying to come to life again. A piece of their past was being exhumed. What a confrontation for a genu-inely reformed Nazi! What a reminder for the conscience-stricken, who had awakened in the night to the clank of the skeleton in the cupboard! The Cologne incident sent a shudder through the nation.

Too much thought on the subject of the Cologne incident would defeat itself. The outrages which followed were largely the work of young men — social misfits, people in search of an ideal where none existed. Was this surprising? Could young Ger-mans find real inspiration in 1960 in normal patriotism? Their country was divided, and, like Humpty-Dumpty, was showing no sign of coming together again. Could European union offer an alternative ideal? The peculiar political antics of France gave one answer to that question. France was moving along a tangent of self-interest, thanks to General de Gaulle, in an independent and self-interested mood. Meanwhile the Six of the Common Market and the Outside Seven were at economic loggerheads. Europe really did not look very united.

The defense of the West, once upon a time, was a worthwhile as well as logical objective. But by 1960 West Germans were aware only of the incubus of foreign troops on their soil, offering no real security. The middle-aged members of the *Bundeswehr* were scornful about their allies, and almost equally scornful about their own West German "citizen soldiers." It might have helped if some traditional German loyalties had survived. But those traditional loyalties had died when Hitler thrust them brutally into the melting-pot. The "solidarity of the West" now seemed merely an uninspiring and very costly business. Since 1952 West Germans had become used to contributing very much less than their fair share to the burden of defense (proportionately, the German contribution was only 30 per cent of the American and about 50 per cent of the British; it was amazing how the West German press scrupulously avoided this aspect of the overall defense problem).

Lack of new ideals, in the 1960 West Germany, was alarmingly, blatantly obvious. Those few Germans who worried often turned to old ones — to the trim, debonair figure of ex-General von Manteuffel standing upright in the dock and explaining how he had fought his bitter, last-ditch battles; to grim, stolid "Papa" Ramcke, utterly confident that he had held the enemy at bay outside the fortress of Brest until the last justifiable moment; to a still vigorous, volatile Hans-Ulrich Rudel, deprecating his own brilliant tank-busting flying exploits, but demanding equivalent dash and daring in young Germans who had no reason to be dedicated to anyone or anything.

Here was incipient anarchy of mind. It is fair to suggest that out of such anarchy of mind sprang the anti-Semitic incidents of December 1959, and of the next three months. Those incidents were out of step with the plodding, insensate pace of the eco-nomically-minded West German community. They represented a reversion to the twisted, dynamic thinking of the Nazis. Anarchy of mind was aptly represented by the synagogue-smearers of Cologne. Arnold Strunk hung pictures of Hitler and Horst Wessel (the young Stormtrooper bully who was killed in a brawl and made into the first Nazi martyr) in his room, painted a cupboard in the old black, red and white national colors, and called his room the "Brown House" after the old Nazi Party headquarters in Munich. But he readily admitted that he had never made any study of the Nazi era, and had read only extracts from *Mein Kampf.*

Paul Josef Schönen, who wore flamboyant red-and-yellow-checked shirts and indulged in ecstatic gestures, maintained that his ideal was "Bismarck's Reich." But in the next breath he agreed that he believed in "modified dictatorship" — which would make government simpler and more efficient — and in political opposition "within our own ranks only." What then was the connection between Bismarck's Reich and such a modified dictatorship? Schönen had not the faintest idea. This introverted, unhappy young man's only counter to questions of this kind was: "I don't want to go into details in public."

Some of the hundreds of swastika-smearers of West Germany were only conventional bullies. Others were brainless louts. Oth-ers, like Strunk and Schönen, were social misfits bulging with complexes. Of the perpetrators of these incidents 80 per cent were young men or mere children. The only common factor about them was that they had read or listened to the wrong kind of stories. (The neo-Nazi publishers, book clubs and discussion groups have never ceased their activities.) Between them Strunk and Schönen had around thirty books extolling the Waf-fen S.S., the *Wehrmacht,* and Nazi leaders in peace and war. Police raids on the homes of other swastika-smearers uncovered copies of *Mein Kampf* (often privately printed), of Alfred Rosen-berg's *Myth of the Twentieth Century,* of *Hitler's Table-Talk,* published ostensibly as offering "new light" on Hitler's character and becoming, in practice, a new political Bible for the younger generation of German Fascists. Strunk and Schönen — and this was true of most of their imitators — read no normal literature, took no interest in day-to-day news, had no friends, no hobbies. In other countries people of this kind turn to the more usual forms of juvenile delinquency; but in Germany there is an obvious temptation to turn to the tradition of political violence which dominated the last years of a unified and powerful nation.

Here, then, is one of the obvious internal stresses which will afflict fifty-four million West Germans for many years to come. There are plenty of others.

The shadow of the past is a dark cloud which can drop only an artificially induced rain of repentance, and which obstinately refuses to disperse. In January 1960, the Federal Minister for Refugees — Professor Theodor Oberländer — appeared before a committee of former members of European Resistance movements to Nazism which convened in The Hague in order to examine accusations that he had taken a personal part in the massacres of Jews in the Southern Polish town of Lemberg (Lwow) in 1941. A Federal Minister was, in fact, under suspicion of having been a mass murderer! Theodor Oberländer had undoubtedly been a convinced Nazi, had belonged to the brownshirted S.A., and had freely subscribed to lunatic Nazi racial theories, but had been "de-Nazified" in the normal way after the war. He had been allowed to return to political life, and became the chairman and the main driving force of the B.H.E. Refugee Party. He took Cabinet office in 1953, switched to the Christian Democratic Union when the B.H.E. quarreled with the West German Government, and withdrew from the coalition. Oberländer was an industrious, efficient Minister.

Yet the past caught up with him; and, like many other Germans, he tried to take the easiest way out by making sweeping denials of all accusations brought against him. He could not deny that he was in Lemberg in 1941, but he did deny that any massacres took place after the Germans occupied the city. He claimed that during his stay he "did not hear a single shot fired." On 3 February, 1960, *Die Welt* published a letter from one of the few Jewish survivors of the Lemberg massacres. Writing from the settlement of Ramat Gan in Israel, Mr. Abraham Goldberg described how he (aged eighteen at the time) and about five hundred other Jews were herded into a yard behind a house in Lemberg's Lackiegostrasse. They were forced to "run the gantlet" between rows of Ukrainian militiamen, who served with the German armies, armed with rifles and mostly with bayonets fixed. The Jews were bayoneted or beaten to death with clubbed rifles. Abraham Goldberg escaped only because he fell under the bodies of dying Jews, and was later able to join a Jewish working party which was shoveling the corpses into lorries.

Of course, this letter did not destroy Oberländer's contention that he did not hear a single shot fired in Lemberg. There was a strong Nazi tradition against using "clean" bullets on "dirty" Jews. But Abraham Goldberg did shake Oberländer's basic argument, that the Lemberg massacres were the work of the retreating Russians. Goldberg did, indeed, see about one hundred corpses of political prisoners murdered by the Russians. But, as he wrote to *Die Welt*, what the Russians did "bore no comparison" to the work of the Ukrainian militia. Professor Oberländer was himself "German political officer," and to all intents and purposes the commander of the Ukrainian "Nightingale" regiment, which was in Lemberg at the time.

The stress imposed on present-day Germany by the Nazi past was equally well illustrated on January 22, 1960, when two young students, Reinhold Strecker and Wolfgang Koppel, issued writs against forty-three former Nazi judges and attorneys, all of whom were still holding posts in public life in West Germany. All of these men had served under the Nazis on special tribunals which carried out acts of legalized murder. The students had procured their documentation from archives in Prague and East Berlin, but a judge of the Karlsruhe High Court had little hesitation in pronouncing it to be genuine.

At least as embarrassing as strictly internal stresses on the new Germany are those which arise directly from the division of Germany. Here are some examples.

East German Communist propaganda is incessant, intensive, diverse. Two of its obvious targets in West Germany have been the trade-unions and the Social Democratic Party. The West German unions have shown commendable resolution in withstanding all the efforts of the "free" East German unions to secure "community of action" in opposing nuclear armament, or in asking for the withdrawal of all "foreign" troops from German soil. In perhaps the sharpest rebuff of all, Willy Richter, Chairman of the United Trade-Union Congress, declared in Berlin in January 1960 that the East German unions were undemocratic, did not attempt to represent the interests of the workers, and were spending one hundred million marks a year in their efforts to dislocate the West German unions. The Social Democrats went even further than Herr Richter. On February 1, 1960, they issued comprehensive instructions to all their members regarding the establishment of personal contact with people or organizations east of the Iron Curtain. They told members that all contact with the East German Socialist Unity Party was forbidden; that any other political contact required party approval; that the Social Democratic Party itself would enter into no relations with any existing Communist or Communist-controlled organization. Social Democrats were told to cultivate personal contacts in East Germany with the maximum discretion; to report any information that they gleaned to party headquarters; and to make it plain, when they went to East Germany, that they utterly rejected the East German Communist claim to represent "pure socialism."

The division of Germany produced the ludicrous "flag controversy" in 1959-1960. (The East Germans had superimposed a hammer and compass onto the black, red and gold national colors.) The flag controversy, in turn, made it nearly impossible for an all-German team for the Rome Olympics to be organized.

The division of Germany produced the spy trial, early in 1960, of Lieutenant-Commander Horst Ludwig, thirty-four years old, an admirably efficient officer and an apparently happy extrovert known by his comrades as "Handsome Horst." Ludwig's father was a Communist agent of long standing, and lived in the

East German town of Erfurt. This did not prevent Ludwig from finding employment with a German labor-service company attached to the American mine-sweeping unit in Bremenhaven in 1954, from graduating from there to a commission in the West German Naval Forces, and from attending NATO courses in Florida and Scotland (where he became engaged to the Beauty Queen of Lossiemouth).

For several years Ludwig passed information to the Russians, making at least a dozen trips to East Berlin in person. The Karlsruhe High Court found him guilty of treason and sent him to prison for five years. It found, too, that Ludwig was primarily concerned with getting as much money as possible out of the Russians. Yet the Court could discover only that he had received around eight thousand marks, or a paltry twenty-six hundred dollars, for extensive information on NATO equipment, organization and morale. There must be at least a fair possibility that Ludwig, who lived in East Germany until 1953, chose to help his father for the latter's sake. His sister and brother-in-law, too, passed on information to the Russians. It would hardly have been surprising had family ties exercised a stronger pull on Ludwig's loyalties than a sense of duty to his country. For had he a country at all — when his home was in East German Erfurt, his heart in Lossiemouth and his Germany divided?

The division of Germany produced, in January 1960, violent attacks on the Evangelical bishop of Berlin and Brandenburg, Dr. Otto Dibelius. These nearly led to a split in the Churches. The Evangelical Churches formed, by 1960, the only all-German institution which preserved its unity. In October 1959, Dr. Dibelius had made what was perhaps an ill-advised attempt to marry religious doctrine with political problems. In a pamphlet circulated to pastors of the Evangelical Churches throughout Germany, he chose the thirteenth chapter of Saint Paul's Epistle to the Romans as the basis for his argument that Christians owed no duty to an authoritarian State. It is doubtful whether Saint Paul, nearly two thousand years ago, had any prophetic vision of the East German Republic of 1960. Although he stated that "there is no power, but of God," and "owe no man anything, but to love one another," he also advised, in the same Epistle, "to render unto all their dues."

East German churchmen who disapproved of Dr. Dibelius's unflinching and sometimes truculent stand against Communism pounced on this piece of loose argumentation. They argued that he was encouraging the Churches to come into open conflict with the Temporal Power (something that Martin Luther did, and then undid). There were demands for the Bishop's resignation. Had they been pressed through, the regime would certainly have been emboldened to reopen its old proposals for the creation of a subservient "State Church" and for the final division of the Eastern from the Western Evangelicals. Dr. Dibelius will survive until his retirement, in 1961. But the situation remains potentially dangerous for the Churches. Here is a stress which Lutherans, with their tradition of quietism and readiness to compromise with the State, may not be well-suited to withstand. Much will depend on the morale of their flocks; and pressure on them will never be relaxed, and is likely to increase.

The very division of Germany is a stress in itself — for the fifty-four million West Germans are continually reminded of what it means to their seventeen million East German cousins. What it does mean was well illustrated by a recent summary of events in East Germany, published by the West Berlin "Association of Free Jurists" on the occasion of the tenth birthday of the East German Republic (October 7, 1959). Here are a few facts from this summary:

> 1950: A Ministry of State Security was created, in order to take over the antidemocratic police powers hitherto exercised by the Russians. A "single-list" election for the new "People's Chamber" (*Volkskammer*) took place, with a 99.7 per cent vote for the selected candidates. During the year, 197,788 East Germans fled to the West.

> 1951: The Ministry of State Security was hard at work. In a single trial, nineteen young people (some of them still at the secondary school of Werdau and seven of them under eighteen) were sentenced to a total of one hundred and thirty years' imprisonment. The workers lost their right to negotiate wage agreements; in future the works manage-

ment merely drew up a "collective agreement." There has been no official wage claim in East Germany since. That year 165,648 East Germans fled to the West.

1952: A "security zone" and a "death strip" were established along the interzonal frontier. A law was passed providing for the confiscation of all property belonging to people who "fled from the Republic." Nevertheless, 182,393 East Germans fled to the West during 1952.

1953: The East German Government raised compulsory work norms by 10 per cent, with no increase of pay. This led directly to the strike of the Stalinallee building-workers in East Berlin, and to the national uprising of June 17 against the regime. Afterwards eighteen people were sentenced to death, and roughly twelve hundred people were sentenced to a total of four thousand years' imprisonment. That year 331,390 East Germans fled to the West.

1954: The second "People's Chamber" was elected, again on a "single-list" system, by a 99.46 per cent vote. The first youth-initiation committees were formed and the Communist campaign against religious teaching in the schools and the homes was under way. During that year 184,198 East Germans fled to the West.

1955: The Communist campaign against private industry moved into top gear, while steady progress was made in the formation of State co-operatives on the land. During that year 252,870 East Germans fled to the West.

1956: The first trials took place of people who had "encouraged flight from the Republic." In a test trial, two men and one woman were all sentenced to life imprisonment for this "crime." The regime introduced its new method of destroying private firms by "offering" State participation in management and financing. During that year 279,189 East Germans fled to the West.

1957: Walter Ulbricht laid down that "anyone leaving the German Democratic Republic is a traitor to the working-class." To back this declaration, a new passport law provided for three years' imprisonment for anyone making an unauthorized journey outside the borders of East Germany. Movement between the two German states was drastically cut down by this law. During 1957, however, 261,622 East Germans fled to the West.

1958: Walter Ulbricht announced a new law under which

any criticism of the regime could be regarded as "slandering the State." Nineteen students of Jena University were sent to prison for breaking this law. Compulsory "polytechnical" education was introduced; it meant that all school children had to work for stated periods in industry and agriculture. During that year 204,092 East Germans fled to the West.

1959: The Ministry for Cultural Affairs ordered a purge of the Universities and technical colleges. At Dresden five students were given sentences totaling 37½ years' imprisonment. Members of the "People's Chamber" received instructions relating to their "duty" to explain and justify every act of the regime to the population. It was not their duty to "represent" the wishes of constituents.

West Germans have had to observe events such as these in angry impotence. This has imposed and still imposes a severe psychological strain. This strain will not diminish in the years ahead.

The main external stress imposed on the people of West Germany is that of a Soviet foreign policy which is absolutely consistent and objective, relentless and unresting, based on the determination to build up East Germany as a Communist State, to push Communism to the Rhine and to absorb the industrial Ruhr without striking a blow for it, and to produce a new "balance of power" in Europe. Mr. Khrushchev has never made any secret of his intention of leading Communism to victory against Western democracy. It is astonishing, often pitiful, that so many clever men in the West have imagined that Mr. Khrushchev's proposal for "peaceful coexistence" could be more than a façade, or that his switch of interest and endeavor from the military to the economic field could be a "hopeful" sign. The story of Communist penetration in Germany is, after all, a very clear one. It is the story of brutal pressure on seventeen million East Germans, an intermittent squeeze on West Berlin, and a careful plan to convince the Western Powers that Federal Germany is simply not worth worrying about and does not deserve their continued military and moral support.

It is a frightening thought that Mr. Khrushchev's expertly calculated policies — with their accompaniment of broad smiles and hearty handshakes — have addled the wits of so many people in the West. If fifty-four million West Germans ever "turn East," and join seventeen million East Germans in satellitedom, it will not be altogether their own fault. German reunification is a legitimate German interest, which the West should never ignore. Yet there are people in the Western countries who are ready, even anxious to fall into the Soviet trap and treat reunification as a "purely German concern." This, for instance, is what an Oxford University historian, Mr. A. J. P. Taylor, wrote in a leading article in the (London) *Sunday Express* in the summer of 1959:

> We have an interest in Germany, a stake of honour which we do not repudiate. That is to ensure that West Berlin remains free from Communist control. Beyond that we have a greater vital interest in Europe. The interest that a new war does not explode there and destroy us all. Beyond that we have no interest worth making a fuss about.
>
> Let every Englishman ask himself the question, "Is it a vital British interest that Germany should be united?"
>
> There can be only one answer, "No, it is not." . . .
>
> Now for another question: "Is it a vital British interest that Germany should be rearmed, especially with nuclear weapons?"
>
> The answer to this is clear too: "No, it is not. Quite the contrary, it is a vital British interest, if we had any sense, that Germany should not be rearmed."
>
> Here is a simple, precise program which Mr. Selwyn Lloyd can offer to the Russians. We want firm, reliable guarantees for the freedom of West Berlin. In return we accept two German states, disarmed. The Germans say they want to be an oasis of peace in the center of Europe. Here is their chance.

For several decades political infantilism in Britain has been regarded as the prerogative of "Colonel Blimp" — that irascible Conservative reactionary immortalized by the political cartoonist Low, and traditionally associated with clubs in Pall Mall, Turkish baths in Jermyn Street, and the suburbs of Cheltenham. A. J. P.

Taylor is a Socialist intellectual. There are too many people of his kind and leanings who would willingly go blindfolded into the battle line of the Cold War, bearing manifestoes of their purblind and puerile "solutions" of the German problem. What a "solution" is Taylor's! Two disarmed German states, in an all-German vacuum: one of them backed by the full power of Soviet propaganda and violently aggressive diplomacy; the other left by the West to get on as best it may with its Communist neighbor and regarded by people like Taylor as an infernal nuisance! This is precisely the situation which the Soviet leaders have been trying to create since 1958, with their proposals for the creation of a "Confederation" of two equally entitled German states, for the creation of social and political conditions in West Germany which would enable a further process of Communist-sponsored reunification, and for the withdrawal of all foreign troops from German soil and the military neutralization of the whole of Germany.

It may seem paradoxical that a left-wing English intellectual like Taylor has hired his pen to the aggressively right-wing Beaverbrook press in London. In fact, it is not. Taylor has written — and there are many people who would do the same — not out of intellectual conviction but out of pathological hatred of Germany and all things German. This is grist to Mr. Khrushchev's mill. It must be immensely comforting to him to reflect that when he asks Western statesmen to commit suicide, there are always Western intellectuals ready to dig graves for them, and for Western democracy.

A. J. P. Taylor qualifies as an outstanding example of misunderstanding of the German problem only because he happens to be an outstandingly intelligent Englishman. His contribution is not unique. Western political and diplomatic leadership has failed, often badly, in post-1945 Europe — not usually in principle, but in method and tactics, and in a due sense of urgency which should be the corollary of the hurrying step of material progress in the Communist world. For that progress will be used, in due course, to reinforce Communist political pressure on the free nations. This is what makes otherwise incidental and uninteresting Western failures so immensely important.

Here are a few of the West's failures:

The Western Powers attached too much importance, initially, to West German rearmament (A. J. P. Taylor would be right here, but for all the wrong reasons! British Socialists made West German rearmament inevitable). Pressure in favor of West German rearmament began in 1950; it overruled the weakly expressed British objection that the measure would not be "popular" in Germany itself, and it overruled Dr. Adenauer's own considered view that what was needed was a para-military force to balance the East German citizen police, the *Bereitschaftspolizei*. The West paid too little attention to the Russian fear of the German soldier — that dedicated automaton who marched to Stalingrad and the gates of Moscow. Being wise after the event, one may write now that West and East German rearmament inevitably made agreement between the Great Powers more difficult.

The Western Powers took too little trouble in the presentation of their views on the German problem, on the possibility of direct negotiations with the Soviet Union, and on new, flexible ideas to break the diplomatic deadlock. The Soviet Union grasped the diplomatic initiative as early as 1948. Western reactions since then have always tended to be slow and surprised, and Western counteraction has been late, hesitant and sometimes bewildered.

The West's powers of endurance have sometimes been insufficient at different levels. By the time that the second Geneva Conference of 1959 had been running for only a week, some observers were already writing of "a mood of exhaustion" in the Western delegations. During pre-blockade negotiations in Berlin, ten years earlier, the American Commandant in Berlin naïvely remarked that he was leaving the conference "in order to get some sleep" (let it be said that Colonel Howley was a vigorous, vital man, and may have had an ulterior motive). But the performance of his British colleague was more revealing. He refused to have his rest disturbed when the news was brought to him — in the middle of the night — of the East Berlin currency reform of June, 1948. Although the Western Powers intended to counter this by announcing a West Berlin currency reform forthwith, the British general preferred to "leave things until the morning." It has been very much to the Russians' advantage to know that they can play on human weaknesses. They, normally, show none themselves; they are not allowed to do so.

There has been a failure on the Western side to realize that — as Walter Lippmann has trenchantly pointed out — the Soviet interpretation of the *status quo* is a temporary acceptance of a given situation, in order to exploit it to their own advantage, thus creating a new *status quo*. For at least five years the Western Powers sat on prepared positions in Germany — those of free all-German elections, the formation of an all-German parliament and government, the signing of a German peace treaty. These prepared positions, according to Dr. Adenauer, would depend on a "policy of strength, but not on a policy of brute force" (October, 1956, speech to the Bundestag). The West was additionally armed by Dr. Adenauer's motto — extreme watchfulness, and a justified distrust of Soviet policies (June, 1956, speech to Yale University).

Western tactics were makeshift, though reasonably sensible. But what of Western strategy? Western diplomats forgot that strategy, most of all in a Cold War, cannot be static. A strong position is valuable, but not in order to dig in for years. Boldness might have paid at the time of the Berlin Conference of 1954, when the West might have bought German reunification on fair terms (free elections and the inception of a democratic all-Germany, in return for Germany's military neutralization). But a Maginot-line mentality obsessed Western statesmen in 1954 and during the next three years. In November, 1958, the Soviet Union launched its threat to free West Berlin; the Western Powers were confronted with negotiations at the pistol-point. They duly negotiated at two Geneva Conferences in 1959, which solved nothing.

347

The Soviet threat produced an agitated wave of activity on the part of the West's unorthodox disciples of "disengagement." Mr. George Kennan and his friends in the American Senate and House of Representatives, the British Labor Party, the West German Social Democrats, and many others who thought like them began to produce plans for a "New Deal" between the West and the Soviet Union in Central Europe. Some of the disengagers were ready to accept the Oder-Neisse line, and so perpetuate the eastern frontier imposed on Germany by unilateral Soviet action. Others thought that the Soviet Union might still grant German reunification, in return for the withdrawal of a united Germany from all military alliances. Others, again, believed that it was possible to pin the Russians down to a step-by-step German reunification, if some sort of "Confederation" were accepted in the first place. None of the disengagers could do more than produce a "paper plan." For Western diplomats were unable to give them any factual clue. Western diplomats had, quite simply, failed to find any.

The disengagers ignored the fact that they were tabling their plans at a time when Western diplomacy (through its own faults of omission) was under duress — in fact, at a time when such plans had least chance of success. The disengagers forgot their own failure to think out something new and positive, during a period of political and diplomatic stagnancy in which the Russians might have been prepared to listen to reason. The disengagers did not realize, at first, that by showing readiness to give away points in advance they were playing into the hands of the Soviet leaders. It is all very well to evolve paper plans for a solution of world problems; but one must have some sense of responsibility for them. It could happen, it did happen, that only the Western Powers were embarrassed by ideas which were new to them.

By 1960 the disengagers were due to spring-clean their ideas. In 1959 Mr. George Kennan asserted that the Soviet Union had three main concerns in Germany — to prevent the armed forces of West Germany, or of a United Germany, from being aligned with those of the United States; to prevent the introduction of nuclear weapons into West Germany; to see that "the Eastern zone was not swallowed up by the Federal Republic." Mr. Kennan added that the Russians wanted the East German leaders to have a voice in a "German Settlement," and, "if possible," the retention of some of the social and economic changes which had already been introduced into East Germany.

What an understatement! The Soviet Union wants a nominally independent but utterly satellite and 100 per cent Communist East Germany. Its social and economic forms would necessarily remain completely intact, and could be extended to West Germany. German reunification would then take place in only one possible form — that of a Communist all-Germany.

Another disengager, Walter Lippmann, maintained that the West Germans did not really want the "absorption" of East by West Germany, "because this would impose a heavy financial burden on them." Integration, Lippmann believed, would be undesirable "because it would change the balance of religious forces and of the political parties." Both arguments were invalid. The fifty-four million West Germans would certainly "absorb" the seventeen million East Germans in any real reunification, and they would certainly want to do so. Naturally, reunification would involve initial sacrifices on the part of the richer West Germans. But East Germany would quickly become a tremendously valuable investment and internal market. All West German parties want "all-German integration," and are ready to exploit it to their own advantage — the Christian Democrats because they could pose as "reunifiers," the Social Democrats because they would pick up a traditional left-wing vote in "Red" Saxony and "pink" Thuringia; as for the Churches, the Evangelicals would reestablish their unity, and the Roman Catholics would recover their East German flock. They would both be supremely thankful.

Roughly fifty years before Mr. Khrushchev posed his destructive threat to Germany — for it struck at the very idea of German unity, and displayed readiness to drive the West to the brink of world war over Berlin — the Under-secretary of State in the British Foreign Office, Sir Eyre Crowe, wrote this:

There is one road which, if past experience is any guide to the future, will certainly not lead to any permanent improvement of relations with any power . . . and which must therefore be abandoned; that is the road paved with graceful British concessions — concessions made without any conviction either of their justice or of their being set off by equivalent counterservices. The vain hopes that in this manner Germany can be conciliated and made more friendly must be given up.

This was written in 1907. In 1960 one need only substitute for "British" the word "Western," and for "Germany" the obvious "Soviet Union." Sound principles of diplomacy remain sound — over a fifty-year span. The Soviet Union can no longer be bought off in Germany. But it can be made to see sense by tough, resilient and flexible diplomacy. Up to 1960, at least, there was no sign of the West evolving such a diplomacy. Dr. Adenauer was ready to be tough, but not flexible. The disengagers were the reverse. In essence, Western diplomacy had all the elements for hard and clear thinking; as served up on the conference table it was flabby, flaccid, filleted.

The Soviet challenge to a peaceful solution of Europe's problems, and even to the *status quo* in Central Europe, is an enduring one. For Soviet policies are founded on the belief, and experience, that pressure will pay — when it is directed against a Europe which is stale and uncertain. Soviet pressure may, therefore, be intensified, applied with extreme force at every weak point in the Western system. Germany is the most obvious weak point.

And for the following reasons. There can be no quick, satisfactory solution of the German problem without Soviet co-operation, and without an active Soviet desire for a solution. Since 1945 the Soviet intention has been to make its zone of occupation into an integral part of the Communist bloc, to use it as a springboard for the ideological conquest of Western Germany and of the rest of Europe. Time tends to favor the Soviet Union. It can steadily strengthen East Germany and bind it more closely into the Communist bloc, whereas West Germany will continue to hanker for reunification, and to arouse suspicions among her allies. The Soviet Union, again, can always apply local pressure on West Berlin, knowing that this will make the West wince.

The Soviet Union can reckon on divisions in the Western camp making a real Western diplomatic initiative improbable. Never were these divisions more evident than in 1959, when Mr. Harold Macmillan evolved his plan for a zone of thinned-out and equalized armaments in Germany. Macmillan did not produce a blueprint, but a constructive idea. It was guided by two arguments: a "pilot scheme" would make general, controlled disarmament more possible, and such a pilot scheme could work to the advantage of the West. Equalization of military forces in an "all-German zone" 120 miles wide would not have impeded the planned build-up of NATO forces. But it would have meant the withdrawal farther east of a great many Russian and East German troops from their half of the "controlled" zone. Whereas there were only five NATO divisions in a sixty-mile-wide belt to the west of the interzonal frontier, there were around twenty Russian and East German divisions in the sixty-mile-wide belt to the east of it.

Of course, the Soviet leaders would not have willingly reduced their forces in this area; but refusal to do so would have put them on the diplomatic defensive. For it would have reduced to nonsense their best-selling propaganda line, that NATO was an aggressive organization which was planning to attack the "peace-loving democracies." Yet Dr. Adenauer, in a rare fit of diplomatic nihilism, refused flatly to consider the Macmillan plan, and sought out General de Gaulle to support him. Did he reflect that there is probably no single French statesman living who really wants German reunification, and who would make the slightest sacrifice to attain it?

The Soviet Union, while refusing to allow free, all-German elections and a genuine expression of the will of the whole German people, can continue to dangle the dummy-carrot of "semi-reunification," in the shape of "Confederation" of the two German states. (Such a Confederation could be eased by stages into the Communist bloc, where it would be sure of most-privileged-satellite status. It would obtain a vital economic role as the work-shop of the Euro-Asian land mass. It would escape the burdens of armament. It would, nominally, restore German unity — at the pleasure of the one power which can withhold unity indefinitely.) At the Leipzig Trade Fair in 1959, Mr. Khrushchev visited the Krupp stand and paid the firm pretty compliments on its products. There was nothing paradoxical about the ruler of Communist Russia hobnobbing with the representatives of the richest capitalist in Europe. For an understanding between them could enable the Soviet Union to take America's place as the strongest industrial power in the world. For that understanding, there would be no need for Alfried Krupp to turn Communist or to forgo one cent of his profits.

Ten years ago it was absurd to think of the people of West Germany "turning East." Memories were still lively of the terrible sack of Berlin, of the suppression of political and personal freedom in the Soviet Zone of occupation, of the thousands of prisoners in Soviet concentration camps and of the countless thousands more in Siberia. The people of Western Germany could not drift into the Communist orbit as long as the Russians pursued their aims with the brutality which they employed in Eastern Germany in 1953, and in Hungary in 1956. Yet Russian tactics are changing. And in 1970 what may the Communist bloc look like to West Germans who have sought but not found unity in the meanwhile? This is one of the strains which will be imposed on half-fledged German common sense in the years ahead.

If Germany is to remain a broken bone of contention for decades to come, what outlet can the intense and restless energies of the German people seek and find? Kirkpatrick, the British High Commissioner, coined his phrase: "I fear German tractors more than German tanks." For these reasons:

The emergence of two mighty world powers, the United States and the Soviet Union, meant that Germany would never again be in a position to play a dominant military role in world affairs. Apart from German lack of terrain, limitation of natural resources and geographical vulnerability, massive rearmament would cost a comparatively small Germany too much. This thought was one of the roots of German disinclination to rearm — a disinclination which has not always been appreciated or understood in the West. In the 1930's the Germany of eighty million industrious, disciplined and brave inhabitants was easily able to envisage its military domination of Europe. In the 1950's and 1960's such a thought was absurd. Far more attractive to Germans is the idea of economic dominance — probably not as an actual end in itself, but as a natural consequence of unlimited expansion.

There are a dozen good reasons for believing that German economic expansion will go on. The German desire to work, earn and spend money is intense. It is founded on the memories of fifteen years of wartime and Nazi-imposed shortages, and on the gaps left in the economy by the destruction of war and postwar Allied dismantling. By 1960 West Germany was losing fewer working hours from strikes than was any other European country. German trade-unions were innately cautious, conservative and accommodating (largely because of their horror of Communism). There was a state of full employment. Professor Erhard's "free-market economy" policies had acquired continuity after a ten-year period which bids fair to be prolonged for another ten years. West Germans, indeed, have learned to glory in free competition and to believe that their talents, techniques and solid determination are sure to give them a clear lead over all European rivals. West Germany, moreover, was less affected than any other European country by the American recession of 1958.

An overemphasized need to expand economically could bring dangers too. In any period of economic stagnancy, or recession, it could lead West Germany into taking too big an interest in the markets of the Communist bloc. Russo-German trade has often flourished in the past, and between 1928 and 1932 was worth two hundred and fifty million dollars a year. The Soviet appetite for German goods has been whetted by the advantageous 1958 trade agreement — Dr. Adenauer's government undertook to send to the Soviet Union heavy machinery, precision instruments, even integrated steel and chemical plants, in return for surplus Soviet raw materials. By 1959 German industry was beginning to toy with the idea of giving the Soviet Union long-term credits. Yet the chief danger in an economic *Drang nach Osten* would lie in its effects on Germany's Western partners. The chronic anti-Germans would have poison to tip their arrows. This is why West Germany must be bound ever more tightly into the Western economic system, implicated ever more closely in the former colonial markets of the Western world, and involved in the development of backward and "politically uncommitted" countries. This is why West Germany should be periodically reminded that economic partnership is preferable to economic domination, is perhaps indispensable — for Germans are still, to some extent, working their passage in the Western boat.

It has become a convention to conclude any book on the Germany of today on a note of extreme gloom. Of course, there are reasons enough for doing so. There is the division of Germany, and Communist pressure on the German problem. There is the startlingly weak position of a geographically isolated West Berlin. There is that endemic lack of understanding, among Germans, of the German past, and the consequently greater difficulties in planning for the German future. There is the unfused West German society, ruled by the thought that riches are power, and riches are all. And there is the smugness born of material success — expressing itself in that frequent phrase, "We can do quite as well as that in Germany, thank you!" — which is a blindworm feeding on the "economic miracle" and which inspired Professor Heuss's trenchant demand for "the ethos of a common responsibility."

There is moreover the certainty that the German character will not change overnight, although the German outlook is gradually emancipating itself from past obsessions. Dust-sheets have been draped over the old stone gods of Might and Glory, of Germanic expansion and self-expression, of racial superiority and a wildly confused sense of mission; but it is too soon for anything positive to have taken their place. It was in July 1959 that the

Frankfurter Allgemeine Zeitung wrote that German students to-day have only one objective — to pass exams and get good jobs, "because everything else seems pointless in a society which offers no ideals." Stark materialism is rampant everywhere in Europe today; it is hardly surprising that the West Germans have fallen the easiest prey to it and will be most vulnerable of all to any check to material prosperity.

Yet the prospect for Western Germany may not be as gloomy as these thoughts suggest. Human ideals are the legitimate off-spring of democracy. Here is one example.

In Düsseldorf a young man, Johannes Wasmuth, founded in 1959 an association which is unique in German history. It has no headquarters, no regular funds, no membership and no name. The twenty-one-year-old Wasmuth has invited people of his own age, as well as teen-agers suffering from mental "ennui" and frus-tration, to help in the work of giving friendship, companionship and love to the children of the poorest families in the land, who are officially homeless, who live in hovels and in a squalor which seems to shut out the very light of the sun. His particular preoc-cupation is the children of the fifty thousand homeless people who live within a radius of thirty miles around Düsseldorf.

Wasmuth, by sheer force of personality, collected enough money to build two kindergartens in a year. He planned and financed a children's holiday camp in the Diemel Valley. He has recruited helpers among people who are themselves poor but who find plenty of hope in life — above all, among the young. For they are the people who can most easily understand and help children; they are not so much older themselves, and they can teach, explain, arouse interest and give affection. "I have looked for helpers in the most unlikely places," Wasmuth told me, "and I have never failed to get the people I want. I am best pleased of all when I find them among those noisy, difficult Teddy-boy gangs which plague the police and their own parents. They are often the readiest of all to help, because part of their trouble is that no one has ever asked anything of them, in the right way."

When Henning von Tresckow compared Germany with Sodom

and asked God to spare his country, he may well have not believed that many people like Johannes Wasmuth existed. Perhaps they did not — in those dark, blood-streaked, latter days of the Nazi nightmare. The work of a man like Wasmuth — and there are plenty of others like him in Germany today — is a reminder that freedom can bring a brighter future for Germany. The Germans lack no human quality, no capability needed to weld them into a community which can make a huge contribution to the free world. They are being given the chance to discover their own soul, not self-consciously, nor in any spirit of arrogance or abasement. But they face strains and stresses in the years ahead which will test them sternly. It should be the duty and privilege of the other free nations to help them along their road.

Bibliography

It is not proposed to give a full list of "authorities," which would run to several hundreds, but to present a selection of the most revealing studies of Germany and German affairs during and after the war. I have added a brief note of description for each book, believing that only in this way has a bibliography any real value for the general reader.

ALEXANDER, H. G.: *Zwischen Bonn und London*. Düsseldorf, Droste Verlag.

This book deals with the tortured subject of Anglo-German relations, and is a balanced attempt to explain the political and psychological barriers between the British and Germans. These barriers have a special impact on the workings of the Western Alliance; hence the importance of this book.

ALLEMANN, FRITZ: *Bonn ist nicht Weimar*. Cologne, Kiepenheuer & Witsch.

Probably the best and most carefully reasoned book on the Federal Republic, from 1949 to 1958, and its domestic and foreign policies. Allemann was for five years (up to 1959) correspondent of the Swiss paper *Die Tat* in Bonn, and a mild but enlightened critic of West German policies.

BALFOUR, MICHAEL, and MAIS, JOHN: *Four-power Control in Germany and Austria: 1945-1946*. London and New York, Oxford University Press.

Michael Balfour has written the German section of this book. This is essentially a textbook, which explains the problems of the victorious Allies in 1945 and the steps which they took to solve them and which led to the splitting of Germany between East and West.

357

BRANT, STEFAN: *East German Rising*. New York, Frederick A. Praeger, Inc.; and London, Thames and Hudson.

Probably the best and certainly the most readable account of the East German rising of 1953. (Published in German as *Der Aufstand* by Stuttgart, Steingruben Verlag.) Another good book on the same subject is *Der 17 Juni*, by Curt Riess (Berlin, Ullstein Verlag).

CLAY, GENERAL LUCIUS D.: *Decision in Germany*. New York, Doubleday and Company, Inc.; and London, Heinemann.

General Clay was first Deputy Military Governor in the United States Zone of Germany, and later became Military Governor. His knowledge of the workings of Allied policies in Germany makes this a valuable book. It is not always easy reading.

CONNELL, BRIAN: *Watcher on the Rhine*. New York, William Morrow and Co., Inc.; and London, Weidenfeld & Nicolson.

A most readable account of the Germany of 1959, with an outline of the most important developments in both parts of Germany since 1945. A book of the same type and length, equally lively and equally critical of German developments, is Charles Thayer's *The Unquiet Germans* (New York, Harper & Brothers).

CRANKSHAW, EDWARD: *Gestapo: Instrument of Tyranny*. New York, Viking Press; and London, Putnam.

The most straightforward account of the organization, aims and methods of the Gestapo.

DALLIN, ALEXANDER: *German Rule in Russia*. New York, St. Martin's Press, Inc.

One of the most valuable of all studies of the Nazi era, this book describes the plans of Hitler and his subordinates for recasting the map of the whole of eastern Europe.

DAVIDSON, BASIL: *Germany, What Now?* London, Muller.

This book has a very obvious left-wing bias, and is not reliable in its treatment of Soviet-Western relations in Germany.

Its value lies in its historical perspective and in its close attention to the past and more recent activities of German industrialists.

ERHARD, LUDWIG: *Wohlstand für Alle*. Düsseldorf, Econ Verlag; and London, Thames and Hudson.

This is the story of the "German Economic Miracle," the rebuilding of an economy shattered by the war and of postwar industrial expansion. There could be no better man to tell it than the Federal Minister of Economics, who has held office since 1949 and who evolved his own "free-market economy" and liberal trade policies.

HISCOCKS, RICHARD: *Democracy in Western Germany*. London and New York, Oxford University Press.

A comprehensive textbook, dealing with Federal, *Land* and local government institutions in Western Germany, and with the organization of the trade-unions and other associations.

KITZINGER, UWE: *German Electoral Politics*. Oxford, Clarendon Press.

An account of the West German political parties, including useful new material on their organization and financing, and of the political habits and trends of the West German public. This book's especial virtue is that it makes a dry subject interesting and is larded with excellent anecdotes.

MORGAN, GENERAL J. H.: *Assize of Arms*. London, Methuen.

Deals with the German Army and the German General Staff from 1919 onwards, and with their impact on German history. Full of bitter wit and savage criticism. The author was able only to begin work on a second volume before his death.

NAMIER, SIR LEWIS: *In the Nazi Era*. London and New York, The Macmillan Company.

This casts a most interesting light on the writing of German history. The book deals with the memoirs of a number of Germans who played important parts in the field of diplomacy, and shows how deep-rooted the habit of miswriting history is in Germany.

REITLINGER, GERALD: *The Final Solution*. New York, Thomas Yoseloff, Inc., and London, Valentine Mitchell.

The classic work on the German concentration camps and the German plan to annihilate the Jewish race. This is a work of real scholarship, and is extremely well-documented. Should be read by every student of anti-Semitism in Germany. The same author has also written *The S.S.* (London, Heinemann), which is the best study of that organization and its work and aims.

VON SALOMON, ERNST: *The Final Solution* (*The Answers*). Hamburg, Rowohlt; and London, Putnam.

This appeared in Germany under the title of *Der Fragebogen* and in England as *The Answers* and is written by the man who helped to murder Germany's Foreign Minister in 1923, Walter Rathenau. Its value lies in the fact that it fully reveals the workings of mind of a German of character. Some of the most violent passages of the German original have been left out of the English translation.

THAYER, CHARLES: *See* CONNELL.

TREVOR-ROPER, H. R.: *The Last Days of Hitler*. New York, St. Martin's Press.

A brilliant account of the last year of the Nazi era and of Hitler's end. The reprint of the third edition contains new material, and this book will remain the most revealing written about Hitler, by reason of its historical exactitude and restraint.

WEYMAR, PAUL: *Adenauer*. London, Andre Deutsch.

The "standard" biography of the Federal Chancellor, written in 1955, after he had been six years in office. The book is pleasantly written and factual, but produces no balanced criticism of Dr. Adenauer's policies.

WHEELER-BENNET, JOHN: *The Nemesis of Power*. New York, The Macmillan Company.

The story of the German General Staff and the German Army from 1919 onwards, highly documented, immensely detailed but excellent reading throughout. This book casts a great deal of light on the politics of the Nazi era and produces by far the best account of the German Resistance to Hitler, superior in every way to Gerhard Ritter's *The German Resistance* (New York, Praeger).

WISKEMANN, ELIZABETH: *Germany's Eastern Neighbors*. London and New York, Oxford University Press.

Germany's relations with these neighbors and a penetrating account of West German refugee-politics, of which the author is sharply critical.

Index

H

Date Due